Marian maternity in late-medieval England

Manchester University Press

MANCHESTER MEDIEVAL LITERATURE AND CULTURE

Series editors: Anke Bernau, David Matthews and James Paz
Series founded by: J. J. Anderson and Gail Ashton
Advisory board: Ruth Evans, Patricia C. Ingham, Andrew James Johnston, Chris Jones, Catherine Karkov, Nicola McDonald, Haruko Momma, Susan Phillips, Sarah Salih, Larry Scanlon, Stephanie Trigg and Matthew Vernon

Manchester Medieval Literature and Culture publishes monographs and essay collections comprising new research informed by current critical methodologies on the literary cultures of the global Middle Ages. We are interested in all periods, from the early Middle Ages through to the late, and we include post-medieval engagements with and representations of the medieval period (or 'medievalism'). 'Literature' is taken in a broad sense, to include the many different medieval genres: imaginative, historical, political, scientific and religious.

38. *Objects of affection: The book and the household in late medieval England*   Myra Seaman
39. *The gift of narrative in medieval England*   Nicholas Perkins
40. *Sleep and its spaces in Middle English literature: Emotions, ethics, dreams*   Megan G. Leitch
41. *Encountering* The Book of Margery Kempe   Laura Kalas and Laura Varnam (eds)
42. *The narrative grotesque in medieval Scottish poetry*   Caitlin Flynn
43. *Painful pleasures: Sadomasochism in medieval cultures*   Christopher Vaccaro (ed.)
44. *Bestsellers and masterpieces: The changing medieval canon*   Heather Blurton and Dwight F. Reynolds (eds)
45. *Medieval literary voices: Embodiment, materiality and performance*   Louise D'Arcens and Sif Ríkharðsdóttir (eds)
46. *The heat of* Beowulf   Daniel C. Remein
47. *Hybrid healing: Old English remedies and medical texts*   Lori Ann Garner
48. *Difficult pasts: Post-Reformation memory and the medieval romance*   Mimi Ensley
49. *The problem of literary value*   Robert J. Meyer-Lee
50. *Marian maternity in late-medieval England*   Mary Beth Long

Marian maternity in late-medieval England

Mary Beth Long

MANCHESTER UNIVERSITY PRESS

Copyright © Mary Beth Long 2023

The right of Mary Beth Long to be identified as the author of this work has been asserted in accordance with the Copyright, Designs and Patents Act 1988.

Published by Manchester University Press
Oxford Road, Manchester M13 9PL

www.manchesteruniversitypress.co.uk

British Library Cataloguing-in-Publication Data
A catalogue record for this book is available from the British Library

ISBN 978 1 5261 5530 6 hardback
ISBN 978 1 5261 9160 1 paperback

First published 2023
Paperback published 2025

The publisher has no responsibility for the persistence or accuracy of URLs for any external or third- party internet websites referred to in this book, and does not guarantee that any content on such websites is, or will remain, accurate or appropriate.

EU authorised representative for GPSR:
Easy Access System Europe – Mustamäe tee 50,
10621 Tallinn, Estonia
gpsr.requests@easproject.com

Typeset by Newgen Publishing UK

Contents

List of plates   *page* vi
Acknowledgments   vii

Introduction: Marian maternity, matricentric reading,
and devotional literacies   1

Part I: The reader: Margery Kempe's devotional literacies and *imitatio Mariae*

1 The Dominican literacies of Margery Kempe's pilgrimages   15
2 Mar(ger)y at the foot of the Cross   55

Part II: The genre: defining Marian absence in legendaries of women

3 The community service of mystics' maternal bodies   101
4 'In Our Lady's Binds': Mary's maternal peers in East Anglian devotion   143

Part III: The author: Chaucer as matricentric poet

5 A Mary for every mother: mothers as agents of orthodoxy   187
6 A Marian, maternal Cecilia   224

Conclusion: 'Show yourself a mother'   261

Bibliography   266
Index   288

Plates

1 Woodcut, Peter Vischer, Nuremberg Relic-Book, 1487. Washington, D.C., Library of Congress, Rare Book and Special Collections Division, Rosenvald 120, fol. 4r
2 Central panel, Rogier van der Weyden, *Altarpiece of the Seven Sacraments*, c. 1445, Royal Museum of Fine Arts, Antwerp
3 Alabaster relief of 'Our Lady of Gesyn', 14th c., Holy Trinity Church, Long Melford, Suffolk. Photo copyright Will Collin (Flickr: d0gwalker)
4 Painted screen at Lady Chapel altar, 15th c., Church of St Helen, Ranworth, Norfolk. Photo copyright Jean McCreanor (Flickr: JMC4–Church Explorer)
5 Page of Chaucer's *ABC*, Glasgow University Library, Hunter MS 239 (U. 3. 12), f. 81r. Courtesy of University of Glasgow Archives & Special Collections
6 Book of Hours, Spain, c. 1461. London, British Library, Additional MS 18193, f. 48v. Copyright The British Library Board

Acknowledgments

This book was mostly a pandemic-era project, when resources, conditions, and outcomes were unpredictable and usually subobtimal. My first thanks are for the flexibility and graciousness of Meredith Carroll and the editorial team at Manchester University Press and Newgen Publishing.

I am heavily indebted to librarians and archivists, particularly the unnamed digital photographers and coders whose work made so many scholarly texts and manuscripts widely available. Robin Roggio at Mullins Library worked minor miracles through interlibrary loan.

I have benefited from institutional time and resources from the English Department and the Fulbright School of Arts and Sciences at the University of Arkansas; thanks especially to Calvin White. Charlena Seymour, Stan Poole, and the National Endowment for the Humanities provided travel support in the work's early stages. I am grateful for the Obama Administration's Family and Medical Leave Act and for the Biden Administration's American Rescue Plan, both of which indirectly protected my time to write.

Arlyn Diamond trained me to trust my own values and timeline as a scholar; although she has not yet read this book, I am indebted to her for its ethos. Ann Higgins has read and gently improved far more of my writing than I've deserved over the last two decades. Isabel Davis, Clare Monagle, and Lucy Allen-Goss have refined my thinking about Marian maternity. Justine Dymond invited me to write about motherhood when I was in the early thick of it: I finally did!

I thank Virginia Blanton, Susan Nakley, Karla Taylor, Samantha Katz Seal, and Nicole Sidhu for generous and edifying critiques of earlier versions of individual chapters. Portions of Chapters 2 and 6 appeared in *postmedieval* and *Studies in the Age of Chaucer*. Jeanette Goddard read the entire manuscript; the remaining flaws are due to my own stubbornness and not her careful eye.

I am grateful to colleagues William Quinn and Lynda Coon for laying the foundations of friendship and mutual support that make the Medieval and Renaissance Studies Program such a joyful and stimulating intellectual space. Joshua Byron Smith and Lora Walsh make the work feel light. Kim Sexton and Lynn Jacobs have inspired and patiently educated me. Lissette Lopez Szwydky and Toni Jensen each offered compassion and wisdom at critical moments.

Jeanette, Ann, Karen, Courtney, Cindy, and ABLM have sustained and mothered me throughout and beyond this project. Chris Long, Casey Cowan, Bill and Liz Barton, Santiago and Lourdes Domínguez, and many wonderful teachers have loved and cared for my children. My mother, especially, has bridged numerous childcare gaps. The Patricolas in Liège housed me and redefined home.

To my mind, the late Jeanne Knight, Dorothy Jean Barton, and Niccolò Domínguez still live in Chapters 2 and 5.

I began the earliest stages of this research when my oldest child was a baby; she is now in college. In that blink of an eye, Rose, Vivian, Laura, and Santi have taught me to view the world matricentrically. To paraphrase Toni Morrison, I am grateful that when they needed and deserved an in-house mother, they accepted a writer.

This book exists thanks to, and for, Freddy. He has habitually sacrificed his own writing and sleeping time so I could have more of both, and he has offered unfailing support for my work and our family. I could not fathom a better partner or parent.

Introduction: Marian maternity, matricentric reading, and devotional literacies

Among several miracle stories in a fourteenth-century sermon collection is an Easter tale featuring a ghastly disembowelment: a Christian cleric's Jewish sworn brother and companions slice open the cleric's torso, scattering entrails in the street to find a glowing Eucharistic wafer embedded in the Christian's broken heart. Once exposed, the host transforms into the Christ child and begins preaching to the Jewish and Christian crowd that has assembled. The child resumes its form as Host in the heart, 'dances' back into the cleric's chest, sucks all the organs back to their rightful place, and revives the cleric's body.[1] The Christians rejoice; the Jews convert. The tale is instantly recognizable as a version of blood libel, an anti-semitic genre that depends for its power on the pathos of children's innocence. It has been categorized as a parody of the Crucifixion.[2] But it also functions as a deconstructed Nativity. While the Virgin Mary is not present, she is certainly referenced by the Eucharist and the incarnation of the child, as well as, less directly, the anti-semitism.[3] The tale makes literal the mystical claim that devoted Christians can conceive Christ in their hearts to imagine a 'birth' outside Mary's womb. The cleric has effectively borne Christ. This is only possible once his body is completely ravaged, a gesture toward the violence of childbirth. His body is resurrected and healed, but not until it has lain exposed for the duration of the Christ child's sermon. Notably, the child does not require care or guidance. The 'maternity' here involves allowing one's body to be tormented for the edification of others, to produce other Christians: a world without Mary is one in which men's bodies get destroyed.

The tale's clear discomfort with the disruption of a man's body by the pain and spectacle of childbearing—of a sort—parallels the intentional erasure of such pain and disruption of Mary's parturient body. Ironically, as Clare Monagle points out, 'the most important and visible mother in the history of Western culture was celebrated precisely because she had *not* been broken by birth'.[4] While the myth of Marian maternity depends heavily on her physical generation of Christ, birth's undeniable physicality is largely erased from Mary's narrative. This was distinct from the cultural expectations of other pregnant or fecund bodies. Aquinas had famously argued that the very purpose of woman's existence was to be a procreative vessel.[5] Bernard of Clairvaux acknowledged the paradox of women enduring physical pain if they have children and social criticism if they don't.[6] While it is Mary's flesh that grants Christ humanity, Mary herself, as perpetual virgin, was not subject to the sin metaphorically associated with female fleshliness. Her virginity was further held as evidence of her beauty and, by extension, sexual potential.[7] In this context, the sermon anecdote above reads like part of a larger cultural experiment in motherless birth, or bodiless mothers.

By the fifteenth century, several of the most popular Marian poems refer to Mary's virginity with an incredulity that the purity of virginity could be congruent with motherhood. In the late fifteenth-century miscellany Ashmole 61, the speaker declares in 'A Prayer to Mary', a text that appears in over forty manuscripts, that 'Modour and mayd was never none/In this werld bot thou alone' (3–4), then addresses her with 'mayden clene' (5), and a few lines later, 'Suete Lady, mayden myld (21). Similarly, a mid-fifteenth-century carol begins its list of Nativity-related paradoxes and miracles by mentioning Mary's virginity no fewer than four times in the first thirteen lines.[8] Once Christ becomes incarnate in the fourth stanza, the 'maiden' in each stanza's closing line is dropped in favor of 'mother': the first three stanzas' 'Mayd mother Marye' (4), 'Maid moder Mary' (13), and 'Born of maid Marye' (22) become in the last three stanzas of the carol 'By his *moder* Mary' (31), 'Of his *moder* Marye' (40), and 'to hys *modere* Mary' (49). Even as the carol's first few lines argue that Mary is mother *and* maid, this shift of nomenclature suggests that the two states are mutually exclusive, as though even Mary's youth ends with the event of Christ's birth. The contrast between the two is underscored by the description of a birth that is 'withouten payne' (3) and Mary's status as virgin 'both after and beforne' (7), claims that, while common to the period, suggest a squeamishness about childbirth and its bodily effects: Mary may undergo pregnancy, but her young, pure, virginal body will not suffer any of its disturbing physical consequences.

This erasure of the physical experiences of Mary's pregnancy and childbirth dovetails with a confusing silence about the daily work of raising a child. In Lydgate's 1420 *Life of Our Lady*, a biography of Mary's early life extant in forty-nine manuscripts, there are only five references to her actions as a mother.[9] All of them concern her breastmilk. There is little attention in Marian lyrics to what Patricia Hill Collins calls 'motherwork', Evelyn Nakano Glenn calls 'reproductive labor', and Sarah Knott calls the 'work' of mothering.[10] Like the Easter sermon anecdote that produces a Christ child only long enough to convert a crowd, the portrayal of Mary's maternity is often devoid of the labor of childraising that is separate from gestation and birth. The 'Five Joys' of Mary—the Annunciation, Nativity, Resurrection, Ascension, and Assumption—skip from Christ's birth to his death, as if the long thirty-three years during which Mary was presumably an active mother are hardly worth mentioning. Even the basic task of putting our baby to sleep has Mary coming up short. One fourteenth-century poem reveals that she doesn't know any lullabies, with the infant Christ asking why Mary doesn't sing to him:

> Ich a moder treuly
> That kan hire credel kepe
> Is wone to lullen lovely
> And singgen hire child o slepe.[11]

Mary knows only what Gabriel taught her at the Annunciation, so Christ teaches her sad songs about his own death. Mary's ignorance about what she has taken on is unexpected, but it is also a reminder that the Mary of the Annunciation is not the same as the one at the Crucifixion. As Andrea O'Reilly has argued, mothering is not an identity or a natural state but the result of acquired skills and commitment.[12] Mary must *learn* how to be Christ's mother.

Given the expectation that readers imitate Mary as they could, the relative absence of such lessons is surprising. Medieval Christian doctrine depended heavily on Mary's role as a human mother of the divine, as it was Mary's humanity that allowed Christ to be fully human. Mary's status as mother gave her divine standing and served as a link to her lay devotees. In the Marian textual corpus, mothering tasks are limited to a few key practices, emotions, and events. For example, visual and textual sources show that she taught Christ to read, as Georgiana Donavin and Laura Saetveit Miles have demonstrated.[13] Mary's affiliation with literacy offers a model for late-medieval readers and literary patrons. Readers relied on their own *devotional* literacies—their familiarity with theology, liturgical ritual and symbol, other devotional texts and performances, and their own practices—to recognize and interpret latent Marian maternal elements.[14]

Reading matricentrically

In this study, I use a matricentric feminist approach to discern how late-medieval readers' devotional literacies reveal or interpret Marian maternity in these texts. I'll define some terms of that approach here. We can think of 'patriarchal motherhood' as a culturally determined performance, and 'maternal practice' as the various transhistorical demands of childraising: feeding, providing shelter and clothing, health care, education, affection.[15] O'Reilly observes that 'Patriarchal motherhood has become the official meaning of motherhood, and as such, it marginalizes and renders illegitimate alternative practices of mothering. As a normative discourse, it polices all women's mothering and results in the pathologizing of those women who do not or cannot perform normative motherhood'.[16] Similarly, Sara Ruddick has described the 'gaze of others' under which mothers 'relinquish authority to others, [and] lose confidence in their own values'.[17] In this system, as Jacqueline Rose argues, society assigns much of the responsibility for a child's well-being to their mother, rather than to culture or other factors.[18]

Dominant Western expectations are, as Monagle has suggested, still rooted in the Marian model of maternity, a subcategory of patriarchal motherhood. Monagle describes the development of that ideal as an inherently misogynistic process:

> Medieval [Christian] thinkers spent a great deal of time thinking about maternity, in fact, and they tore themselves into a great many logical knots trying to work out how it could be sanctified. ... The

[scholastic] theologians make Mary perfect, and to do so they have to define what is normatively imperfect about women and about motherhood.[19]

Developed alongside the theology of Marian perfection by Cistercians and other theologians, Marian maternity expects the natal, adoptive, or metaphorical mother to shape her maternal behaviors into a deferential form of *imitatio Mariae*.

As we have seen above, however, the late-medieval Church's construction of Marian maternity is tied to Mary's inimitable biology. This is important because while clerics who were instrumental in *constructing* the ideals of Marian maternity were heavily invested in Mary's bodily connection to Christ, the *performance* of Marian maternity is not necessarily tied to biological reproduction at all. This matters when we consider maternity as a metaphor, as when maternal metaphors are employed by convents; when maternal care is administered by anyone other than the natal mother, as often happened in a culture with high maternal mortality rates; or when we consider maternal practice that includes childraising responsibilities shared between a couple, among friends or peers, or through collective community investment in a child. Ruddick and others have made clear that anyone can commit to mothering work; it is not linked to birth or gender. One of the most useful tools of matricentric feminism is its examination of maternal qualities, behaviors, and needs outside the natal maternal body.[20] As Tatjana Takševa has noted, defining motherhood 'as a category of existence rather than a performative role' means that the 'ethics of care' that is a key part of maternal experience is not taken seriously.[21] A maternity that depends on biology rather than the relational leaves many who care for children out of mothering.

Devotional literacies

To my mind, the notion of devotional literacies is no more or less feminist than that of reading matricentrically. Both force an unwinding of assumptions and a de-centering of patriarchal expectations. This study discusses Mary's maternity as both theological concept and imitable practice. To read matricentrically, here, is to seek out Marian expressions of maternity, and to notice the ways those expressions reflect and encourage lived maternal practices. I focus on the books that fifteenth-century patrons chose for their private devotional reading to complement explicitly Marian texts. The primary texts analyzed here do not announce themselves as Marian at all, and yet they are saturated with indirect reference to and imitations of her. The details of Marian maternity are frustratingly elusive in explicitly Marian texts and can be fleshed out more thoroughly with what might look like displacement or proxy in the devotional texts under discussion. While a handful of scholars have acknowledged the roles of Mary or maternity in some of these texts, those topics have not been the focus of sustained study.[22] I take as premise that the writers who developed Mary's maternity considered her maternal practice ideal as they considered her body ideal, and that through their own devotional literacies, those who read these texts would recognize elements of her maternity, whether or not they consciously emulated her. By accreting what are sometimes thinly dispersed hints about Mary's maternity from these texts into a concentrated picture, we can see the perceived maternity of Mary through a lens that permits a view closer to that of medieval devotees.

As much as this is a book that will define Marian maternity through these not-so-Marian texts, it is also very much a book about what readers might have made of those texts given their own devotional, emotional, and relational circumstances. I consider how the maternal status of these texts' patrons and readers might affect the content and interpretation of their books within a Marian devotional practice, particularly because so many of these readers claimed social, literate, and spiritual authority through that maternity. This necessarily results in revisionist readings. What emerges from employing this matricentric lens is a thematically coherent package of subtly-Marian devotional materials that depend for their success on the reader's literate engagement with practices such as *imitatio Mariae*. All of these factors feed into my use of the term 'devotional literacies'.

I examine these materials in three sections that focus on, respectively, a reader, a genre, and an author, with attention to the various aspects of Marian maternity that each favors. The first section considers Margery Kempe as a reader or consumer of Marian texts, with attention to her pushing at the far edges of literacy and of *imitatio Mariae* under the guidance of a Dominican anchorite whose influence is often buried beneath Margery's own voice. The second section examines the seemingly conventional genre of the legendary of women, zeroing in on the patrons, compilers, and local cultures of origin of individual *vitae* and their manuscripts that build out their Marian canons in idiosyncratic ways. The third section focuses on the late fifteenth-century manuscripts that include Chaucer's Marian poems to identify how his characters and potentially his readers incorporate Marian maternity into their own maternal practice, sometimes to their detriment.

Chapter 1 argues that Margery Kempe's embrace of Marian maternity begins with her Dominican confessor, who mediates her access to textual culture and trains her for her largely arts-based *imitatio Mariae* program. Her pilgrimages are thus not a separate spiritual endeavor from that program or her engagement with books, but integral to each. Gothic cathedrals, for example, offer material reinforcement of Margery's maternal status and of her view of Mary's role in and as the Church. Our understanding of Margery's attempted supersession of Mary depends on how we interpret her use of liturgical space, validated through the medieval concept of Ecclesia. Margery's version of *imitatio Mariae* ultimately includes seeing her own body as a sacred house of God. This clarifies and expands what many scholars have called her 'authority', a reading that emerges from attending to Mary's maternal presence in the *Book*.

Chapter 2 examines Margery's *imitatio Mariae* across two types of performative episodes, the Eucharist and the Crucifixion. The Christian appreciation of the body as metaphor encourages Margery's appropriation of maternal imagery such as the Eucharist, *Maria lactans*, and the foot of the Cross. Her engagement with these elements is evident from her repeated bodily maneuvering into recognizably Marian spaces. I consider Margery's inhabitation of Marian and Ecclesian roles and her predilection for spatial play as ways to define and claim authority through her maternity, often as she employs antisemitic tropes. We see this clearly in the chapter's concluding study of Marian maternity alongside medieval maternal practice through the shared cultural experience of reproductive loss.

Chapter 3 focuses on Oxford, Douce MS 114, which contains Middle English versions of three mystics' *vitae* affiliated with the thirteenth-century beguine movement and its hospital culture: Elizabeth of Spalbeek, Christina *mirabilis*, and Marie d'Oignies; a letter in support of Catherine of Siena's canonization; and Henry Suso's *Orologium Sapientiae*. The *vitae* position their subjects' bodies as venues of spirituality and community service, much in the model of *Maria medica* and her body's use for public benefit in miracle tales. In each of the *vitae*, the mystic fulfills a responsibility to the public rather than simply seeking her own holiness. Drawing from pain theory, I show that these texts frame such behaviors as Marian.

Chapter 4 considers British Library MS Arundel 327 and Cambridge University Library Add. MS 2604, two mid-century East Anglian legendaries. Their contents are almost exclusively female saints' lives that acknowledge the natal families of their subjects; they both also include intriguing allusions to Mary's social support system, echoing the visual contexts of their patrons' worship spaces. The importance of birth as a social event helps explain the space that these texts and spaces make for 'maternal peers', friends and family in Mary's early motherhood who shift the portrayal of her maternity further toward the relational. The emphasis on mothering as a shared enterprise may be a function of their patrons' investment in social connections.

Chapter 5 argues that the manuscripts that situate Chaucer's poems among other Marian texts encourage readers' matricentric interpretation. The visual form of Chaucer's *An ABC* grants power to create new Marian narratives, both visual and textual. The autonomy suggested by these letters allows embroidery to become literary, narrative, and devotional practice. The *Prioress's Tale* continues Chaucer's assumption of a reader's direct engagement with a Marian narrative and interest in maternal teaching. The plot relies partly on familiarity with Marian maternal mourning and its anti-semitic themes. Maternal grief becomes raw material to be shaped and processed into devotion, but it also becomes a test of maternal competence.

Chapter 6 traces how the *Second Nun's Tale* recalls Mary, Queen of Heaven as the model of persuasion and intercession for Cecilia's wifely behaviors. The tale connects the 'Marian Chaucer' that Heather Blurton and Hannah Johnson describe with *imitatio Mariae*; the Cecilia who is as much wife as virgin reflects the Virgin

Introduction 9

who acts like a wife. Mary's appearance in the *Second Nun's Prologue* underscores the need for careful reading and for the theological understanding central to the *Tale* that makes a metaphorical mother of its virgin subject. Cecilia's invocation of Mary's maternity means that her public and political engagement with Almachius also puts motherhood in the public sphere. Mary's model allows us to interpret Cecilia's rapport with men in the text as maternal rather than [merely] confrontational.

There is no shortage of cultural analyses of modern Western ideals of motherhood now, especially after the flush of attention to maternal labor during lockdown and subsequent pandemic-related conditions. There has been less attention to the premodern roots of those ideals. Recognizing that medieval Marian maternity anticipates and influences modern patriarchal motherhood is important, but we need also to know just what it comprises. Making Mary's maternal practice legible is part of making maternal labor visible. By centering Marian maternity, this study asks new questions of texts that reinforced its cultural dominance.

Notes

1 'Et cor saltabat in corpus'. British Library, Royal MS B XXIII, fols 70–1. The collected sermons of the Latin and English manuscript are in *Middle English Sermons*, ed. Woodburn O. Ross, EETS o.s. 209 (London: Oxford University Press, 1940), 63–5; this anecdote appears in Latin.
2 See Denise Depres, 'Cultic anti-Judaism and Chaucer's litel clergeon', *Modern Philology* 91.4 (1994), 413–27; like other scholars of the genre, she notes its use in answering Christian doubts about transsubstantiation. This tale is clearly meant to critique the company the cleric keeps, since his Jewish sworn brother organized his assault. The harsh response to an interfaith sworn brotherhood suggests such relationships were plausible and common enough to be perceived as a threat to the Church. Such narratives certainly contributed to Christian violence against Jews.
3 Miri Rubin observes that '[i]n vernacular literature, a strong bond was created between the Eucharistic body reborn at the mass and the original body born from a virgin womb' in *Corpus Christi: The Eucharist in Late Medieval Culture* (Cambridge: Cambridge University Press,

1991), 142. Rubin describes the convergence among the Incarnation, Passion narrative, and Eucharist at 142–7 and 230–2.

4 Clare Monagle, *Scholastic Affect: Gender, Maternity and the History of Emotions* (Cambridge: Cambridge University Press, 2020), 4, emphasis mine. Monagle offers a lucid meditation on the modern implications of Marian maternal expectations created by scholastics. Her book has indirectly shaped my thinking throughout much of this study.

5 'I answer, it was necessary for woman to be created, as the Scripture says, as a helper to man, not in just any work, as some say, since *in any other work man can be more suitably helped by another man than by a woman*, but [only] as a help in the work of procreation'; translation mine. 'Respondeo dicendum quod necessarium fuit feminam fieri, sicut Scriptura dicit, in adiutorium viri: non quidem in adiutorium alicuius alterius operis, ut quidam dixerunt, cum ad quodlibet aliud opus convenientius iuvari possit vir per alium virum quam per mulierem; sed in adiutorium generationis'. Thomas Aquinas, *Summa theologiae* (Rome: Marietti Taurini, 1950), I, q. 92. a. I.

6 Homily 3.7.

7 This was a later development: Bernard of Clairvaux, whose homilies provoked and promoted widespread devotion to Mary in the west, barely mentions Mary's bodily experience, discounting the relevance of her physical virginity. He instead emphasizes her humility. See especially Homily 1.5–6. 'Humility' is significantly less honored in the Marian texts that emerge in the two centuries following Bernard's sermons. For virginity as a sexuality, see Sarah Salih, *Versions of Virginity in Late Medieval England* (Woodbridge: Boydell and Brewer, 2001); on the late-medieval depiction of Mary's sexuality, see Emma Maggie Solberg, *Virgin Whore* (Ithaca: Cornell University Press, 2018).

8 'Blissid be that lady bryght', in Oxford, Bodleian MS 29734 (Eng. Poet e.1), fol. 52v–53r. Edited as poem 15 in *Middle English Marian Lyrics*, ed. Karen Saupe (Kalamazoo, MI: Medieval Institute Publications, 1998); [hereafter Saupe, poem 15].

9 Sarah McNamer discusses Lydgate's avoidance of Christ's adulthood and Passion in *Affective Meditation* (Philadelphia: University of Pennsylvania Press, 2010), 201.

10 See Patricia Hill Collins, 'Shifting the center: Race, class, and feminist theorizing about motherhood', *Mothering: Ideology, Experience, and Agency*, ed. Evelyn Nakano Glenn et al. (New York: Routledge, 1994), 45–65, at 47; Evelyn Nakano, 'From servitude to service work: Historical continuities in the racial division of paid reproductive

labor', *Signs* 18.1 (1992), 1–43; and Sarah Knott, *Mother Is a Verb* (New York: Sarah Crichton Books, 2019).
11 Edinburgh, National Library of Scotland Advocates MS 18.7.21, fols 3v–4v, lines 15–18 (Grimestone's commonplace book, 1372); Saupe, poem 25.
12 Andrea O'Reilly, *Matricentric Feminism: Theory, Activism, and Practice* (Ontario: Demeter Press, 2016), 14.
13 See Georgiana Donavin, *Scribit Mater: Mary and the Language Arts in the Literature of Medieval England* (Washington, DC: Catholic University of America Press, 2012), and Laura Saetveit Miles, *The Virgin Mary's Book at the Annunciation* (Woodbridge: Boydell & Brewer, 2020).
14 Though she does not employ this term, an exemplary study of the phenomenon is Naoë Yoshikawa's *Margery Kempe's Meditations: The Context of Medieval Devotional Literatures, Liturgy and Iconography* (Cardiff: University of Wales Press, 2007).
15 Adrienne Rich first distinguished these concepts in *Of Woman Born: Motherhood as Experience and Institution* (New York: Norton, 1976).
16 O'Reilly, *Matricentric Feminism*, 58.
17 Sara Ruddick, *Maternal Thinking: Toward a Politics of Peace* (Boston: Beacon Press, 1989), 111.
18 Jacqueline Rose, *Mothers: An Essay on Love and Cruelty* (New York: Farrar, Straus and Giroux, 2018).
19 Monagle, *Scholastic Affect*, 10, 14.
20 A similar model is the isolation of masculine traits outside the cisgendered male body in Jack Halberstam, *Female Masculinity* (Durham: Duke University Press, 1998).
21 Tatjana Takševa, 'One is not born but rather becomes a mother: claiming the maternal in women and gender studies', *Journal of the Motherhood Initiative* 10.1–2 (2019), 27–44, at 29 and 32.
22 Notable among those are Yoshikawa, Laura Kalas, Tara Williams, and Gail McMurray Gibson, on whose work the following chapters build.

Part I

The reader: Margery Kempe's devotional literacies and *imitatio Mariae*

The subtext of readerly participation is made explicit in Margery Kempe's *Boke*: she determines Marian meaning in texts and images and adapts it for her own purposes. Margery's book makes clear that she is familiar with the *vitae* of Marie d'Oignies, Bridget of Sweden, Catherine of Siena, and the Virgin Mary that are extant in multiple manuscripts owned by women. But Margery's behaviors as a pilgrim, and her multivalent interpretations of the Virgin Mary, also indicate engagement with mendicant textual and visual culture at a level that suggests purpose-based training. While there is visual and textual support for each of her devotional practices, the sum of her behaviors would have been unpredictable and thus was untenable for the Church authorities she encounters. Margery represents the outer limits of how far one reader might take *imitatio Mariae*, seeing herself not merely as imitator of but as replacement for Mary, using texts to enable and justify her self-authorizing behaviors. She explodes both the conventional definition of 'literacy' and what we normally consider 'maternal', drawing from multiple seemingly non-maternal depictions of Mary to shape her own metaphorical maternal practice. Her pilgrimages and her embodiments of the Virgin Mary take seriously the medieval view of reading as a physical experience, putting her devotional reading into bodily practice and developing new depictions of maternal authority.

1

The Dominican literacies of Margery Kempe's pilgrimages

In chapter 58 of her *Boke*, Margery Kempe tells us that she '*hungryd* ryth sor aftyr Goddys word'.[1] She is fed within a few sentences, when a new priest spends seven or eight years reading her a 'Bybyl wyth doctowrys therupon, Seynt Brydys boke, Hyltons boke, Boneventur, *Stimulus Amoris, Incendium Amois*'.[2] Such a list promises insight into Margery's literary diet, offering a metaphorical feast of fourteenth-century mysticism. Much has been made of its connection to Franciscan spirituality. But our scholarly glee at the bibliographical details can obscure exactly how and why Margery came to read these books with this priest—a sequence of events so important that it is explained twice in the same chapter. This is not the only time in her *Boke* that Margery mentions this particular set of texts, which first appear in chapter 17, or this priest, whose story is told again in chapter 60. If we attend to narrative function rather than content, we see that the list is wielded in this passage to confirm Margery's credibility as a mystic and to reduce suspicion that her visions are not of God.[3] Further, this episode tacitly reveals the text-based relationship Margery expects between herself and her spiritual advisors. That list of titles, which initially looks like her characteristic name-dropping, instead clarifies the importance of a bookish confessor to Margery's devotional program.

Margery's sense of entitlement in this passage is clear, as she demands of Christ 'that thu ne woldyst sendyn me on of hem that myth fulfillyn my sowle with this word and wyth redyng of Holy Scriptur'.[4] In other words, she wants a new priest because she needs access to books. Christ's response sounds almost obedient, but his words, 'Ther schal come on fro fer that schal fulfillyn thi desyr', are framed as a minor mystery in the narrative: *will* this new priest be the one who fulfills Margery's desire? Is she wrong to express such a demand? Is Margery misinterpreting a demonic vision as a conversation with Christ? Without the affirmation of the Dominican anchorite who has previously approved her visions one by one, the validity of the conversation and the meaning of Christ's words are unclear. It is only when this new priest establishes rapport with Margery and reads her the books, which turn out to be 'to gret encres of hys cunnyng and of hys meryte', that Margery's own discernment is no longer in question. The priest can be accepted as sent from God, and Margery's status as visionary appears trustworthy, *because the books are good*: 'And than wist sche that it *was* a spirit sent of God whech seyd to hir, as is wretyn a lityl beforn, whan sche compleynyd for defawte of redyng, thes wordys, "Ther schal come on fro fer that schal fulfillyn thi desyr"'.[5] The books confirm both the priest's legitimacy and Margery's, since their quality reframes Christ's response to her request as prophecy. This is the conclusion the narrative offers in its own analysis: Margery requires reading material, and Christ has provided it through this priest.

This portrayal of Margery's active participation in textual culture is itself enough to combat the *Boke*'s occasional claim of her illiteracy, but it masks the breadth and depth of what appears to have been her longtime text-based practice. Christ's brief and enigmatic response, 'Ther schal come on fro fer that schal fulfillyn thi desyr', is provoked by what turns out to be Margery's most impassioned *j'accuse* to Christ in the *Boke*: '*thu hast takyn awey* the ankyr fro me whech was to me synguler solas and comforte and many tymes refreschyd me wyth thin holy worde'.[6] With this line, she claims a debt that awaits payment: Christ *owes* her a confessor. The new priest who reads books to her in chapter 58 is meant to replace the loss of the Dominican anchorite and his unspecified textual influence, an equation that strongly implies that the anchorite's relationship with Margery was also rooted in texts. Ultimately, Margery gets access to *more books*, and thus more literacy, as a direct result of the anger she expresses over the death of the anchorite.

Here I want to acknowledge that literacy represents a set of social practices, as explained by education researchers David Barton and Mary Hamilton.[7] It is helpful to think of Margery's textual discussions with the Dominican anchorite and the priest as 'literacy events', social activities that are centered on a text, and on her pilgrimages and time in churches as the resulting 'literacy practices', the activities that are prompted by specific literacy events.⁸ When we see how crucial the literacy *event* of shared reading is to the literacy *practice* of pilgrimage, Margery's urgent need to replace the Dominican anchorite makes more sense.

We should, then, recognize Margery's prior encounters with the late, unnamed Dominican anchorite and his also-unnamed books as her first training in *devotional* literacies—training that led her to the extensive pilgrimage and practice of *imitatio Mariae* that distinguish her narrative. The Franciscan origins of the titles in her cited list should not obscure the Dominican origins of her dependence on texts. More generally, this passage reminds us that book ownership was not required for book access. Medieval women benefited from the large physical and mental libraries available to their confessors, who could provide through summary, suggestion, and discussion the content from books they might not lend out. As we see here, Margery's demand for regular access to such content also wins her the collaborative interpretation and informal religious community that comes with sharing books. But Margery's behaviors as a pilgrim, and particularly her multivalent interpretations of the Virgin Mary, also indicate engagement with mendicant textual and visual culture at a level that suggests purpose-based learning. Margery's is not a typical literacy, but she demonstrates just how far the boundaries of devotional literacy and *imitatio Mariae* could conceivably be pushed. She could easily claim literal maternal authority from her bodily experience, but instead aims for oblique, theoretical maternities that access Marian power.

Margery articulates the Dominican's importance in chapter 69, when she augments her reproach of Christ and her loyalty to the anchorite: he is now 'þe most special & synguler comforte þat euyr I had in erde, for he euyr louyd me for thy lofe & wold neuyr forsakyn me for nowt þat any man cowd do er seye', to which Christ replies defensively, 'Dowtyr, *I* am mor worthy to thy sowle than evyr was the ankyr'.⁹ This man whose loyalty inspires a touch of jealousy from Christ flies mostly under the radar in the *Boke* and in scholarship, but his influence is crucial.[10] In chapter 16, he categorizes Margery's permission from Archbishop Arundel to choose her own confessor—the anchorite himself—a 'gret myracle', a declaration Hope Emily Allen explains would have 'marked her for sanctity'.[11] The anchorite risks important relationships to continue confessing

Margery.[12] He assures her in chapter 19 that her tears are indeed a heavenly gift. He expects to be consulted for approval of her visions, and he clearly has an understated hand in her visits to various pilgrimage sites in England and on the continent. It is the anchorite who in chapter 26 predicts both Margery's traveling troubles in Germany and the 'brokebakkyd' Richard who will help her communicate with priests in Italy, and who must have himself arranged for Richard's services through the extensive Dominican communication networks in those regions.[13] By the time Margery leaves for the continent, she has established herself as a prophet, as controversial, as 'chosen', and as well-connected: the Dominican anchorite has quietly overseen it all, and he has died by the time she returns. While Margery never quite recovers the Dominican support she enjoyed under the anchorite's direction, Dominicans feature regularly as low-key heroes in the narrative to advance her arc toward the holy.[14]

I regard Margery's first choice of spiritual advisor as a deliberate and literate act, rooted in her educated preference for a Dominican lens through which to view and read the world.[15] The order's longstanding interest in women's mystical practice and the material focus to its devotional theories are well documented.[16] In selecting as confessor a Dominican anchorite who offers her access to literate culture, Margery begins training that shadows the more formal arts program of German women under Dominican direction and that requires her to engage not only with Christ but with Mary, especially through visual stimuli.[17] Her devotional practices draw from both German sources and locally produced books. As we'll see, Dominican theories regarding Mary, art, and the interaction of the two offer a cohesive way to interpret Margery's time in so many faraway churches.[18] Her absorption and assessment of liturgical visual components via an earnest, if inconsistent, *imitatio Dominicani* also affirm her impulses toward *imitatio Mariae*.

Margery *Ecclesia*

Throughout the narrative, Margery's frequent jockeying for position with the Virgin Mary may be among the most disconcerting of her many surprising self-disclosures. Tara Williams has written compellingly about Margery's emphases on her own physical maternity and sexuality toward this end, noting that 'in her intimacy and authority, Margery eventually seeks to *exceed* the Virgin Mary herself'.[19] I would go further: the *Boke* offers ample evidence that Margery meant to supplant Mary in aspects well beyond the sexual, particularly in her role as representative of and interchangeable with the Church. Specifically, German mystics' metaphors of incarnation through images and local travel guides' advice to pilgrims about engaging with liturgical art provide a textual foundation for Margery's idiosyncratic *imitatio Mariae* program. The liturgical art and architecture she encounters in her travels, then, act as material reflections and reinforcements of her attempt to supersede Mary and help explain her view of Mary's role in and as the Church. Margery's pilgrimages and multiple visits to churches are thus not a separate spiritual endeavor from her *imitatio Mariae* or her engagement with literate culture, but an integral piece of both.

Signposts to this appear early in the *Boke*. The moment in the Proem that finds Margery 'sekyng socowr undyr the wengys of hyr gostly modyr, Holy Cherch' signals that the slippage between 'Holy Cherch' and 'gostly modyr' will play an important role in the narrative. These terms are worth parsing, given late-medieval England's association of Marian maternity with the Church and Margery's own complex relationships with each. Specifically, the period's multivalent concept of *ecclesia* offers support for eliding the 'gostly modyr' figure with the 'Holy Cherch' building.[20] One dedication sermon ascribes four different meanings to *ecclesia*: as 'the Virgin, who became a church through the Incarnation; the material church, made holy through the celebration of Mass and the representation of the Passion; the soul, a church by the infusion of grace; and lastly, the heavenly mansions'.[21] The first several chapters of *Boke* blend various Ecclesian narratives into Margery's own, as she merges the 'soul' and 'church building' definitions—and multiple Marian identities—into one. Inhabiting the role of *Maria Ecclesia* meant not only being maternal and bridely, as other scholars have noted,[22] but also interpreting and taking on characteristics of the Church as physical building and as institution. As we will see, Margery's implicit constellation of logic alleges that she is analogous to Mary, that the church building itself functions like a maternal body to the point of fungibility, and that her own maternal body can take on many of the functions of that building and institution. Her attempted replacement of Mary draws from her experience of the spaces and visual art most associated with 'Holy Cherch'. The connections of these seemingly disparate themes are best explained by Dominican interpretations of mysticism, maternity, material culture, and faith practice.

Incarnation, reflection, and inhabitation

For Dominican mystics, birth was a crucial metaphor, and imagery was both central to devotion and a point of contention.[23] As Meister Eckhart saw it, the 'birth' of God in the Christian soul is the focus of all creation, evidence of God's creativity, and signified by all devotional images.[24] God's engagement with humanity replicates Mary's experience of the Incarnation in each Christian; however, for Eckhart, once God has been 'born' in an individual soul, devotional images are no longer necessary.[25] Henry Suso departs slightly from Eckhart by recommending continued engagement with images: successful visual contemplation results in an ontological exchange between the soul and the divine truth signified by the image. For Suso, devotional practice *requires* the image, for it is the image's absorption of a soul that makes each individual incarnation, or union with Christ, possible.[26]

The circulation and translation of Suso's *Horologium Sapientiae* in multiple manuscripts across England and its connections to Mountgrace Charterhouse suggest that Suso's embrace of devotional images was well-received by the community that ultimately preserved Margery's *Boke*.[27] Several passages in *Horologium* reflect the Dominican conception of humans as images of the divine, as when Suso's Disciple declares to Wisdom, a stand-in for Mary, 'I lift up myne eyene, myne handes to þe ... deuowtly besekynge þe þat þe ymage and likenesse of þi wirchepfulle passione be effectuelye pryntede in mye sowle'.[28]

Margery as (Marian) mirror

Margery's absorption of these Dominican ideas is evident in her description and imitation of Mary's bodily maternity.[29] In chapter 77 of the *Boke* Margery prays that her Marian spiritual gift of holy tears be removed or made more discreet. Christ explains his intention that 'my modrys sorwe be knowyn by the that men and women myth have the mor compassyon of hir sorwe that sche suffyrd for me': people would know the grief of *Mater dolorosa* through their encounters with Margery's involuntary tears. Further, he clarifies, even the intercession of Mary herself would not sway him ('thu schalt not han thy desyr in this thow my modyr and alle the seyntys in hevyn preye for the'). That is, Margery's behavior as Mary's proxy is more important than the actual Mary's wishes. Lest Margery miss the implications of this, Christ adds in the next chapter, 'Nevyrthelesse, dowtyr, I have ordeynd the to be a *merowr* amongys hem for to han gret sorwe that thei schulde takyn exampil by the for to have sum litil sorwe in her hertys for her synnys that thei myth therthorw be savyd'.

Aside from the shocking revelation that it is now through Margery, not Mary, that sinners will find grace, Christ's choice of 'mirror' ('merowr') had special resonance for medieval believers. Per the Apostle Paul, God could be known only 'per speculum in aenigmate' (through a mirror, dimly)[30]—that is, only through signs and representations, which were not to be mistaken for God himself, and whose interpretations were dependent on faith. And yet Mary as mirror of Christ was described by the Dominican Jacobus de Voragine in his popular Mariale sermon cycle, *Sermones aurei de beata Maria*, as comparable to the 'speculum sine macula' in the Book of Wisdom, so pure nothing could taint her purity or her clear reflection of Christ.[31] From that point, mirrors in visual art had Marian inflections,[32] as we see when Suso's Disciple addresses Wisdom as 'þou *myrrour* of clannesse and of alle vertues'.[33] Further, in the *Liber Celestis* of Bridget of Sweden, a text with which Margery was familiar, Mary confides that 'God is so ner to me þat he þat sese him sese me: and whoso sese me sese þe godhede and manhede in me as in a *mirowe*'.[34] Margery as 'merowr' thus serves a double function: She herself acts as a representation, a dim reflection of Christ, and as such also embodies a new version of Mary.[35]

Margery would have known that this concept of mirrors containing or reflecting an ideal was frequently applied to religious texts. The Augustinian Rule, adopted by Dominicans, ends with the instruction, 'That you may see yourself in this little book *as in a mirror* and may not neglect anything through forgetfulness, let it be read to you once a week'.[36] Bernard of Clairvaux described meditation on scripture and of hagiography as profitably analogous to spiritual mirror-gazing.[37] Margery may have imagined her *Boke* as a retaining mirror that would offer Christ's words, and her own, direct to the reader after her death.[38] If holiness can be absorbed by ideal bodies such as Mary's and Margery's, then it might also be reflected by the narratives that describe them: this thinking, rooted in Augustine's and Bernard's observations about sacred texts, renders Christ's assignment of 'mirror' to her body extendible to her text.

Margery's trip to Aachen in 1433 to see relics such as Mary's birthing smock and Christ's swaddling clothes augments the import of her function as 'mirror' and her purpose on pilgrimages.[39] According to Heinrich Schwarz, commemorative handheld circular mirrors were sold by the thousands to pilgrims during the *Heiligtumsfahrt*, Aachen's Holy Week event, an enterprise with such lucrative potential that Johannes Gutenberg tried to enter the market in 1438.[40] These were not merely souvenirs: in a gesture eerily similar to that of taking a snapshot, pilgrims aimed their new mirrors at the display of relics to capture their visual and spiritual power so that holders could share the holy place's essence upon their return home.[41] (See Plate 1.) Just as pilgrims' badges were commonly believed to retain some of the sacred nature of their sites of origin, and a copy of a holy painting thought to distribute some of the original's power,[42] so too could a mirror absorb visually the power of relics and pilgrimage sites. If Margery is herself a 'merowr', she potentially retains and can distribute the powers of Christ as well as the holiness of the many sacred sites she has visited.[43]

Margery *Ecclesia*: inhabitation, incorporation, incarnation

This line of thinking has remarkable affinity with modern geographical theories holding that repeated presence in a place allows one to become part of or absorb the power of that place. Richard Lang has argued that 'Inhabiting is an act of incorporation; it is a situation of active, essential acquisition ... embracing and assimilating a certain sphere of foreign reality to its own body. In this sense, incorporation is essentially the movement from the strange to the familiar'.[44] Karen Franck explains, 'Through our patterns of inhabitation, space becomes a kind of possession ... Through our daily pattern of activities and routines, we acquire the space we are using; we lay claim to it by our actions' and 'incorporate these places and spaces into ourselves'.[45] Reading Margery's significant time spent in churches through this theoretical lens, with an eye toward Dominican interests in the powers of devotional art, creation, and incarnation, suggests that she absorbs liturgical space and power into her own body, to reflect and distribute as she sees fit. Taken to its conclusion: she gradually threatens to become the site of another 'church', another route toward becoming another, better Mary.

We see a hint of how literally—and playfully—this possibility could be interpreted in Jan van Eyck's *The Virgin in the Church*, the left half of a diptypch depicting Mary as Queen of Heaven with the Christ child in a Gothic nave.[46] The church interior surrounding her includes tracery and carvings that show scenes from multiple maternal stages of her life, including the Annunciation, Crucifixion, and Coronation, as well as a Madonna statue that mirrors the live Virgin and child in the foreground. The image works as a visual chicken-and-egg puzzle: is Mary emerging from the architectural fabric of the church as if invoked, or was the church simply built up around her? The presence of the Christ child and of the art in the background underscores the blurriness of the line between incarnation and incorporation. It is that grey area that allows Margery to try on Marian identity through the Dominican blending of incarnation, incorporation, and reflection. The *Boke* assumes that the reader understands as well as Margery does that her presence in a holy space matters. Her proactive inhabitations of churches are clearly an important narrative thread, but it is not always obvious how we are meant to understand her effect on the churches or their effects on her. Knowing that she approaches these spaces with Dominican concepts in mind helps clarify her function there.

Christ's frequent communiques affirm Margery's potential to *become* liturgical space just as his mother Mary has.[47] He seems to think of Margery's as a holy body, a sacred place capable of bypassing or replacing ecclesiastical architecture, and he underscores her role as a mirror reflection of himself. When Margery decides in chapter 10 that her body is healed and healthy enough to go on pilgrimage, he assures her, with Dominican phrasing, that 'thei that worshep the thei worshep me; thei that despysen the thei despysen me ... *I am in the, and thow in me*. And thei that heryn the thei heryn the voys of God'.⁴⁸ He again makes Margery his proxy in chapter 34, 'as long as he spekyth ageyns the, he spekyth ageyns me, for I am in the and thu art in me',⁴⁹ in terms that echo both John 14:20 and the Dominican ideas of incarnational and ontological exchange. Christ's assurance in chapter 14, 'the how thow art wretyn in myn handys and my fete', is often glossed as Isaiah 49:16. The full biblical passage reveals architectural metaphors: 'Behold, I have graven thee in my hands: *thy walls* are always before my eyes. *Thy builders* are come: they that destroy thee and make thee waste shall go out of thee' (Isaiah 49:16–17). Later in the same passage Christ identifies Margery as his daughter, mother, sister, wife, spouse. Like Mary, she fills all roles, acting as Christ's mirror and even, here, as his house. It is only a short, audacious step from being recognized as *like* Mary to trying to replace her.

Dominican devotional literacies

Margery's wealthier, literate contemporaries had their own bespoke or spot-customized books to guide them to an orthodox Marian relationship. As we've seen, Margery engages with books through confessors' summaries, explanations, and oral performance. In addition to the seven or eight years she spent with a priest reading her mystical texts and her time with the anchorite before that, she mentions the psalter and the Gospel, and she once makes casual mention of 'hir boke in hir hand'.⁵⁰ She speaks more directly of social encounters in specific places, often churches, that train her to compare herself to Mary honestly. ('Sum gret clerkys seyden owyr Lady cryed nevyr so', she admits when her inexplicable gift of holy tears is criticized.⁵¹) More direct still is the disarmingly causal relationship between what Margery sees in churches and what she experiences in visions. At multiple points, Margery describes visionary episodes that occur in close proximity to a liturgical space or specific monument (such as the Great East Window at York Minster), trusting the curious reader to deduce the visual stimulus from her location.⁵² This connection between art and vision might be read simply as adherence to mystical manuals' instructions, which famously relied on visual stimuli. Barbara Newman details how Margery developed a practiced talent for 'scripted visions', calling hers a 'mimetic mysticism' and suggesting that Christ's early advice for Margery to think of his mother is meant to signify her entry-level status as a visionary.[53]

We should note, then, that the chapter immediately preceding the moment that Christ instructs Margery 'Dowtyr, thynke on my modyr' also marks the first appearance of her Dominican anchoritic confessor, at Christ's prompting. In chapter 5, Christ instructs Margery to stop eating meat, to start taking communion, to accept her visions passively, and, crucially, to go to the Dominican anchorite, who remarks upon meeting her, 'ye sowkyn evyn on Crysts brest'. It's an odd comment until we remember that Suso often described himself as 'nursing' at Christ's or Mary's breast; Catherine of Siena, too, a mystic with a Dominican confessor, consistently focused on this image.[54] The anchorite, then, seems to recognize Margery not simply as a novice visionary, but as one whose insights ground her in maternity and in recent Dominican mystical imagery.[55]

Similarly, Margery's linking of her first Marian meditation to the anchorite appears an attempt to credit him, and perhaps Dominicans generally, for the Marian turn in the narrative. Margery's vision places her at the Nativity in a caretaking scene similar to the following vision of Suso's:

> He looked at its pretty little eyes, gazed as its tiny hands, and kissed its tender little mouth. All the tiny limbs of the heavenly treasure he looked at carefully and, raising his eyes, he cried out in amazement in his heart that the bearer of the heavens is so great and so small, so beautiful in heaven and just a Child on earth. He busied himself with him as the occasion allowed, with singing, with weeping, and with spiritual exercises.[56]

The nurturing of baby Christ that Suso describes appears in a handful of female mystics' visions, as well, but given his popularity in England, Suso is Margery's most likely source. (Margery's role model Bridget of Sweden, though not Dominican, was also a reader of Suso's.) In this light, Margery's meditation on Mary and the infant Christ in chapter 6 helps establish her not only as a visionary but as a Dominican protégé.

This first meeting also makes clear that the Dominican and Christ are on the same page: 'I charge yow receyveth swech thowtys whan God wyl geve hem as mekely and as devowtly as ye kan', the anchorite says, echoing Christ's admonition a few lines earlier to 'thynk swych thowtys as I wyl putt in thi mend'. Instant credibility! As Margery's new confessor, the Dominican anchorite will decide whether her visions are from God or Satan. Once she receives a vision, he explains, she should 'comyth to me and tellyth me what thei be, and I schal, wyth the leve of ower Lord Jhesu Cryst, telle yow whether thei ben of the Holy Gost or ellys of yowr enmy the devyl'. He does not state outright that in addition to exercising his own discernment for her benefit, he will train her to assess and evaluate her visions and their stimuli when she travels alone, but that is clearly what must happen as she prepares to go on pilgrimage.

Margery's art literacy and performance

Margery often employs tangible objects or images to demonstrate her connectedness to Christ, Mary, or other holy women: white clothing, the love-token ring from Christ, the baby-Christ dress-up dolls, even the conspicuous lack of distaff that distinguishes her from ordinary women in chapter 53. Those she encounters in person or through the text are expected to 'read' the objects appropriately. Taken at face value, Margery's faith journey as described in *Boke* offers a series of material alternatives to literate Marian devotion. To a textually biased reader, her literal interpretations of theological nuances appears to reveal a ham-fisted grasp of doctrine and practice. But that interpretation misreads Margery's visual literacy and her application of her confessor's books and Dominican training. Particularly at Töss and other convents in Germany, as Jeffrey Hamburger and others have documented, women under Dominican tutelage were trained not only to contemplate but to create images in paint or textiles.[57] While Margery never indicates that her confessor encourages her to paint or stitch, her scene descriptions often create living tableaux, as if she is staging the visual art she sees in liturgical spaces. Her use of props such as the ring, dolls, and white clothing might be better understood as artistic performance of the ideas with which she is already familiar.

Chapter 22 offers one example: when Margery expresses her desperate fear of death, Christ promises her a welcome in heaven almost identical to depictions of Mary's assumption there. She'll be greeted by the twelve Apostles and multiple saints; Christ will take her in one hand, Mary in the other. Margery, Christ's 'own derworthy derlyng', will be granted the role of Queen of Heaven, appropriating Mary's place. The mere assurance of welcome must have seemed insufficient: Margery requires the starring role in a scene she recognizes from liturgical art. This insertion of herself into an important position is not far removed from the common practice of pious art patrons having themselves painted into key biblical scenes, as Virginia Chieffo Raguin has described.[58] Margery offers a live-action version of the way surrogates functioned in visual art. Laura Gelfand and Walter Gibson explain that patrons whose images appeared in altarpieces and book illuminations with Mary, Christ, or the saints 'could communicate with the divine through their own likenesses, and continue to do so even after death'.[59] But while Margery's process may be conventional, her results are not: she not only empathizes with the Virgin Mary, but actively projects herself into or beyond Mary's role.

Certainly Margery's behaviors are not quite the docile 'reading' that Pope Gregory I had in mind when he outlined his argument for what became known as *libri laicorum*,[60] or that justified Abbot Suger's preference for fancy materials in cathedral building.[61] But the *Boke*'s matter-of-fact acknowledgment that Margery's visions occur in response to visual catalysts in liturgical spaces takes a definite orthodox position within a contemporary debate, both within and outside the Dominican community. Challenges from iconoclasts had theologians carefully re-articulating the role of liturgical images.[62] Archbishop Arundel's statement at a heresy trial in 1407 publicly affirmed their importance:

> I graunte wel þat no liif owiþ to do worschip to ony siche ymage for itsilf. But a crucifix owiþ to be worschipid for þe passioun of Crist þat is peyntid þereinne, and is brouȝt þereþoruȝ into manus mynde. And þus þe ymage of þe blessid virgyne Marie, Cristis modir, and oþer ymagis of seyntis owen to ben worschipid.[63]

In the vein of Gregory I and Abbot Suger, the late fourteenth-century *De Adoracione Ymaginum (On the Worship of Images)* essentially re-stated that laypersons *required* physical representations of spiritual ideas: with their impoverished faith and their lukewarm love, they needed to ingest not solid food but the infant 'milk' of corporeal signs.[64] (We might here remember Suso's contention that images were required for devotional meditation.) However justified it was, lay engagement with liturgical art required careful discernment. In aiming to resolve lay confusion with explicit instruction, *Dives and Pauper*'s dialogue on the First Commandment spells out how high the stakes are:

> wurshepe [God] abouyn alle thyngge, nought þe ymage, nought þe stok, stoon ne tree, but hym þat deyid on þe tree for þin synne and for þin sake, so þat þu knele, ȝyf þu wylt, aforn þe ymage nought to þe ymage. *Doo þin wurshepe aforn þe ymage nought to þe ymage. … For ȝyf þu doo it for þe ymage or to þe ymage þu doist ydolatrye.*[65]

Margery seems unworried. In all her time spent in church and arguing with clerics, she never challenges whether art should be visible or how it should function. Liturgical material culture, including art, relics, and architecture, matters to her: she comments on individual depictions of the Pietà and of the Crucifixion with an awareness of technical terms such as 'Pietà' ('pyté') and who's who in Crucifixion scenes.[66] As Richard Marks explains, the popular 'our lady of pity', like Suso, originated in south Germany.[67] The Gesine chapel where she spent so much time was likely named for (and may have housed) a 'gesyn' sculpture of postnatal Mary. Margery's domestic visual education was German-influenced, rooted in the imagery of Christ's birth.

Mary's arts knowledge emerges in the text in unexpected ways. In chapter 32, when Margery cannot find a confessor in Rome, Christ sends her John the Evangelist—who was often depicted alongside Mary as her chosen caretaker at the foot of the Cross. (Mirk's Assumption Day sermon also features John spontaneously appearing to help the Virgin.) As she develops her practice of *imitatio Mariae*, Margery pays attention both to what she is supposed to do in the face of liturgical monuments and also to the monuments themselves: she knows what they mean and what they're for. Her visions are sourced in images and experiences housed and approved by the church. Her interpretation of liturgical aesthetics is both affirmation of what the church claims and a path toward what her visions tell her directly. As the text reveals, she regularly 'reads' Crucifixion scenes, Nativities, and pietàs, and spends considerable time in chapels, praying near relics, stained-glass windows, and statuary.[68]

Pilgrimage as Marian performance

Some of this expertise doubtless results from Margery's travel preparations under the Dominican anchorite's guidance.[69] Pilgrims were encouraged not only to attend masses and collect indulgences while traveling but to seek out specific relics and works of art, which they would presumably know not to worship. For example, in its description of Rome's Basilica of Santa Maria Maggiore, *Stacions of the Cross* (c. 1370) first lists the church's relics, such as 'the bodi of seint Jerom' (479), the cloth Mary put Christ in at his birth, and the hay he lay on in the manger.[70] Margery spent time in Santa Maria Maggiore during her Lenten visit to Rome, about which she offers an account clearly connected to her encounter with Jerome's relics:

> On a tyme, as this creatur was in a chirche at Rome wher the body of Seynt Jerom lyth biriid ..., to this creaturys gostly sygth aperyng, Seynt Jerom seyd to hir sowle, 'Blissed art thow, dowtyr, in the wepyng that thu wepyst for the peplys synnes, for many schal be savyd therby. And, dowtyr, drede the nowt, for it is a synguler and a specyal gyft that God hath govyn the, a welle of teerys the whech schal nevyr man take fro the'.[71]

It is striking that Jerome, like Christ, encourages Margery's *imitatio Mariae* in the form of holy tears. As we have seen above, Christ agrees that her tears are the venue by which 'many schal be savyd'. Jerome has his own associations with Mary ('Mors per Evam: vita per Mariam'/'death through Eve, life through Mary', Epistle 22.21).[72] He, like John the Evangelist, frequently appears alongside the Virgin in Crucifixion and other scenes.[73] His blessing acts to legitimate Margery as a version of the *dolorosa*, and the whole episode confirms her as a careful observer of the site-specific Marian attractions that pilgrim guides such as *Stacions of the Cross* offer.

This vision, which occurs near the end of Margery's stay in Rome, tends to be overshadowed by the more titillating account of her wedding to the Godhead in chapter 35 and Christ's subsequent love-talk, when he invites her to 'take me to the as for thi weddyd husbond, as thy derworthy derlyng, and as for thy swete sone, for I wyl be lovyd as a sone schuld be lovyd wyth the modyr and wil that thu love me, dowtyr, as a good wife owyth to love hir husbonde'.[74] Although not atypical of mystical texts, this language of intimacy does not fit the rest of Margery's Rome travel narrative. What has sparked this nuptial joy, particularly Christ's synonymous use of 'son' and 'husband'? That Margery has prepared to enhance her Marian identity in Rome is hardly in question: she accepts her gift of tears and visits Mary's burial place in Jerusalem (chapters 28 and 29) and has recently seen the 'kerche' or veil Mary wore in Assisi, prompting a flood of those tears in chapter 31. It certainly seems possible that Margery's development of *new* aspects of her Marian persona relies at least partially on her interpretations of the jumble of Byzantine and Italian images of Mary that she sees in Rome.[75]

The pilgrim's guide *Stacions of the Cross* describes a Marian icon in Santa Maria Maggiore about which the *Boke* is silent: 'an ymage sikerly/Wonder feir of vre ladi./Seint Luik while he lyuede in londe/Wolde haue peynted hit with his honde/And whon he hedde ordeyned so/Alle colours þat þer to/He fond an ymage al a-pert/ Mad with Angel hone and not with his' (505–13). This late sixth-century icon portraying the Madonna with child had accrued its own local history connected to Mary's role as Queen of Heaven by the time Margery saw it. A twelfth-century cleric claimed that the 'image … began to stir' the night before the Assumption feast in anticipation of 'meeting' the Christ icon from St John Lateran in a procession meant to re-enact their reunion in heaven, an anecdote and practice that was still repeated in the fifteenth century.[76] Given Margery's preoccupation with Mary and the Christ child, it is hard to imagine that she missed this icon that lusted for Christ or Santa Maria Maggiore's other Marian depictions. Viewing the apse there, for example, she would see a dazzling mosaic of the Coronation of Mary, who is seated next to an enthroned and crowned Christ. Just below the mosaic, an inscription of text borrowed from Assumption feast antiphons reads, 'The Virgin Mary is assumed into the ethereal bridal chamber, in which the King of Kings is seated on a starry throne; the holy Mother of God is exalted above the choirs of angels to the celestial realm'.[77] Margery might also have noticed the triumphal arch mosaic that Maria Lidova argues depicts *Maria Regina* as *Mater Ecclesia*.[78] In all of these, the dominant note is of Mary as regent of heaven and bride to Christ, an encouraging prelude to an aspiring Mary's vision of marrying God. Here, again, Margery's familiarity with her confessor's books' instructions about what and how pilgrims should see—to 'read' images for meaning, to allow them to shape her devotion, to 'birth' Christ in various manifestations—would allow her to make an on-the-spot assessment of the nature of Mary and Christ's relationship.

The dual themes of *Maria Regina* and as *sponsa Christi* intensify across the river at another eponymous church, Santa Maria in Trastevere ('seinte Marie in trismere' in *Stacions*), a station that Margery would have visited in the second week of Lent. There, the connection of Mary's regency with her motherhood remains strong: its façade mosaic features an enthroned *Maria lactans* surrounded by virgins approaching with offerings. Even the sixth-century icon of Mary holding the Christ child depicts her as queen.[79] In another monument at Trastevere, the overlap of Mary with *Ecclesia* is more explicit than her role as mother: the apse mosaic's crowned heavenly bride is spectacularly enthroned and embraced by Christ. She displays a scroll identifying her with the Bride (or Church) in Song of Songs ('His left hand is under my head, and his right hand shall embrace me'), while the pages of Christ's book connect her to the Mary of the Assumption ('Come, my chosen one, and I will place in you my throne'), dueling captions that, for those versed in biblical typology, agree only if the viewer interprets the bride as simultaneously both *Ecclesia* and *Maria Regina*.[80] Looking at this mosaic, it is difficult to ignore the accoutrements of Mary's regency as Christ's bride and as Ecclesia.

The apse mosaic in Trastevere encourages a nuanced understanding of Mary's many functions, one for which Margery's multi-pronged approach to *imitatio Mariae* and to liturgical art suggests she was ready. She may have seen similar images before, perhaps in a priest's or anchorite's book, and she certainly would have heard about the concept in sermons. So many depictions of *Maria Regina* in one place—and Margery's clear response to them in the form of her nuptial visions—invite us to consider more carefully *Maria Ecclesia*, a figure who offers a plausible model for Margery to think of herself not only as Christ's bride but as the church, as Mary was understood to be.[81] The beginning of chapter 41 suggests Margery was thinking along these lines while in Rome. Frustrated by her incomprehension of the sermons preached in foreign languages, Margery is comforted by 'Crist Jhesu, whos melydiows voys swettest of alle savowrys softly sowndyng in hir sowle, seyd, "*I schal preche the and teche the myselfe*, for thi wyl and thy desyr is acceptabyl unto me"'.[82] It is not the first time Christ has indicated that Margery is superior to the church, but it is followed by the confirmation episode of Roman locals acknowledging her good influence. Identifying as a church might not come as naturally to Margery as being Christ's bride or *dolorosa*, but outdoing Mary would require embodying all of the Virgin's attributes, not only the easy or obvious ones. Her becoming the bride of Christ is signaled explicitly by his request to join her in bed, but we might not as easily recognize how Margery is performing other components of *imitatio Mariae*, such as Mary's interchangeability with the church.

Imitatio Mariae via Ecclesia and Gothic spaces

The theoretical gap between Margery's general attempt to supersede Mary while she happens to be visiting multiple churches and her ambition to *become* symbolically synonymous with the church, as was Mary, begins to close when we fully consider the rich theological concept of Ecclesia depicted in several liturgical images. According to Ruth Horie, the term *ecclesia* as deployed in sermons could indicate 'the clergy, the Virgin Mary, the material church, the soul, or the universal Church'.[83] Mary herself had been widely considered a type for the church at least since Isidore of Seville stated explicitly, 'Mary is the figure of the Church'.[84] Further, Honorius of Autun explained that 'everything that is said of the Church can also be understood as being like the Virgin herself, the bride and mother of the Bridegroom'.[85] The interchangeability of the two female figures is evident across multiple visual media, where the young woman representing Ecclesia appears dressed in Mary's signature blue, and at least once is shown holding a book.[86] Each is a favorite subject in Crucifixion depictions and in illustrations of Song of Songs 1.1.[87] Ecclesia's flexibility as a symbol in vernacular sermons and in liturgical art fruitfully collapses the feminine spiritual church and

The Dominican literacies of Margery Kempe's pilgrimages 33

Mary's maternal body with the church building. Ecclesia's extreme metonymic function derives partly from the Pauline Epistle to the Ephesians 5.21–25 and from enthusiastic applications of the wife-as-church metaphor to the Song of Songs. Images of and references to Ecclesia had long been proliferating, and it is unlikely that Rome was the first place Margery encountered her.[88]

Ecclesia provides a concrete model for Margery to apply the Dominican idea of incorporation to her own Marian agenda. The anchorite, whose identity and spiritual experience were fused with his cell, could also help expand Margery's connection of her spirituality with the spatial.[89] As her pilgrimages revealed examples of the various forms that *imitatio Mariae* could take, liturgical spaces offered opportunities for her to absorb and, like a mirror, reflect. Seeing Rome in shambles and eventually participating in the restoration of her home church,[90] the Margery who narrates is simultaneously aware of the impermanence of architecture and a believer in *genius loci*, the power of place. Margery rarely mentions the architectural aspect of her travels but regularly describes the results of her presence in churches. She 'reads' liturgical spaces and alters them with her sonic and visual inscriptions: other pilgrims would remember *her*, weeping noisily and reflecting colored beams broadcast from stained-glass windows to her white garments, as well as the space.

The conflation of Mary with the church building is most evident in the Marian visual cues of Gothic architecture to which Margery's travels exposed her in England and elsewhere. The Gothic style had developed in tandem with theories of Mary as the Church and as *sponsa Christi*—van Eyck's *Virgin in the Church* depicts a Gothic space—and its connection to those Marian metaphors is often made explicit in the number of churches named in honor of Our Lady.[91] These edifices not only contained the relics, floor plan, and radiating chapels that allowed ordinary pilgrims to express devotion, but suggested the Marian physique more literally. The miraculous architecture of Mary's womb was deconstructed in multiple large, liturgical spaces within which pilgrims could wander after entering through suggestively-shaped vulvic doors: dark and mysteriously scented, with rose windows to acknowledge Mary's virginity, skinlike walls stretching between visible supports, tracery branching out like veins.[92] The old metaphor of the church as body was fully unpacked, with reliquaries shaped as body parts and whole skeletons brought from the crypt to new tombs on the ground floor. In their external display of framing supports such as flying buttresses and vaulting ribs that eerily replicated the body's bones, and light through windows that suggested ethereal breath, Gothic architectural structures also visually affirmed the possibility that a physical, maternal body could access and express the divine. The cross shape of the floor plan has traditionally signified Christ himself, so that entering the church allows the worshipper metaphorically inside Christ's body.[93] But given the common theoretical slippage in defining Ecclesia, these eponymous churches could be equally coded as Marian. Medieval theologians regularly described Mary's body as the church and her womb as the site of incarnation—Ecclesia offers validation for this—making explicit the Gothic connections of the body to the spiritual.

The sophistication of churchgoers' interpretation of stylistic elements as Marian is demonstrated by the *Marienschrein* that housed the Marian relics Margery saw in Aachen. As Lisa Victoria Ciresi has explained, the reliquary is shaped like a small Gothic cathedral. Its only clue to the Marian contents within is its resemblance to the church style developed in her honor.[94] The visual effectiveness of the reliquary depended on viewers' understanding of Mary's inextricable, symbiotic connection to the Gothic church. Mary (or, here, her secondary relics) inhabits the church, and it is her presence that renders it holy.

Margery is fully capable of this level of interpretation; she does not mention maternity, architecture, or shrines in her book because she considers their meanings, like those of the visual art described above, self-evident. For example, we learn in chapter 10 that York is the first place she visits on pilgrimage, probably to see the Corpus Christi plays in June 1413—York, with the gigantic Gothic cathedral she says nothing about, where the expensive and imported blue glass in the windows should have dazzled her.[95] Yet she does highlight the places she visits that happen to have Gothic cathedrals, barely mentioning those without them. Virginia Raguin has discussed Margery's liturgical spaces and provides many intriguing leads in *Mapping Margery Kempe*, the wide-ranging online compendium of resources that she and Sarah Stanbury host at Holy Cross.[96] Their list of the English cathedrals Margery visited gives a sense of her steady exposure to Gothic architecture, largely at home

The Dominican literacies of Margery Kempe's pilgrimages 35

in England: Bristol, Canterbury, Ely, Lincoln, Norwich, York. Margery also visited Aachen and may well have passed through Liège on her way back home.

As Franck explains, architectural elements suggest what bodies are meant to do in a space: doorways let human bodies pass in and out; windows in doors suggest we pause and peer through before opening; towers and building height mean bodies will move up and down.[97] Design organizes movement. As Franck puts it, 'we *learn* ways of inhabiting space'.[98] Church architects had a particular use in mind for what Gothic liturgical space would encourage bodies to do: just as radiating chapels encouraged pilgrims to take certain pathways, screens and narrow passages were intended to keep people out. As a visitor, Margery often thwarts this order: she gains access to normally off-limits places, moving wherever she wants. Further, she alters the spaces, dressed in white within dark cathedral spaces; the noise of her weeping would be unabsorbed, bouncing off stone. She defies male use and rules of these spaces, as we see when various clerics protest her presence.[99]

More importantly, Margery is not merely trespassing, but absorbing liturgical power with the goal of inhabitation, as defined by Lang and Franck above. Margery exploits these spaces for their Marian potential to add to her own spiritual authority. As pilgrimage is a way for Margery to experience Christ *in situ*, so do her visits to various Gothic spaces allow her to repeat the experience of inhabiting or absorbing the church as a form of Marian power. She continually returns to similar floor plans, lighting, and shapes. Gothic churches contain relics and icons, of course, but also body-like spaces and architectural elements. Given the regular conflation of the church building with Mary's body in sermons and in liturgical art, Margery's *imitatio Mariae* easily encompasses regarding her own body as a sacred site, a dwelling-place of God. Becoming like Mary also meant becoming a church. We see her practicing this frequently in her home church of St Margaret's Lynn, particularly in the Gesine chapel where she often prays.[100] With her repeated, consistent presence there and her frequent announcements of such in the book, Margery trains the reader to associate her body with the Gesine space, and she slowly accumulates encounters with clergy that further demonstrate her Marian authority. Of course, each new church she visits requires Margery's negotiation of similarly powerful spaces, and she spends most of her narrative energies describing these negotiations rather than the spaces themselves.

Margery makes these built environments her own both aurally and visually, with loud weeping and visual spectacle, so that to fully comprehend her Marian maternity requires the context of her temporary inhabitation of churches. She also renders many different spaces, such as prisons, domestic spaces, and sickrooms, 'holy', as Margaret Hostetler's definition of her term 'performance of enclosure' makes clear.[101] These behaviors cohere around Margery's understanding her body as a church site from the early pages of the book. She wasn't the first to aspire to holiness through extending her own identity to a Gothic church: Abbot Suger's identity was likewise fused with that of St Denis, and he saw the visual glories of the church as a way to his own redemption.[102] Constant liturgical reinforcement of the body as temple—the Eucharist, the focus on Mary's womb, the sumptuous vestments worn directly on the priest's body as though he is himself the fabric of the church—would hardly dissuade her from the bold step of expanding this notion of her body's function. Margery considers her authority both bestowed by and beyond the power of the church.

As Gillian Rose puts it, women's use of space is a 'complicated and never self-evident matrix of historical, social, sexual, racial and class positions which women occupy, and its geometry is one strung out between paradoxical sites'.[103] Laura Varnam, discussing the *Boke*'s use of symbolic and physical space, notes its transition from metaphorical to literal interpretations of space when Christ, in the 'highest possible authorization', calls Margery a 'peler of Holy Cherch'.[104] Pillars were a common visual trope in depictions of the Annunciation, so Christ is doubly assigning Margery a Marian role. Margery takes this authorization further when she bestows on herself church authority independent of the building, replacing the body-like spaces of the Gothic with her own body. Much of her conflict with clerics concerns how she conducts her body in church spaces. In an exploitation of the body-as-church metaphor shared by Mary and Ecclesia, Margery does not relinquish her role as a Mary substitute when she steps into literal church territory, largely because she sees her own body as a functional church.

Some theoretical tools may be helpful in thinking this through. Margery's architectural literacy reveals her ongoing dialogue with built space as a means of *imitatio Mariae*. Linda McDowell's work on bodies within spaces and on bodies *as places*, or what she calls 'embodied geographies', further clarifies Margery's actions: 'The body is the place, the location or site, if you like, of the individual, with more or less impermeable boundaries between one body and another'.[105] In accepting the role of performing liturgical functions, Margery grants her body the status of place and affirms its churchlike spiritual power. Reading Margery's body as a 'place' invites us to employ geographical theory not only for the Gothic churches she visits, but for Margery herself. For example, André Corboz famously applied the metaphor of the palimpsest to landscape, noting that landscape is constantly 'rewritten and erased' with new buildings and new uses for old buildings.[106] If we see church architecture as palimpsest, then a particular building is only a process or placeholder—a temporary phase, much like, say, pregnancy in the 'place' of a human body.[107] Corboz also borrowed the archaeological term 'stratification' for the study of architecture, a helpful concept as we observe Margery's Marian development. As she moves among various churches, she accumulates and layers depictions and interpretations of Mary, in dialogue with past versions of the churches as well as the metaphorical palimpsest of Mary's body. Margery's own body is being 'rebuilt' as a space for evolving purposes, as she goes from baby-producer to grace-bestower during the years documented by her book. The accumulated meanings of Mary and Ecclesia as church, and of Marian womb as sanctuary, implicate Margery in chronological as well as spatial geographies. We see this in chapter 67, shortly after Margery's prayer has prompted a miraculous snowfall to save her parish from fire. Margery considers others' judgment of her *imitatio Mariae*, which they consider overwrought: '*owr Lady, Cristys owyn modyr*, cryed not as sche dede, and that cawsyd hir to seyn in hir crying, "Lord, I am not thi modir. Take awey this peyn fro me, for I may not beryn it. Thi passyon wil sle me"'. Margery's experience of Mary's tears is beyond her abilities, beyond a temporal identity that she can bear ('I am not thi moder'), but it provokes others' recognition of her status as Marian reflection.

 Writing about the relationships of texts, image, and sacramental changes, Maidie Hilmo reminds us that medieval visual art—and, I would add, architecture, including Margery's transition of herself into a holy space—was meant to produce particular effects in the viewer.[108] Art could plausibly depict what someone or something looked like or, more importantly, could interpret scriptural truth, which invested artists with spiritual authority. Hilmo cites John of Damascus, who considered visual images a 'bridge' to connect the physical to the divine world because people could 'see' beyond the material representation to the art's true meaning.[109] Margery did not have access to modern theories of absorbing space into self (or the inverse) as we see in Lang and Franck's definition of inhabitation, or of nuanced theoretical concepts of bodies in or as space and place. But thanks to the anchorite's Dominican influence, she did have the concept of incorporation to complement her understanding of similar metaphysical feats such as transubstantiation. Her maternal body in church thus offers a multivalent platform: it accords not only temporal or spatial splits, but metaphysical ones. She herself is a bridge from the concrete to the divine. Her body has the capacity not only to physically host Christ, as Mary did through the miracle of incarnation, but also to function as the site of holy rituals.

Margery's body as church

Two episodes early in the *Boke* read quite differently if we consider Margery's absorption of liturgical space to allow her own body to function as a church. First, in chapter 9, a stone and beam fall on Margery's head, as she holds 'hir boke in hir hand' while praying in the Gesine chapel. She interprets her survival and healing as miraculous, and the ensuing debate in the congregation concerns whether the stone should be displayed as a relic.[110] The event is treated as a blessing rather than a condemnation of Margery. Yet the detail most alarming to the modern reader goes unremarked in the narrative: the very fabric of the church building has begun to crumble *on her*. By contrast, Margery's body—her soul's 'house'—survives the injury and remains strong. She outlasts the physical building that has singled her out. The scene ties Margery's spiritual legitimacy to the building; the Holy Spirit, echoing the earlier words of the Dominican anchorite, calls it a 'gret myracle', and promises more to come.

Second, in a much-cited passage from chapter 13, Margery has been abandoned by her husband at the Gothic cathedral in Canterbury, left to severe daylong judgment from monks and priests. Just before she is accused of Lollardy and threatened with burning,

> an eld monk ... toke hir be the hand, seying unto hir, 'What kanst thow seyn of God?' 'Ser' sche seyth, 'I wyl bothe speke of hym and heryn of hym', rehersyng the monk a story of scriptur. The munke seyd, 'I wold thow wer closyd in an hows of ston that ther schuld no man speke wyth the'.

The 'house of stone' here is often glossed as an anchorhold or prison, a space to contain Margery: stone is silencing of her and protective of those who might encounter her. In this view, enclosure in the form of a 'hows of ston' will shape her behavior and limit her influence. Yet his frustrated comment might as easily mean: *I wish you were a stone church instead of a human one.* Here, the 'hows of ston' refers to the many churches she has already visited, perhaps even the one in Canterbury, and absorbed into herself. Rather than contain her, they strengthen and encourage her. 'Thow' imparts Margery's Marian soul into stone rather than flesh. It is a remark with architectural theory built into it. After all, the monk 'toke hir be the hand' before conversing with her: seeking her out, he changes his mind upon hearing her speak. The stone church, in his view, is unchanging, not dynamic and interactive like Margery.

The *Boke* is full of similar moments that grant Margery access to spiritual power outside the church building, some well before she begins her local pilgrimages. Much of this power is connected to her or to Mary's maternity. For example, Williams observes that in the opening chapter, Margery does not undergo a public churching ceremony: instead, her postpartum purification occurs outside the church building, because Christ himself sanctifies her in her bed. Williams reads this moment as highly sexualized. But the more startling element is its implication that Margery's body renders the church unnecessary: she, with direct access to Christ, can practice rituals extra-liturgically.

Margery deploys her power like the judicious Virgin who appears in miracle stories. In chapter 12, she extends a kind of absolution (and apophatic confession) for a lecherous monk, administering

Marian grace. In chapter 24, a priest praises Margery as a better judge of character than another priest who'd been easily fooled. In chapter 26, she admonishes disdainful fellow travelers: 'Christ is just as important here as in London'. In chapter 60, she is deeply moved by a Pietà; when a priest reminds her, 'Damsel, Jhesu is ded long sithyn', Margery retorts, 'Sir, hys deth is as fresch to me as he had deyd this same day'. Like Mary, who experienced labor pains only at the Crucifixion, Margery's tears are outside the Church's version of history, outside even chronology. Emboldened by frequent practice as a Mary/Ecclesia substitute, Margery has no need of church authority to tell her what happened or how to feel about it.

Once Margery's body becomes an extension of the church, her social encounters with critics, especially with priests, become a test of their discernment rather than hers: they must decide whether to recognize her Christ-sanctioned authority. Although Margery attempts to maintain access to clergy, the *Boke* suggests that it is she who functions as a Marian bodily portal to the divine, not the men in pulpits wearing vestments. Of course, many clerics whom Margery encounters cannot conceive of a church or even a faith without the conventional church building. If a woman's own body is the site or space that is sacred, she doesn't need liturgical space (or its infrastructure, including clergy) because she has a direct connection to God.

The potential theological danger of this situation is clear, and the Dominican anchorite's early insistence on vetting Margery's visions seems less controlling and more prudent than when he first voices it early in the *Boke*. So, too, does Margery's demand for a spiritual guide with access to good books. Knowing what, how, and whom to read as she ventured on pilgrimage, absorbing liturgical space and art, training to try on the role of Mary as well as that of the church: Margery was building meaning and accumulating authority from multiple sources. As we will see in Chapter 2, the performative devotional literacies that Margery learns from the Dominican anchorite see her through several episodes: inserting herself into Nativity scenes, engaging directly with Christ and Mary at the Crucifixion, staging her own performances of the Eucharist. We can't rely merely on a book list to tell Margery's story of devotional practice. She doesn't limit herself this way, after all: her account of her visions and travel is studded with references to specific people, places, events, and conversations. As writer of her own *vita* and reader of many more, Margery must have been thinking proactively of how to place these elements in a wider literary and intellectual history.

Notes

1 Marjory Kempe, *Book*, 140, emphasis mine: all quotations of the *Boke* are from *The Book of Margery Kempe*, ed. Lynn Staley (Kalamazoo, MI: Medieval Institute Publications, 1996).
2 *Ibid.*, 141: A well-glossed Bible, Bridget of Sweden, Walter Hilton, St Bonaventure, the Franciscan text *Pricking of Love*, Richard Rolle.
3 Karma Lochrie discusses similar connections among orthodoxy, authority, and texts in *Margery Kempe and Translations of the Flesh* (Philadelphia: University of Pennsylvania Press, 1992), at 98–134.
4 Kempe, *Book*, 140.
5 *Ibid.*, 141.
6 *Ibid.*, 140.
7 Barton and Hamilton's chapter 'Literacy practices' shows the connection, and distinction, between literacy events and literacy practices. In *Situated Literacies: Reading and Writing in Context*, ed. David Barton, Mary Hamilton, and Roz Ivanič (New York: Routledge, 2000), 7–14. Brian Stock explores a similar dynamic among medieval monastic and heretical communities in *The Implications of Literacy* (Princeton, NJ: Princeton University Press, 1983), 88–240. In *Margery Kempe and the Lonely Reader* (Ithaca: Cornell University Press, 2017), Rebecca Krug fruitfully enlarges our understanding of Margery's textual communities and literacy practices but leaves her overt connections to the Virgin Mary unexamined. See also the recent erudite and evocative study by Anthony Bale, *Margery Kempe: A Mixed Life* (London: Reaktion Books, 2022). While I developed my analysis of Margery's devotional literacies independently of Bale's, I am delighted that my readings tend to complement rather than contradict his.
8 These concepts were first developed by Shirley Brice Heath in her classic study of childhood literacy acquisition; they have since become important terms in describing engagement in activist communities. See 'What no bedtime story means', *Language in Society* 11.1 (1982), 49–76.
9 Kempe, *Book*, 162–3.

10 To date, Hope Emily Allen, who calls the anchorite 'a fanatical type of mystic', has given him more attention than has recent scholarship. See Allen's contributions to *The Book of Margery Kempe*, ed. Sanford Brown Meech, EETS o.s. 212 (London: Oxford University Press, 1940), 264, n. 17/31. Allen argues that pious women in Lynn had access to and knowledge of German mystical texts. In *Margery Kempe's Meditations*, Yoshikawa mentions the anchorite explicitly only twice (5, 65), musing that 'Margery may have learned the basic principles of memory through her Dominican confessor', at 5. According to Mary Carruthers, the Dominican order was 'responsible for developing many of the most useful tools for the study of written texts during the thirteenth century' and 'simultaneously the most active single proponent and populizer of memory as an art' in *The Book of Memory* (Cambridge: Cambridge University Press, 2008), 193. Dominicans supported contemplative practice in England; the best known anchorite is John Lacy, who composed a book of hours (now St John's College, Oxford MS 94) during enclosure. See C. Pepler, 'John Lacy: A Dominican contemplative', *Life of the Spirit (1946–1964)* 5.57 (1951), 397–400. Janet Wilson describes the complex dynamics of local factions in 'Communities of dissent: the secular and ecclesiastical communities of Margery Kempe's *Book*', in *Medieval Women in Their Communities*, ed. Diane Watt (Toronto: University of Toronto Press, 1997), 155–85.

11 Hope Emily Allen, Notes. *The Book of Margery Kempe*. Ed. Sanford Brown Meech. EETS o.s. 212 (London: Oxford University Press, 1940), 275.

12 In his words: 'I have herd mych evyl langwage of yow syth ye went owt, and I have ben sor cownseld to leve yow and no mor to medyl wyth yow, and ther is behyte me gret frenschepys wyth condycyon yf I leve yow. And I answeryd for yow thus: "yyf ye wer in the same plyte that ye wer whan we partyd asundyr, I durst wel say ye wer a good woman, a lovere of God, and hyly inspyred wyth the Holy Gost"', Kempe, *Book*, 49.

13 The narration makes clear that Richard's duties include communication on Margery's behalf. Its reluctance to address directly who does what (such as whether Margery's son is her first scribe) leaves room for Richard's being the interpreter in the following passage, as well as for the Dominican arranging Richard's hire: 'Than sche preyd hir man wyth the brokyn bak for to gon to the preste and preyn hym to spekyn wyth hir. Than the preste undirstod non Englysch ne wist not what sche seyd, and sche cowde non other langage than Englisch, and therfor thei spokyn be an interpretowr, a man that telde her eythyr

what other seyde', 88. Richard, from Ireland but traveling from Venice to Rome to England, may have been a merchant in Lynn's extensive trade network, or he may have been affiliated more directly with Dominicans in England and on the continent. The book suggests his facility with English, German, and perhaps Italian and Latin, and he is probably present, if not mentioned, in most of the liturgical scenes in Rome. Kate Parker suggests merchants from Lynn could read and write and that 40 percent knew Latin in 'Lynn and the making of a mystic', *A Companion to the Book of Margery Kempe*, ed. John Arnold and Katherine Lewis (Cambridge: D.S. Brewer, 2004), 55–74, at 64.

14 In chapter 54, the 'Frer Prechowrys' of Lynn, apparently influenced by the anchorite, are disapprovingly credited with having preventing Margery's burning at the stake by another Dominican, intent on accusing Margery of heresy. In chapter 68 a 'Maister Custawns' from the Norwich house tells her about Marie d'Oignies to confirm that her tears are orthodox and welcomes her weeping during his sermon.

15 Since studies of medieval religion have become less confessionally biased, scholars have sometimes glossed over the differences among orders. In doing so, we risk losing a theological literacy that Margery and her contemporaries had and employed in carving out their religious identities. Margery regularly mentions 'blackfriars', for example, and she knows and acknowledges when a convention of Franciscans, as opposed to just a bunch of preachers, comes to town.

16 Apart from numerous continental holy women who worked with Dominicans (discussed in Chapter 3) and artistic practices such as *nunnenarbeiten*, the rosary was first given to St Dominic during an apparition of Mary and was named by Thomas of Cantimpré. Fifteenth-century Dominicans strongly promoted rosaries (also called 'pasternosters') as tools of lay devotion. See Anne Winston-Allen, *Stories of the Rose: The Making of the Rosary in the Middle Ages* (University Park: Pennsylvania State University Press, 1997).

17 Ute Stargardt details similarities between Margery's behaviors and German religious in 'The beguines of Belgium, the Dominican nuns of Germany, and Margery Kempe' in *The Popular Literature of Medieval England* (Knoxville: University of Tennessee Press, 1985), 277–313. See also Jeffrey Hamburger, 'The use of images in the pastoral care of nuns: The case of Heinrich Suso and the Dominicans', *The Art Bulletin* 71:1 (1989), 20–46.

18 Laura Varnam focuses on Margery's interactions with her parish church in 'The importance of St Margaret's Church in "The book of Margery Kempe": A sacred place and an exemplary parishioner',

Nottingham Medieval Studies 61 (2018), 197–243. Varnam's monograph, *The Church as Sacred Space in Middle English Literature and Culture* (Manchester: Manchester University Press, 2018), fruitfully examines parishioners' investments in and integration with their liturgical spaces, with particular attention to Margery in chapter 4.

19 In Tara Williams, 'Manipulating Mary: Maternal, sexual, and textual authority in *The book of Margery Kempe*', *Modern Philology* 107.4 (2010), 528–55, at 531, emphasis mine. See also Wendy Harding, 'Medieval women's unwritten discourse on motherhood: A reading of two fifteenth-century texts', *Women's Studies* 21 (1992), 197–209, and Liz Herbert McAvoy, *Authority and the Female Body in the Writings of Julian of Norwich and Margery Kempe* (Woodbridge: Boydell & Brewer, 2004).

20 Previous readers of the *Boke* have occasionally mentioned the concept of Ecclesia; Staley touches scantly on the concept in a chapter title and connects Ecclesia to the *mulier fortis* of Proverbs 31 (123–6); Yoshikawa invokes the idea but doesn't quite define it in *Margery Kempe's Meditations*.

21 (Pseudo-)Albertus Magnus, 'Dominus in templo sancto suo', in *Sermones de tempore et de sanctis* (Cologne, 1475); qtd. in Ruth Horie, *Perceptions of Ecclesia: Church and Soul in Medieval Dedication Sermons* (Turnhout: Brepols, 2006), 40.

22 The *Boke* has no shortage of maternal imagery. For example, McAvoy notes that Margery's description of physical suffering from taking on Mary's grief employs a 'discourse of maternal suffering', primarily of childbirth, in 'Virgin Mother Whore', 128. On Margery's bridely mysticism, see Yoshikawa.

23 The use of birth metaphors to describe *priests*' work was nothing new: Augustine exclaimed, 'Oh revered dignity of priests in whose hands the Son of God is incarnated as in the Virgin's womb'/'Vere veneranda sacerdotum dignitas, in quorum manibus Dei Filius, velit in utero Virginus, incarnatur'. Bernard called priests 'parentes Christi', with the 'Pater Christi generando' (begetting him) and the 'Mater Christi pariendo' (birthing him). In this context, Margery's confessor's declaration 'You are nursing from Christ's breasts!' merely conflates Mary's nourishing milk with Christ's saving blood in images that were already understood. See Caroline Walker Bynum, *Jesus as Mother: Studies in the Spirituality of the High Middle Ages* (Berkeley: University of California, 1984), 132–4, for the ungendered nature of birthing metaphors. In many contexts, *imitatio Christi* and *imitatio Mariae* were not mutually exclusive. By the sixteenth century, preaching was described as helping birth a Christian.

24 The birth metaphor is described in Suso's German sermon 2; the images in his instructional talks 21.
25 For differences between Eckhart's and Suso's approaches, see Niklaus Largier, 'The poetics of the image in late medieval mysticism', *Image and Incarnation: The Early Modern Doctrine of the Pictorial Image*, ed. Walter Melion and Lee Palmer Wandel (Leiden: Brill, 2015), 173–86. Jeffrey Hamburger offers further summary in *Visual and the Visionary: Art and Female Spirituality in Late Medieval Germany* (New York: Zone Books, 1999), at 202–3, and at note 40, 526. Stargardt explains how Eckhart's theology requires the spiritual birth of God in each Christian's soul, at 292.
26 As Hamburger explains, monks kept images of the Crucifixion, of the Virgin, and of St. Dominic in their cells for this purpose; see 'Use of images', 27. Hamburger highlights Suso's brief comment on the usefulness and biblical precedent of images and material objects: 'Multi quoque sancti novi testamenti in transactis ante nos temporibus pro incitamento suae devotionis picturas diversas sibi fecerunt; quidam imagines vel cruces iuxta se habuerunt; nonnulli etiam reliquias vel cetera similia apud', at 29.
27 Nicholas Love, first prior of Mountgrace Charterhouse, used Suso's *Horologium* as a source for his *Mirror of the Blessed Life of Christ*. Its English translation may have been commissioned for Margery, Duchess of Clarence and sister of Thomas Holland, Mountgrace's founder. For the English manuscripts, see Dick Schultze, 'Wisdom in the margins: Text and paratext in *The seven points of true love and everlasting Wisdom*', *Études Anglaises* 66.3 (2013), 341–56. See also McNamer, *Affective Meditation*, 60. Suso's influence is evident in Love's recommendation of the types of Christ-focused visions Margery often describes: 'contemplacion of þe monhede of cryste is more likyng, more spedefull, & more sykere þan is hyȝe contemplacion of þe godhed ande þerfore to hem is pryncipally to be sette in mynde þe ymage of crystes Incarnacion, passion & Resurreccion so that a symple soule þat kan not þenke bot bodyes or bodily þinges mowe haue somwhat accordynge vnto his affecion wher wiþ he maye fede & stire his deuocion', in *The Mirror of the Blessed Life of Jesus Christ*, ed. Michael G. Sargent (Exeter: University of Exeter Press, 2004), 10.
28 Emphasis mine; Henry Suso, 'Orologium sapientiae or the seven poyntes of trewe wisdom, aus MS. Douce 113', ed. Carl Horstmann, *Anglia* 10 (1887), 323–89, at 341. Hereafter Suso, 'Orologium'.
29 As Stargardt points out, the nuns at Töss were similarly obsessed with Mary's bodily maternity, 'Beguines', 293.

30 The Authorized Bible's translation is 'through a glass darkly', I Corinthians 13:12. Corinth was known for its mirror industry, and Paul was familiar with Plato's allegory. See Benjamin Goldberg, *The Mirror and Man* (Charlottesville: University of Press of Virginia, 1985), 112.
31 Sermon 137 focuses on this comparison: 'solis radius specular penetrat, et soliditatem eius insensibili subtilitate pertransit'. Wisdom is the 'unspotted mirror of God's majesty and the image of his goodness' (Book of Wisdom 7:26). *Sermones aurei de Maria Virgine Dei Matre, omni doctrina & magnis Sacre Scripture Sensibus Referti* ... (Venice, 1590), 171–3, at 172.
32 Heinrich Schwarz observes that mirrors appear frequently in late medieval paintings of the Virgin and Child in 'The mirror of the artist and the mirror of the devout', *Studies in the History of Art*. London: Phaidon, 1959, 90–105, at 99–100. The titles of Love's *Mirror*, the Birgittine liturgy *Myroure of Oure Ladye*, and the late fourteenth-century English translation of Marguerite Porete's *Mirror of Simple Souls* testify to the symbol's popularity among Margery's contemporaries. For a comprehensive approach to the mirror as symbol, see Goldberg.
33 Wisdom answers that tears of compassion, like rivers, are pleasing; Suso, 'Orologium', 339.
34 Book I, Ch. 42 in *The liber celestis of St Bridget of Sweden*. Vol. 1, ed. Roger Ellis, EETS 291 (Oxford: Oxford University Press, 1987), 74.
35 The association of Mary with mirrors extended to fourteenth-century women's jewelry: Joan Evans mentions circular-mirror pendants containing images of the Virgin in her *History of Jewellery 1100–1870* (London: Faber and Faber, 1953), 80.
36 The line appears in chapter 12 of the Augustinian Rule and chapter 8 of the Dominican adaptation: 'Ut autem vos in hoc libello tanquam in speculo possitis inspicere, ne per oblivionem aliquid negligatis, semel in septimana vobis legatur'. Ep. 211, 'Ad Virgines', or *Regula ad Servos Dei* (PL, XL, 1384).
37 'Specula earum sunt exempla sanctorum, sive testimonia Scripturarum: in his animae justorum velut in speculo se considerant, et quidquid deformitatis in se deprehenderint castigant'. In *Instructio Sacerdotis*, ii, caput xi (PL, Vol. 184, 788BC). Ritamary Bradley contextualizes Bernard's and Augustine's uses of 'speculum' as spiritual metaphor among an astonishing array of other medieval writers in 'Backgrounds of the title *Speculum* in mediaeval literature', *Speculum* 29.1 (1954), 100–15.

38 The *Boke* includes quite a bit of dialogue from Christ, as Barbara Zimbalist shows in *Translating Christ in the Middle Ages* (Notre Dame: University of Notre Dame Press, 2022), 178–89. Capgrave's *vita* of Katherine also includes quotations of Christ's direct speech. James Simpson implies that including '*Christ's own words*' (428, original emphasis) may be a fifteenth-century trend in *Reform and Cultural Revolution*, The Oxford English Literary History, Vol. 2 (Oxford: Oxford University Press, 2002).

39 A few years after Margery's visit to Aachen, Jan van Eyck's painting *Arnolfini Wedding* would feature a mirror prominently to suggest Christ's wedding to the Church. See Robert Baldwin, 'Marriage as a sacramental reflection of the Passion: The mirror in Jan van Eyck's *Arnolfini Wedding*', *Oud Holland* 98.2 (1984), 57–75.

40 Gutenberg was a year or so off in his projections of profit; the Marian relics were and are only displayed every seven years. In 1426 a different mirror merchant had claimed the Aachen market, so Margery's 1433 pilgrimage there could theoretically have been enhanced with a mirror sold *in situ*.

41 Schwarz, 'Mirror', 101–2. Schwarz offers visual evidence of this practice in a mid-fifteenth painting in Naples, a mid-fifteenth-century pilgrim's badge, and a 1487 woodcut by Peter Vischer (in Library of Congress, Rosenwald 120, fol. 4r); he cites evidence of a Nuremberg guild for makers of mirror-glass by 1373; that merchants sought to sell mementos in 1426; and that *Spiegile* were documented for sale on site by 1431. The trend was established in previous decades at southern European pilgrimage sites such as Santiago de Compostela, where, of course, Margery visited.

42 On copies of paintings wielding the power of originals in Rome, see Kirstin Noreen, 'The icon of Santa Maria Maggiore, Rome: An image and its afterlife', *Renaissance Studies* 19.5 (2005), 660–72.

43 Notably, Margery's near-contemporary Chaucer deploys secular examples of mirrors as recording devices. The *Merchant's Tale* imagines a mirror set down in a marketplace to capture a record of all the women milling around (1580–85), and Troilus's remembering Criseyde's appearance is described as making a 'mirour of his mynde' that retains her in *Troilus and Criseyde* (I.365–7).

44 Richard Lang, *The Dwelling Door*, in D. Seamon and R. Mugerauer, *Dwelling, Place and Environment* (Dordrecht: Martinus Nijhoff, 1985), 202.

45 In Karen A. Franck and R. Bianca Lepori, *Architecture from the Inside Out*, 2nd ed. (Chichester: Wiley-Academy Press, 2007), 51, 52.

46 Gemäldegalerie, Staatliche Museen, Berlin, c. 1438. Yoshikawa mentions this painting as an example of Margery's being a 'peler of Holy Cherch' in 'Searching for the image of new Ecclesia: Margery Kempe's spiritual pilgrimage reconsidered', *Medieval Perspectives* 11 (1996), 125–38, at 134.

47 Similarly, in a discussion of the Digby *Candlemas Day*, Theresa Coletti argues that the late fifteenth-century play 'stresses that Mary herself is such a [sacred] space' in 'Genealogy, sexuality, and sacred power: The Saint Anne dedication of the Digby *Candlemas Day and the Killing of the Children of Israel*', *Journal of Medieval and Early Modern Studies* 29.1 (1999), 25–59, at 31.

48 Staley, 36, emphasis mine.

49 Staley, 90.

50 The texts are listed and specified as yet unread in chapter 17; the list is repeated, as we've seen, in chapter 58. In chapter 27, Margery cites a text of the Gospel to companions at dinner. Some readers have assumed that 'hir boke in hir hand' refers to a book of hours, but the *Boke* does not specify.

51 This happens in chapter 28 and again in chapter 67.

52 Since Caroline Walker Bynum's *Holy Feast and Holy Fast*, a rich body of scholarship on the affective piety wrought from images has developed; see e.g., McNamer, *Affective Meditation*. For Margery's engagement with the visual, see Laura Varnam, 'The crucifix, the pietà, and the female mystic: Devotional objects and performative identity in *The Book of Margery Kempe*', *Journal of Medieval Religious Cultures* 41.2 (2015), 208–37.

53 Barbara Newman, 'What did it mean to say "I saw"? The clash between theory and practice in medieval visionary culture', *Speculum* 80 (2005), 1–43, at 31.

54 See the discussion in Bynum, *Holy Feast*, 166–80 and 270–6, and Raymond of Capua, *The Life of St Catherine of Siena*, trans. George Lamb (Charlotte, NC: Tan Books, 2009). In her note on this line, Staley describes images of Christ's nurturing as 'conventional', but this was so only within a small group of mystical writers, not in general lay practice or parlance.

55 It may also connect her to the literal interpretations of and concerns about Mary's maternity by the nuns at Töss, the likely first audience for the Suso text that would be used as a source by Nicholas Love. See note 27 above.

56 *Henry Suso: The Exemplar, with Two German Sermons*, trans. and ed. Frank Tobin (New York: Paulist Press, 1989), 80–1 (hereafter Suso, *Exemplar*).

57 Hamburger summarizes Dominican investment in art and visual language as teaching tool; see note 17 above. See also *Visual and the Visionary*, 197–278.
58 Virginia Chieffo Raguin, 'Real and imaged bodies in architectural space: The setting for Margery Kempe's *Book*', *Women's Space: Patronage, Place, and Gender in the Medieval Church*, ed. Virginia Chieffo Raguin and Sarah Stanbury (Albany: SUNY Press, 2006), 105–40.
59 Laura D. Gelfand and Walter S. Gibson, 'The "Rolin Madonna" and the late-medieval devotional portrait', *Simiolus: Netherlands Quarterly for the History of Art* 29.3/4 (2002), 119–38, at 131. This practice could work textually as well, as in John Clopton's 1496 inscription at the Lady Chapel of Long Melford ('christ' sit testis hec me no'exhibuisse ut merear laudes, sed ut spiritus memoretur'/ 'let Christ be witness this shows not that I deserve praise, but that the soul be remembered'). See Nikolaus Pevsner, *Suffolk*, 2nd ed. (Harmondsworth: Penguin, 1974), 345. I discuss Long Melford patronage further in Chapter 4.
60 'Nam quod legentibus scriptura, hoc idiotis praestat pictura cernentibus, quia in ipsa etiam ignorantes vident quid sequi debeant, in ipsa legunt qui litteras nesciunt. Unde et praecipue gentibus pro lectione pictura est'. Pope Gregory I, 'Epistola XIII ad Serenum Massiliensem Episcopum', PL, Vol. 77, c. 1128.
61 Suger's reasoning was that 'de materialibus ad immaterialia transferendo' ('transferring that which is material to that which is immaterial') would allow ordinary people to understand God's glory viscerally, in *Abbot Suger on the Abbey Church of St.-Denis and its Art Treasures*, ed. and trans. E. Panofsky, 2nd edn by G. Panofsky-Soergel (Princeton: Princeton University Press, 1979), 62–5. Even his contemporary Bernard of Clairvaux, whose rant against conspicuous clerical wealth was appropriated by Lollards, conceded pragmatically in his *Apologia*, 'Assentio: patiamur et haec fieri in ecclesia, quia etsi noxia sunt vanis et avaris, non tamen simplicibus et devotis' ('I agree, let us put up with these things which are found in the church, since even if they are harmful to the shallow and avaricious, they are not to the simple and devout'). In Conrad Rudolph, *The 'Things of Greater Importance': Bernard of Clairvaux's* Apologia *and the Medieval Attitude Toward Art* (Philadelphia: University of Pennsylvania Press, 1990), 282–3.
62 See Kathleen Kamerick, 'Art and moral vision in Angela of Foligno and Margery Kempe', *Mystics Quarterly* 21.4 (1995), 148–58, and Margaret Aston, 'Gold and images', *Faith and Aire: Popular and*

Unpopular Religion 1350–1600 (London: Hambledon Press, 1993), 219–29. On preachers' criticism of images, see G.R. Owst, *Literature and the Pulpit in Medieval England*, 2nd ed. (New York: Barnes and Noble, 1961), 561.

63 From 'The testimony of William Thorpe' in *Two Wycliffite Texts*, ed. Anne Hudson, EETS OS 301 (Oxford: Oxford University Press, 1993), 24–93. Derek Pearsall briefly discusses this passage in the context of Lollard-driven public conversations, concluding that 'the cult of images was now an emotional rallying cry for orthodoxy' in 'Hoccleve's *Regement of Princes*: The poetics of royal self-representation', *Speculum* 69.2 (1994), 386–410, at 406. Simpson observes that saints' lives regularly include the devaluing and destruction of images in *Reform and Cultural Revolution*, The Oxford English Literary History. Vol. 2 (Oxford: Oxford University Press, 2002), 406.

64 'Habet tamen ecclesia alios filios paruulos in fide et caritate tepidos, inperfectos scilicet laicos simplices: hos lacte potat corporalium signorum', in *Walter Hilton's Latin Writings*, ed. John P.H. Clark and Cheryl Taylor, 2 vols, *Analecta Cartusiana* 124 (Salzburg: Institut für Anglistik und Amerikanistik, 1987), 175–214, at 189. The passage's attribution to Hilton is tantalizing, since the *Boke* tells us Margery's priest read her Hilton's *Scale of Perfection*, but Nicholas Watson argues that the evidence falls short in '"Et que est huius ydoli materia? Tuipse": Idols and images in Walter Hilton', *Images, Idolatry, and Iconoclasm in Late Medieval England*, ed. Jeremy Dimmick, James Simpson, and Nicolette Zeeman (Oxford: Oxford University Press, 2002), 95–111.

65 *Dives and Pauper*, ed. Priscilla Heath Barnum, EETS 275. Vol. 1, pt. 1 (Oxford: Oxford University Press, 1975), 85, emphasis mine.

66 Margery comments on the Pietà at St Stephen's of Norwich by name in chapter 60, and mentions a 'crucyfyx' in chapters 4, 46, and 78. I discuss Margery's readings of depictions of the Crucifixion further in Chapter 2.

67 Richard Marks, *Image and Devotion in Late Medieval England* (Stroud, Gloucestershire: Sutton, 2004), 123–43.

68 For a catalog of sculptures similar to those Margery would have read, see Joanna E. Ziegler, *Sculpture of Compassion: The Pietà and the Beguines in the Southern Low Countries, c.1300–c.1600* (Rome: Institut Historique Belge de Rome, 1992).

69 Early-fifteenth-century Rome was even less intuitively navigable for the traveler than it is now: visitors oriented by churches rather than often-unnamed streets. Most of its accommodations to outsiders, such as obelisks to mark the plazas of important pilgrimage churches,

would be sixteenth-century achievements. Rome had only one bridge until 1450, when a bucking mule near the Ponte Sant'Angelo would force 200 pilgrims to their deaths by trampling or drowning in the Tiber. Textual or human guides, such as the Irish man Margery met in Venice, were a necessity. See the colorful account by Loren Partridge, 'Urbanism: Rotting cadeavors and the New Jerusalem', *The Art of Renaissance Rome, 1400–1600* (New York: Harry N. Abrams, 1996), 19–40. The papacy's return to Rome would require significant civic planning and liturgical renovations, but most of these changes were undertaken long after Margery's visit in 1414–15, when Rome was in 'a shambles', as Laura Howes puts it in 'Romancing the city: Margery Kempe in Rome', *Studies in Philology* 111.4 (2014), 680–90, at 682.

70 *Stacions of the Cross*, ed. Frederick Furnivall, EETS 25 (1867), 16–17, at 476–534. The church also claims boards from Christ's manger.
71 Kempe, *Book*, 103.
72 PL, Vol. 22, c. 408.
73 They were also associated in manuscript; e.g., Lydgate's *Life of Our Lady*, Huntington Library, MS 115, was once bound with the lives of Jerome, John the Baptist, John the Evangelist, and St Catherine. A loggia mosaic at Sta Maria Maggiore depicts Mary sharing her good news with John; see *The Virgin Announcing the Miracle to John*, in Robert Vicci, *The Major Basilicas of Rome* (Florence: Scala, 1999).
74 The full passage appears in chapter 36 of Staley, 94–5. Yoshikawa argues that this passage marks 'a new era in her spiritual progress—a fruit of her pilgrimage', *Meditations*, 54.
75 Mary Morse explores this possibility with respect to Venetian images of Mary nursing and as the Dolorosa in 'Margery Kempe, Venice, and Marian iconology', *Studia Mystica* 19 (1998), 56–67.
76 See Hans Belting, 'St Luke's Picture and "Unpainted" Originals', *Likeness and Presence: A History of the Image Before Art*, trans. Edmund Jephcott (Chicago: University of Chicago Press, 1994), 47–81, 68. See also Noreen, 'Icon'.
77 'Maria virgo assumpta est ad etherum thalamum in quo Rex regum stellato sedet solio/exaltata est sancta Dei genetrix super choros angelorum ad coelestia regna'. Qtd. in Joan Barclay Lloyd, 'The river of life in the medieval mosaics of S Maria Maggiore in Rome', *Reading Texts and Images*, ed. Bernard Muir (Exeter: University of Exeter Press, 2002), 35–55, 37. The antiphons appear in PL 78.798–9.
78 Maria Lidova, 'Empress, Virgin, Ecclesia: The icon of Santa Maria in Trastevere in the early Byzantine context', *IKON* 9 (2016), 109–28, at 117, 120.

79 As Lidova suggests, this image also represents the church, a common association in Byzantine depictions, 'Empress', 22. Michael Camille describes the Lady of Walsingham as an 'enthroned Madonna', but there she was in a modest wooden chapel and only occasionally displayed, possibly surrounded by devotees' offerings; Margery mentions having visited Walsingham in Book II. See Michael Camille, *The Gothic Idol: Ideology and Image-making in Medieval Art* (Cambridge: Cambridge University Press, 1990), 228–9.

80 The Virgin's scroll reads: 'Leva eius sub capite meo et dex(t)era illius amplesabit(ur) me' from Song of Songs 2:6 and 8:3; Christ's book reads 'Veni electa mea et ponam in te thronum meum' from the Assumption feast liturgy. Judith Wechsler traces the development of theologians' assignment of Ecclesia, and later Mary, to the Bride in Song of Songs in 'A change in the iconography of the Song of Songs in 12th and 13th century Latin Bibles', *Texts and Responses: Studies Presented to Nahum N. Glatzer*, ed. Michael Fishbane and Paul Flohr (Leiden: Brill, 1975), 73–93, at 76–80.

81 Wechsler detects a shift from Ecclesia to Mary as *sponsa Christi* beginning in the twelfth century that led to the widespread acceptance of Mary as Ecclesia, 'Change', 78. By the thirteenth century, she adds, artists were beginning to illustrate the Song of Songs with Madonna and child, an image meant to prefigure their nuptial roles.

82 Kempe, *Book*, 102.

83 Horie, *Perceptions of Ecclesia*, 43.

84 Qtd. in Emile Mâle, *The Gothic Image: Religious Art in France of the Thirteenth Century* (New York: Harper and Row, 1972), 190. This association between Ecclesia and the Church was so widely accepted that the sources that distinguish between the physical building and the feminine figure tend to be explicitly anti-clerical. The Lollard text *The Lanterne of Liȝt* employs gendered imagery to distinguish Christ's church, 'a clene chaast maiden', 'Cristis spouse', 'a womman wiþ childe ... whanne she traueiliþ' (23, 25) from the categorically negative description, via Bernard of Clairvaux's *Apologia*, of the material building, compared to a gold-bedecked whore who neglects her children: 'O vanite among alle vanites & no more vanite þan as miche woden drem þe chirche schynneþ in wowis & sche nediþ in þe pore/ sche wlappiþ hir stoones in gold & hir owene sones sche forsakiþ nakid/of þe spensis of nedi is mad a veyn seruise to riche mennes iȝen' (38), in *The Lanterne of Liȝt*, ed. Lilian M. Swinburn, EETS o.s. 151 (London: Kegan Paul, Trench, Trübner & Co., 1917).

85 'Omnia quae de Ecclesia dicta sunt, possunt etiam de ipsa Virgine, sponsa et matre sponsi, intelligi', in *Expositio in Cantica Canticorum*, PL 172. c. 494.

86 For visual depictions of Ecclesia, see Miri Rubin, 'Ecclesia and Synagoga: The changing meanings of a powerful pairing', *Conflict and Religious Conversation in Latin Christendom*, ed. Ram Ben-Shalom and Israel Jacob Yuval (Turnhout: Brepols, 2014), 55–86, at 65. On Mary's association with books and literacy, see Saetveit Miles, *Virgin Mary's Book*, and Donavin, *Scribit Mater*.
87 In addition, Ecclesia's foil, Synagoga, was associated with the Crucifixion, the moment at which the Church was thought to triumph over the Synagogue. Margery's disdain for Jews is in accord with visual art, which began depicting Synagoga as haggard and undesirable in Crucifixion scenes as opposed to the young, beautiful *Maria Ecclesia*. See Nina Rowe, who argues this rivalry emerges over time in *The Jew, the Cathedral, and the Medieval City* (Cambridge: Cambridge University Press, 2014), 40–78. Mâle explains that John the Evangelist eventually replaces Synagoga in Crucifixion scenes as symbol of the synagogue.
88 For an overview of *Maria Ecclesia*, see Jo Spreadbury, 'The gender of the church: the female image of *Ecclesia* in the late Middle Ages', *Gender and Christian Religion*, ed. R. N. Swanson (Woodbridge: Boydell, 1998), 93–103.
89 Liz Herbert McAvoy has done extensive work on this topic, particularly *Medieval Anchoritisms: Gender, Space and the Solitary Life* (Cambridge: D.S. Brewer, 2011).
90 Margery's parish church, St Margaret's, was almost completely rebuilt in the thirteenth century; in the fifteenth century, the Trinity Guild (which Margery herself joined near the end of her life) added Gothic elements. See www.stmargaretskingslynn.org.uk/history/.
91 See Lisa Victoria Ciresi, 'Maria Ecclesia: The Aachen Marienschrein as an alternate body for the Virgin Mary', in *Binding the Absent Body in Medieval and Modern Art*, ed. Emily Kelley and Elizabeth Rivenbark (London: Routledge, 2017), at 58.
92 The multiple spaces of the church correspond particularly with the multi-chambered womb. Joan Cadden explains the understanding of the uterus as a five- or seven-celled organ; the cell in which a fetus grew determined its sex. See Joan Cadden, *Meanings of Sex Difference in the Middle Ages* (Cambridge: Cambridge University Press, 1993), 198. Katherine Park writes of the womb having 'special, symbolic weight', a 'privileged object of dissection in medical images and texts' in *Secrets of Women: Gender, Generation, and the Origins of Human Dissection* (New York: Zone Books, 2006), 26–7.
93 Leopold Schmidt observed that the shape of a church represented not only the crucifix but Christ himself. Horie points out that 'Entering the church is thus symbolically equated with entering the body of Christ', *Perceptions*, 53.

94 Ciresi, 'Maria', 58.
95 See Philip Ball, *Universe of Stone: Chartres Cathedral and the Triumph of the Medieval Mind* (London: The Bodley Head, 2008), 251.
96 See https://college.holycross.edu/projects/kempe/.
97 Franck and Lepori, *Architecture*, 55. Related: nave seating was not common until the sixteenth century.
98 *Ibid.*, 49.
99 E.g. Margery documents her own presence in the choir in chapters 23, 57, 70, 75, and 85.
100 The Old French term *gesir* indicates the act of childbirth.
101 Margaret Hostetler, '"I wold thow wer closyd in an hows of ston": Re-imagining religious enclosure in the Book of Margery Kempe', *Parergon* 20.2 (2003), 71–94.
102 See Panofsky, 11, 31, 81.
103 Rose, *Feminism and Geography: The Limits of Geographical Knowledge* (Minneapolis: University of Minnesota Press, 1993), 155.
104 Varnam, 'Church', 304. Varnam employs Lefebvre's concepts of perceived, conceived, and lived space to explain how the physical building connects to ritual and to devotional practice: parishioners' liturgical engagement depended on deep shared understanding of what spaces were for.
105 Linda McDowell, *Gender, Identity, and Place: Understanding Feminist Geographies* (Minneapolis: University of Minnesota Press, 1999), 34.
106 See André Corboz, 'Le territoire comme palimpseste', *Diogène* 121 (1983), 14–35, at 35.
107 McAvoy coins the phrase 'palimpsestic unity' to describe Margery's particular embrace of maternity and virginity in her practice of *imitatio Mariae* especially at Jerusalem; see 'Virgin, Mother, Whore', 127ff.
108 In Maidie Hilmo, *Medieval Images, Icons, and Illustrated English Literary Texts from the Ruthwell Cross to the Ellesmere Chaucer* (New York: Routledge, 2004), at 3.
109 See Hilmo, 19.
110 Anthony Goodman dates this event to 1413, so this occurs before her pilgrimages to Jerusalem and Rome. It is the Friday before Whitsun, just after Christ has promised Margery to 'slay your husband'. See *Margery Kempe and her World* (London: Routledge, 2002).

2

Mar(ger)y at the foot of the Cross*

Margery not only processes her confessors' books as she travels on pilgrimage but draws from her own maternal identity as a source of Marian authority.[1] The depiction of her as a mother who fits Marian conventions begins with the *Boke*'s opening chapter in childbed. It collapses Margery's suffering with the 'chylding', a dynamic familiar from Mary's maternal narrative: we learn about the birth only in the context of her pain.[2] But while the *Boke* is suffused with Marian motherhood, it withholds many concrete details we might expect of a memoir by a mother. In a narrative spanning forty years, Margery describes only her first childbirth and her last pregnancy. There is no mention of the feeding, educating, caregiving, or general childrearing in between.[3] Other readers have examined how Margery exhibits maternal attributes such as nurturing through a *Maria medica* role, healing and midwifing real or envisioned mothers.[4] Margery ministers this way to Anne, to Mary, and to a postpartum woman in Rome, among others. Each time, her presence is requested by the laboring mother, her competence implied or praised as crucial. The text capitalizes on Margery's expertise for symbolic effect: she moves in such close proximity to childbirth that we accept her as maternal despite her children's absence.

Amid these examples of motherhood-once-removed we can miss how Margery also choreographs her readers' Marian and Dominican literacies to expand her own maternal authority. This chapter examines the ways that this authority depends not on Margery's maternal practice but on her readers' devotional reading lenses. As Naoë Yoshikawa explains, the *Boke* is a text for those well-versed in the liturgical calendar.[5] It rewards experienced readers. Margery's maternity, like Mary's, is therefore depicted through subtle and sophisticated image and metaphor, apart from her own parenting or her participation in other women's births. The *Boke* thus speaks at multiple levels of Marian maternal literacies. I consider these across two types of performative episodes, the Eucharist and the Crucifixion, with attention to their connections to the functions and form of Mary's body. For the devotionally literate, these scenes and spaces, mostly set in Jerusalem and Rome, are useful backdrops to demonstrate Margery's orthodoxy, specifically a mendicant-inflected Christianity set against Judaism. As we'll see, articulating anti-Jewish tropes and sentiments further confirms Margery's inhabitation of Marian and Ecclesian roles, and by extension, her fully Marian maternity.

Just as the *Boke* largely deflects guesses about the prosaic details of Margery's parenting, Margery herself seems indifferent to clarifying her own maternal circumstances except as they elevate her spiritual status. Even her eyebrow-raising remark about bearing children during a long stint of hairshirt-wearing highlights her discretion rather than the conceptions or births themselves.[6] Most of the references to 'modir' or 'chyld' and like terms indicate Mary and Christ, or even Margery and Christ, rather than Margery and her flesh-and-blood offspring, to the point that it is impossible to know whether the few references to Margery's own 'children' indicate biological or spiritual ones. In chapter 8, Christ promises Margery that 'alle thi chylderyn' will be allowed into heaven. In chapter 57, she prays that 'Jewys, Saracinys, and alle fals heretikys' might become 'children of salvacyon'.[7] Most tellingly, Christ indicates Margery's use of her maternal status as spiritual metaphor when he observes, 'thu art mekyl the boldar to askyn me grace for thiselfe, for thin husbond, and for thi childryn and *thu makyst every Cristen man and woman thi childe in thi sowle for the tyme and woldist han as meche grace for hem as for thin owyn childeryn*'.[8] The ambiguity in Margery's use of the term 'children' is so strong that the *Boke*'s closing prayer in Book Two clarifies that 'I cry the mercy, Lord, for *alle* my childeryn, *gostly and bodily*', as if we (or Christ) might interpret only one or the other.[9] In doing so, the prayer allows Margery the spiritual benefits of both types of motherhood.

Margery's midwifery, too, sacralizes her, allowing her to act as *Maria medica* and to demonstrate her orthodoxy. The frequent requests for her presence at births show that other women believe she participates *correctly*. A proper birth meant invoking Mary and the saints and included the possibility of baptizing a baby or offering last rites to a mother. According to Sue Niebrzydowski, 'women were able to appropriate those aspects of Mary's pregnancy and childbirth with which they might empathize'.[10] Niebrzydowski calls attention to the tokens women used to this purpose: birth girdles bore Mary's name alongside Margaret's, or the words of the Magnificat. Margery was qualified to invoke them. Margery's continued repetition of the experience, as laborer or midwife, offers a meditative focus on birth as metaphor and process.[11] In chapter 6, Margery is commended for her competence by both Mary and Elizabeth at births considered crucial to Gospel narrative ('Dowtyr, me semyth', seyd Elysabeth, 'Thu dost ryght wel thi dever'). At Christ's birth, especially, the text focuses on Margery's essential role as mentor to Mary and comforter to Christ: 'Lord, I schal fare fayr wyth yow; I schal not byndyn yow soor'. Unlike Mary, Margery has foreknowledge of 'the scharp deth that he schuld suffyr' and acts accordingly; her gentleness with the infant is informed by her accurate recall of the Crucifixion. The birth setting allows Margery's Gospel knowledge to fuel her prophecies: she tells Mary she will be Mother of God, Elizabeth that her son will be a holy man.

Margery's spiritual interpretation of childbirth departs from mystical and liturgical acknowledgments of its physicalities. For Suso, contemplating Christ's birth means a three-day meditation on Mary's pure body, followed by visionary engagement with Christ's infant body:

> He knelt down in front of [Mary] and, raising his hands and eyes, asked her to show him the Child and also to let him kiss it. And when she kindly offered it to him, he spread out his arms to the ends of the earth, took the beloved Child, and embraced it countless times. He looked at its pretty little eyes, gazed at its tiny hands, and kissed its tender little mouth. ... He busied himself with him as the occasion allowed, with singing, with weeping, and with spiritual exercises.[12]

This description ends Suso's description of Candlemas, the feast that celebrates Mary's churching. Other liturgical celebrations also attend to the physical experience of childbearing. Mary Erler describes the popularity of the Feast of the Visitation, an event which must have seemed all the more miraculous because all birth participants survived.[13] In Mirk's *Festial* description of the Visitation, Mary learns how to undergo childbirth from helping with Elizabeth's delivery.[14] Gail MacMurray Gibson explains that St Anne's feast was important to East Anglia because she was patron of safe childbirth.[15] The *Revelations* of Bridget of Sweden recreate the Nativity, Crucifixion, and Pietà in descriptions less delicate than Margery's: Bridget 'feels her belly full of Christ', as if to imitate Mary's pregnancy.

Like her theologian contemporaries, Margery is more interested in Mary's role as bodily founder of the church than as physical mother of Christ, a preference that may explain her squeamishness about divulging the gritty details of birthing. In adapting so many birth experiences into spiritual metaphor, she offers a reinterpretation of Abbot Suger's phrase 'de materialibus ad immaterialia' from a theology of light to one of birth. As we saw in Chapter 1, Dominicans appreciated birth imagery in their understanding of conversion.[16] When a new Christian achieved true mystical union with God, that Christian's heart became a metaphorical womb in which God was re-incarnated, becoming flesh, or 'born' again just as he was in the Virgin Mary's womb. Dominicans such as Eckhart and Suso described the sensation of Christ's rebirth in one's heart as a 'burning'. The quickest, most reliable way to achieve that burning was by meditating on visual art. Eventually, through the Dominican Observants, a fundamentalist offshoot of the order, this focus changed to the devotional act of *creating* art, known as *nonnenarbeit*.[17] The prayer books created in convents were made as an act of devotion, a hope of achieving a burning, a birthing, in the heart. Margery's own creative meditation includes active performing in Marian postures and spaces. Her predilection for spatial play may be read as a form of *nonnenarbeit*, an attempt to capture spiritual rebirth.

Ecclesia, birth, and labor

Reading Margery through the lens of Ecclesia suggests additional options of how she understood Marian maternity. In the *Boke*'s opening chapter, for example, Margery's first postpartum vision is of Christ, who materializes only long enough to say, 'Dowtyr, why hast thow forsakyn me, and I forsoke nevyr the?' before disappearing gracefully into thin air. Although she has been in delirium and actively self-harming for 'half yer eight wekys and odde days', the vision instantly restores Margery to her old self: immediately upon seeing her husband, she requests the keys to the 'botery', or pantry. Against their servants' advice, he gives them to her. On its surface, this anecdote appears to mark a simple return to managing household duties. Critical analyses of the passage have taken it more or less at gendered face value, marking Margery's dominion over the domestic sphere.[18] Margery knows, however, of the role keys played in ecclesiastical establishment and power, that in Matthew 16:19, Christ promises to build the church in passing the 'keys' to Peter, and in Bede's interpretation, at least, the keys are passed to 'ecclesia'.[19] The Proem prepares us for this moment with no fewer than eight references to the Holy Ghost, and the Boke later references the flames of Pentecost with burning sensations in Margery's chest.[20] A woman who has control over her own household can also have power in Christ's kingdom, to the point of being its representative on earth. Reinventing the birth of the church in this way gives Margery license to gestate and revise other theological ideas.

Traditionally, Mary was present at Pentecost, the founding of the church (Acts 1:14). With her selectively literal interpretation of the passing of the keys, Margery has here cleverly offered her own version of Pentecost, removing Mary and inserting herself. Margery's reclaiming of the keys marks not only her entry into public life, but, here on her postpartum bed, multiple 'births'. As understood by medieval Mariology, Mary's presence at Pentecost suggests a kind of double conception in her by the Holy Spirit: first to birth Christ, then to birth the Church, both sired by the Holy Spirit.[21] Margery's re-creation sets her own two 'births' nearly in tandem. Iris Marion Young's description of the temporal and spatial splits in a pregnant body are pertinent here: 'the pregnant subject, I suggest, is decentred, split, or doubled in several ways ... her body boundaries shift ... Pregnant existence entails, finally, a unique temporality of process and growth in which the *woman can experience herself as split between past and future*'.[22] To borrow Young's framing: Margery merges the literal birth of her child with this metaphorical 'birth' of her own body as a potential church. In line with Dominican interpretations such as those of Eckhart and Suso, there is a third 'birth' as well: in Origen's homily on Luke 1:35, he explains, 'when you have been made worthy of the shadow [of the Holy Spirit], His body from which the shadow is born, will in a manner of speaking come to you'.[23] That is, Mary's conception is replicated in every Christian convert as Christ is reborn in each Christian. Christ's appearance at her bedside restores Margery to herself in part because it confirms that he and his church have been born[e] in her, but he also helps her collapse the confusing past and future split of Young's theory into a present that Margery can control. In Origen's terms, Christ does 'come to' Margery, verifying her worth and her potential to persist as a Marian and Ecclesian figure in the narrative.

The Christian appreciation of the body as metaphor for all Christian experience encouraged such maternal imagery. When Margery, steeped in devotional training, adopts the metaphor of the Marian maternal body, she also takes on all its symbolism. Her nurturing is almost wholly spiritual and metaphorical; we hear nothing, for example, of Margery's own *pappes*, although Mary's were a favorite topic of poets and preachers. Margery speaks more often of Mary's virginity and her role as incubator of the church, almost entirely ignoring her lactation. But she is well aware of the importance of Mary's body to her spiritual authority: it always signified the Incarnation. Symbols such as the Eucharistic cup or the position at the foot of the Cross made this embodiment of incarnational theology available to figures such as Ecclesia and Margery. Medieval writers deduced that the church must have been 'born' from the wound in the crucified Christ's side, rendering the Cross, too, a natal space.[24] John 19:25 is the only Gospel text to place Mary in the Crucifixion scene, but it is the kind of detail that sticks, especially given its metaphorical association with birth. Ecclesia is routinely shown as a feminine figure at the foot of the Cross holding a communion chalice, also signifying the incarnation for its connection to Christ's flesh.[25] As we'll see, images of *Maria lactans* equally connoted the Eucharist and thus the Incarnation; the visual depiction of Christ's blood gushing straight into Ecclesia's cup from the wound in his side was less visually subtle but imparted the same message.[26] The *Boke* assumes its readers recognize the maternal threads connecting the Eucharist to the Crucifixion; these are as important as Mary's or Margery's reproductive body.

Two passages in the *Boke* play on these associations with Crucifixion-related staging and the Eucharist to evoke Marian or Ecclesian elements. Margery's engagement with these elements is evident not only in her meditations on art and Christ but in the way she repeatedly maneuvers her body into recognizably Marian spaces.[27] Her practices include re-enacting the kinds of Crucifixion scenes that appear in devotional tableaux featuring Ecclesia or Mary at the foot of the Cross, creating an active form of liturgical art with her body placement. Shortly following the memorable debate with her husband about whether their marriage will proceed chastely (chapter 11: 'ye arn no good wyfe'), Margery and John argue at the foot of a cross, forming visual parallels with Mary and John the Evangelist. She carries a bottle of beer, he a cake—Eucharistic props for a conversation centered partly on whether she will resume normal dining with him. Echoing the married virgin martyr Cecilia, Margery reminds John that he will be 'slayn' if he touches her. Margery tearfully negotiates terms with both Christ and John, making clear that by clerical standards she is, in fact, a very good wife whose concerns extend to her husband's soul, not only his body.[28] As a maternal figure under the Cross, Margery receives much more explanation than Mary got at the Gospel version of the Crucifixion. Christ acknowledges her prayer with considerable detail about how he will help her reach her goals through transactional bargaining with John. The scene ends in convivial triumph:

> Thys creatur thankyd god gretly, enjoyng that sche had hir desyr, preyng hir husbond that thei schuld sey three Pater Noster in the worshep of the Trinyté for the gret grace that he had grawntyd hem. And so they ded, knelyng undyr a cros, and sythen thei etyn and dronkyn togedyr in gret gladnes of spyryt.

If not literally the sacrament of communion, their meal seems intentionally ceremonial, with incarnational overtones. Margery and John proceed from the Cross having reborn their marriage into a mutually satisfying arrangement. John no longer questions her motives or reasons for their chastity. Margery has, in effect, brought another believer into the fold. Their 'communion' together reads like vows with a wink: Margery has colluded with Christ as a

Marian problem-solver, so that John comes away feeling he's won something, too. This passage is mostly suggestive and symbolic— the beer and cake, the Cross, the dwelling on food and sex, the tears that arguably evoke Mary's and Ecclesia's postures at the Crucifixion. The scene usually gets scholarly attention for the focus on chastity rather than on communion or the Incarnation, but its achievement of a spiritually fruitful marriage depends at least partly on its setting. Otherwise, why mention that the conversation takes place under a cross, or that the beer and cake are consumed 'togedyr in gret gladnes of spyryt'? Even a husband as demanding as John can be transubstantiated into a supportive one: the process is presented as a miracle, confirmed with communion. Visually, set beneath a cross, it is a reminder of the potential of Mary's transformative womb.

The connection between the Eucharist and Mary's womb was more conspicuous in liturgical settings, where the Church was understood to be continually reborn with each offering of the Host. The play on Christ's flesh as fruit of Mary's womb could be endless. Caroline Walker Bynum lists material Eucharistic elements that feature Mary's body as physical container of Christ: tabernacles, retables, *Vierges ouvrants*, and monstrances, along with several homiletic references.[29] Christ's announcement to Margery in chapter 10 that 'I am in the, and thow in me' echoes Suso's incarnational language generally; specifically, the line anticipates the Eucharistic scene in chapter 11: Christ *in* Margery, perhaps as ingested by her, has worked that miracle. The blend of Eucharistic and Crucifixion imagery recalls Christ's fleshly nature, inherited from Mary. Given the overlap between that spousal and filial relationship, this also invites the erotic language that pops up from time to time in mystical texts. As Yoshikawa notes, Suso's Wisdom describes taking Eucharist as a marital encounter: 'Afterwards, filled with the most ardent desire, let your heart reach out and draw him within you, receive him, so glorious a spouse, and take delight in his sweetest presence.'[30] Ecclesia's communion chalice keeps her in the same category, bearing a container of Christ's blood, if not his flesh. In reality, late-medieval women's access to Communion and to the Eucharistic vessels was strictly regulated.[31] Apart from its symbolic significance, this depiction of physical contact with Christ's body seems to celebrate that Ecclesia, a woman, had direct access to Christ—a worthy model for Margery, who sometimes managed to talk her way into areas of the church normally off-limits to the laity.[32]

Margery does not fetishize the Eucharist as much as do some of the continental mystics, but she cannot seem to get through her brief tour of Calvary-related sites without craving it. In chapter 29, she receives 'howseling' twice, at the Mount of Calvary and at the site of Christ's Last Supper. These 'howselings' prepare us for Margery's desire and quest for weekly Eucharist while in Rome, a motivating factor in her search for an Anglophone confessor there. The tracing of this Eucharistic craving to her Dominican training is suggested twice. First, Christ congratulates her: 'I am wel plesyd wyth the, dowtyr, for thu stondist undyr obedyens of Holy Cherch and that thu wylt *obey thi confessowr and folwyn hys cownsel*'.[33] The confessor in question is the Dominican anchorite. Then, at the end of chapter 29, Margery takes the Franciscans' desire for her company as confirmation of Christ being *in her*, in a union of Dominican and Eucharistic language:

> she wist wel that it was trewth that owyr Lord seyd to hir er sche went owt of Inglond, 'Dowter, I schal makyn al the werld to wondryn of the, and many man and many woman schal spekyn of me for lofe of the and worshepyng *me in the*.'[34]

This last is the same phrasing that confirms her as potentially Marian elsewhere in the text.

Marian lactation

In Rome, Margery's desire for the Eucharist was perhaps a nod to the significance of Mary's lactation as well as the ingestion of Christ. Breastmilk was believed to be merely a more-processed form of uterine blood. Isidore of Seville had explained that milk 'becomes what it is through a transformation of blood, for after birth, if any blood is not consumed as nourishment in the womb, it flows along a natural passageway to the breasts and, whitened due to their special property, it takes on the quality of milk'.[35] Mary's milk was thus a stand-in for the redemptive blood of the Eucharist, since it could theoretically have nourished Christ in the womb. Toward this end,

Isidore provided a useful etymological segue: 'The female breasts (*uber*) are so called, either because they are abundant (*ubertus*) with milk, or because they are moist (*uvida*), that is to say, filled with the liquid of the milk as if they were grapes (*uva*).'[36] Accordingly, images of the Madonna with child often include grapes or cheese to nudge viewers toward Eucharistic thoughts.[37] Margery knew of this connection as she set up Eucharistic scenes. In Rome, her visit to a poor woman in chapter 39 offers a tableau reminiscent of *Maria lactans* and the Eucharist:

> ryth as sche cam be a powr womanys hows, the powr woman clepyd hir into hir hows and dede hir sytten be hir lytyl fyer, gevyng hir *wyn to drynke in a cuppe of ston*. And sche had a lytel manchylde sowkyng on hir brest, the which sowkyd o while on the moderys brest; an other while it ran to this creatur, the modyr syttyng ful of sorwe and sadnes.

Like a living, multitasking version of the Madonna of Humility, the poor woman gives Margery wine as she feeds her toddler. The narrative does not explain the mother's emotional state, though her 'sorwe and sadness' echo the Virgin Mary's tears. Margery's response suggests a Marian interpretation is correct.

> Than this creatur brast al into wepyng, *as thei sche had seyn owr Lady and hir sone in tyme of hys Passyon,* and had so many of holy thowtys that sche myth nevyr tellyn the halvendel, but evyr sat and wept plentyuowsly a long tyme that the powr woman, havyng compassyon of hir wepyng, preyd hir to sesyn, not knowyng why sche wept. Than owr Lord Jhesu Crist seyd to the creatur, 'Thys place is holy'.

The scene is both indirect and literal: the mother provides both milk and wine; she not only shows humility but is actively poor; Margery herself bursts into Marian tears. Franciscan devotion encouraged meditation on the Marian breast's nourishment of Christ. The woman's breast is not *necessarily* Mary's. But there is enough here for us to understand the encounter as Eucharistic and that Margery, confirmed by Christ's affirmation, reads it as such.

This brings us to chapter 86, Christ's final address in the *Boke*, the only passage in which Margery connects Mary's breasts explicitly to the sacrament.[38] Christ first praises Margery for her frequent reception of the Host. Then he reveals her vision: 'Dowtyr, thu clepist my modyr for to comyn into thi sowle and takyn me in hir armys and leyn me to hir brestys and gevyn me sokyn'. Having commissioned and directed this performance of lactation—which otherwise passes without comment—Margery accepts Christ's praises for her successful ingestion of the Eucharist and subsequent generous hosting of him and multiple others in her soul: the twelve Apostles, Mary Magdalene, all the holy virgins, the rest of the Trinity. Margery employs the mystical idea of the heart as a 'house' that Jeffrey Hamburger has described.[39] The virgins decorate; various members of the Trinity repose on cushions; presumably the Apostles come and go as they wish. The image invokes the vièrge ouvrante, with multiple key biblical figures present and interacting with each other, and a German devotional poem addressed to Mary: 'You, mirror, without any blot, you enclosed the one and threefold God in your heart'.[40] We see here how Mary's role as bearer of the Church looks on Margery. Her soul is capacious: she has, through her devotions, incarnated and hosted not only Christ but most of the Gospel cast. It is here that Christ says, 'thu makyst every Cristen man and woman thi childe in thi sowle for the tyme and woldist han as meche grace for hem as for thin owyn childeryn'.[41] Mary's lactation at the chapter's opening, then, was a lesson. Margery's request to witness it demonstrates her awareness of the connections among the Eucharist, lactation, and incarnation.

Along with the offhand remark by her Dominican confessor ('you are nursing from Christ's breasts!'),[42] the *Boke*'s most prominent mention of Mary's breasts is in a similar deflection of authority from Mary to Christ. Margery undercuts praise for Mary's maternity when she interprets Luke 11:27–28 in chapter 52:

> the gospel makyth mencyon that, whan the woman had herd owr Lord prechyd, sche cam beforn hym wyth a lowde voys and seyd, 'Blyssed be the wombe that the bar and the tetys that gaf the sowkyn'. Than owr Lord seyd agen to hir, 'Forsothe so ar thei blissed that heryn the word of God and kepyn it'. And therfor, sir, me thynkyth that the gospel gevyth me leve to spekyn of God.

Seizing on Christ's response rather than the woman's blessing of his mother, Margery justifies her own speech about God. Hearing and doing God's word is what's important, not praising (or mimicking) Mary for her bodily contribution.

Mary's divisive breasts

The relative scarcity of breasts and breastmilk in the *Boke* contrasts with their ubiquity in Marian texts. A popular miracle tale that appears in the late fourteenth-century Vernon manuscript concerns the healing of Bishop Fulbert of Chartres during a bout with tonsillitis.[43] Even before Mary's appearance, the tale hints at the complex interplay of healing, sensory experience, and Mary's body:

> Whon he herde of hire eny speche,
> Of al his dissese that was his leche.
> That hedde he levere then drinke or ete.
> For ioye the teres wolde he lete. (7–10)

Merely *hearing* talk about Mary serves as Fulbert's 'leche', or medicine, a term that plays on *lactatio* as the shared etymological root of both 'milk' and 'leech' and foreshadows the tale's titular event, Mary's restorative suckling. While Mary's role in the scene is unmistakably curative, it is also vaguely maternal and unsettlingly erotic: her breast in Fulbert's mouth, Mary's voice soothing, her arm supporting his neck as she strokes his throat.[44] The milk's healing effect is, naturally, instantaneous ('The swellyng slaked. He feld no sore'). Fulbert's emotional response is complex. Just as hearing talk of Mary was a cure-all that could replace food or drink, provoking tears of joy, so does his healing result in disorientation and misuse of his newly soothed throat. He blames bystanders for Mary's departure, screaming at them for not providing enough quiet space or praise to encourage her to stay longer. Suddenly, his tantrum inexplicably over, he 'wepte for ioye wel glad' (69), now Mary's lifelong devotee. The tale's closing invocation subtly repeats the pun on *lactatio*:

> Othur help or othur leche
> Us nedeth not no forthere seche
> But Mari, modur and maiden clene. (73–5)

Leche might mean medicine or doctor; it might also be literal milk. Mary's healing powers draw directly from her maternal body. Here she fulfills her role as *Maria medica*, but she also acts as a mild chaos agent, unsettling Fulbert's and the bystanders' emotional equilibrium.

This tale is typical of Marian texts and images in its treatment of Mary's breasts: they are simultaneously maternal, erotic, available, and disruptive. They are often parsed for further symbolic meaning, the threat of salaciousness staved off by the milk's sacred essence. Fulbert was not the only cleric to confront them up close.[45] As Bernard of Clairvaux sang the hymn 'Ave, stella maris', a statue of Mary projectile-lactated on his face, sometimes directly into his eyes or lips, when he reached the line asking her to prove herself a mother.[46] The milk was thought to provide him wisdom. Suso's *Exemplar* repeats a similar anecdote involving John Chrysostom, who knelt at an altar with a wooden statue of *Maria lactans*. Mary suggests that the Christ child 'stop drinking for a while and allowed the aforementioned student to drink from her heart, too'. The scene is re-enacted between the Virgin and Suso, bestowing eloquence on him: 'the teaching that comes from his mouth from now on will be heard with more longing and joy than before'.[47]

That Mary's breasts were depicted in a constant state of ready lactation was surely as relevant to devotees as her permanent state of virginity. In the sermon cycle that prompted her high medieval cult, Bernard emphasized Mary's humility over her virginity, which seemed to him overrated. But he was mostly ignored on this point. It was only in the fourteenth century, when Bernard's own encounter with Mary's breasts became a popular sermon anecdote and friars embraced the nursing Virgin, that *Maria lactans* and the Madonna of humility gained traction as visual subjects.[48] These maternal images coexisted with references to Mary's breasts as young, pert, and pleasingly virginal.[49] However incidentally appealing, Mary's breasts always answer some deeper spiritual need in their viewer: forgiveness, healing, intercession, conversion, the nurturing of the holy that only she can provide. In the collection of miracle tales by Guibert of Coinci, they convert a Saracen, who contemplates doctrine as her breasts miraculously appear on an icon.[50] In multiple paintings, Mary flashes her nipples at Christ to remind him that the breasts that nurtured him belong to a woman whose authority should be respected.[51] Medieval pilgrims' comfort with Mary's breasts as object of devotion is clear from the many shrines to her milk, such as at Walsingham and the milk cave at Jerusalem.[52]

Margery visited many such sites. But for all her interest in relics of Mary's lactation, she barely mentions Mary's breasts as a subject of meditation. I want to suggest that Marian breasts presented a theological conundrum for Margery and for her *Boke*'s earliest readers. For many theologians, Mary's lactation was evidence of her thoroughly human physiology.[53] Augustine, and later Aquinas, explained that women's bodily maternal functions ultimately derived from original sin, inherited by all through sex. Because of this argument, Dominicans felt that to accept the idea of Mary's immaculate conception was to impose biological and theological gymnastics on her reproductive system.[54] A Marian body that lactated only through miracle and not through ordinary human function meant, among other things, that Christ could not have inherited his full humanity from Mary. Throughout the fourteenth and fifteenth centuries, then, Dominicans promoted *Maria lactans* images and other references to Mary's functional breasts as important indicators of her full, genetic humanity, supporting Bernard's emphasis on humility rather than immaculate conception.[55] Franciscans argued in favor of both Mary's immaculate conception *and* her functioning reproductive physiology, worrying less about any indiscrepancies.[56] Intriguingly, the Franciscan Nicholas Love doesn't mention the conception of Mary in *Mirror of the Blessed Life of Christ*, a book with which Margery claimed familiarity. As a trainee of both Dominicans and Franciscans, Margery may have worried that to assert a definite pro-mammary stance was to deny Mary's immaculate conception. In short, to speak of Mary's lactating breasts in the fifteenth century, amidst an audience full of or friendly with mendicants, sent a potentially divisive message.

Mary's antisemitic body

Even as Margery tiptoes around possible interpretation of Mary's breasts, she embraces the powerful image of Mary's womb as the site of Christ- and church-gestation. Her dual interests in Mary's maternal body and in the Eucharist allow her, along with confirming her role as *Maria Ecclesia*, to assert herself as Christian against Judaism. Marian stories and poems had long depicted Jews as actively disliking Mary and disbelieving details of her maternity.[57]

One of the alleged Jewish accusations was that Mary hadn't actually borne Christ; in such texts, proving her physical motherhood became all the more important. In the *Mirk's Festial* sermon for the Nativity of Mary, she introduces herself to one such non-believer: 'I am Mary, þat þou and alle þine nacion despysuth and seyne þat I bare neure Godys Sone of my body'. She later offers him a chance to convert based partly on the belief that 'Goddys Sone of heven was borne of me, and I clene maydon beforyn and aftyr'.[58] To judge from clerical writings, the perceived Jewish rejection of Mary as Mother of God had long rested on their disgust with uterine filth. In 1106, the Benedictine Odo of Cambrai claimed to record the words of Leon, a Jewish man mocking the idea that God would deign to be born of a woman:

> Here's something for which we really laugh at you and think you're insane. You claim that God suffered for nine months locked up in his mother's obscene bowels, in the fetid prison of a sealed belly, then finally emerged disgracefully in the tenth month (which can't even be imagined without shame), bringing dishonor with Him.[59]

Clerical emphases on Mary's virginity, purity, and cleanness spoke to such hypothetical allegations. To speak of the details of her physical childbirth, then, was also to assert one's stance against Jewish unbelief.

Marian maternity thus offered Margery theological rationale and venue for expressing antisemitism.[60] Bernard had described Jews as inferior; Aquinas argued that Jews purposefully killed Christ. Popular culture amplified these claims. In the early fifteenth-century poem 'O litel whyle lesteneth to me', Mary casually mentions the 'fikell Jewes, without othe,/Jewes stone-hard, with synnes merke' (216–17).[61] That Jews were 'hard-hearted', refusing to consider the truth of Christianity, was a popular trope. It emerges in a late fifteenth-century poem in which the speaker, perhaps Jewish, describes himself as 'so harde-hartid' he couldn't show empathy for Mary's grief; she replies, 'Nature shall move thee, thou must be converted' (12, 14).[62] She describes Christ's body as 'so beyn, so wowndid, entreted so Jewlye' (22). Similarly, the N-Town Plays, which Margery likely saw performed multiple times, feature Jews whose lack of empathy is meant to contrast with the humanity that Mary's own tears prove. By the time Margery began spiritual training, such anti-Jewish sentiment had long been part of mendicant culture in England. The Dominicans' first priory had been established in Oxford's Jewish quarter, and Franciscans played a large role in the expulsion of Jews from England.⁶³ Despite those expulsions and papal legislation enacted in attempts to exclude Jews from many aspects of public life (e.g., the Fourth Lateran Council required Jewish persons to wear identifying badges), the 'stubborn Jew' remained a constant bugbear in Christian theological treatises masquerading as dialogues or in mystery plays masquerading as histories.

The treatment of Mary's body as a foil to Jewishness extended to Eucharistic practice. Kathleen Biddick notes the overlap of Eucharistic shrines with the sites of massacres of Jews, explaining that blood libel narratives developed alongside Jewish persecution.⁶⁴ Depictions of the Eucharist thus carry a subtext of antisemitism or anticipatory violence against Jews. Biddick's work has implications about Margery's frequent use of Eucharistic images and her redirecting attention from Mary's lactating breasts to the meanings behind them or to the womb beneath them. To focus on Mary's body and her emotional response at the Crucifixion, then, was to affirm Mary's humanity and Margery's own orthodoxy at the same time. The Cross was considered the site of both Mary's doctrinal turn away from Judaism and the birth of the Church through her [now Christian] maternal body. The two pivotal moments dovetail in Mary's swoon.

The swoon: a more literal birth

What had transpired beneath Christ's cross—Mary's labor, tears, and voiced lament—was much-discussed throughout the late-medieval period. As Siegfried Wenzel has shown, the faithful were to spend midday prayers contemplating the Virgin under the Cross.⁶⁵ *Imitatio Mariae* by its nature required compassion for and emulation of Mary's sorrow. The connection of Margery's performative use of the Crucifixion to the Incarnation is clearer when she recreates Mary's swoon at the foot of the Cross:

> And whan thei cam up onto the Mownt of Calvarye sche fel down that sche mygth not stondyn ne knelyn but walwyd and wrestyd wyth hir body, spredyng hlr armys abrode, and cryed wyth a lowde voys as thow hir hert schulde a brostyn asundyr, for in the cité of hir

sowle sche saw veryly and freschly how owyr Lord was crucifyed. Beforn hir face sche herd and saw in hir gostly sygth the *mornyng of owyr Lady*, of Sen John and Mary Mawdelyn, and of many other that lovyd owyr Lord.

In the next chapter, Margery returns to the swoon:

> And sythen sche ros up ageyn wyth gret wepyng and sobbyng as thow sche had seyn owyr Lord beriid even befor hir. Than sche thowt sche saw oywr Lady in hir sowle, how sche mornyd and how sche wept hir sonys deth, and than was *owyr Ladiis sorwe hir sorwe*.

Further:

> And her gydes teld wher owyr Lord bare the cros on hys bakke, and wher hys Modyr met wyth hym, and how *sche swowynd, and how sche fel down* and he fel down also.

Scholars have noticed the similarity of Margery's swoon to the labor of childbirth.[66] Importantly, it is specifically *Mary's* labor that Margery is imitating, not simply childbearing generally, and it is Mary's sorrow that she imagines and portrays. Theologians debated whether Mary's expression of that sorrow through swooning or otherwise visibly emoting called her self-restraint or strength into question, with some writers declaring that surely she must have remained unfazed.[67] Margery's witness to Mary's swoons at least three different times in chapters 79–81 and her re-enactments of them in the above passages affirm that she has picked her side: she is definitely not standing still or stoically at the foot of the Cross.

The swoon was not only a demonstration of sorrow. Amy Neff's work on visual depictions of the Crucifixion makes clear why Margery's swoon, imitating Mary's, is so reminiscent of the labor of childbirth.[68] The popular view, strongly promoted by Dominicans, was that the labor pains Mary did not experience while delivering Christ were delayed until the Crucifixion, when she experienced a second, physically painful labor.[69] Following Rupert, the thirteenth-century Dominican Albertus Magnus described how Mary labored at the Cross, suffering childbirth pains to give birth to mankind; these ideas were echoed by the Franciscans Anthony of Padua and Bonaventure.[70] Mary's pain, signified by the swoon, was a required component of the birth of the church and sometimes held up as parallel to the Crucifixion itself. The pain showed her full humanity. Hamburgh explains that the birth of the Church 'is not only through the death of Christ but through the *agonia* of the mother'.[71] The Cistercian Ogier of Locedio invokes Mary directly: 'Now, Virgin, you repay with interest what you borrowed from nature in giving birth. You did not feel pain in bearing your son; you suffered a thousand times more in the dying of your son'.[72] This suffering was often understood to produce the Church, making Mary mother of all Christians. Ambrose had argued that Mary's adoption of John the Evangelist as son marked the first moment of her universal motherhood; accordingly, Margery describes Mary swooning as soon as Jesus introduces her to John in chapter 80.[73] Ambrose also saw motherhood as an attribute shared by Mary and the Church itself. Margery's acting out the Crucifixion labor would seem to confirm her wish to be Ecclesia and universal mother, as well.

Further, for theologians looking to justify Christian antisemitism, the painful labor of Mary beneath the Cross was a convenient setting for her turn from Judaism. Visual art sometimes depicted this moment with a triumphant Ecclesia and disgruntled (or blinded, or unhearing) Synagoga at the foot of the Cross.[74] Mary's swoon offered a useful shorthand for the same event. Years after Margery's trip to Rome, Rogier van der Weyden's *Altarpiece of the Seven Sacraments* makes these connections visually. (See Plate 2.) In the central panel, Mary swoons within the sightline of the priest offering the Eucharist, while Synagoga turns, face hidden, from the viewer.

Not only does Margery experience Marian contemplative tears in Jerusalem, then, but in symbolically swooning the birth of Christ or of the Church, she demonstrates that Christ has been *in* her, incarnated perhaps by her fruitful devotions and birthed on Calvary, just as Mary's delayed labor pains produced the Church. Margery appropriates Marian maternal identity to become *Maria Ecclesia*, birthing the church. She is not merely exploiting her own maternal status, but staking a claim in a particular realm of theological debate.

The poetry of maternal despair

Margery's investment in the swoon speaks to the emotional power and reach of Marian art and poetry. Depictions of Mary's maternal loss were uninhibited. Thomas Hoccleve's early fifteenth-century

Mar(ger)y at the foot of the Cross 73

poem 'Complaint of the Virgin' verbalizes a keening.[75] It depicts, unflinching, the frantic mental energies of fresh grief: a mother in the shocked early acknowledgment of her child's death. Mary blames biblical figures for the cruel surprise of the Crucifixion, beginning with her direct address to God himself as 'fers' and 'cruel':

> O fadir God, how fers and how cruel,
> In whom thee list or wilt, canst thow thee make.
> Whom wilt thow spare, ne wot I neuere a deel,
> Syn thow thy sone hast to the deeth betake. (1–4)[76]

How could God be trusted to keep anyone safe if he won't protect his own sinless, harmless son? Mary indicts others who opted not to prepare her for this moment: her parents, the Holy Ghost, Gabriel, Elizabeth, the Samaritan women who praised her womb and teats. Trapped as awkward witness, the reader might be briefly distracted by the potential blasphemy of this bereaved Mary. But as harsh as her words are, they are clearly meant to be read as symptoms of her grief, not her lack of faith. This scene and others like it aim in part to cement Mary's identity as Christian rather than Jewish, as her loyalty is to Christ above all.[77]

What *is* radical in this poem is Mary's occupation of verbal and affective spaces for her mourning, trusting that the reader will accept its necessity. Mary's case for the reader's empathy in the first several stanzas relies largely on antithesis, evoking the stark contrasts of her emotional life before and after grief. Built into her borderline-blasphemous accusations is the ruing of her past naïveté in having trusted her protectors. Similarly, she highlights the distinction between her memory of Christ's infancy and the pain of the current moment, describing her current condition primarily as abruptly deprived of maternal joy:[78]

> I hadde ioye entiere and also gladnesse
> Whan thow betook Him me to clothe and wrappe
> In mannes flessh. I wend, in sothfastnesse,
> Have had for euere ioye by the lappe.
> But now hath sorwe caught me with his trappe.
> My ioye hath made a permutacioun
> With wepyng and eek lamentacioun. ...
> Syn my ioye is me rafte, my grace is lorne. ...
> My blissyng into peyne Retorned is. Of ioye am I bareyne.
> (8–14; 35; 39–40)

Mary's loss of 'joye' is here portrayed as a theft. Joy was rightfully hers, to be expected with the territory of maternity. The rest of the poem delves into the complex wrinkles of maternal grief. Fourteen stanzas in, she justifies her long, public lament:

> How may myn yen þat beholde al this
> Restreyne hem for to shewe by weepynge
> My hertes greef? Moot I nat weepe? O yis. (99–101)

Here, and in the very act of narrating a thirty-five-stanza lamentation, Mary argues for the ability to express sorrow in public discourse, especially the maternal sorrow born of the stripping of hard-won 'joye'. Herein lay much of the poem's appeal for medieval readers. The author rightly assumes that readers need not be persuaded that the loss of a child is devastating. As Katharine Goodland has observed, 'To medieval audiences it seems to have been impossible to imagine a mother who did not wail her child's death.'[79] In her confidence that the audience shares her indignation, Hoccleve's Mary identifies and cultivates an emotional community of grieving mothers.[80] She focuses on the depth and range rather than the existence of that grief, and, as we see here, the need for a means to articulate it. Her tears, long understood as a spiritual gift, become a legitimate means of acknowledging and sharing grief and anger with that emotional community. Their use as social indicators is consistent with modern theories on grief; her tears' potential to assert (or subvert) power is clear from textual attempts to silence them in other maternal mourners, as we'll see.[81]

Hoccleve's poem is among the best known of a body of Marian lyrics in English known as *planctus Mariae* or *quis dabet*, a genre that emerged in Latin poetry of the thirteenth century and developed in several vernacular languages. As we see in the deployment of 'ioye' above, these poems depend for their power not only on a grasp of established Marian legend but on the reader's intuitive understanding of the physical and emotional joys that parenting a healthy, unharmed infant is supposed to bring. They refer to breastfeeding, to painless (in Mary's case) labor, and to the aesthetic appeal of a thriving infant rather than a bloodied adult. Intended as a venue for affective piety, the poems inadvertently allow readers to achieve *imitatio Mariae* not only through empathy but through their own experiences of maternal grief. With their emphasis on wholesome, nostalgic images of infancy, they speak, especially, to the mother who has lost a child and feels similarly deprived of a promised joy. The memory of such loss was readily available to a great many medieval women and easily imposed on Mary's lament. The *planctus Mariae* poems were so susceptible to this off-label use that by the end of the fifteenth century they explicitly warn women *not* to think of their own children: 'make ye no mone for your chyld'.[82] The attempt to manipulate mothers' emotions through empathy with Mary's sorrow seems to have backfired in part because writers underestimated readers' familiarity with and tendency to focus on their own maternal grief to the perceived exclusion of piety.

As template for readers' mourning, these poems filled a gap in devotional literature. Marian lyrics, spiritual autobiographies, and Crucifixion depictions are not simply avenues toward Christian or Marian meditation. Grieving mothers could read them as a means to project or inscribe their own experiences. By legitimizing space for maternal grief, Mary as speaker reveals the tension for those who seek to mourn within a culture that resists accommodating their pain emotionally or spatially. Drawing from one's memory of maternal affection to join Mary's emotional community was permitted; drawing from one's personal experience of grief was deemed insufficiently reverent of the Crucifixion. A generous reading of the *planctus* poems' limiting readers' responses in this way suggests an attempt to channel readers' pain into a more socially manageable form of piety. A more cynical interpretation is that the poems' authors wish to minimize maternal readers' grief or pre-empt its power. Such erasure of common maternal experience does both medieval and modern readers a disservice, given both cultures' default of silencing maternal grief. These texts' overt recognition of the deep connection between birth and death provides spaces to address failed pregnancy and maternal sorrow.

Silencing maternal grief

In contrast to Hoccleve's Mary, medieval mothers understood, thanks largely to horrifying perinatal and child mortality rates, that to give birth was also to create a death, be it imminent or distant, and, possibly, to hasten one's own. Here they were ahead of us. We in the modern world are still taken by surprise when an advanced pregnancy isn't viable, stunned when birth results in infant or maternal mortality. Western cultural taboos obscure that up to one-fifth of clinically recognized pregnancies end in loss and that, in the United States, more than two women die every day in childbirth.[83] Similarly, for reasons that include personal sorrow, readers' aversions or disinterest, and our own misreading of literary cues, we shy from serious discussion of miscarriage, stillbirth, and infant and maternal mortality. These phenomena were both more common and less stigmatized in the late-medieval period than they are now, referenced and depicted, if unnoticed, in multiple literary texts.

Scholars who do address medieval reproductive loss focus on its physical causes rather than emotional anguish.[84] Katherine French and Theresa Earenfight have acknowledged the difficulty of confirming failed pregnancies with historical evidence such as wills and records of gifts to convents and monasteries.[85] Evidence sometimes lies only in an absence of or gap between children. For example, we know that Christine de Pizan had a child who died young. Margery claims to have borne fourteen children, but confirms only one who survived to adulthood. Hoccleve's own patron, Joan FitzAlan de Bohun, managed only two live births in nine years; in comparison, Blanche of Lancaster delivered seven babies in the same time frame, three of whom survived to adulthood. Such lacunae suggest reproductive losses that remain unconfirmed in the historical record.

Medieval mothers could hardly ignore statistical realities: Nicholas Orme estimates child mortality rates at over 40 percent, not counting stillbirth or perinatal deaths, whose frequency was so high that baptisms were only performed and recorded at least ten days after birth—a practice that both suggests how high infant loss rates were and precludes our having accurate records of failed births.[86] Accordingly, it is clear from the material evidence of medieval rituals, amulets, charms, prayers, and images for births that negative outcomes to childbearing were expected in the Middle Ages.[87] Certainly they were included in the cultural conversation about birth. Because nutritional deficiencies commonly obfuscated signs of early pregnancy, medieval pregnancies often remained unconfirmed until the quickening in the fifth month, when most people would be visually pregnant and could feel fetal movement.[88] Early miscarriages could therefore go unnoticed even by the mother, while late-term losses were, then as now, less likely to be private—and, because of environmental factors, more likely to occur. The frequency and visibility of loss led to medical and theological speculation about its causes, though with less room for maternal mourning than we might expect: the pregnant body was a public one, but maternal emotion was to remain private. Central to those discussions was the belief that a pregnancy's success could be controlled by known factors, and that, by extension, failed pregnancy was preventable. Primary among the causes for miscarriage imagined by medieval writers was sex during the pregnancy, which was thought to lead to fetal death or birth defects.[89] Penitentials thus often forbade it.[90] Clerical writers were particularly concerned that certain sexual positions might be harmful to the fetus.[91] Jacques de Vitry held a husband's alcohol-fueled lust to blame for pregnancy loss, preaching against 'a drunk, returning from the tavern with the stink of wine on his breath to know his pregnant wife, who killed the child in his mother's womb when she went into labor prematurely'.[92] The medical treatise known as the *Trotula* offers a range of possible causes for fetal and maternal mortality, including the size of the mother's pelvic cavity,[93] the intensity of her desires,[94] her health and behaviors,[95] and the quality of her care during labor and delivery.[96] Tinctures are recommended to prevent fetal loss and for recovering and reviving a stillborn infant.[97] While medical treatises are more thorough and nuanced in their assessment than are religious sources, the burden of sustaining a pregnancy still falls on caregivers and the mother, with the implication that a woman whose pregnancy failed simply wasn't trying hard enough. Potential maternal grief for such a loss goes unmentioned.

Foremost among medieval clerical writers' concerns about preventing pregnancy loss is not the emotional state of the mother but the status of the fetal soul. 'Ensoulment', or the entry of the soul into the fetal body, was thought to happen at quickening, so that confirmation of pregnancy often coincided with the recognition of the fetus as a potentially Christian soul, thus rendering willful termination of the pregnancy as murder. There was some legal danger of being suspected of having induced miscarriage, with varying penalties assigned according to the stage of the pregnancy and the perceived intent.[98] Jacques de Vitry addresses ensoulment in a sermon anecdote:

> I have heard of some who obstinately distress their pregnant wives who are about to give birth, because they are unwilling to abstain for a short time to spare a woman heavy with child and thus kill the son in the mother's womb and deprive him of baptism. Cursed be this lust *that steals his son's soul from God.*[99]

The *Trotula* suggests that the soul's presence in a fetus helps stabilize it in the womb: 'when the soul is infused into the child, it adheres a little more firmly and does not slip out so quickly'.[100] Failed pregnancy, then, was a spiritual concern of the church, and cause for pious, rather than personal, lament, a perspective that lingers in some factions of the anti-abortion movement today. The linking of ensoulment to abortion and to miscarriage in medieval law and theology, and the disregard of the mother's emotional state in favor of the fetal soul's status, has had lasting effects.[101] Even now, medical treatments available for miscarriage are significantly limited by a state's laws (or a private hospital's policies) restricting abortion rights. Similarly, in their haste to disregard a mother's needs for those of the fetus, authors of anti-abortion policies often overlook the effects on miscarriage patients. In this context, a mother's private grief takes a backseat to the perceived spiritual loss of a soul.

Antithesis and the Crucifixion

These attempts to assign spiritual weight to the health of the pregnancy are out of tune with the grief Mary expresses at Christ's death, and presumably with what in the *planctus* poems appealed to women grieving perinatal or filial loss. Mary's ruthless narrative probing of her own experience contrasts with the abstract concern with souls that we see elsewhere in medieval writing about infant and child mortality and affirms that maternal grief was normative. Built into the *planctus Mariae* poems, along with the confirmation that maternal grief merits poetic space, is the recognition that new life brings death. Here the Christian fondness for inverting life and death does not hold: death and its implicit heavenly rewards are not cause for rejoicing, but for sorrow. Mary does not recover her Christian world-upside-down lens by the end of the poem: while her tone has softened, she is still grieved, even angered, by the paradox that invites death to the nursery and birth pains to a death scene.

As Rosemary Woolf and Amy Vines have each made clear, that duality is not exclusive to *planctus Mariae* but is also common to Nativity lyrics. Woolf observes that 'there is no [Nativity] lyric which does not ... look forward to the Crucifixion'.[102] Vines sees antithesis as a didactic strategy, arguing that 'Mary's shift from lullaby to lament in many of the Nativity lyrics model the emotional shift that is intended to take place within the reader'.[103] But poems meant to teach empathy to those unfamiliar with such loss through affective meditation would instead articulate and reinforce the emotional trauma of readers experiencing perinatal or filial grief. The imagery takes on a more visceral, personal meaning for a grieving audience, for whom any portrayal of the Madonna and child bears the pentimento of the Pietà. The fifteenth-century Nativity lyric 'Dear son, leave thy weeping', relies on multisensory, almost ekphrastic imagery in its depiction of a Madonna-and-child dialogue.[104] As Mary sings gently, presumably cuddling Christ in her arms, the infant points to his own body parts 'that ye may see' and predicts that men who later see those same limbs pierced with nails will 'wepe' just as he does now. Mary's response draws on stereotypical maternal imagery: 'A, dere Son, hard is my happe,/To see my child that sokid my pappe,/His hondes, his fete, that I dide wrappe,/ Be so naylid, that neuer did amysse' makes clear the imbalance of her maternal investment. The Mary of this lullaby does not relax and enjoy the infant body she is holding, though she clearly feels entitled to since he has enjoyed her 'pappes'.[105] Given the familiar visual appeal of a baby in its mother's arms, *imitatio Mariae* would require little emotional transfer for those enmeshed in perinatal or filial loss: the poem becomes a venue to process their own experience. It offers language for the unfairness that cheats them of their bodily investment and grants status for biological motherhood. Like the *planctus Mariae*, they also allow a space for personal grief.

To return to 'Complaint of the Virgin': we know a fair amount about the personal losses and emotional communities of the patron Hoccleve claims for the poem, Joan FitzAlan de Bohun. Countess of Hereford and sister to Archbishop Arundel, Joan is known for her management of massive landholdings in Essex, for her loyalty to the Edwardian court, and for her religious patronage, especially to Walden Abbey. She also experienced multiple forms of maternal loss: at least two of her grandchildren died in infancy or childhood, with one daughter's first pregnancy ending in stillbirth.[106] One of Joan's daughters and one of her granddaughters died in childbed; another granddaughter died while pregnant. Joan outlived her husband, both daughters, and nearly all of her grandchildren, and spent the last several years of her life 'like Anna in the temple'.[107] It is unclear whether she herself experienced miscarriage or perinatal loss, but Hoccleve's connection of her with a poem featuring a deeply grieving mother is suggestive, as is the relatively long gap between her daughters' birth dates.

That grieving women such as Joan were using these poems to process their own mourning is also suggested by the way the poems' content evolves over the course of the fifteenth century. In Hoccleve's poem, as in the Nativity lyrics, Mary focuses on the physical affection between mother and infant and the implied reciprocity it sets up.

> Thow in myn armes lay and on my knee
> Thow sat and haddist many a kus of me.
> Eek, thee to sowke, on my brestes yaf y
> Thee norisshyng faire and tendrely.
> Now thee fro me withdrawith bittir deeth
> And makith a wrongful disseuerance. (74–9)

The mother has given ample sacrifice of her own body—'many a kus' and 'norisshynge faire and tendrely' from her breasts—so that the child's physical death rather than, presumably, persisting bodily intact, is 'wrongful disseuerance'. More than once, Mary suggests that it's the unjustness of this unreturned maternal physical connection that intensifies her pain:

> A modir þat so soone hir cote taar
> Or rente, sy men neuere noon or this,
> For chyld *which þat shee of hir body baar*
> *To yeue her tete*, as my chyld þat heere is. (239–42)

It is not only that her memories of Christ's infancy have been tainted by his gruesome death, but that she as a parous woman is owed some filial recompense for the child's use and benefit of her body.

This equation seems to appeal to women with some experience of early motherhood and related grief. We see a twist on the same concept in another *planctus* poem, 'An Appeal to All Mothers', in which Mary addresses maternal readers directly, again employing antithesis:[108]

> Your childur ye dawnse upon your kne
> With laghyng, kyssyng, and mery chere:
> Behold my childe, beholde now me,
> For now liggus ded my dere son, dere. (5–8)

The poem continues with eleven stanzas of overt comparison between the perceived ideal nursery interactions of readers with their healthy, happy children and Mary's having only her child's corpse. Here, Mary criticizes mothers who don't respond to her harrowing maternal loss: 'If your childe had lost his life/Ye would wepe at euery mele;/But for my son wepe ye neuer a del' (67–9). Grieving readers, however, would have no need for this attempt to teach empathy. They could instead simply step into the speaker's role, chastising other mothers—in Mary's voice—for not recognizing their plight. Read this way, the poem is cathartic rather than accusing. The author seems to have anticipated some readers would, indeed, project themselves into the poem, potentially to the exclusion of the devotion it means to provoke: in the penultimate stanza, mothers are cautioned, 'Wepe not for yours, but wepe for hit' (75)—that is, weep for Christ rather than your own child. For readers with their own experience of perinatal or filial loss, these poems attempt to control rather than to provoke their tears. Shared motherhood is suitable for stimulating empathy in the reader, but relevant personal grief is viewed as rivalry.

Other poems in the *planctus* tradition similarly acknowledge maternal grief but encourage readers to redirect their weeping on behalf of Christ. In one fourteenth-century version of the hymn 'Stond wel, Moder, under Rode', filial loss is explicitly mentioned ('Moder, mitarst thi mith leren/Wat pine tholen that childre beren,/ Wat sorwe haven that child forgon'),[109] but in another manuscript of the same hymn, simply bearing children is the source of sorrow, so that the specific grief of losing an infant or child is effectively erased ('Moder, nou thou miht wel leren/Whet sorewe haveth that children beren,/Whet sorewe hit is with childe gon').[110] By the late fifteenth century, the 'Lament of Mary' articulates the existence of other mothers' filial loss but chastises them for indulging their own grief:

> Than seyd Oure Lady bothe meke and myld
> To all women: 'Behold and se,
> And make ye no mone for your chyld,
> Of Godys sond if it dede be.
> For if ye do, ye be not wyse
> To se my sone as he lyghet here.
> Now he is dede—lo, were he lyes.
> For thi sone dyghd my dere son dere.[111]

A few stanzas later, grieving mothers are advised, 'Woman, now thou canste thi wyte./Thou seyst thi chyld whether it be seke or dede./*Wepe thou for myn and not for it,*/And thou schall have mych to thy mede' (81–4).

Here the *planctus* walks a fine line between exploiting the intuitive connection maternal readers had to natal imagery—which was useful in expanding the reach of these poems—and downplaying its association with readers' actual perinatal and filial losses, which may have limited the poems' appeal or, more immediately, overshadowed Mary's sorrow. The emotional communities first recognized and cultivated by Mary now needed to be controlled, lest they interfere with the intended effects of the poems. Even as the *planctus* carves out space for mourning, filial loss permits tears only if they are ascribed to sorrow for Christ. These poems make clear that filial lamentation should be framed as empathy for Mary or sorrow for Christ rather than personal mourning.

Margery Kempe, *Planctus* reader and re-interpreter

Margery was both contemporary with Hoccleve and demonstrably familiar with his poem's genre; she was a close and critical reader of the *planctus*. Modern medicine tells us that the number of miscarriages per woman increases with parity and age.[112] Given the uncertainties of medieval obstetrics, Margery was unlikely to have known the total number of her pregnancies. She never indicates that fourteen children survived to adulthood or even childhood. And there is a palpable absence of actual (rather than potential, envisioned, or metaphorical) babies and children in the *Boke*. While she often claims authority through her experiences in childbirth and postpartum care, the only actual children are those who prompt her tears in the streets of Rome or witness them in England. It is unclear whether Margery's attempt at *imitatio Mariae* includes the denial of personal filial grief that the *planctus* recommends, but the odds are high that she did have some experience of failed pregnancy and infant mortality.

Margery's recounting of the Crucifixion scene makes clear that she has been attentive to the *planctus Mariae* genre, and her engagement with the form demonstrates the tensions for grieving readers I've already suggested. She is certainly mindful of the connection between Christ's birth and death that holds in the *planctus*. In chapter 6, caring for the newborn Christ, she 'swathyd hym wyth byttyr teerys of compassyon, havyng mend of the scharp deth that he chuld suffyr for the lofe of synful men'.[113] Lest we miss her internalizing of the *planctus*, Margery describes in chapter 29 how closely she engaged with Mary's grief:

> And sythen sche ros up ageyn wyth gret wepyng and sobbyng as thow sche had seyn owyr Lord beriid even befor hir. Than sche thowt sche saw owyr Lady in hir sowle, how sche mornyd and how sche wept hir sonys deth, and than was owyr Ladiis sorwe hir sorwe.[114]

In phrasing reminiscent of one of the *planctus* or Nativity poems, Mary tells Margery, 'yyf thu wylt be partabyl in owyr joye, thu must be partabil in owyr sorwe'.[115] But when Margery does try to partake of that sorrow, both Christ and Mary remind her that *she's* not his actual mother, implying that only Mary is worthy of public grief. Chapters 79–81 depict Margery as witness to Mary's lament as she collapses to the ground and begs Christ to let her die first to avoid sorrow.[116] Upon seeing the interaction between Mary and Christ that is recounted in several *planctus* poems, Margery replicates the same sequence, asking Christ to kill her and claiming to be unable to remain in a world without him: she 'cryid ful lowde and wept rith sor'.[117] While Margery constantly affirms that she is grieving *with* Mary (perhaps disregarding her own filial losses, exactly as the Mary of the *planctus* lyrics expected), she is still chastised for attempting to share in Mary's sorrow. Christ tells her, 'Be stille, dowtyr, and rest wyth my modyr her and comfort the in hir, for *sche that is myn owyn modyr* must suffyr this sorwe'. A few lines later, when Margery remarks, '*I may not dur it, and yyt am I not hys modyr*', Mary replies tartly, 'Dowtyr, thu herist wel it wil non otherwise be, and therefor *I* must nedys suffyr it for *my sonys lofe*'.[118] Only Christ's mother has a right to this mourning; only Christ's body is worth maternal grief.

Trying a different tack, Margery returns to a fundamental purpose of the Crucifixion scene: distinguishing Mary from other Jewish persons.[119] Antithesis could involve inserting a villain to contrast with the virtuous sufferer, and for *planctus*, this was the Jew.[120] To appropriate Marian motherhood in the context of *planctus* meant to shrug off the humanity of Jews, an especially problematic decision for Margery to take in Jerusalem but one for which she is rewarded. It is only when Margery explicitly attributes the violent details of Christ's torment to Jewish behaviors in chapters 79 and 80 that she is permitted to speak to Mary on more equal terms. Miri Rubin has pointed out that it is during the period of *Mater dolorosa*—that is, as *planctus Mariae* develops as a genre—that the blame of Jews for Christian and Marian suffering increases.[121] The poems' teaching of Mary's maternal sorrow was also meant to set Christian empathy versus what the genre presented as the foil of Jewish cold-heartedness. Margery's acceptance of this connection is clear. In her view, othering the Jews temporarily allows her closer communion with both Mary and Christ. Her first run at describing Christ's torments at their hands results in his acknowledgment that she, too, deserves to grieve for him: 'Dowtyr, thes sorwys and many mo suffyrd I for thi lofe ... Therfor, dowtyr, thu hast gret cawse to lovyn me right wel, for I have bowt thi lofe ful der'.[122] As Margery continues to build a case against the perceived atrocities of the Jews in chapter 80, she and other devout women begin to form a coalition roughly allied with Mary.

No longer advised that she must respect Mary's exclusive right to mourn Christ, Margery feels emboldened to offer advice to the grieving Mary: 'I prey yow, Lady, cesyth of yowr sorwyng ... for me thynketh ye han sorwyd anow. And, Lady, I will sorwe for yow, for yowr sorwe is my sorwe'.[123] Not only does Margery minimize the need for Mary's grief, but she names herself as a sharer in the mourning. This is a step too far. When Margery again urges

Mary to end her grieving, Mary argues sharply that, because her son is the best who ever lived, she has more right to sorrow than anyone else: 'certeyn was ther nevyr woman in erth had so gret cawse to sorwyn as I have, for ther was nevyr woman in this world bar a bettyr childe ne a mekar to hys modyr than my sone was to me'.[124] At this dressing-down, Margery silently withdraws from the conversation: uncharacteristically, she cedes the argument. The rest of the chapter consists of her passively reporting Mary's interactions with John the Evangelist and Mary Magdalene. The generic parameters of the *planctus* that require the centering of Mary's grief have triumphed; Margery's attempt to reconstruct the *planctus* has failed.

What is only implicit in the *planctus Mariae* poems is fleshed out in Margery's prose version: regular women are not quite worthy of grieving for Christ, or for their own children, as Mary does. Margery's version of the *planctae* confirms the tension the genre acknowledges in demanding (controlled) affective piety while not granting public space for grieving. Telling Mary to 'cesyth of [her] sorwyng' seems ridiculous in the context of the rest of the *Boke*, given that much of the narrative involves Margery seeking acceptance for her own ostentatious weeping. But it also reflects late-medieval culture's resistance to public grieving. In thirteenth- and fourteenth-century Italy—not long before Margery traveled there—public displays of mourning such as

> appearing bareheaded, clapping, tearing one's own hair or clothing and ripping at one's own face as a sign of grief, became punishable by a fine by law. While weeping was tolerated, public wailing and loud crying was penalised even if lamentations were permitted indoors ... in certain cases even widows could be perceived as too sorrowful.[125]

Public mourning was coded as feminine and excess. In a letter to his patron, Petrarch argued that women's displays of grief disturbed peace and order:

> A coffin is carried out, a crowd of women bursts forth, filling the streets and squares with loud and uncontrolled shrieks ... Order that no woman should set foot outside her house on this account. If weeping is sweet for those in misery, let her weep at home to her heart's content, and *not sadden the public places*.[126]

These edicts decry women's public mourning merely as disturbances of the peace or of dignity, but Katharine Goodland has identified how, when deployed as residual practices of ritual lament, it also threatens foundational power structures. Discussing the Lazarus plays, Goodland notes that 'inconsolable grief seems to subvert the Christian promise of redemption and eternal life, and the belief that women's cries could commune with the dead challenges the Christian belief in Jesus as the mediator between the human and heavenly realms'.[127] In her study of the Corpus Christi plays, Goodland again addresses the power of women's mourning, comparing Mary's lament to the responses of mothers to the Slaughter of the Innocents: their anger effects justice in various ways, often articulated through echoes of Mary's words. As Goodland puts it:

> Their cries reflect upon the joy and pain of childbirth, their efforts to feed and rear their sons, and the appalling waste of all their labors as they witness the horror of evil and the fragility of human life. ... their sorrow testifies to Herod's cowardice and inhumanity, the injustice of the powerful preying upon the helpless and innocent. Herod's ultimate fate is conceived in the maternal mourning of Mary and the mothers.[128]

Here maternal grief is not merely a rival to Mary's status, but a threat to government stability. The play's treatment of grieving mothers as a collective makes clearer why the Mary of Margery's *Boke* and of the *planctus* poems are so eager to shut down the tears of individual mothers. If the mothers of innocents are able to bring down Herod with phrasing parallel to Mary's, what kind of power might lie in other grieving mothers' voices? Maternal grief as a latent, fearful power that can be channeled and directed at targets is more troubling than the idea of pain or grief as merely outside the verbal, as Elaine Scarry has described it, or uncontrollable.[129] It also suggests that Mary's attempts to quell or redirect mothers' mourning aim to minimize their likelihood of challenging other forms of authority—or the possibility that their grief, like her own, might manifest into anger and blame. Margery appropriates Mary's sorrow, perhaps disregarding her own filial losses, on good authority: that's exactly what the Mary of these lyrics expected. Margery's misbehavior mimics what the Virgin does in *planctus Mariae*: it too is *imitatio Mariae*.

Margery's prose rendition is one among multiple versions of the *planctus Mariae* in which we can discern the potential power of pain. Margery's temporal distance from childbirth as she narrates the Crucifixion scene and others in her *Boke* does not protect her from its potential emotional wounds. Grief is, whatever its source, unpredictable and chronologically untethered. The Crucifixion scene with Mary in which tears connote power suggests Margery has an inkling of the importance of her weeping, and the two chapters that follow (82 and 83) are mostly a long justification and defense of her holy tears. She describes them as delicious relief, as providing access to prayer, as provoked by new mothers' churching ceremonies and, later, witnessed by children as priests test their authenticity. These chapters serve as the response to Mary that she could not give in the moment of accusation. The cause of Margery's tears, a source of public conflict and her own comfort throughout her book, is now contestable: is she truly seeking permission to practice an *imitatio Mariae* that expresses sorrow over Christ, as she claims, or does her determination to weep assert the ability to mourn her own personal losses, which she doesn't mention? Margery's insistence on crying in church and out, in the streets and in private conversations, until Mary tells her to stop, is also a refusal to allow her grief— over Christ, or over her personal losses—to be erased or unseen. *Her* mourning knows no stigma, and is frequently affirmed by Christ himself. Mary's chastisement of her at the Crucifixion only highlights how openly and defiantly Margery has grieved to that point, and how much weeping might be left to do.

Notes

* Portions of this chapter first appeared in Mary Beth Long, '"Woful womman, confortlees": Failed maternity and maternal grief as feminist issues', *postmedieval* 10.3 (2019), 326–43.
1 See Williams, 'Manipulating Mary'; Liz Herbert McAvoy, *Authority*.
2 Sarah Salih cautions against over-interpreting the juxtaposition of Margery's madness to her postpartum state, arguing that is 'tenuous and accidental' in *Versions of Virginity*, 178–9.
3 Scholars explain Margery's childcare arrangements along two possibilities: either the children really are absent (with other caregivers, or dead), or they are unmentioned because Margery prioritizes promoting her

spiritual superiority. McAvoy (*Authority*, 61) posits that Margery and her husband utilized the extramural fostering described in John Boswell, *The Kindness of Strangers* (New York: Pantheon, 1988), 356–60. However, the Kempes' circumstances do not match those Boswell describes. Laura Kalas argues that Margery depends on wetnurses; she sees Margery as a 'surrogate' mother who produces spiritual fruits in *Margery Kempe's Spiritual Medicine: Suffering, Transformation and the Life Course* (Woodbridge: Boydell and Brewer, 2020), 15.

4 See Yoshikawa, *Medicine, Religion and Gender in Medieval Culture* (Cambridge: D.S. Brewer, 2015), at 12. Diane Watt reads Margery's healing of a postpartum woman as implicit acknowledgment of *Maria medica* in 'Mary the physician: women, religion and medicine in the Middle Ages', in Yoshikawa, *Medicine, Religion and Gender*, 27–44. Kalas discusses Margery's nursing in *Margery*, 127–60. I discuss *Maria medica* further in Chapter 3.

5 See Yoshikawa, *Margery Kempe's Meditations*.

6 'Than sche gat hir an hayr of a kylne swech as men dryen on malt and leyd it in hir kyrtylle as sotyllych and prevylich as sche mygth that hir husband schuld not aspye it, ne no mor he dede, and yet sche lay be hym every nygth in his bedde, and weryd the hayr every day, and bar chylderyn in the tyme', Kempe, *Book*, 27. She does not specify whether the hairshirt was also kept hidden from the infants or midwives.

7 *Ibid.*, 139.

8 *Ibid.*, 199, emphasis mine.

9 *Ibid.*, 232, emphasis mine.

10 Sue Niebrzydowski, 'Marian literature', in *The History of British Women's Writing, 700–1500*, ed. Liz Herbert McAvoy and Diane Watt (Basingstoke: Palgrave Macmillan, 2012), 112–20, at 116.

11 See Yoshikawa, *Margery Kempe's Meditations*.

12 Suso, *Exemplar*, 80–1.

13 Mary C. Erler, 'Home visits: Mary, Elizabeth, Margery Kempe and the Feast of the Visitation', in *Medieval Domesticity: Home, Housing and Household in Medieval England*, ed. Maryanne Kowaleski and P.J.P. Goldberg (Cambridge: Cambridge University Press, 2008), 259–76.

14 She delivers him 'from the earth' in *Mirk's Festial*. Vol. 1, 94. Bridget of Sweden's description from Book Seven of her *Revelations* was influential: Mary 'tuke him and laide him, firste, in on linen clothe, and sithen in one wolle, and band his bodi, his armes and his legges with one band; and þan shoe band two linen litill clotþis, þat sho broght with hir, about his heued'. *The liber celestis of St Bridget*

of Sweden. Vol. 1, ed. Roger Ellis, Early English Text Society 291 (Oxford University Press, 1987), 486.

15 Gail MacMurray Gibson, 'Saint Anne and the religion of childbed: some East Anglian texts and talismans', *Interpreting Cultural Symbols: Saint Anne in Late Medieval Society*, ed. Kathleen Ashley and Pamela Sheingorn (Athens, GA: University of Georgia Press, 1991), 95–110.

16 Francis of Assisi employs birth imagery differently: '[we are] mothers when we carry Him in our heart and body through love and a pure and sincere conscience; and give Him birth through a holy activity, which must shine before others by example'. From 'Letter to the Faithful', www.vatican.va/spirit/documents/spirit_20020203_lettera-fedeli-2_en.html

17 Hamburger's *Nuns as Artists* offers a brief history of this phenomenon.

18 Staley calls the keys 'tokens of female authority ... symbols of admission into the territory that her gender allows her', in *Margery Kempe's Dissenting Fictions* (Pennsylvania: Pennsylvania State University Press, 1994), 89. Williams agrees that 'the keys signify that Margery's power is still limited to and by her earthly roles as wife and mother', 'Manipulating Mary', 535. Sarah Salih interprets the resumption of pantry duties as a move from confinement to authority over her household in 'At home; Out of the house', *The Cambridge Companion to Medieval Women's Writing*, ed. Carolyn Dinshaw and David Wallace (Cambridge: Cambridge University Press, 2006), 124–40, at 124.

19 'Data est *ecclesiae* in christo omnis potestas in coelo et in terra, clavibus ei ligandi atque solvendi dimissis/All authority has been given to the Church, in Christ, in heaven and on the earth, the keys with the power of binding and of loosing having been sent unto him', PL 93, col 163, emphasis mine. Bede speaks here of the general church, not the figure of Ecclesia who appears in art, although Spreadbury, 'Gender', 95, reads it as the latter. I thank Stephen Harris for clarifying this point to me: 'Bede, interested first in the literal, would understand that the keys pass to Peter not as an individual, but as a foundation, that is, as the first holder of an office around which is organized the *universa ecclesia* of Acts. ... Ecclesia is found throughout Bede's work in a variety of forms. In his commentary on Solomon, Bede says that the Strong Woman of Proverbs is a type of *ecclesia*. In his hymns, Mary becomes a type of *ecclesia*'. Private communication, May 2017.

20 Kempe, *Book*, 93.

21 Acts 1:13, and see Hilda Graef, *Mary: A History of Doctrine and Devotion* (Notre Dame: Ave Maria Press, 2009).

22 Iris Marian Young, 'Pregnant embodiment: Subjectivity and alienation', *On Female Body Experience: Throwing Like a Girl and Other Essays* (Oxford: Oxford University Press, 2005), 46–61, at 46–7.
23 Cited in Miri Rubin, *Mother of God: A History of the Virgin Mary* (New Haven: Yale, 2009), 15.
24 The wife-as-church metaphor was applied to the description of husband and wife as 'one flesh' in Genesis 2; see Mâle, *Gothic*, 187–8; Spreadbury, 'Gender', 94. Perhaps equally relevant are the body-as-temple analogies scattered throughout the Pauline letters, such as in II Corinthians 6.16, and faith described as an athlete's footrace in I Corinthians 9.
25 Rubin, *Mother of God*, 61, and Spreadbury, 'Gender', 95–8 offer several examples of this depiction, although to different ends. Bynum lists several examples of the Virgin Mary's association with the Eucharist.
26 See Mâle, *Gothic*, 187ff.
27 Raguin examines this phenomenon in donor portraits produced in the decades after *Boke* in 'Real'.
28 This persuasion ties her to the good wife St Cecilia; see Chapter 6.
29 Bynum, *Holy Feast*, 268.
30 Qtd. in Yoshikawa, *Meditations*, 115.
31 See Spreadbury 95–7.
32 See Bynum, *Holy Feast*, 227–37 for women getting communion without priests. Women were forbidden as 'potential polluters' in certain areas or practices of the church; see Gilchrist, *Norwich Cathedral Close*, 16.
33 Kempe, *Book*, 79, emphasis mine.
34 *Ibid.*, 80, emphasis mine.
35 *The Etymologies of Isidore of Seville*, ed. and trans. Stephen A. Barney et al. (Cambridge: Cambridge University Press, 2006), book XI, 236.
36 *Ibid.*, 236. See also Megan Holmes, 'Disrobing the Virgin: The Madonna lactans in fifteenth-century Florentine art', *Picturing Women in Renaissance and Baroque Italy*, eds. S. Matthews Grieco and G. Johnson (Cambridge: Cambridge University Press, 1997), 167–95.
37 Cheese, milk, and honey were used in the early church's Eucharistic practices and remained popular visual cues. In the sixteenth century, Gerard David would paint a series of Mary feeding the infant Christ milk soup, often depicting grapes as well, as if to layer as many Marian and Eucharistic tropes as possible.
38 Yoshikawa offers a thorough analysis of this chapter as a meditation on the Eucharist as spiritual espousal, *Margery Kempe's Meditations*, 111–16.
39 See Hamburger, *Nuns*, 151–7.
40 'Du speigelglaß, on allen rums, den ein und den druvalten, versluß du in dins Herzen schrein', qtd. in Hamburger, *Nuns*, 151.

41 Kempe, *Book*, 199.
42 Clare of Assisi, among others, also claimed to have drunk milk from Christ's breast.
43 French and Latin versions of the tale identify him as Fulbert, a theologian who devoted significant energies to raising Mary's profile in the liturgy. See Margot Fassler, 'Mary's nativity, Fulbert of Chartres, and the *Stirps Jesse*: liturgical innovation circa 1000 and its afterlife', *Speculum* 75.2 (2000), 389–434. The episode appears on fol. 126va of the Vernon manuscript, Bodleian MS Eng. Poet. A. 1. and is edited in Adrienne Williams Boyarin, *Miracles of the Virgin in Middle English* (Peterborough, ON: Broadview Press, 2015), 87–90.
44 The illumination in the Vernon is less suggestive than the text: Mary's arm rests on Fulbert's shoulders, and she holds her own breast, preparing to administer the milk, while two bystanders look on. I am grateful to Cynthia Rogers for sharing a scan of this image when I could not easily access it.
45 The story was embedded in liturgical practice at Chartres, with the milk left from Fulbert's encounter preserved as a relic: 'unde accidit tres guctas dicti lactis super faciem remanisse, quas recollegit et in precioso vase ad hoc aptato reposuit, que usque ad presens, in ecclesia, certis temporibus, venerantur' ('and so it happened that remaining on his face were three drops of this milk, which he collected and placed into a precious vase appropriate for storing them, so that even now, they are venerated in church at certain times'). E. de Lepinois and Lucien Merlet, *Cartulaire de Notre-Dame de Chartres*, 3 vols. (Chartres, 1865), 1:14.
46 The line: 'Monstra te esse matrem'. The anecdote does not appear in Bernard's own writings but became popular in the fourteenth century. For medieval sources, see Léon Dewez and Albert van Iterson, 'La lactation de saint Bernard: legende et iconographie', *Citeaux in de Nederlanden* 7 (1956), 165–89. See also Jutta Sperling, 'Squeezing, squirting, spilling milk: The lactation of Saint Bernard and the Flemish *Madonna Lactans* (ca. 1430–1530)', *Renaissance Quarterly* 71.3 (2018), 868–918.
47 Suso, *Exemplar*, 96. Suso cites fellow Dominican Vincent de Beauvais, *Speculum Historiale* 8.84, as his source.
48 Holmes warns that humility was often conflated with lactans, 'Disrobing', 169.
49 While sermons emphasized Marian breasts' maternal and spiritual functions over their sexual appeal, visual depictions of Mary's breasts often maintained erotic tensions. See Margaret R. Miles, *A Complex Delight: The Secularization of the Breast, 1350–1750* (Berkeley: University of California Press, 2008). See also the lyrics discussed in Holmes, 'Disrobing'. Mirk's Feast of Assumption sermon

includes an anecdote of a man willing to be blinded so he could look lustily at Mary. Lydgate's *Life of Our Lady* describes Mary's entire motherhood mostly with reference to her 'smale pappes'.

50 'deus mameles/si glorïeuses et si beles,/si petites et si bien faites', Gautier de Coinci, *Miracles de Nostre Dame*, ed. Frédéric Koenig. Vol. 3 (Librairie Droz, 1966), 25, lines 58–61.

51 E.g., the late-fourteenth-century *Intercession of Christ and the Virgin*, Lorenzo Monaco, now at the Cloisters (1953, 53.37); London, British Library MS Additional 37049, fol. 19r; and the fifteenth-century Day of Judgment painting over the chancel arch at St Mary Magdalene, Ickleton. Such images echo Arnold of Bonneval, whose sermon imagines Christ and Mary baring their torsos to promote mercy: 'Securum accessum iam habet homo ad Deum, ubi mediatorem causae suae Filium habet ante Patrem, et ante Filium matrem. Christus, nudato latere, Patri ostendit latus et vulnera: Maria Christo pectus et ubera' ('Man now has sure access to God, where he has the Son as mediator of his cause before the Father, and the mother before the Son. Christ, baring His flank, showed the Father His side and wounds; Mary to Christ her breast and paps'). *De Laudibus Beatae Mariae Virginis*, in J.P. Migne (ed.), *Patrologina Latina*, 189, 1726. On Mary's intercessory breasts, see Ryan, 'Persuasive' and Yoshikawa, *Margery Kempe's Meditations*.

52 Waller offers a colorful description of the English 'milk trail' in *Virgin Mary*.

53 See Charles T. Wood, 'The doctors' dilemma: Sin, salvation, and the menstrual cycle in medieval thought', *Speculum* 56.4 (1981), 710–27. See also J.A. Tasioulas, 'The portrayal of Mary in the N-Town Plays', in Diane Watt (ed.), *Medieval Women in Their Communities* (Toronto: University of Toronto Press, 1997), 227.

54 For the long history of the doctrinal controversy and Dominicans' perspective, see Thomas Izbicki, 'The immaculate conception and ecclesiastical politics from the Council of Basel to the Council of Trent: The Dominicans and their foes', *Archiv für Reformationsgeschichte* 96 (2005), 145–70.

55 Ryan argues that *Maria lactans* fell out of favor as theories of immaculate conception took hold.

56 See Holmes, 'Disrobing', 171, for their focus on her nursing.

57 For what Jewish thinkers actually were saying about Mary, see Ephraim Shoham-Steiner, 'The Virgin Mary, Miriam, and Jewish reactions to Marian devotion in the High Middle Ages', *AJS Review* 37.1 (2013), 75–91.

58 *John Mirk's Festial*, ed. Susan Powell. Vol. 2 (Oxford: Oxford University Press, 2010), 225.

59 Translation mine. 'In quodam vos valde ridemus et insanos judicamus. Dicitis enim Deum, in maternis visceribus ob[s]ceno carcere fetidi ventris clausum, novem mensibus pati, et tandem pudendo exitu (qui intuitum sine confusione non admittit), decimo [sic] mense progredi, inferentes Deo tantum dedecus'. *Disputatio contra Iudaeum, Leonem Nomine, de Adventu Christi Filii Dei*, PL 160: 1110C.
60 The biblical reference to Mary at the Crucifixion is minimal; see John 19:19–27. The scholarship on antisemitism in Mariology is extensive; see e.g. Thomas H. Bestul, *Texts of the Passion: Latin Devotional Literature and Medieval Society* (Philadelphia: University of Pennsylvania Press, 1997), and Adrienne Williams Boyarin, *Miracles of the Virgin in Medieval England: Law and Jewishness in Marian Legends* (Woodbridge: D.S. Brewer, 2010).
61 BL Royal 18 A 10, fol. 126b; Saupe, poem 43.
62 Manchester Rylands Library 18932 (Latin 395), fol. 120a-b; Saupe, poem 39.
63 See Jeremy Cohen, *The Friars and the Jews: The Evolution of Medieval Anti-Judaism* (Ithaca, NY: Cornell University Press, 1982), 43, and 'The Jews as the killers of Christ in the Latin tradition, from Augustine to the friars', *Traditio* 39 (1983), 1–27.
64 Kathleen Biddick, 'Genders, bodies, borders: Technologies of the visible', *Speculum* 68.2 (1993), 389–418, at 402.
65 Siegfried Wenzel, 'The Dominican presence in Middle English literature', ed. Kent Emory and Joseph Wawrykow (South Bend: University of Notre Dame Press, 1998), 315–31, at 323–4. Yoshikawa describes Margery's meditation on the Passion in *Meditations*, 81–92. See also McNamer, *Affective Meditation*.
66 See e.g. Hope Phyllis Weissman, 'Margery Kempe in Jerusalem', in *Acts of Interpretation: The Text in its Contexts, 700–1600*, ed. Mary Carruthers and Elizabeth Kirk (Norman, OK: Pilgrim Books, 1982), 201–17, at 209–15; Karma Lochrie, *Margery Kempe*, 192; see also Williams, 'Manipulating'.
67 Harvey Hamburgh lists several thinkers' interpretations from the fourth through the fifteenth centuries in 'The problem of Lo Spasimo of the Virgin in cinquecento paintings of the Descent from the Cross', *The Sixteenth Century Journal* 12.4 (1981), 45–75, at 46–56.
68 Amy Neff, 'The pain of *compassio*: Mary's labor at the foot of the cross', *The Art Bulletin*, 80.2 (1998), 254–73.
69 *Ibid.*, 255.
70 See *ibid.*, 256, and corresponding notes 27–30. Neff also describes devotional art that emerged in Germany after Rupert's death as spotlighting a laboring Virgin under the Cross.
71 Hamburgh, 'Problem', 51.

72 'Nunc soluis, virgo, cum vsura quod in partu mutuasti a natura. Dolorem pariendo filium non sensisti; milies replicatum, filio moriente, passa fuisti', from *Meditacio Bernard de lamentacione beate virginis* (London, British Library, MS. Cotton Vespasian E.i, s. xiv), in Bestul, *Texts*, 176. As Neff notes, Simeon had predicted this pain as the 'sword' Mary would endure, 'Pain', 256. Margery may have known that Bridget of Sweden mentions this sword in her *Revelations*. Esther Cohen's observation that late medieval women might scream in childbirth, while saints suffered pain silently, is pertinent in thinking through how theologians affirmed Mary's humanity through that pain. See Esther Cohen, 'The animated pain of the body', *American Historical Review* 105.1 (2000), 36–68.

73 See Graef, *Mary*, 67, for an explanation of Ambrose's view.

74 See Spreadbury, 'Gender'.

75 Hoccleve's loose translation of Guillaume de Deguilleville's 'Le pèlerinage de l'âme' was completed before 1413 and is extant in ten manuscripts.

76 Thomas Hoccleve, *Hoccleve's Works: The Minor Poems*, ed. F. J. Furnivall and I. Gollancz, EETS e. s. 61 (London: Kegan Paul, Trench, and Trübner, 1892), 1–8.

77 See Bestul, *Texts*, 69–110.

78 For antithesis in this poem, see George Keiser, 'The Middle English *planctus Mariae* and the rhetoric of pathos', *The Popular Literature of Medieval England*, ed. Thomas J. Heffernan (Knoxville: University of Tennessee Press, 1985), 167–93, and Jennifer E. Bryan, 'Hoccleve, the Virgin, and the politics of complaint', *PMLA* 117.5 (2002), 1172–87.

79 Katharine Goodland, '"Veniance, Lord, apon thaym fall": Maternal mourning, divine justice, and tragedy in the Corpus Christi Plays', *Medieval & Renaissance Drama in England* 18 (2005), 166–92, at 188.

80 I apply Barbara Rosenwein's term loosely here, as it is unclear from the texts whether the mourners engaged with or socialized each other. See her *Emotional Communities in the Early Middle Ages* (Ithaca, NY: Cornell University Press, 2006).

81 On tears as a physical manifestation of grief see Catherine Sanders, *Grief: The Mourning After: Dealing with Adult Bereavement*, 2nd ed. (New York: Wiley, 1998).

82 Line 11 in the lament that appears in Ashmole 61, discussed further below.

83 The statistics for Black women, poor women, and women in developing countries and rural areas are far more troubling. In my home state of Arkansas, Black women are three times more likely than white women to die in childbirth; in the state's poorer counties this disparity doubles.

84 Monica Green's body of work, aimed at both academic humanists and medical professionals, has been foundational in that conversation.
85 E.g., Katherine French, 'The material culture of childbirth in late medieval London and its suburbs', *Journal of Women's History* 28.2 (2016), 126–48. Theresa Earenfight has written extensively on childless queens and is preparing a relevant database.
86 Nicholas Orme, *Medieval Children* (New Haven: Yale University Press, 2001), 93–128.
87 See Peter Jones and Lea Olsan, 'Performative rituals for conception and childbirth in England, 900–1500', *Bulletin of the History of Medicine* 89.3 (2015), 406–33. For an overview of humanities scholarship on medieval birth, including rituals, see Rebecca Wynne Johnson, 'Divisions of labor: Gender, power, and later medieval childbirth, c. 1200–1500', *History Compass* 14.9 (2016), 383–96.
88 Barbara Duden cites archival evidence of public announcements of this recognition dating from as late as the eighteenth century in *Disembodying Women: Perspectives on Pregnancy and the Unborn* (Cambridge, MA: Harvard University Press, 1993).
89 See Cadden, *Meanings*, 149.
90 See James A. Brundage, *Law, Sex, and Christian Society in Medieval Europe* (Chicago, University of Chicago Press, 1987), 156.
91 Albertus Magnus was a notable exception, arguing that pregnant women's physical needs justified sex, although he, too, approved only a limited range of positions. See Brundage, *Law*, 451–3.
92 Sermon CCXXVI is in Bibliotheque Nationale de France, MS lat. 17509, fol. 136 v b: 'Audivi de quodam ebrioso, cum rediret de taberna et uxorem cognosceret pregnantem, ex fetido et vinoso hanelitu puerum in ventre matris necavit ita quod mulier abortivum edidit'. It appears in *The exempla or Illustrative Stories from the Sermones Vulgares of Jacques de Vitry*, ed. Thomas Crane (London: Folklore Society, 1890), 94.
93 'Galen says that women who have narrow vaginas and constricted wombs ought not have sexual relations with men lest they conceive and die. But all such women are not able to abstain, and so they need our assistance', *The Trotula: An English Translation of the Medical Compendium of Women's Medicine*, ed. Monica H. Green (Philadelphia: University of Pennsylvania Press, 2002), 78. The *Trotula* lists possible causes of stillbirth and failed delivery and offers treatment options, 79.
94 'when a women is in the beginning of her pregnancy, care ought to be taken that nothing is named in front of her which she is not able to have, because if she sets her mind on it and it is not given to her, this occasions miscarriage', *Trotula*, 77.

95 'a woman on account of coughing or diarrhea or dysentery or excessive motion or anger or bloodletting can loose the fetus', *Trotula*, 79.
96 'There are some women for whom things go wrong in giving birth, and this is because of the failure of those assisting them: that is to say, this is kept hidden by the women', *Trotula*, 93.
97 *Trotula*, 77, 111, 92, 103.
98 For discussion of legal penalties for ending a pregnancy, see Wolfgang Müller, *The Criminalization of Abortion in the West: Its Origins in Medieval Law* (Ithaca, NY: Cornell University Press, 2012), and Fiona Harris-Stoertz, 'Pregnancy and childbirth in twelfth- and thirteenth-century French and English Law', *Journal of the History of Sexuality* 21.2 (2012), 263–81, at 269–71.
99 Emphasis mine. 'Audivi de quibusdam qui uxores pregnantes propinquas pertinacia vexant, cum per modicum tempus abstinere non velint, nec parcere gravidis quod puer in utero materno occiditur et baptismo privatur. Maledicta sit ista libido, que animam filii sui aufert deo'. BN lat. 17509, fol. 136 vb; Latin transcription from DL d'Avray and M Tausche, 'Marriage sermons in *ad status* collections of the Central Middle Ages', *Archives d'histoire doctrinale et litteraire du Moyen Age* 47 (1980), 99. Augustine uses similar language: 'Sometimes, indeed, this lustful cruelty, or if you please, cruel lust, resorts to such extravagant methods as to use poisonous drugs to secure barrenness; or else, if unsuccessful in this, to destroy the conceived seed by some means previous to birth, preferring that its offspring should rather perish than receive vitality; or if it was advancing to life within the womb, should be slain before it was born'. *De Nube et Concupiscentia* 1.17 (15).
100 *Trotula*, 79.
101 Duden offers a brief overview of the distinction between theologians' focus on ensoulment and legal and medical professionals' interest in viability, 56–61.
102 Rosemary Woolf, *English Religious Lyric in the Middle Ages* (Oxford: Clarendon Press, 1968), 149.
103 Amy Vines, 'Lullaby as lament: Learning to mourn in Middle English nativity lyrics', *Laments for the Lost: Medieval Mourning and Elegy*, ed. Jane Tolmie and M. Jane Toswell (Turnhout, Belgium: Brepols, 2010), 201–23, at 202.
104 The poem appears as poem 152Aa in R. L. Greene, ed., *The Early English Carols*, 2nd ed. (Oxford: Clarendon Press, 1977), 100.
105 As in the lament, she rebukes Gabriel here, too, for not warning her ('Whan Gabryell called me full of grace,/He told me nothyng of this').

106 Jennifer C. Ward, 'Joan de Bohun, Countess of Hereford, Essex and Northampton, c. 1370–1419: Family, land and social networks', *Essex Archaeology and History* 32 (2001), 146–53.
107 W. Dugdale, J. Caley, H. Ellis, and B. Bandinel, eds, *Monasticon Anglicanum* (6 vols, London, 1817–30), iv, 134, 140.
108 CUL MS Ff. 5. 48. Printed in Carleton Brown, ed., *Religious Lyrics of the Fifteenth Century* (Oxford, Clarendon Press, 1939), 13.
109 BL Royal 12 E 1, fols 193a–94b, lines 37–9; Saupe, poem 87.
110 British Library MS Harley 2253, fol. 79a.
111 Bodleian Library MS Ashmole 61, fol. 106r, lines 9–16.
112 See Judy Slome Cohain, Rina E. Buxbaum, and David Mankuta, 'Spontaneous first trimester miscarriage rates per woman among parous women with 1 or more pregnancies of 24 weeks or more', *BMC Pregnancy and Childbirth* 17 (2017), 437.
113 Kempe, *Book*, 33.
114 *Ibid.*, 78.
115 *Ibid.*, 80.
116 *Ibid.*, 179.
117 *Ibid.*, 180.
118 *Ibid.*, emphasis mine.
119 See Bestul, *Texts*, 69–110.
120 Rubin also notes this parallel. See also Keiser, 'Middle', 177ff.
121 Miri Rubin, *Mother of God*, especially chapter 15. See also Bestul, *Texts*.
122 Kempe, *Book*, 182.
123 *Ibid.*, 184.
124 *Ibid.*, 186.
125 Mia Korpiola and Anu Lahtinen, 'Cultures of death and dying in medieval and early modern Europe: An introduction', *Collegium: Studies across Disciplines in the Humanities and Social Sciences* 19 (2015), 4.
126 *Letters of Old Age (Rerum Senilium Libri)* I-XVIII. Vol. 1, trans. by Aldo S. Bernardo, Saul Levin, and Reta A. Bernardo (Baltimore: Johns Hopkins University Press, 1992), 552, emphasis mine.
127 Katharine Goodland, '"Vs for to wepe no man may lett": Accommodating female grief in the medieval English Lazarus Plays', *Early Theatre* 8.1 (2005), 69–94, at 72.
128 Goodland, 'Veniance', 177.
129 Elaine Scarry, *The Body in Pain: The Making and Unmaking of the World* (Oxford: Oxford University Press, 1987), 4.

Part II

The genre: defining Marian absence in legendaries of women

We now turn to English legendaries of women—here, collections of female saints' lives commissioned for the use of women readers, a genre in which we might expect extended focus on the Virgin. Although her influence is implicit in the saints' maternal behaviors and persuasive powers, Mary herself only rarely appears in the narratives as a central or supporting figure. Instead, her influence is through proxy and external prompts. Via their saintly protagonists, the texts discussed here invoke Mary's body's availability to the whole Church and her role as a community member. I focus on three books: Bodleian Library MS Douce 114; the convent collection in Cambridge Addit. MS 2604; and Osbern Bokenham's legendary in Arundel 327 to discuss the maternal concerns that emerge from women's engagement with these texts' concepts of Marian maternity, including *Maria medica* and the communal use of bodily pain, maternal peers, and shared maternal labor, and connections among natal and metaphorical families. In deference to those subtexts, this section is particularly interested in reading and mothering as collective and communal acts. It looks to the friendship and community imagined for Mary by devotional texts, visual art, and performances outside the legendaries, as well as to the uses to which Mary's body and those of her proxies were put.

3

The community service of mystics' maternal bodies

The figures of *Maria medica* and *mater misericordia* derive from Mary's role at and after the Crucifixion. The concept of *compassio* allowed for Mary's comforting of Christ to include her bodily sharing of his pain.[1] Mary was considered the authority on *compassio*, having born witness to and duplicated Christ's agony as he suffered it. The Pietà is the best-known depiction of Mary's body suffering in tandem with Christ's, but her *compassio*, with its centering of physical pain, could take many forms, including the healing of others.[2] Mary's penchant for physical healing is well established: at Rocamadour in twelfth-century southwestern France, at Walsingham and elsewhere on the 'milk trail' in late-medieval England, at various shines, Notre Dames, and indeed all churches, as Marian feasts were observed or prayers said.[3] Dee Dyas has established that requesting healing, offering thanks for such healing, and sending surrogates to pray for healing were among the main reasons penitents went on pilgrimage; Mary was often the target of such devotions.[4] As Carole Rawcliffe puts it, Mary was 'a ubiquitous presence in the wall paintings, statuary and altarpieces of hospital chapels and infirmaries throughout Christendom'.[5] The numbers of pilgrims seeking healing miracles at Mary's shrines illustrate her importance to sufferers of injuries, chronic illnesses, and infectious disease such as leprosy and the plague.[6]

The medieval pious, too, could feel Christ's pain through directed meditation; such suffering was highly desirable and coded as maternal. Angela Foligno, a Dominican tertiary, asked Mary rather than Christ to give her access to the pain that Christ had felt and Mary had witnessed: 'Oh Holy Mary, tell me about that pain of your son, since you saw the passion more than any other saint ... so that I can see what you saw both with my physical eyes and with my imagination.'[7] Henry Suso depicts a more personal connection between maternity and *compassio* in an anecdote about his own mother's Lenten meditation on a carving of the descent from the Cross: 'In front of this piece of art she somehow felt the intense pain that the gentle *Mother* had felt beneath the cross' and 'suffered so much pain out of sympathy that her heart palpably burst'. Suso's mother fainted, was carried home, and died on Good Friday as the passion text was read aloud; she simultaneously appeared in a vision to her son. There, she announces her own death to Suso even as she 'gave [him] a motherly kiss on the mouth'.[8] Christ's pain is borne by the mother Mary, then perceived and transmitted by Suso's mother. No one else comforts Suso; his dead mother's kiss is the only balm to his grief. Maternity is the intermediary to pain.

Mary's healing powers often depend on the use of her body, which becomes a means of sharing and curing the pain of suffering sinners. We saw in Chapter 2 the miracle tale of Fulbert, whom Mary heals from quinsy with her milk. As 'leche', her maternal emission functions as medicine, her touch as healing.[9] The Vernon manuscript offers another miracle tale set at the Abbey of Notre Dame at Vivier, a Cistercian abbey just outside Namur in modern Belgium.[10] A man with extreme pain in his lower leg waits in line for days among others seeking a miracle at the site of an image of the Virgin. After a few days of unanswered prayers, he decides 'beter legles/Then so to suffer' (691–2). Despairing, he amputates the leg below the knee and applies salves to help it heal. In a dramatic plea, he speculates to the Virgin that he must be 'cleynt' by his own sin, as all the afflicted around him have their prayers answered 'save I, sunful caytyf, outcast'. He weeps, swoons, and falls into deep slumber in which he has a vision of a 'fer ladi' who touches his knee and, with her hands, coaxes a new leg out from the stump. When he awakens, his leg is fully restored. The text is not shy about crediting her with healing powers:

> Heo is solase in eueri serwe and Medicyn in Mischeef.
> In eueri serwe or seknesse ouþer *Heo* is sovereynest leche.[11]
> ...
> In alle Mischeues heo is Medecyn aȝeyn seknesse obstacle.[12]

But Mary does not quite nurse the man to health: it is her touch—her body—that restores his leg. The text articulates the connection between Mary's healing of 'sorrows' as well as 'sickness', and is literal in its phrasing about her being the 'leche' or medicine that does the actual healing.

Mary's body as spiritual aid

Sara Ritchey eloquently explains the flexible medieval term *salus* that could indicate both 'health' and 'salvation': a 'full semantic range that included body and soul, the individual and community, the temporal fluidity of cosmic past, present, and future, and the whole spread of healing technologies used in the treatment of these varied aspects of self'.[13] Esther Cohen has demonstrated that medieval preachers made little distinction between physical and spiritual pain.[14] The connections and conflations among Mary, healing, and spiritual and physical nurturing that would have seemed obvious to the first readers of the Douce 114 texts are spelled out in a fourteenth-century devotional book. Henry of Lancaster, a second-generation hospital patron, wrote *The Book of Holy Medicines*, a set of personal devotions that praises Mary's milk and tears as soothing to his spiritual wounds.[15] Henry took seriously the connection between spiritual and physical health; he revised his own hospital's regulations to require would-be patients and beneficiaries to confess to the priest-warden.[16] In his text, Mary's healing 'bandages' work spiritually as well as physically. Henry describes bodily wounds as metaphors for his sins, explaining that he can heal through strength gained from the Virgin's milk and cleansing and cooling from her tears. He builds the case that Mary might have stronger healing abilities than Christ, for women are better nurses: 'they handle a patient more sweetly and more graciously and do all things more pleasantly than a man would do'. His devotions key the healing of particular sins or wounds to Mary's corresponding bodily joys. He speaks casually of exploiting her body: 'And, most sweet Lady, as it seems to me, I may say that to drink your sweet milk would be good for my wounds, just as those who are wounded drink a little salve'.[17] Her corpus is medicinal, there to be applied or depleted as needed. Henry imagines each of the physical sites of Mary's joys as a vein he can tap for his spiritual healing: her ears that heard the annunciation can soothe his ear wound; the thought of her joy in breastfeeding Christ can heal his heart.

In a widely circulating portion of *Horologium Sapientae*, Suso adds antithesis to Henry's transactional formula. When addressing Mary, Suso asks her to extract from her memories of the pain of *compassio* the strength to make Suso's life easier: 'May your loving kissing of his wounds reconcile me to him. May your deathly wounds gain for me sincere sorrow. May your intense groans bring me constant zeal. And may your bitter tears turn my hard heart soft.'[18] For both men, Mary's body and painful experiences exist for the purpose of healing *them* rather than prompting empathy as we saw in Chapter 2.

Medieval Marian maternity thus developed a working equation of maternal pain, compassion, and the healing of others: ultimately, Mary's body remained available as a vessel for public benefit. In one late-medieval poem, she is 'oleum effusum, to languentes medsyne'.[19] This easy slippage among Mary's body, the cause and purposes of her pain, and the needs of others accords with Sarah McNamer's argument for the gendered nature of medieval compassion for female mystics and devotees.[20] The perception and depiction of pain, too, was gendered. Cohen argues that women had to lose dignity though 'pain scripts' to gain power, while male mystics generally did not record details of their pain.[21] Amy Hollywood notes that male authors focus on women's suffering when they write about them, although the women themselves do not. Clerics fetishized the women's bodies and sufferings partly in an attempt to benefit themselves spiritually, in what Hollywood calls 'ventriloquizing orthodoxy'.[22]

Mary's *compassio* and its derivative pain created a model of *Maria medica* that attributed healing power to the maternal body, and more widely, the enduring belief that women's bodies are available for public benefit. Mothers were already expected to sacrifice their own youth, bodily comfort, and status to tend the health of their own children. This expectation of service was not limited to physical maternity, although the hyper-focus on bodily suffering often meant other modes of healing and maternal care, such as intercession and community-building, got less attention. The belief that women should be unendingly sacrificial was deeply entrenched, as we still see in modern anti-abortion rhetoric. And so even a woman's body that was not procreating, whether because it was past childbearing years or opting out of them, might also still be exploited to minister to and heal others. Bodies unavailable to birth children could thus be expected to continue physical work to nurse others.

Douce 114 and its beguine-influenced culture of origin

The fifteenth-century English devotional book Oxford, Douce MS 114 champions the Marian model of women's bodies as healing and spiritual aid. Taken as a whole, the manuscript's focus concerns the spiritual elements of both suffering and healing. In addition to the beguine-affiliated *vitae* of Elizabeth of Spalbeek, Christina *mirabilis*, and Marie d'Oignies, the manuscript includes a copy of Stephen Maconi's letter supporting the canonization of Catherine of Siena.[23] The second half of the manuscript is a translation of part of Henry Suso's *Orologium Sapientiae*, known as *The Seven Poyntes of Trewe Wisdom*, a treatise on preparing spiritually for death.[24] Brian Vander Veen notes that several manuscripts of *Seven Poyntes* credit its translation into English to the Carthusian monastery of Mount Grace, which also preserved Margery's *Boke*.[25] Douce 114 has received a healthy share of scholarly attention because of its texts' connection to the thirteenth-century beguine movement, but the book's inclusion of Maconi's letter and *Seven Poyntes* suggests a more diffuse focus than its scholarship has reflected.

The manuscript's depictions of holy behaviors are rooted deeply in its source texts' caregiving cultures of origin, whose values emerge in the texts even when an actual hospital does not. The geographical center of the beguine movement was the diocese of Liège; by the end of the thirteenth century the city had twenty-four beguinages.[26] The influence of the beguines in and around Liège lingers; its archives boast ample textual evidence in wills, legal statutes, and legendaries.[27] The *vitae* of Christina *mirabilis*, Elizabeth of Spalbeek, and Marie d'Oignies appear in manuscripts throughout Liège and across modern Belgium.[28] Liège is still a city of churches, and its central plaza and street names reflect the influence of medieval religious figures: Place St-Lambert, Rue

Lambert-le-Bègue, Impasse des Ursulines, and, still, the abbeys of multiple orders. Not coincidentally, Liège is also a city of modern hospitals, visually as well as practically; the Citadel, site of a large hospital, sits dramatically atop a cliff overlooking the city center. Nursing was perhaps the most encompassing of medieval beguines' charitable activities, with some beguines highly trained in medical care, as Ritchey has shown.[29] Most beguinages were associated with a hospital or lepers' house.[30] They were often affiliated with Mary, as evident in their frequent choice of Mary as patron and as subject of visual art, notable even within a deeply Marian culture.[31] Beguine *vitae* were initially meant to assert the church's authority and control over the hospitals where they worked.[32] Marie d'Oignies is still known for her work in a lepers' community; her contemporary Juetta of Huy abandoned her children to minister to lepers and was ultimately enclosed as anchoress to their hospital chapel.[33] Juliana of Mont-Cornillon, just east of Liège, was briefly head of the religious community that ran a lepers' hospital.[34] Beguines' presence was especially desired at funerals and at births, the most vulnerable and intimate moments of their neighbors' lives. All of the cities in the southern Low Countries had a hospital by 1200, with Liège an especially important care center.[35]

The texts of Douce 114 do not discuss the hospital cultures that produced them, but the collection's attentions to pain and to the demands of ministering to one's community align with the physical and psychological challenges of caring for the unwell. The subjects of its *vitae* and spiritual narratives were intimately involved with pain and illness as both sufferers and nurturers. I am not the only reader to notice a health-based theme in these texts: Amy Appleford and Corinne Saunders see Elizabeth's *vita*, along with Margery Kempe's *Boke*, as disseminating medical and theological information in what they call a 'deinstitutionalization of knowledge' about the body.[36] Speaking more generally about other beguine-related texts, Ritchey has argued that the spiritual framing of medieval medical work camouflages what she terms the 'therapeutic treatments' female mystics were doing. However, such framing provided orthodox cover. Marian precedent allows the women's pain and healing work to be presented as maternal care and gendered as appropriate for women. As we've seen, Marian miracle stories position Mary's body as communal property while suggesting her power to heal is solitary. This portrayal misrepresents how both healing and maternal caregiving take place within community contexts. As we'll see, the mystics of Douce 114 rely on supporters and networks to help them do this care work, making visible the arguments by Sarah Knott and Evelyn Nakano Glenn that mothering is shared labor.[37]

Partly because the original contexts are missing and partly because of Marian texts' depiction of healing as an individualistic act, Douce 114 presents an incomplete picture of the mystics' functions in their communities. The clerical hagiographers of the source texts not only take for granted that the women's bodies, like Mary's, are available for public benefit but also minimize how mystical 'mothering' requires the company and support of others for the mitigation of pain. Healing and caregiving are complex, holistic acts. A matricentric reading of the Douce 114 texts illuminates how the mystics' holiness derives from both their embeddedness in the community and from the physical availability of their bodies to bear and sometimes treat others' suffering, elements that would have been clearer in their healing-rooted cultures of origin. As such, they offer another version of the inhabitation and incorporation discussed in Chapter 1. Drawing from pain theory and from what we know of medieval hospital cultures, we can see how readers of these texts would interpret such self-sacrificial behavior as maternal and Marian.

Jacques de Vitry and Marie's finger

Jacques de Vitry's Latin *vita* of Marie d'Oignies is often considered central as a source for this manuscript and, more broadly, to convincing the future Pope Gregory IX to approve the beguine movement. The conditions of that papal persuasion matter. Jacques' beliefs about the purpose and use of Marie's story are inseparable from his own use of her body as healing relic. In the *Supplement* to Marie's life by Thomas of Cantimpré, Marie, horrified at 'hearing the grating of the pliers' as the prior, Gilles d'Oignies, removes the teeth from a holy man's corpse, expresses dismay that he might colonize her own body for relics after her death and promises to clench her postmortem jaw against it. When this prediction comes true—despite multiple tools and brute strength, the prior cannot even part her lips—Gilles is chastened and prays Marie's forgiveness. In answer, her corpse generously spits seven teeth into his hand.[38]

Despite Marie's aversion to having her body repurposed for relics, Jacques wore her finger in a silver locket for years after her death, believing it kept him safe on multiple occasions. It is that disregard for Marie's bodily autonomy that earned papal approval for the beguines. According to Thomas of Cantimpré, Ugolini, the future Pope Gregory IX, confided to Jacques that he was suffering from spiritual doubts: 'When my spirit has been worn out by countless thoughts, it drives my nearly exhausted body to destruction.'[39] Jacques replied that Marie had been famous for expelling blasphemous spirits and recommended that Ugolini read her *vita*. At Ugolini's request to borrow a relic of Marie's, Jacques 'smiled happily' and offered the finger he'd been wearing for years to help assuage Jacques' despair, the 'spirit of blasphemy', as Jan Vandeburie explains.[40] It is not only the *vita* itself but the inclusion of Marie's healing body part as relic that, through curing Ugolini of his spiritual depression, persuades him of Marie's power and by extension the beguines' usefulness. Thomas tells us that when Ugolini next felt 'the lethargy of his familiar temptation' he 'grasped (Marie's) finger … clasping it tightly to his breast' to find relief.[41] Michel Lauwers has described how common the dismemberment of holy corpses for distribution into reliquaries and jewelry was in this period.[42] Still, the direct connection of Marie's disembodied finger to stability and support for the beguines is disconcerting. Marie's relic becomes a shared talisman for clerical benefit. Jacques wore it around his neck; Ugolini clutched it in prayer: both men consistently touched and exploited her postmortem body, so it should not surprise us that her living body, too, is treated as community property in her *vita*.

The Marian, maternal pain of Douce 114

The other bodies of Douce 114 appear as similarly exploitable, especially when stripped of the biographical context such as the *Supplement* that appears with the Latin versions of the texts. Because they are so closely documented, the women's private practices of pain are made public. Even the parts of their devotion that were not initially intended to benefit the community become matters of public consumption. Granted, the hagiographers' frequent misreading of their subjects might be explained by the distracting spectacle of their bodily pain. Marie d'Oignies cuts out and buries a piece of her own flesh; Christina *mirabilis* cooks herself in hot ovens; Elizabeth of Spalbeek contorts her limbs and bears the stigmata; Catherine of Siena slices up her feet; Henry Suso bloodily carves Christ's initials into his own chest.[43] These semi-public displays are central to the subjects of Douce 114. The pain is legible, in a world that knows how to read it.[44] Voluntary pain had been steadily accruing theological meaning in pious practices, especially for women.[45] Cohen explains that between the thirteenth and fifteenth centuries, pain came to be seen as so useful a spiritual benefit that the involuntary pain of illness was grouped theologically with the voluntary pain of the saints.[46]

More troublingly, observers who attempt to document another's pain, such as the hagiographers who write the *vitae* of Douce 114, alter the subject's experience of self. As Ariel Glucklich puts it, '*Modulated* pain weakens the individual's feeling of being a discrete agent; it makes the "body-self" transparent and facilitates the emergence of a new identity. Metaphorically, pain creates an embedded 'absence' and makes way for a new and greater "presence".'[47] In other words, a patient or sufferer who is being monitored, described, or coached feels less like herself and more like a conduit. A bit of humanity is lost. Bernardino of Siena argued that something similar happened to Mary, whose grief at the Cross was so intense that '*nothing of herself* remained in her'.[48]

In their attempt to document their subjects' pain, the *vitae* explain the *use* of the women's bodies to the community, implying that the mystic's body must be a productive, constantly helpful site in order to justify the space and resources it requires. This approach has the benefit for its writers of affirming the need for clerical interpretations of orthodoxy and intervention: someone must explain how physicality is holy. Mary's body is used for multiple clerically approved purposes: her womb births the Church, her breasts offer grace and forgiveness, her tears remind penitents of Christ's sacrifice. And her touch, as we see in miracle stories, offers healing. Popular depictions of Mary's aid to Christians suggest it occurs in isolation. The lyrics, miracle stories, and poems depend on her singular power, a singularity often articulated in her isolated experience of pain or in the penitent's use of her body. No one, as the *planctus* reminds us, can feel the maternal pain that the Virgin has. But as we saw in Chapter 2, the Virgin's ability to help people also has the effect of creating communities that then have their own, less-regulated power. She brings together clerics with laypersons. She can restore the healed to the wider population, ending their isolation.

The narrators of the *vitae* that appear in Douce 114 are so focused on the mystics' pain and their bodies as visible and accessible objects that they miss the critical importance of companions and caretakers—that is, the healing community around hurting people. They, and we, easily miss the embeddedness of the subjects, their roles as potential connectors within communities. These are stories about networks and connectedness, not isolation. As several scholars have shown, observers are crucial to the performance of asceticism and pain.[49] Mary Suydam argues that the public nature of beguine life meant that 'all aspects of their devotional practices had a marked communal component ... the ecstatic visionary is often surrounded by other people who benefit from, often participate in, and react to her experiences'.[50] Pain's advantage was often to someone other than the one suffering. Cohen notes that when describing the torments of purgatory, preachers invoked listeners' relatives and friends rather than listeners' own future there.[51] Through her pain, the beguine becomes a vector that connects potential caregivers with suffering. The clerics frame these women as maternal because of the perceived availability of their bodies. I suggest they are also acting maternal and Marian in the way they prompt and harness the goodwill of their peers. Their maternity lies not only in the absence of self or subjectivity forced by pain, but equally in their commitment to building communities beyond themselves.

Elizabeth

In Douce 114, we see this play out first in the Cistercian Philip of Clairvaux's thirteenth-century account of Elizabeth of Spalbeek. It reads almost as a medical case study, with a detailed daily account that includes the observable symptoms of the spiritual rapture she experiences each Friday. We learn of her stigmata, which include the marks of a crown of thorns; the 'ravishings' or passions she acts out at specific times during the day; and the physical miracles her body regularly undergoes. Philip focuses on Elizabeth's body and physical performance to the exclusion of their effects on her audience and community. The medical format of the text highlights the disconnect between the clerical audience whom Philip imagines as her community and the caretakers who actually are.

Elizabeth's passion enactment, described by several scholars as a 'dance', encompasses scenes in which she is untouchable and unmoveable, 'alle starke as an ymage of tree or stoon' and more active ones during which she contorts her arms and paces like Jesus before Pilate, then lies, ravished.[52] She slaps herself, dashes her head upon the ground, and beats herself on the chest; her eyes bleed. Under what is described as an involuntary trance, she acts out various roles of the passion narrative, including those of tormentors as well as Christ and his followers. Among her assorted characters is, briefly, that of the Virgin Mary:

> Ferþermore þe same frydaye sche figured vnto vs how oure blessyd lady, Crystes moder, stood be-syde þe crosse: puttynge hir left hande vndir hir lefte cheek & bowynge hire heed and hir nekke to þe same syde, and holdynge hir riȝthe hande vndir hir riȝhte pappe.[53]

Elizabeth's channeling of Mary remains a pantomime; she shifts quickly into the posture of John the Evangelist to flesh out the Crucifixion's composition. In addition to these dramatic performances, Elizabeth's body bears stigmata

> in her handys, feet and syde with-outen any dowte, similacyone or fraude fresshe woundys are ful euydently shewed, often and namely bledynge on fridayes. Þe woundys of handes and feet are rounde, þe wounde in the syde is auelonge, as hit were of a speer, and þat oþere foure woundes of nayles.[54]

Philip suggests that these afflictions have strengthened what was previously a weak body: at five years old, he says, Elizabeth was so feeble she could hardly move without assistance, but by age twenty, she has so mortified her own flesh that she is 'merueylously strong' rather than 'weyke & vnmyghty'[55]. It is, according to his analysis, her bodily sufferings that give her the power to function physically, her weakness that makes her strong. Philip is careful to delineate how Elizabeth's physical experiences communicate spiritual truth. When he describes her lack of bodily fluids and inability to ingest certain foods, he explains 'þat þe vtward clennes of þe same virgyn Elizabeth beeriþ witnesse and open euydens of hir inwarde clennes'.[56]

As plausible as these interpretations are, Philip's methods of obtaining these data limit his understanding. He writes as observer of rather than participant in her experiences, depending for corroboration on the testimony of 'booþ abbotes and monkes' who also observe her from relative distance. The text's accuracy depends on what they notice as her audience, as reflected in its phrasing: Philip often specifies whether an action '*is seen in* hir', for example, so we remember that she is being watched, or names 'y and my felawes' as witnesses to her behavior.[57] Throughout the first half of the *vita*, there is little mention of a community or public except implicitly through these witnesses. Elizabeth does not engage directly with the clerics who are so intrigued by her performances. She remains only an object of their curiosity.

Philip's star-struck interest in her performance and his status as interloper dull his sensitivity to how deeply Elizabeth is embedded in her community. Sometimes this is revealed through her engagement with visitors: she advises a lewd young friar whom she recognizes as truly good; she receives a visit from the King of France, who gives her money for a chapel.[58] More consistently, she benefits from the care of other women. When she meditates with a 'tabil' to the point of ecstasy, her companions are prepared to help.

> sche keueriþ and closeþ þe same tabil and takith hit to sombody bisyde hir, and strikeþ for the hire armes to her moder, and to her sostres ʒonger thane sche þat serue hir; and þey take and liftes hir vp fro þe erthe and berith and leyeþ hir in her bedde. And she schewith to hem cleernesse of cheere, charite of herte, gladnesse of mynde, and swetnesse of goostly woordes. *Netheles, she is but of fewe woordys, the whiche woordes are [not] ful spoken oute, but sche makith hem swete, with an esy and mylde gladsumnes and maidenly schamefastnes.*[59]

It seems clear both that her 'moder' and 'sostres' are accustomed to her trances and have a good rapport with Elizabeth, but Philip declares, apparently based on her reticence with *him*, that she is 'of fewe woordys'. In another scene during which she enthusiastically takes the Eucharist, 'hir sistres and hir moder lifte vp and vndirsette hir wiþ cloþes or wiþ two piloues'.[60] Elizabeth's companions keep showing up for her to make sure she is safe and comfortable, and yet Philip is convinced that it is only her physical suffering, performed for and observed by him and other clerics, that has strengthened her body.

Philip provides his interpretation of her behavior 'þat maye stir all cristen pepil to deuocyone'.[61] Elizabeth herself appears oblivious to the public function her performances may serve; she reserves her conversation for the 'mother and sisters' who tuck her in and prop her up. And so while Philip and other clerics are passive consumers of her performance—watching without intervening as she self-harms, looking for spiritual meaning as they observe her in pain—Elizabeth serves and is served by the women who anticipate and attend to her physical needs. In his neglect of this reality, Philip reveals the invisibility of care: these women are clearly crucial to Elizabeth's well-being, and he barely sees them. She is not merely a conduit of spiritual truth to her community but a beneficiary of their ministry to her. Philip sees only her pain.

Pain as social experience

We can better understand the connection between the mystics' pain and their human interactions—and by extension, the suffering and community experienced within caregiving contexts—through Sara Ahmed's question: 'How are lived experiences of pain shaped by contact with others?' Ahmed explains that 'stories of pain involve complex relations of power'.[62] When we are asked to feel empathy for those in pain, 'we feel sad *about* their suffering, an "aboutness" that ensures that they remain the *object of* "our feeling"'.[63] It seems clear that hagiographers were objectifying their subjects' pain in this way. Henry of Lancaster, Henry Suso, and Jacques de Vitry, as we have seen, go a step beyond simply objectifying Mary or Marie d'Oignies or Elizabeth of Spalbeek; they acknowledge their pain, document it, and then ask the sufferers to help *them*.

Medieval devotion had higher expectations of empathy in the practice of *compassio*. Mary's emotional connection to her son is so strong that she feels his pain in her body. Elizabeth V. Spelman discusses the empathy of 'co-suffering', which seems close to what those practicing affective piety tried to achieve, and what some of the subjects of Douce 114 evidently did achieve. Kalas has called such sharing of another's suffering 'pain surrogacy', which she defines as 'necessarily maternal activity legitimised through the female mystic's physiology and capacity to (re)experience, or to bear, productive and physical pain'.[64] Bridget of Sweden equated her own skill in *compassio* with Mary's healing: 'And therefore I can well say that my Mother and I have saved man as it were with one heart, I by suffering in my heart and flesh, she in the sorrow and love of her heart.'[65] Bridget's claim anticipates what Ahmed argues: 'an ethics of responding to pain involves being open to being affected by that which one *cannot* know or feel'.[66] This is, I suggest, where healing another's pain differs from *compassio* or affective piety, and why the social bridges we see hints of in Douce 114 are crucial. The first step toward this ethics is recognizing that pain is necessarily social. It gives us a visceral sense of the limits of our own experience. As Ahmed puts it, pain is 'bound up with how we inhabit the world, how we live in relationship to the surfaces, bodies and objects that make up our dwelling places'.[67] That is, pain is *contingent* because it attaches us to the world of other bodies. Further, as Ahmed notes, *contingere* is the etymological root of both 'contingency' and 'contact': 'Contingency is linked in this way to the sociality of being 'with' others, of getting close enough to touch.'[68] The Douce 114 texts include admiring descriptions of the subjects' ascetic pain but say less about how they relieve others in pain, including their healing by touch. A corollary of the social nature of pain is the requirement of human contact for healing. In Douce 114 and in the Marian tales of healing, that means the availability of a willing maternal body.

What Ahmed calls the 'sociality of pain' also explains another dynamic across multiple texts in Douce 114, that of suffering being *communicated*, either with or by a text's subject. In Marian miracle tales, Mary often swoops in to erase penitents' suffering. It is never clear when or where she will appear. Sinners need her at their deathbed, in church, on a roadside, in ovens. She is never too busy or too distant; her healing powers await only the end of a prayer. She is not, as Queen of Heaven, capable of co-suffering;

she (and the sufferer) must rely on her willingness to believe that someone else is feeling pain or suffering illness outside her experience. To heal or nurture another requires humility and 'being open' to what one cannot feel. It is here that the unequal relationships between maternal and filial, Mary and penitents, and mystic and community demand mutual valuing of social ties, that is, trust. The hagiographers of Douce 114 see the medical usefulness of maternal bodies, but in minimizing the importance of the sociality of pain, they misrepresent the shape of healing practice.

Christina and maternal pain

Because mystics' pain is so frequently seen as symbolic, the degree of pain in devotional texts is sometimes ambiguous. The descriptor of 'a woman in labor' used to describe so many subjects of the Douce 114 texts is to categorize its intensity. Of Christ's suffering at the Crucifixion, Jacobus de Voragine said, 'This pain is similar to torture, *childbirth pangs*, and the pain of parents weeping for [losing] an only child. These are the greatest pains that can be found.'[69] Experiencing the pain of giving birth, then, could be construed as a shortcut to the most intense *imitatio Christi* experience. And Mary, of course, experienced two of the three pains Jacobus lists. At the same time, the childbirth comparison permits categorizing the subjects' behaviors into a gendered slot, even as their biographers are writing *vitae* and letters of support that would seem to elevate them. It marks them as maternal: holy men's pain is not described this way. Comparisons to Mary tend to occur to the hagiographers at the very moments the women lose control of their own bodies. The Virgin Mary's swoon, unconstrained by the time and space of her child's birth, shows that intense emotional or spiritual grief could manifest as temporally mobile birth pains. Similarly, these women might at any time suffer the indignity and instability of the pain of childbirth. However voluntary their circumstances, the perceived spontaneity of their pain provides useful narrative tension, even in the case of Elizabeth, whose daily regimen assigns rotations of her pains.

The voluntary nature of their participation is highlighted by the life of Christina *mirabilis*, who both explicitly agrees to take pain on and takes the option to reject it midway through the text, when she moderates her behavior to a more conventional standard. Christina's body is up for anything: as a healing medium, it appears available to all. God has made hers, like Mary's, a public body. Much of the 'mirabilum' is that she moves so freely, unlimited by the usual constraints on deviant bodies. Unlike Elizabeth, who is always in the same small room, her pain on a strict schedule, her contortions more shocking within a nondescript cell, Christina moves vertically and laterally: to the tops of trees, to the wilderness, to a basement, through rivers, into graves, into baptismal fonts and ovens. Even death does not hold her. She moves to hell and to paradise. In contrast to Margery, Christina does not become the spaces she transgresses; she is moving *through*, not into. Her body neither absorbs nor inhabits. God has promised that pain will not mark her body, either, but it comes to her unpredictably, often from beyond her physical experience, beyond life, even: from purgatory.

The reader's shift from Elizabeth's narrative to Christina's in Douce 114 is abrupt. It implies pain is random. Elizabeth's performance of *imitatio Christi* is understandable: we know whom she is portraying as she progresses through the Passion chronology. Christina's is less legible. To share or perform the pain of Christ or of Mary, as many mystics did, was to sacralize one's own body. Christina instead takes on the consequences of sin. In doing so, she embodies the *compassio* that was commonly affiliated with devotion to Mary and to Christ. Confident in her own salvation, Christina joins Mary and Christ to share sinners' burdens. Her body is similarly universally available, ready to perform necessarily painful maternal functions.

Doctrinally, Christina's bodily experiences remind readers that purgatory is painful. Thirteenth-century preachers were, as Cohen explains, generally promoting the fear of pain that could be experienced in the afterlife. In his *Art of Preaching*, Thomas of Chobham included a whole chapter on how sermons could frighten people into compliance through *stories* of pain.[70] For Christina to be effective, her pain must be believed. Writing after her death, Christina's Dominican hagiographer Thomas of Cantimpré hedges against readers' incredulity with eyewitness corroborations, ultimately crediting the recluse Ivette as his main source. Everything can be verified. From the beginning, he sets Christina's story in the public sphere: 'Nor þese thinges were not done in corners & hyrnes, but openly amonge the pepil'.⁷¹ Her pain, in other words, must be communicated.

It becomes clear early on that Christina is moving not only in many spaces but among multiple publics. This begins with her funeral. After she 'wex seck in bodily myghte, and dyed', her body is laid out and wept over until 'sodeynly þe body steried and roos vp in þe bere, and anoon lifte vp as a bridde, stei3h in to þe beemes of þe kyrke'. Unsurprisingly, the sudden ascension of Christina's corpse scatters the mourners. Meanwhile, her soul travels to witness the tortures in purgatory. Then she is taken to paradise to consider two options posed by God: she may stay in heaven, or

> turne ageyne to þy body, þere to suffre peynes of an vndeedly soule by a deedly body wiþ-outen harme of hit-self, and to delyvere wiþ þy peynes alle þos soulles of þe whiche þou haddest pite in þe place of purgatorye, and also with ensaumple of þy peyne and lyfe stir men to repentauns & penauns and to forsake her synnes & be trewly turnyd to me.⁷²

The correct choice is obvious. Christina will undergo dead sinners' physical torment. Simultaneously, she must also inspire the living community to turn to God. They must believe—be open to—her pain. The *vita* plays up the tension of her responsibilities to these two communities. From this point, her body becomes a text to be read.

Because Christina's arrangement with God requires witnesses—and because a healing practice will require her openness to others' pain—her intolerance of living bodies is a problem. Almost immediately upon divulging her heavenly assignment, Christina displays her incompatibility with her friends: she 'fledde þe presens of folke wiþ a wonder loþinge into wildernesse & in to trees, into þe coppys of tourys or chirches or of oþere hye thinges'.⁷³ Though she is caught and bound with iron chains, she still escapes to solitude in the wilderness. She nourishes herself for nine weeks by miraculous lactation until she is recaptured and bound again.

Christina's community is determined to re-socialize her. When she flees again to dwell in treetops, her embarrassed sisters hire a bounty hunter to break her leg and bring her home. A doctor binds her with chains in a cellar to allow the bone to heal, but

Christ releases her. Christina walks freely, and her frustrated and bewildered relations tie her to a tree and 'fedde hir as a dogge with a litil breed & watir alone'.[74] Christina's breasts again miraculously nourish her, with flavored oil that serves as condiment for her bread and salve for her wounds. This time, she is observed. It is only when Christina's behavior becomes recognizably maternal that she is compared to 'þe imcomparabil & singler virgyne Cristes moder';[75] this is the only explicit mention of the Virgin Mary in the *vita*. This physical demonstration of maternity and implied alignment with Mary convince her friends to show compassion: they 'bigan to wepe & fro þen forþ þey sturglid nor enforced no-thinge ageyne goddes wille in Cristyns miracles, but lowsed hir of bondys & knelyd doun, preiynge forgifnes of the wronge þat þey hadde done to hir, & so let hir go'.[76] Now perceived as Marian, Christina's productive breasts thus allow her to accomplish the more difficult part of her task: to inspire the living to turn to God. The supernaturally maternal nature of her body saves her from public scorn and, ultimately, the living community from its own disbelief.

Still, her progress toward local acceptance, and thus full maternal healing practice, is slow. Her purgatorial torments are numerous, driving her to cry 'as a womman þat travells wiþ childe': she enters 'hoot-brennynge ouenes', holds her hands and feet in open flame, immerses herself in scalding water, submerges herself in the Meuse river for six winter days at a time, stretches herself on the rack, hangs on the gallows, enters graves, leads a pack of dogs to chase her through briars and thorns, and mutilates her flesh barehanded. The narrator emphasizes her pain throughout; for example, she is 'turmentyd wiþ brennynges & heet *as oon of vs*'.[77] It is easy to forget that her suffering is voluntary.

Thomas's dependence on eyewitnesses for his material may explain his close attention to the evolving dynamic between Christina and the living community. Christina's agreement with God requires that her body be a spectacle. People must see it. They must also learn to read it, as the *vita* makes clear. The sociality of *her* pain permits her healing practice. Upon her now-predictable escape from witnesses, her friends pray for God to 'tempir his myracles in Cristyn after þe comun state of men' so that she may live a more normal life. Accordingly, Christina immerses herself in a baptismal font and 'fro þen forþe þe manere of hir lyfe was more tempyrde to men, & hadde hir-selfe afterwarde more esely, & better myghte suffre þe taste of men & dwelle amonge hem'.[78] This self-baptism, much like her self-nourishing lactation, leads to Christina's proactive engagement with others: she coaxes alms from sinners so that she can suffer their punishment; she begins to preach and prophesy; she discerns the true characters of those wrongly dismissed as sinful. Christina's behavior remains unusual: she undergoes 'ravishings' during which her body whirls like a top; she occasionally cries 'as a womman trauelynge'.[79] But as she becomes more responsive to others, the living community begins to accept these actions as spiritually beneficial. For example:

> whanne any was deed in þe cite wham she knewe in spirite dampned for synne, she wepte and turmentid hir-self and croked hir armes & fyngers as if þey were wryþabil for softenesse & with-outen bones. ... for hem þat steygheþ vp and shulde be saued, she hoppyd and dauncyd, at hit was a wonder maruaile tosee hir in so grete myrþe. Wherfore þey þat knew the vertue of hir spirite, lightly myghte perceyue in hir ioye or sorow what shulde falle to hem þat dyed in þe cite.[80]

The community thus learns to interpret Christina's suffering based on their correct reading of her body. Christina commands respect for her political prophecies and her counsel. She privately admonishes sinful clergy. She develops close relationships with a nobleman who calls her 'mother' and with the recluse Ivette, with whom she lives for nine years and who later becomes Thomas's chief informer. Christina thus successfully carries out her responsibilities to both the living and the dead communities, her maternal body the medium that connects them.

Christina's final loss of bodily control occurs after her second 'death' when a nun, Beatrice, begs her to revive to answer a question.[81] The seemingly outrageous demand illustrates Beatrice's power over Christina's body. Christina returns to life, grumbling, and answers before dying for the third and final time. Her revival at Beatrice's request reveals that Christina has finally become wholly functional in her community: her public *wants* her presence, and she is obliged to provide it.[82] Her full availability to Beatrice marks her body as maternal. This second resurrection, like her first lactation, confirms her as analog to Mary, available for intercession to anyone who asks directly. Christina's answer to Beatrice may not read as 'maternal' to modern readers, but medieval readers would have recognized its Marian frame.

Marie and the sociality of pain

John Coakley observes that Marie's 'powers of intuition and revelation give her precisely an ability that priests themselves lacked, namely to use *direct interventions* to bring souls to penitence or protect them from harm', whether this was through spying via visionary powers, exorcising demons, or enacting vengeance on her critics.[83] In other words, Marie behaves like Mary, capriciously choosing whom to help. Marie's interactions with demons are largely on behalf of other people: she cures a young man who is possessed and cures a blasphemous nun through her fasting. She drives a 'multitude of fendes' from a nun's bed and prays devotedly for the same sister when she is shown the nun's diseased soul.[84] Her holy tears also generally take place in a public setting.

What sets Marie apart from Elizabeth and Christina are the consistently healthy relationships she maintains with multiple constituencies, not only the clerical community Jacques recognizes, throughout the *vita*. She has mastered mutual empathy: she interacts with a wide range of people who seek help from her, offering prayers for 'friends', delivery of a 'special friend' from their sins, and the admonishment 'I weep for you' to a knight who has sought her counsel. Marie's deeds are recognized by her immediate public as beneficial and useful to the community itself. Her work on behalf of the poor is admired by those who see it; her friends depend on her advice; and a steady stream of visitors throughout her life imply that Marie is one sought out for, not ostracized by, her unusual behavior. Marie's community depends on her much more than does Christina's or Elizabeth's, and the *vita* thus focuses more closely on Marie's effect on those around her. She resists judgment by others: 'she gat so grete prerogatif of fredome, þat no man durste saye: "why dost thou so?", and for hir lyfe passed mannes resone, wiþ a specyalle priuilegge she, lafte to go and to hir-selfe, demed alle, but of no man was demyd'.[85] Already respected among her peers, Marie enjoys further encouragement and protection from the clerics around her. The narrator speaks in the first-person plural to indicate a group of observers who share Jacques's clerical perspective. For example, he remarks that many of her confessions were so insignificant that '*wee* myghte absteyne fro laghter'.[86] She does not, as does Christina, seek to interpret her own behavior or bodily experience to others; that is left for Jacques to do.

The only hint of real conflict is her marriage, but even that is framed as doctrinally perfect. Marie's parents disdain her ascetic practices and arrange her marriage at age fourteen. As a result of her prayers, her husband John is 'enspyred' to keep the marriage chaste; the more they are separated from 'carnelle affeccyone' the closer they grow in spiritual wedlock 'in a blessed kynde of martirdome'.[87] Marie's marriage allows her to appear more conventional than the other subjects of Douce 114. Though he is mostly under the radar in this *vita* except as evidence of her chastity, Marie's husband allows her to enter more public spaces than she otherwise could and probably to interact more deeply with visitors: chaste marriage is a stronger shield than virginity for erasing her sexuality. Marie gets most of the spiritual benefit of the 'fruits' of the marriage, but it's John's cover that gives her spiritual privilege so that a Marian maternal mode is possible. Importantly, the marriage is what permits her to move into the lepers' community. A single woman would have to work under priests or be grouped with semi-deviant beguines. Marie has already left her husband for a female community at Oignies by the time Jacques comes along. Her marriage is effectively moot: like the impotent Joseph, John is out of the picture, useful mostly for having gotten her into the lepers' colony and as a means to Jacques' end.

Confident her pain will be witnessed and understood, Marie undergoes mortifications such as self-mutilation, fasting, and sleep deprivation. She cuts out portions of her own flesh, once as penance for requiring food and wine to recover from an illness, another time to demonstrate (by slicing skin from her feet) the sinfulness of the places she walks through. She is more famous for her holy tears, a phenomenon that by the time of Douce 114 was 'classified, according to cause, and ... sharply differentiated from "natural tears"'.[88]

> she fonde so mykel grace of compunxyone, so grete plente of terys, þristyd oute in þy passyone with þe pressure of thy crosse, þat hir teerys copiously doune rennynge on þe kirke-paumente shewed where she ȝeed.[89]

A priest who chastises Marie for weeping during Mass succumbs later that same day to his own mid-service fit of holy tears. Similarly, when a pilgrim's companion ridicules him for seeking out Marie, he too is overcome with weeping. Marie describes her tears as 'refresshynge' and as 'sustynauns', though she must change her soaked veil and linen clothes frequently. Her weeping prompts comparisons with Mary Magdalene, a figure popularly associated with holy tears in the Middle Ages, as well as with the Virgin.[90] By the fifteenth century, such tears also evoke Bridget of Sweden, whose weeping saves her son Karl from damnation. Margery's *Boke* explicitly mentions Marie d'Oignies in the context of a priest's rejection of Margery until he notes her similarity to Marie.[91]

Marie's prayers and actions on behalf of those in the wider, non-clerical community offer physical and spiritual healing. Like Mary, Marie can heal others with her touch, and she sometimes hosts others' sickness in her own body, suffering empathetically with or for them. We have already seen how her hagiographer Jacques de Vitry felt entitled to her postmortem body's power; an irony of his text is that Marie's healing practice depends more on mutual relationships than on the availability of her body to others. While she experiences a healthy number of bodily miracles, she tends to help people more frequently through powerful intercessory prayer. Marie does not take on purgatorial suffering, as does Christina, but she does pray and encourage others to pray for those in purgatory, drawing the community into the kind of spiritual work she is known for. Physical healing always occurs in tandem with spiritual health; by building networks of praying people to ease others' pain, Marie strengthens both.

Catherine

Although she was not canonized until 1461, the story of Catherine of Siena was well known to fifteenth-century English readers, thanks in part to her connection to Syon.[92] Her *vita* by Raymond of Capua, translated into Middle English in 1493, emphasizes the bodily manifestations of her holiness: receiving the stigmata, a literal exchange of hearts with Christ, and spiritual marriage to Christ, with his foreskin used as a wedding ring.[93] These are not the focus of the letter from Brother Stephen Maconi to Frere Thomas Anthony, both of Siena, which functions more as documentation of the author's interactions with and impressions of Catherine than as a narrative of all her deeds. In Douce 114, the letter works to shore up some of the understated themes of Elizabeth's, Christina's, and Marie's lives: political engagement, physical suffering, and maternal caregiving. The letter describes less how engaged Catherine is with her community peers than how closely she interacts with clerics and public figures. A prolific letter-writer, she was heavily involved in regional and papal politics. Brown has argued that Maconi downplays Catherine's political involvement in his letter, which is true in the context of her active public life.[94] But among her textual neighbors in Douce 114, Catherine is by far the most politically engaged: she is advising the Pope, not merely the aristocrats or clerics who are name-dropped into Christina's and Marie's lives. She is, like Mary, the 'moste brighte myrrour of Goddes god men'.

What's left out of the letter is the context that makes clearer how it fits among the other care-based cultures of the source texts of Douce 114. Catherine was born in 1347, just before the plague began decimating the population. Half of her twenty-two siblings died, including her own twin. Catherine fasted to avoid having to marry the widower of her older sister, who died in childbirth. Surrounded by illness and death, and herself sick enough to negotiate permission from her parents, she became a Dominican tertiary. This let her remain at home, with a father whose time in purgatory she hoped to shorten by suffering pain herself and a mother whom Catherine's prayers later resurrected from death. In her capacity as tertiary, Catherine also worked in a hospital.

Maconi's letter assumes his readers' familiarity with that caregiving background. When the narrator Maconi becomes ill, Catherine is stirred with 'modirly charite', and shows up with a whole team of nurses to help.[95] She heals him, stating that his work is too important for him to remain sick. Maconi also mentions other examples of her healing, a step beyond the more general nursing ministry that Marie does. In the context of Catherine's intimate knowledge of illness and grief, this power to heal is not only impressive, but poignant: the letter's depiction shows her at the height of her spiritual power, now able to heal those she cares about, in contrast to her helpless witnessing of suffering in her early life. As Maconi tells it, her later life remains marked by physical suffering. At one point, Maconi notices she is in sockfeet; it turns out she has pricked her feet so much that they are almost entirely covered with open bloody wounds.[96] Late in her life, Catherine returns to the self-starvation that prevented her arranged marriage. She ingests only the Eucharist every day, presumably purifying her body to be filled only with Christ's flesh and blood. Maconi's text implies that this malnutrition leads ultimately to her death. But it also allows her belly, like Mary's, to host only Christ in the last few weeks of her life.

Catherine's *vita* and correspondence beyond Maconi's letter show her ready engagement with real-life mothers who fall short of her own spiritual standards. The *vita*'s account of the resurrection of her mother, Lapa, emphasizes Lapa's spiritual shortcomings: Catherine's prayers restore her life but imply that Lapa doesn't really deserve it. Catherine's extant letters to Maconi's mother are clearly responses to Monna Giovanna di Corrado Maconi's complaints of not seeing her son enough.[97] In what might have been intended as an awkward joke, Catherine volunteers the sacrifice of her body to 'birth' him and the whole family in 'tears and sweat'. At first glance, such a remark acknowledges the physical sacrifice of his natal mother. But to say, even in jest, that the birth experience is Catherine's for the taking effectively erases his natal mother's claim to him, particularly after Catherine has spent most of the letter chiding Signora Maconi for her 'selfish' maternal love, implying that her devotion to Christ is in question until she is cured of it.[98] Neither the letters nor the *vita* is included in Douce 114, but Maconi would have, by time of writing, been well aware of them. His letter would have been intended to supplement them in the case for Catherine's sanctity—and her maternity.

Brown points out that Catherine is standing in for Mary as well as Maconi's natal family. It's the obvious conflation of these two mother figures that is meant to demonstrate Catherine's holiness in Maconi's own letter of support. Catherine judges herself so suitable a maternal figure that she can admonish Maconi's mother and her own. Her relationship with Maconi makes explicit the vaguely maternal role so many of these hagiographers outline for their subjects: her maternal legitimacy is the ultimate proof of her authority. The 'real' Mary's appearance is postponed until the end of the letter, when the Virgin appears to validate the Marian devotee Raymond of Capua as Catherine's confessor, and in doing so, affirms Catherine as worthy of a Marian visitation.[99] Mary's appearance elevates Raymond's status, but also Catherine's: Mary is her peer, the company she keeps. Otherwise, Catherine herself fulfills the roles of Mary, healing the sick, negotiating politics, invoking the sacred through the theater of her own body.

Women's bodies in English hospitals

I want to pause here to acknowledge the appeal that these four maternal subjects would have had to the late-medieval English readers of Douce 114. Continental holy women were often affiliated with caregiving centers: Elizabeth of Hungary famously chose her hospital over more socially acceptable options, and Bridget of Sweden sponsored hospitals and nursed lepers herself. Had Margery Kempe less of a taste for travel, she might have ended up in a healing or hospital ministry. She frequently describes herself offering comfort to the sick or ailing. Her peers held her responsible for her husband's health: 'þe pepil seyd, ȝyf he deyd, hys wyfe was worthy to ben hangyn for hys deth, for-as-meche as sche myth a kept hym & dede not'. Diane Watt has deduced from this criticism that 'nursing was a key element of medieval housewifery, and that fulfilling this role was expected of women'.[100] Bynum notes that even as men took control of professional medicine, women 'retained the right and the obligation to nurse the aged, the young and the ill'.[101] Monica Green maintains that while men were often professionally involved in women's health, limiting our scholarly attention to 'explicitly labelled practitioners' ignores the medical care women routinely provided.[102]

As Erler has shown, it was not uncommon for pious English laywomen to spend their last years in residence and service at hospitals. Erler suggests that 'the altered and expanded social functions of hospitals at the end of the middle ages offered particular opportunities for lay women', especially widows 'seeking to progress spiritually, reading and studying, connecting with female friends, carrying out family obligations, advocating for members of one's circle, choosing particular charities to support'.[103] Hospital work was seen as a natural extension of the maternal caregiving such women were already doing as mothers and grandmothers. Closer to charity wards than medical institutions, late-medieval English hospitals were often attached to religious houses and were sometimes sponsored by individual philanthropists.[104] Joan FitzAlan de Bohun lived her last years at Walden Abbey, whose hospital she and her husband Humphrey de Bohun had endowed.[105] Hospitals served the community at large, as well; Nicole Rice has shown links between religious pageants and sponsoring hospitals.[106]

Devotional reading was an important part of late-medieval English hospital culture, with the larger ones maintaining libraries for their workers and guests.[107] These collections might range from a handful of prayer books for use in services to several dozen volumes including theological texts such as Augustine, Richard Rolle, and the *Golden Legend*. Erler describes the hospital master's direction of the widows' devotions, especially their reading.

I propose that when the English compiler of Douce 114 anticipates 'alle men and wymmen þat in happe rediþ or heriþ þis englyshe', this potential readership includes those in a fifteenth-century English hospital or healing setting.[108] Such an audience would have their own ideas about the use of maternal bodies, the sociality of pain, and the empathy required for healing practices. Recognizing the collection as one rooted in healing culture also affirms Brian Vander Veen's theory that Douce 114 was a response to Lollards.[109] By the fifteenth century, English enthusiasm for hospitals was waning, with many having tightened budgets or closed.[110] Lollards criticized hospitals as church institutions, calling for reform. They were particularly upset that hospital-based clerics had been taking fees for their own use rather than spending it on care for the ill and impoverished, and took their concerns to Parliament in 1415.[111] At Nottingham, where Douce 114 was copied, the local hospital, St John Bridgwater, was unpopular in the community.[112] With its centering of clerical perspectives in a hospital-dense culture of origin, the manuscript may have been commissioned in part to support the local hospital's ministry, either as an attempt to build rapport or as a gesture of goodwill toward a potential donor with the means to support it.

Henry Suso and hospital readers

Given that some hospital-based readers would be active as nurses while others would be convalescing or near the end of their lives, it makes sense for Douce 114 to change direction midway through, from the duties one might owe her community to the obligation to establish or maintain one's own orthodoxy as a means of preparing for the afterlife. Suso's *Seven Poyntes of Trewe Wisdom* is addressed to 'my moste worschipful lady' and 'goostly douȝhter', misleading phrasing that Dirk Schultze has shown was attached to most English manuscripts of this text and thus does not tell us much about the book's first owner.[113] Suso's *ars moriendi* treatise offers a doctrinal dialogue between a 'disciple' and 'Wisdom', who alternately represents Christ or Mary.[114] Like the *vitae*, it ties bodily pain to spiritual achievement: in a vision of his own death, the disciple realizes that 'þe frendes of the bodye ben enmyes to þe soule'.[115] However, Suso's text does not maintain the previous texts' interest in the social context of caregiving; there is little awareness of mothering or healing others outside the self.

Suso's text shifts the manuscript's physical focus slightly, from the mystics' maternal pains to the heart, an organ by which readers of all genders could benefit spiritually. Memorably, Suso's memoir describes his cutting Christ's initials into his chest.[116] In the Latin *Horologium*, the servant wishes he could carve and even gild Christ's name into his own heart, a winking allusion to what Suso actually has done.[117] The Disciple in Douce 114's *Seven Poyntes* also references Suso's heart-carving, but uses a gentler, more literate image, asking Wisdom 'þat þe ymage and likenesse of þi wirchepfulle passione be effectuelye *pryntede in mye sowle* þorhe þi veruese grace, & þat it worche in me continulye his helefulle effecte to þe loovyng & wirchepynge of þi blessed name'.[118] As Steven Rozenski notes in his study of the Latin text, Suso continually uses images of literacy to express devotion.[119] The shift to a more literate, individual devotion echoes similar images in Proverbs, but is also appropriate to an aging readership that was not necessarily exclusively female and might connect more readily with heart preparation than to labor pains.[120]

Mary is an active figure in Suso's oeuvre, but rather than embodying or emulating Mary, the Disciple treats her as someone who confirms his own urges. Her answers to his questions about the Crucifixion parallel his urge to imprint Christ on his heart: Mary speaks of her heart being *knit* to Christ's: 'he knitte and constreynede mye herte to hym with so brennynge love'.[121] Like the ascetic Suso described in the autobiography, Mary's devotion to Christ results in a drenching of blood that confuses identity: 'with a grete luste I kissede þe hote blode þat droppede downe in to erþe owt of þe wondes of mye der sone, in so miche þat þe moder face was alle blodye of þe slayne sones blode'.[122] Her compassion allows the brief merging of mother with son. Such loss of self is outside the experience of the Disciple. When Wisdom advises the Disciple that 'þou schalt have alleweye in þine herte þe mynde of myne passione, & alle tribulaciones and aduersitees þat þou suffreste referre to hit, & in as miche as hit is possible to þe, þou schalt as hit were cloþe þe with þe likkenesse þer-of', it is clear that the Disciple will be honing Marian skills of *compassio*, but not to help or heal anyone beyond himself.[123] Similarly, chapter 6 is devoted entirely to his own meditation on and preparation for the Eucharist.[124] All his bodily practices are in service to his own piety. After so many *vitae* in Douce 114 that highlight the mystic's mutual obligations to her community, the focus on orthodoxy, *imitatio Mariae*, or suffering for its own sake seems abrupt, even selfish.

Even reproducing Christ is, in this text, death preparation rather than gestating or populating the church. As we saw in Chapter 1 of this study, Suso was invested in the Christian's replicating or reproducing Christ through meditation. Wisdom's advice in *Seven Poyntes* to conjure thoughts of the Crucifixion allows this to happen. The depiction of such an act as solitary reinterprets and expands the applications of the Marian maternity invoked in the mystics' *vitae*. Community-building has become irrelevant. Further, reproducing Christ is an activity that can be performed by men as well as women: spiritual maternity need not be gendered, a point emphasized by the fluidity of Wisdom's identities between Christ and Mary and by the centrality of the gender-neutral heart to Suso's asceticism.

These changes allow Douce 114 to remain thematically cohesive: they respond to the different life stages of readers in a hospital setting. While the whole manuscript is concerned with healing practice, not all readers would be women; not all would be in a position of active caregiving service. Hospitals could also be sites of healing and of death, places to ponder theological issues that justify Suso's inclusion among so many female mystics. With that in mind, I want to return now to the thirteenth-century hospital contexts that produced so many of these texts and, in later manifestations, received the fifteenth-century English version in Douce 114.

Healing practice, orthodox practice

While Douce 114 does not make its cultural origins in hospital culture clear, that embeddedness remained in the institutional memory of the orders that preserved the texts. As we've seen, hospitals were important sites of religious practice in the Low Countries. They were also important to Catherine of Siena, whose poor health impelled her family's permission for her to become a Dominican tertiary and who, as such, did hospital work. Her protégé, Stephen Maconi, had at least tangential connections to a hospital.[125] Both Catherine and Marie d'Oignies are portrayed as concomitant physical sufferers and healers. Adam J. Davis observes that the initial rise in the founding of hospitals reflects 'a renewed concern with the poor and sick among theologians and canonists, and a rise in lay spirituality'.[126] The twelfth and thirteenth centuries had seen, as André Vauchez has observed, 'une véritable révolution de la charité'.[127] Hospitals were primarily religious institutions whose main purpose was to care for the sick and weak.[128] Different types served various constituencies: lepers, travelers, the seriously ill, and the poor, with significant overlap among them. Both hospital workers and patients were told their time in the hospital could shave time off their stay in purgatory. As Davis points out, 'by helping sick inmates become physically stronger, the hospital workers helped heal themselves spiritually through the penitential and potentially salvific effects of doing works of mercy'.[129] Despite the distinction between the two groups in sermons, there was sometimes overlap in their practices: patients might perform some care duties, and nurses could age into patient status.[130] They also shared reading interests. Douce 114, with its attention to the spiritual use of pain and to death preparations, could be useful to either hospital audience.

Working in hospitals was initially meant to divert pious women, including mothers and grandmothers, from being tempted by heretical sects, be they Cathars in the thirteenth century or Lollards in the fifteenth. An important part of patients' care, too, involved keeping them orthodox.[131] Confession and the Mass were central, as Carole Rawcliffe has shown in her work on lepers' hospitals.[132] Patients were expected to attend church services and say prayers.[133] Jessalyn Bird explains that 'the first line of treatment for bodily illness was reconciliation with God, and spiritual healing and preparation for death by confession and enjoined penance preceded bed-rest and medical treatment'.[134] To this end, hospital infirmaries were often set up in the chapel. Simon Roffey notes that such a layout allowed patients to complete all the worship that founding documents required, and that it demonstrates 'the clear relationship between the care of the afflicted body and spiritual provision for the soul through proximity to the high altar'.[135] The layout imitated those of monasteries. Emilia Jamroziak shows that in Cistercian houses, 'infirmaries were a sort of 'mini-monastery' where the patients were expected to observe the offices as far as possible'.[136]

In fifteenth-century English hospitals, the Eucharist was especially valued for its health-restoring abilities. Accordingly, hospitals arranged beds around the altar so patients could see the host. John Mirk reminds parish priests what Augustine had promised: just seeing a priest bearing 'goddes body' guaranteed sufficient 'mete & drynke' for the day, God's forgiveness of oaths or idle words, and the avoidance of blindess or 'soden deth'.[137] That Mirk specifies the Host's prevention of *sudden* death seems significant for its witnesses in hospitals: presumably a death suffered in the infirmary would not be considered 'soden'. Other sermon anecdotes vouch for the host's spiritually healing properties: the mid-fifteenth century British Library, Royal MS B XXIII includes a promise from Christ himself: 'take', says Crist, 'and ete of þis brede, for it is my body in þe forme of brede, þe wiche brede is a full good *medecyn to þi soule*'.[138] Christ's language here echoes Lateran IV's canon 21, which compares the priest and Host to a doctor with healing medicine. As Ritchey explains, canons 21 and 22 articulated how the Eucharist's 'sacramental efficacy became canonically linked to bodily health'.[139]

That healing, restorative quality of the Eucharist is also present in Douce 114, where it is a favored ritual and substance. Elizabeth is depicted taking it; Christina requests it on her deathbed; Marie could distinguish whether it was consecrated, performed several related miracles, and at some points ate no other food; Catherine deprived herself of all other nourishment; Suso devotes a whole chapter to its appreciation.[140] Vander Veen argues convincingly that Douce 114 was compiled to offer an orthodox argument against fifteenth-century Lollards, who in addition to their criticisms of hospital administration questioned the concept of transubstantiation.[141] As we saw in Chapter 2, the Eucharist has affiliations with not only Christ's flesh but Mary's womb. Its centrality to both fifteenth-century English hospital design and to the *vitae* in Douce 114 reflects the stability of its perceived role in the health of body and soul. It is also a reminder that the holy body is not one's own: Christ's body, via transubstantiation, becomes medicine, as Mary's did post-Assumption.

Jacques de Vitry, promoter of beguines, as hospital preacher

The availability of the maternal body as spiritual medicine that we saw in Jacques de Vitry's use of Marie's finger is articulated in his sermons to hospitallers. Jacques preached in and out of hospitals in a public ministry that began with observing Marie's holiness in a hospital context, with separate messages to hospital workers and to their patients.[142] Jacques applauded the workers for renouncing the world to 'refresh Christ' by performing acts of mercy in hospitals: 'Spiritually, we could say that *you are the mother of Christ* for whom you feed and nurture Christ in his members.'[143] To the patients, he explained that God 'used bodily afflictions to punish sinners and convert those he loved from sin, inflicting suffering on earth to spare them the agonies of purgatory or hell'; rather than complain, they should pray, praise God, and exercise patience.[144] In other words, he told the sick that their suffering was penance and told the hospital workers to think of those sick bodies as *containers for the suffering Christ*—whom they should nourish as Mary would. When he preached to lepers, Jacques championed spiritual healing as more important than physical health or money: 'no corporeal alms can soothe pain as effectively as the word of comfort, which is like a sweet ointment'.[145] Sick bodies existed for spiritual use.

These sermons and the *Supplement* itself are absent from Douce 114, so that the Marian element of his work in hospitals and with Marie are understated in the legendary. Instead, the subjects' bodies are there for the male authors to interpret. The frustration of losing autonomy over one's body or relinquishing it involuntarily to men's use is not as articulated in Douce 114 as in the full source texts and contexts. The anecdote about Marie's finger, conversations about body parts as relics, and the threat of despair are missing from the English compilation. Only a well-read Carthusian scribe might notice their absence; the intended recipient(s) of Douce 114 would likely never know. Deprived the context of the *Addendum* to Marie's *vita*, or Catherine's illness-soaked youth, or Suso's depression, the *vitae* here contain only the pain that the clerical observers can recognize and voice. The pain of lost agency doesn't count. Nor does the threat of despair that appears in the *Supplement*'s anecdote about Ugolino. Further, the complex duality of the subjects' lives as both sufferers and nurturers, perhaps too obvious to state in the source texts, is barely perceptible in Douce 114.

Still, the authors and their texts have been shaped by these contexts. The ghosts of such focus on the physicality, for example, keep the concept of pain narrowed to the physical. The texts are so focused on women as physical spectacle and as individual healers that they minimize the role community members play in their successful healing practice. The authors of the source texts clearly look to their subjects as maternal figures—as bodies to be exploited for their spiritual usefulness—and additionally as workers in hierarchical charitable institutions where the clerical authors, not the women themselves, would have authority. Relationships among women, as in childraising or community care work, do not merit comment. Instead, by performing pain publicly, Christina and Elizabeth, and to a lesser extent Marie and Catherine, invite the reader to step into the role of Mary feeling *compassio*. Like the hospitallers working through the theological implications of their work, readers of Douce 114 become witnesses who must work out themselves what the pain is for and what it means.

Notes

1 Theologians debated whether Mary suffered purely emotional grief or additional physical pain, as in the swoon. Donna Spivey Ellington traces the evolution of Mary's *compassio* in *From Sacred Body to Angelic Soul: Understanding Mary in Late Medieval and Early Modern Europe* (Washington, DC: Catholic University of America Press, 2001).

2 R. C. Finucane notes that the medieval experience of affliction differed from ours: 'To be ill was not a trivial matter, and to recover from

illness was not always the usual outcome. In their eyes, recovery was, sometimes, a miracle'. Disabilities could simply be altered: a 'cure' or miracle need not be permanent or complete. See 'The use and abuse of medieval miracles', *History* 60.198 (1975), 1–10, at 7–8.

3 Rubin summarizes the establishment of some of these sites in *Mother of God*, 182–6.
4 See her *Pilgrimage in Medieval English Literature, 700–1500* (Cambridge: D.S. Brewer, 2001).
5 Carole Rawcliffe, 'Medicine for the soul: The medieval English hospital and the quest for spiritual health', in *Religion, Health and Suffering*, ed. John Hinnels and Roy Porter (New York: Routledge, 1999), 316–38, at 323.
6 Mary 'healed' disabilities, too, as Anne Clark shows in 'Guardians of the sacred: The nuns of Soissons and the slipper of the Virgin Mary', *Church History* 76.4 (2007), 724–49.
7 'O santa Maria ... dime di quela pena del tuo Fiolo, inperzioché tu vedesti de quela passione più che nessuno santo ... poi ch'io vezo che tu la vedesti con li ochi del capo e con la inmaginazione'. In *Il libro della Beata Angela da Foligno*, ed. Ludger Their and Abele Calufetti (Grottaferrata: Ed. Collegii S. Bonaventurae ad Claras Aquas, 1985), 293. Translation mine.
8 From *The Life of the Servant*, chapter 42, in Suso, *Exemplar*, 167.
9 While most texts attribute his cure to the Virgin's milk, one version has Mary lay fingers on his cancered tongue instead. See Ruth Tryon, 'Miracles of Our Lady in Middle English verse', PMLA 38.2 (1923), 308–88, at 350.
10 The tale's setting varies depending on the version. Tryon mentions that 'mal des ardents', a bacterial infection known as St. Anthony's fire, spread widely in northern France in 1128–29, 336. Boyarin glosses the Vernon version in her edition as Viviers, in southern France. With thanks for Boyarin's generous response to my queries, I propose that Namur was the place readers of the Vernon manuscript would have imagined as 'Viuari': it was on a pilgrimage route; it was a 'munstre ifoundet .../In honour of Ure Ladi'—named, like all Cistercian houses, for Mary; and it maintained a hospital. The compilation of the Vernon manuscript has traditionally been attributed to Bordesley Abbey, a Cistercian house in Worcestershire; its connection to the house at Namur is geographically and ideologically close.
11 *The minor poems of the Vernon Manuscript*, ed. Carl Horstmann, EETS o.s. 98, 117 (London: K. Paul, Trench, Trübner & Co., 1892), 138–9, lines 21–3; lines 635–8 in Boyarin, *Miracles*, 75–9.
12 Line 70 in *Vernon*; lines 730–1 in Boyarin.

13 Sara Ritchey, *Acts of Care: Recovering Women in Late Medieval Health* (Cornell University Press, 2021), at 32.
14 Esther Cohen, *The Modulated Scream: Pain in Late Medieval Culture* (Chicago, University of Chicago Press, 2010).
15 Henry's book appears in Stonyhurst College, Blackburn, MS 24, and Cambridge, Corpus Christi College MS 218. For a French edition, see *Le Livre de seyntz Medicines: The unpublished Devotional Treatise of Henry of Lancaster*, ed. E. J. Arnould, Anglo-Norman Text Society. Vol. 2 (Oxford: Basil Blackwell, 1940). See also Henry of Grosmont, First Duke of Lancaster, *Le Livre de seyntz medicines/The Book of Loly Medicines*, ed. Catherine Batt (Tempe, Arizona: ACMRS, 2014).
16 Naoë Kukita Yoshikawa, 'Holy medicine and diseases of the soul: Henry of Lancaster and le livre de seyntz medicines', *Medical History* 53 (2009), 397–414, at 402.
17 *Le Livre* (ed. Batt), 190.
18 Suso, *Exemplar*, 299–300; Suso, 'Orologium', 346.
19 'Oil poured out, medicine to the languishing', from Canticles 1:2. Fifteenth-century poem added to London, British Library Additional MS 20059, fols 99v–100v, line 17; Saupe, poem 50.
20 Sarah McNamer, *Affective Meditation*.
21 Cohen, *Modulated*, 129.
22 Hollywood, *Sensible Ecstasy*, 253–7.
23 The beguine *vitae* and the letter on Catherine of Siena (fols 1–88) are in a separate quire from Suso's treatise (fol. 89ff). The hand of the Suso treatise differs from that of the *vitae* and letter, although the inkwork was completed by the same artist. Both letter and treatise appeared widely in medieval texts and in print. For discussion of the manuscript and the three beguine *vitae*, see *A Critical Edition of and Commentary on MS Douce 114*, ed. Jennifer N. Brown (Turnhout: Brepols, 2003); for discussion of versions of Suso's text see Amy Appleford, *Learning to Die in London: 1380–1540* (Philadelphia: University of Pennsylvania Press, 2015).
24 The letter on Catherine of Siena appears along with the three mystics' lives in 'Prosalegenden: Die legenden des MS Douce 114', ed. Carl Horstmann, *Anglia* 8 (1885), 119–34, hereafter 'Prosalegenden'. Horstmann also edited Suso's treatise in 'Orologium'. For consistency, page numbers given here correspond with Horstmann's editions.
25 Brian C. Vander Veen, 'The *vitae* of Bodleian Library MS Douce 114'. Unpub. Ph.D. thesis (University of Nottingham, 2007), 187. Michael G. Sargent considers the translator's mention of 'þis place of grace' possible confirmation of that attribution. Sargent, 'Introduction' to Love's *Mirror*, lvi–lvii, lxv, 326.

26 The term 'beguine' began as a mild slur and remained so until the beguines adopted it for themselves. None of the *vitae* translated in Douce 114 uses 'beguine' to describe their subjects. See Walter Simons, *Cities of Ladies: Beguine Communities in the Medieval Low Countries, 1200–1565* (Philadelphia: University of Pennsylvania Press, 2001), 124.

27 Les Archives d'État de Liège holds beguine wills such as the testament of Kathline de Haneffe, October 6, 1291 (Charte no. 4, Hôpital Tirebourse et St Christophe), the testament of Ode de Naiverule, November 14, 1302 (Charte no. 7, Hôpital Tirebourse et St Christophe), and the Testament of Beatrice de Stavelot, dated April 24, 1307 (*Fonds Tirebourse et S Christophe* April 24, 1307), all in the vernacular. For a comprehensive list of extant documents related to the beguines, see Pascal Majérus, *Ces Femmes qu'on dit béguines … Guide des béguinages de Belgique. Bibliographie et sources d'archives*, 2 vols. (Bruxelles: Archives générales du Royaume, 1997).

28 For example, the thirteenth-century Université de Liège MS 260 contains the *vita* of Marie d'Oignies in a careful hand. In Université de Liège MS 135, a group effort of many different hands, are the *vitae* of Elizabeth of Spalbeek (fols 119r ff) and Marie d'Oignies (fols 171 ff). Bibliothèque du Grand Séminaire, MS XV 6L21 contains the life of Christina *mirabilis* (fols 346–59). At the Bibliothèque Royale Albert I in Brussels, the fifteenth-century MS 7917 has the *vitae* of Marie d'Oignies (fols 120v–140v) and Christina *mirabilis* (fols 169r–174v), together with the lives of a significant number of other beguines and virgin saints, including English ones. Likewise, the fourteenth-century Latin B.R. MS 8609–20, created for La Cambre, contains the *vitae* of beguines and female saints, among them Mary Magdalene, Elizabeth of Hungary, the Virgin Mary, Lutgard, Christina *mirabilis*, Alice of Schaerbeek, Ida of Leuven, Odonis, Elizabeth of Schoenberg, Ursula, and Margaret; its treatise on the Eucharist references Marie d'Oignies. See Ritchey, *Acts* 229–43, for a full discussion of the La Cambre manuscript.

29 See Ritchey, *Acts of Care*. See also Simons, *Cities*, 77.

30 E.g., the beguinage at Nivelles built their own hospital in the period 1281–85. See Ernest McDonnell, *The Beguines and Beghards in Medieval Culture, with Special Emphasis on the Belgian Scene* (New York: Octagon Books, 1969), 67.

31 See Simons, *Cities*, 87, and Ziegler, *Sculpture of Compassion*, 117–52.

32 Simons, *Cities*, 37–8.

33 *Ibid.*, 39.

34 *Ibid.*, 42; see also Miri Rubin, *Corpus Christi: The Eucharist in Late Medieval Culture* (Cambridge: Cambridge University Press, 1991).

35 Liège had fifteen hospitals by the fifteenth century. See Pierre de Spiegeler, *Les hôpitaux et l'assistance à Liège Xe-XVe siècles: Aspects institutionnels et sociaux* (Paris: Les Belles Lettres, 1987); see also Simons, *Cities*, 76.

36 Amy Appleford and Corinne Saunders, 'Reading women in the medieval information age: *The life of Elizabeth of Spalbeek* and *The book of Margery Kempe*', *Studies in the Age of Chaucer* 42 (2020), 253–81, at 257.

37 See Sarah Knott, 'Theorizing and historicizing mothering's many labours', *Past and Present* Supplement 15 (2020), 1–23; see also Knott, *Mother Is a Verb: An Unconventional History* (New York: Sarah Crichton Books, 2019); Evelyn Nakano Glenn, 'Social construction of mothering: An overview', *Mothering: Ideology, Experience, and Agency*, ed. Evelyn Nakano Glenn, Grace Chang, and Linda Renney Forcey (New York: Routledge, 1993), 1–32.

38 Thomas of Cantimpré and Jacques de Vitry, *Two Lives of Marie d'Oignies*, ed. and trans. Margot King and Hugh Feiss (Toronto: Peregrina Press, 1987), 202–4. Sharon Farmer discusses Marie's own devotion to relics in 'Low Country ascetics and Oriental luxury: Jacques de Vitry, Marie of Oignies, and the treasures of Oignies', *History in the Comic Mode: Medieval Communities and the Matter of Person*, ed. Rachel Fulton and Bruce W. Holsinger (New York: Columbia University Press, 2007), 205–22. But Jan Vandeburie suggests Marie found relics off-putting. He describes similar negotiations between Thomas of Cantimpré and Lutgard for her finger as a relic: again, a woman leverages the power of her own body parts. See Jan Vandeburie, '"Sancte fidei omnino deiciar"': Ugolino dei Conti di Segni's doubts and Jacques de Vitry's intervention', *Studies in Church History* 52 (2016), 87–101.

39 Thomas, *Two Lives*, 205.

40 *Ibid.*, 206; Vandeburie, 'Sancte', 31. Corroborating this tale of doubt with other documents, Vandeburie dates this meeting to 1226, the same year Marie's body was exhumed and another finger removed for the monastery at Oignies; others have dated the meeting as early as 1216. Besides casually passing Marie's stolen body part to another bishop, Jacques took another one for the Oignies monastery at large. This second finger remained on site. Farmer, 'Low Country', 209.

41 Thomas, *Two Lives*, 206.

42 Michel Lauwers, *La mémoire des ancêtres, le souci des morts: Morts, rites et société au Moyen Age: Diocèse de Liège, XIe–XIIIe siècles* (Paris: Beauchesne, 1997), 410–13.

43 The carving is depicted in *The Life of the Servant* in Suso, *Exemplar*, 70–1; the Servant references it in *Seven Poyntes*. Suso also attaches

sharp implements to his clothing and sleeping surface so that a cross is secretly cut into his back in Suso, *Exemplar*, 89.

44 These voluntary pains distinguish them from leprous patients, who did not feel pain in their affected extremities: pain could thus be a sign of health. See Rawcliffe, *Leprosy*, 2. Earlier, Augustine had noted that pain was an indicator of life, as evidence that gangrene was not present: 'in corpore dolorem facit sensus resistens corpori potentiori ... item in corpore melius est vulnus cum dolore, quam putredo sine dolore, quae specialiter corruptio dicitur', PL 42: 556–7, qtd. in Cohen, *Modulated*, 267, n. 32.

45 Amy Hollywood puts this pithily: 'The identification of women with the body demands that their sanctification occur in and through that body', *The Soul as Virgin Wife: Mechthild of Magdeburg, Marguerite Porete, and Meister Eckhart* (Notre Dame: University of Notre Dame Press, 1995), 35.

46 Cohen, *Modulated*, at 32–7.

47 Emphasis mine. Ariel Glucklich, *Sacred Pain: Hurting the Body for the Sake of the Soul* (New York: Oxford University Press, 2001), 207.

48 'de se enim nihil in se remanserat', qtd. in Ellington, *From Sacred Body*, 92.

49 See Marla Carlson, *Performing Bodies in Pain* (New York: Palgrave Macmillan, 2011); Gavin Flood, *The Ascetic Self: Subjectivity, Memory, and Tradition* (Cambridge: Cambridge University Press, 2004).

50 Mary Suydam, 'Beguine textuality: Sacred performances', *Performance and Transformation: New Approaches to Late Medieval Spirituality*, ed. Mary Suydam and Joanna Ziegler (New York: St. Martin's Press, 1999), 169–210, at 172.

51 Cohen, *Modulated*, 49.

52 'Prosalegenden', 108, 111. Simons notes, 'From the early Middle Ages onwards church councils prohibited dancing in churches or in religious ceremonies; the endless repetition of these decrees must prove that such dances were not unusual, however, and some texts appear to single out women as the prime suspects', 'Reading' 13.

53 'Prosalegenden', 114.

54 *Ibid.*, 107.

55 *Ibid.*, 108.

56 *Ibid.*, 118.

57 *Ibid.*, 109, 113.

58 *Ibid.*, 116, 118.

59 'Prosalegenden', 110, emphasis mine. Appleford and Saunders have described Elizabeth's interaction with this 'tabil' as a form of *askesis*, 'Reading', 264–6.

60 'Prosalegenden', 115.
61 *Ibid.*, 107.
62 Sara Ahmed, 'The contingency of pain', *The Cultural Politics of Emotion* (Edinburgh: Edinburgh University Press, 2004), 20–41, at 20, 22.
63 *Ibid.*, 21, emphasis mine.
64 Kalas, *Margery*, 129.
65 Qtd. in Graef, *Mary*, 243.
66 Ahmed, 'Contingency', 30, emphasis mine.
67 *Ibid.*, 27.
68 *Ibid.*, 28.
69 Emphasis mine. 'Iste dolor assimilator torsionum et dolori parturientium et dolori flentium unigenitum. Isti enim tres dolores sunt maiores qui inueniri possunt'. Jacobus de Voragine, *Sermones quadragesimales*, ed. Giovanni Paolo Maggioni, Edizione Nazionale dei Testi Mediolatini 13 (Florence: Sismel, 2005), 296.
70 Thomas's strategy was for preachers to emphasize how painful hell is. See his *Summa de arte praedicandi*, ed. Franco Morenzoni, CCCM 82 (Turnhout, 1988); 'Quomodo auditors abterrendi sunt' (how to terrify listeners) is at 32–53. See also Cohen, *Modulated*, 40–41. Thomas's *Art of Preaching* appears in Cambridge, Corpus Christi College MS 455 and would have been long circulating in England by the time Douce 114 was compiled. Christina's hagiographer, Thomas of Cantimpré, a traveling preacher across the Low Countries, likely knew this preaching manual.
71 'Prosalegenden', 119.
72 *Ibid.*, 120–1.
73 *Ibid.*, 121.
74 *Ibid.*, 124.
75 *Ibid.*, 121.
76 *Ibid.*, 124.
77 *Ibid.*, 122.
78 *Ibid.*, 125.
79 *Ibid.*, 126, 129.
80 *Ibid.*, 126, emphasis mine.
81 This nun assigned to nurse Christina may have prepared her body for burial: Rawcliffe explains that nurses were considered analogous to priests and wrapped the dead in funeral shrouds in *Leprosy*, 49.
82 The Middle English translation does not include accounts of Christina's post-mortem miracles, which would provide further evidence that she participates fully in both the living and dead communities.
83 John Coakley, 'Thomas of Cantimpré and female sanctity', in Fulton and Holsinger, *History in the Comic* Mode, 45–55.

84 'Prosalegenden', 155.
85 *Ibid.*, 162.
86 *Ibid.*, 139, emphasis mine.
87 *Ibid.*, 136. Marie thus acts as a successful 'Cecilia' to counterpoint Margery Kempe. For comparison to Margery, see Sarah McNamer, 'The Middle-English version of Jacques de Vitry's *Life of Marie d'Oignies*', *Medieval Hagiography*, ed. Thomas Head (New York: Routledge, 2001), 709–28, at 711, and Allen's notes to Kempe's *Book*.
88 See Allen's notes to Margery Kempe's *Book*, 256.
89 'Prosalegenden', 137.
90 See Michel Lauwers, '"Noli me tangere": Marie Madeleine, Marie d'Oignies et les pénitentes du XIIIe siècle', *Mélanges de l'École Française de Rome: Moyen Age* 104 (1992), 209–68.
91 Kempe, *Book*, 148–50.
92 See Jennifer N. Brown, *Fruit of the Orchard: Reading Catherine of Siena in Late Medieval and Early Modern England* (Toronto: University of Toronto Press, 2019).
93 In the sixteenth century, Catherine would be strongly associated in iconography with Dominicans and the rosary, and thus Mary. This connection is unstated in the letter, perhaps because it was obvious to one Dominican writing to another.
94 Brown, *Fruit*, 52–3.
95 'Prosalegenden', 189.
96 *Ibid.*, 188.
97 Catherine of Siena, *The letters of Catherine of Siena*. Vol. 2, ed. Suzanne Noffke (Tempe: Arizona Center for Medieval and Renaissance Studies, 2000), 209.
98 Catherine, *Letters*, 255, 257.
99 'Prosalegenden', 195.
100 Watt, 'Mary the Physician', 30.
101 Caroline Walker Bynum, *Fragmentation and Redemption: Essays on Gender and the Human Body in Medieval Religion* (New York: Zone Books, 1991), 181–238, at 197.
102 Ritchey's *Acts of Care* addresses this gap. See Monica Green, 'Documenting medieval women's medical practice', in *Practical Medicine from Salerno to the Black Death*, ed. Luis García-Ballester, Roger French, Jon Arrizabalaga, and Andrew Cunningham (Cambridge: Cambridge University Press, 1994), 322–52, at 329. See also Green, 'Women's medical practice and health care in medieval Europe', *Signs* 14.2 (1988–89), 434–73, and 'Gender, health, disease: Recent work on medieval women's medicine', *Studies in Medieval and Renaissance History*, ser. 3, 5 (2005), 1–46.

103 Mary Erler, 'Widows in retirement: Region, patronage, spirituality, reading at the Gaunts, Bristol', *Religion & Literature* 37.2 (2005), 51–75, at 53.
104 Simon Roffey lists evidence of later medieval leper hospital chapels in 'Medieval leper hospitals in England: Archaeological perspective', *Medieval Archaeology* 56 (2012), 203–33, 213–14.
105 See note 106 in Chapter 2 above. See also David Andrews, 'A lost Essex hospital: The College of St Mark at Audley End', *Essex Archaeology and History* 26 (1995), 276–7.
106 See Nicole R. Rice, 'The feminine prehistory of the York Purification: St. Leonard's Hospital, civic drama, and women's devotion', *Speculum* 94.3 (2019), 704–38.
107 Nicholas Orme and Margaret Webster, *The English hospital, 1070–1570* (New Haven: Yale, 1995), 64–5. Such 'guests' might include anchoresses and anchorites.
108 'Prosalegenden', 195.
109 Vander Veen, 31–2.
110 Orme and Webster, *English Hospital*, 129.
111 *Ibid.*, 134–6.
112 *Ibid.*, 103.
113 Suso, 'Orologium', 325. See Schultze, 'Wisdom'.
114 Writing about a different manuscript's 'death texts', Appleford comments, 'Nowhere in the book … are sophisticated reading practices more seductively urged' (*Learning to Die*, 121) than in its version of *Learn to Die*, which appears as chapter five (357ff) in *Seven Poyntes*.
115 Suso, *Exemplar*, 362.
116 *Ibid.*, 70–1.
117 *Ibid.*, 231.
118 Suso, '*Orologium*', 341, emphasis mine.
119 See Steven Rozenski, Jr., 'Henry Suso's *Horologium Sapientiae* in fifteenth-century France: Images of reading and writing in Brussels Royal Library MS IV 111', *Word & Image* 26.4 (2010), 364–80.
120 Mercy and truth, and God's law, should be written 'upon the tables of thy heart' in Proverbs 3:3 and 7:3, respectively.
121 Suso, 'Orologium', 344.
122 *Ibid.*, 345.
123 *Ibid.*, 343.
124 *Ibid.*, 366–78; Suso, *Exemplar*, 276–86.
125 'in the early period of their acquaintance he allowed himself to be drawn into some plots against the government, and attended the secret meetings of the conspirators, held in the vaults of La Scala [the charitable hospital]. Catherine, who knew by revelation what was going

on, sent for Stephen, and, severely reproving him, bade him take a discipline, and shed as many drops of his own blood as he had spoken words in the unlawful assembly. (de vita et moribus beati Stephani Maconi, lib. v. c. 2.)'. In *The History of St. Catherine of Siena and Her Companions*, Herbert Cardinal Vaughan, Abp of Westminster, December 15, 1898, 343. www.archive.org/stream/MN5127ucmf_1/MN5127ucmf_1_djvu.txt

126 Adam J. Davis, 'Preaching in thirteenth-century hospitals', *Journal of Medieval History* 36 (2010), 72–89, at 73.

127 André Vauchez, *La spiritualité du Moyen Âge Occidental (VIIIe–XIIIe siècles)*, 2nd edn. (Paris: Editions du Seuil, 1994), 118.

128 See Lucy Barnhouse, *Houses of God, Places for the Sick*, forthcoming from Amsterdam University Press.

129 Davis, 'Preaching', 80.

130 *Ibid.*, 76.

131 Peregrine Horden demonstrates how central religious practices such as the liturgy, sacraments, and relics were to patient care in 'A non-natural environment: medicine without doctors and the medieval European hospital', *The Medieval Hospital and Medical Practice*, ed. Barbara S. Bowers (Aldershot, 2007), 133–45. See also Tiffany Ziegler, *Medieval Healthcare and the Rise of Charitable Institutions* (London: Palgrave, 2018).

132 Carole Rawcliffe, *Leprosy in Medieval England* (Woodbridge: Boydell & Brewer, 2006), 337–43.

133 Orme and Webster, *English hospital*, 52–3.

134 Jessalyn Bird, 'Medicine for Body and soul: Jacques de Vitry's sermons to hospitallers and their charges', *Religion and Medicine in the Middle Ages*, ed. Peter Biller and Joseph Ziegler, 91–108, at 103.

135 Roffey, 'Medieval leper hospitals', 224.

136 Emilia Jamroziak, *The Cistercian Order in Medieval Europe 1090–1500* (London: Routledge, 2013), at 58. In Coletti's view, such observation meant that the inmates' sleeping quarters also became 'performance spaces'. Theresa Coletti, 'Social contexts of the East Anglian saint play: The Digby Mary Magdalene and the late medieval hospital?' in *Medieval East Anglia*, ed. Christopher Harper-Bill (Woodbridge, UK, 2005), 287–301, at 297.

137 John Myrc (Mirk), *Instructions for Parish Priests*, ed. Edward Peacock and F.J. Furnivall, EETS o.s. 31 (London: Oxford University Press, 1868, rev. 1902), 10.

138 *Middle English Sermons*, 126. The same edition, at 127, echoes language about the graven and smooth sides of the wafer that appears in Suso.

139 Ritchey, *Acts of Care*, 233.

140 For a full treatment of the Eucharist in thirteenth-century Liège see Rubin, *Corpus Christi*.
141 Vander Veen, *Vitae*, 31–2, 188–9.
142 For contextualizing of Jacques' sermons with those of other hospital preachers, see Davis, 'Preaching'.
143 Emphasis mine. 'Spiritualiter dicitur quod estis mater Christi eo quod Christum in membris suis pascitis et nutritis', in Jessalyn Bird, 'Texts on hospitals: translation of Jacques de Vitry's *Historia occidentalis* 29', in *Religion and Medicine in the Middle Ages*, 109–34, at 115.
144 Bird, 'Medicine', 102.
145 Elma Brenner, 'The leprous body in twelfth- and thirteenth-century Rouen: Perceptions and responses', *The Ends of the Body: Identity and Community in Medieval Culture*, ed. Jill Ross and Suzanne Akbari (Toronto: University of Toronto Press, 2013), 255.

Plate 1 Woodcut, Peter Vischer, Nuremberg Relic-Book, 1487. Washington, D.C., Library of Congress, Rare Book and Special Collections Division, Rosenvald 120, fol. 4r

Plate 2 Central panel, Rogier van der Weyden, *Altarpiece of the Seven Sacraments*, c. 1445, Royal Museum of Fine Arts, Antwerp

Plate 3 Alabaster relief of 'Our Lady of Gesyn', 14th c., Holy Trinity Church, Long Melford, Suffolk. Photo copyright Will Collin (Flickr: d0gwalker)

Plate 4 Painted screen at Lady Chapel altar, 15th c., Church of St Helen, Ranworth, Norfolk. Photo copyright Jean McCreanor (Flickr: JMC4–Church Explorer)

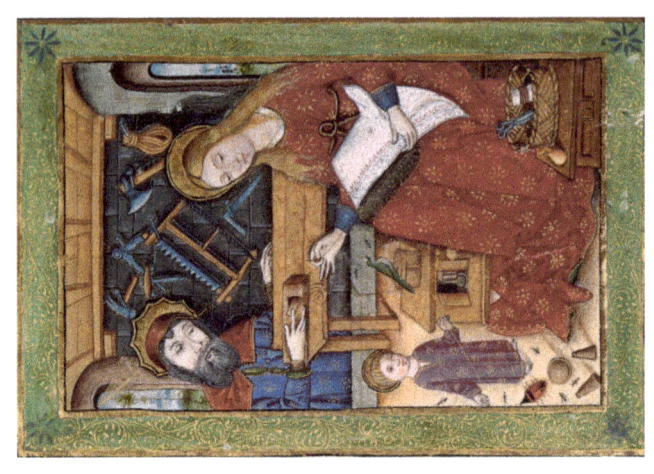

Plate 5 Page of Chaucer's *ABC*, Glasgow University Library, Hunter MS 239 (U. 3. 12), f. 81r. Courtesy of University of Glasgow Archives & Special Collections

Plate 6 Book of Hours, Spain, c. 1461. London, British Library, Additional MS 18193, f. 48v. Copyright The British Library Board

4

'In Our Lady's Binds': Mary's maternal peers in East Anglian devotion

The version of the fifteenth-century poem 'How the Goodwife Taught her Daughter' that appears in Oxford, Bodleian Library MS Ashmole 61 predicts that both church attendance and traumatic birth events will be accompanied by 'friends':

> When thou arte in the chyrch, my chyld,
> Loke that thou be bothe meke and myld,
> And bydde thi bedys aboven all thing.
> *With sybbe ne fremde* make no jangelyng. (19–22)
>
> ... And if it thus thee betyde,
> *That frendys falle* thee fro on every syde,
> And God fro thee thi chyld take,
> Thy wreke onne God do thou not take. (171–4)[1]

The speaker does not think highly of these friends. The scenes depicted here shift abruptly from a group of teenagers giggling during Mass to a socially isolated woman grieving pregnancy loss. Neither quite portrays the listener as capable of building her own emotionally and spiritually supportive social network. As Felicity Riddy has shown, 'How the Goodwife Taught her Daughter' likely took a fictional premise to impart bourgeois and clerical values to household employees, rather than relating authentic instruction from a real mother to an actual daughter.[2] Yet its casual assumption that 'friends' will be part of going to church, raising children, and running a household—whether those 'friends' are extended family members or social acquaintances—makes clear that mothering and worshipping were not considered solo tasks any more than running a household was.

I want to acknowledge the ways that these friends, whom I am calling 'maternal peers', both socialize young women into new roles of responsibility and offer a less-proscriptive form of support and companionship. These are relationships often rooted or reinforced, as line 169 implies, in birth events. Birth, like attendance at the parish church, was and is an important social event for all involved.[3] Family members, friends, and midwives create a specialized social dynamic before and during the birth; afterward, relationships are often formed based on the age and status of one's child(ren). Births are also events that cement friendships and mark or foreshadow parallels, such as whose son will be martyred, or who will be widowed. Considering birth a social event affirms the values of both Aquinas, who saw reproduction as the point of women's existence, and of the readers of the texts considered in this chapter, for whom so much status is wrapped up in whom, or whose, they birth. As we have seen in Chapter 2, the solidarity that forms among maternal peers can be perceived or enacted as politically powerful. Such power can be disruptive or additive to the status quo. Medieval narratives about Mary recognize birth as the event that creates her social and emotional world. Both of Mary's most important female friendships emerge from and are centered around her pregnancy and childbirth. They become foundational to her identity and maternal practice.

As a pregnant teenager and teenaged mother, Mary needs as much social support from other women as does the addressee of 'Goodwife'. Lydgate reminds us just after Christ's birth in *Life of Our Lady* that Mary is only sixteen. Her youth offers a parallel with the adolescent virgin martyrs whose *passiones* anchor so many of the legendaries of women that appear in the fifteenth century. Mary and the female saints are exceptional for their age in their avoidance of behavioral and doctrinal mistakes. The conventional wisdom is that adolescent girls are difficult to control: they are high energy; they question authority; they require a lot of calories and a lot of space.[4] As Riddy has shown, the practice of sending adolescents to live in other households as workers was one way to attempt to contain them. Mary Erler has posited that some girls were sent to visit older relatives to be socialized properly.[5] The affluent readers of women's devotional books were less likely to undergo a recognized period of adolescence. For them and their daughters, marriage or the convent shortened or eliminated this developmental phase.

Both marriage and the convent required a kind of matrescence, the anthropological term for the social and intergenerational process of becoming maternal, the skills learned en route to a new identity.[6] Matrescence is not strictly biological, although biology may play a role. This may explain why narratives about teenaged girls continued to appeal to affluent women, and why the texts in these collections are so invested in teenaged girls and their proximity to birth and death. As Catherine Sanok has shown, 'exemplarity' does not always indicate the most obvious connection between reader and subject.[7] Maternity was an important metaphor for convents, places where teenagers and geriatric women cohabited. Nuns' socialization into their new roles was both more regimented and less literal and transactional than that of pregnant women: only one nun could be Prioress at a time, and any maternity would only ever be symbolic. The efforts of devotional texts to provide holy women's social and familial context suggests readers were interested not only in genealogy—which they certainly were, as Pamela Sheingorn shows—but in how Marian and saintly matrescence developed.[8] Importantly, Mary's maternal peers are also her family members. That her social network is rooted in her genealogy reinforces the values of affluent devotional readers, for whom birth could be an opportunity to strengthen or wield social power, as well as of nuns, who often depended on the familial connections of their peers to stay solvent. It is also a reminder of medieval readers' layered social contexts, which might include parasocial relationships with ancestors and saints as well as living relations. As Erler argues, such networks could also develop from shared access to their devotional books.[9] The assumption is that religious devotion and maternal practice, broadly defined, benefit from a social network.

This chapter broadens our consideration of English legendaries of women, collections of female saints' lives for the use of both household and conventual readers, a genre in which we might expect extended focus on the Virgin. Mary herself does not appear in these *vitae* as a central or supporting figure. Instead, her influence is through proxy or through other media that contextualize the legendaries. Via their saintly protagonists, these hagiographical texts invoke Mary's role as a family member and incorporate her social ties into her maternal identity. We might even consider a legendary of women a collection of maternal peers, with their production of a cult or mass conversions at the end their own offspring, their network burgeoning as readers seek communion with them through prayers.

There is significant overlap among the subjects of such manuscripts.[10] Manchester, Chetham MS 8009 includes the *vitae* of Dorothy, Anne, and Katherine; Arundel 168 includes Christine, Dorothy, and Katherine; Harley 4012 includes Katherine, Margaret, and Anne; Cambridge Addit. MS 2604 includes Agatha, Cecilia, and Barbara. Arundel 327 contains most of the universal female saints' lives that are in these books, as well as Ursula, Faith, Agnes, Mary Magdalene, Lucy, and Elizabeth of Hungary. I focus here on two manuscripts, Cambridge Addit. MS 2604 and Osbern Bokenham's legendary in Arundel 327, with reference to how other fifteenth-century texts, images, and performances infuse them with Marian presence. Both Arundel 327 and MS 2604 were owned by religious houses. Other than size, their chief distinctions from larger, better-known collections such as the *Golden Legend* or the *South English Legendary* are the gender of their subjects and the self-conscious attention to the natal families of their subjects and readers. Taken together, these texts offer an extended meditation on the nature of natal and spiritual family, entities strongly associated both with Mary and with convents. Several texts begin with Mary's genealogy, including most versions of her mother Anne's *vita* and the Saint Margaret in Harley MS 4012. The saints interact with their own natal families, sometimes with their genealogies included. The *vitae* highlight family links among patrons and among saints, but they also stress the importance of community generally, as we've already seen in Douce 114.

Mary's relational self

The focus on Mary's kinship ties and the resulting blurred lines of her maternal territory highlight that maternal peers are a crucial component of the birth and parenting experience that clerical writers denied Mary. To judge from most of the clerically-authored miracle stories and poems, Mary was alone at the painless birth of Christ, alone as she grieved his death later, alone when supplicants asked her for intercession or when she answered their pleas with miracles. She was 'peerless': a brutal loneliness. In the fourteenth and fifteenth centuries, despite clerical attempts to paint Mary as isolated from all other women, we start to see richer depictions of the postpartum Mary in company, as well as developments of what we now know as 'othermothering' among her maternal peers, a recognition that the work of raising a child cannot be limited to one person. The recognition and requirement of maternal peers expands and softens the borders of Marian motherhood.

The women permitted within Mary's inner circle must prove their loyalty and strength. Elizabeth caresses Mary tenderly at the Visitation, then during the Massacre of the Innocents fiercely commands a mountain to open. Salome stands guard as the Magi visit, then asserts herself in Mary's defense after the Crucifixion. Both are willing to cede some of their own maternal territory to Mary. To qualify as Mary's maternal peer also requires filial sacrifice. Elizabeth suffers her adult son's death (to the dance of a young girl also, confusingly, called Salome). Mary Salome's sons, disciples of Christ, will be martyred shortly after the Crucifixion. The women's loyalty to Mary is borne not only of sharing a family tree, but of bearing sons who show loyalty and deference to her holy child.

The depiction of mothering as a shared enterprise suggests that an important developmental milestone is not only in martyrdom or reproduction itself but in choosing one's maternal peers, be they friends, family, or saints. This possibility helps us conceptualize virgin martyrs as maternal, as well: it is not only a physical act to 'mother'. Using Mary's matrescence as a lens for the saints' vitae, we can see that the social connections built around birth—whether that 'birth' is physical or metaphorical—can determine whether maternity will be successful and sustainable.

To clarify, while birth and matrescence are social events, the performance of maternal work is separate from pregnancy and birth.[11] Childraising, motherwork, or parenting does not require a natal mother and can be done outside the household or natal family.[12] The emphasis of constructed Marian motherhood on Mary's physiology and domestic engagement resists this broader definition of maternity, but even Marian narrative allows Mary's physical maternity to exist apart from her emotional and spiritual maternal work. As we've seen, Mary's breastmilk is often deployed in an essentialist way, her maternity embodied rather than enacted. But it is clearly not a purely biological function, since she continues to lactate for others' benefit after Christ's death. Similarly, the deconstruction of Mary's childbirth labor so that the pain occurs separately from the birth, coupled with the distancing of her maternal peers from the event of her solitary childbirth, distinguishes maternal work and practice from the birth process. Mary's adoption of John the Evangelist at the Crucifixion and her maternal care of John the Baptist before Christ is born show that even Marian mothering can be performed by someone besides the natal mother.

The acknowledged gap between biology and maternity can be filled by 'othermothering', the term and concept now known most prominently through the Black community's routine sharing of mothering roles.[13] Describing West African traditions that persist in the diaspora, Patricia Hill Collins explains that 'while the biological mother-child bond is valued, child care was a collective responsibility, a situation fostering cooperative, age-stratified, woman-centered "mothering" networks'.[14] In an essay that sees 'maternal bonding as inseparable from action and from context, and makes no presumption that care is given by a single, "natural" mother', Sarah Knott highlights Sarah Hrdy's anthropological identification of a similar form of maternal cooperation called 'alloparenting' that de-emphasizes birth and attends to multiple care practices and caregivers.[15] Othermothering and alloparenting are useful concepts for medieval cultures that routinely raised children apart from their natal mothers, even as the primary exemplar of motherhood was officially depicted as handling it alone. It illuminates the necessity of maternal peers, not only for their emotional support to a mother but for their sharing of maternal work.

Cambridge University Library MS 2604

The legendary in Cambridge University Library MS 2604 invokes these concepts. Like Arundel 327, it is a book first created for an East Anglian convent.[16] Half its twenty-two saints are English natives, half are universal; nineteen are women. The legendary opens with the male saints John the Baptist and John the Evangelist and closes with Leonard, all common dedicatees of convents.

The manuscript's modern editors Veronica Mara and Virginia Blanton note these male saints' popularity in visual art and describe them as thematically relevant to a women's legendary because of their virginity. For example, Leonard was patron of the Denny convent, an institution that has also been affiliated with Bokenham; he relieves a queen from labor pains in his *vita* and was thus invoked by those undergoing childbirth.[17] Within the collection, the women's *vitae* are arranged roughly in the order of the liturgical year, like other local collections that often rounded out major collections such as the *Golden Legend* or *South English Legendary* with their own offerings. As Mara and Blanton explain, the manuscript's *vitae* 'serve not only to put these nuns firmly in touch with their historical past but to provide models for their contemporary lives'. Most noticeably, it offers mini-genealogies of the saints between *vitae*, opening and sometimes closing each saint's narrative with acknowledgment of her known relatives.[18] The *vitae* of nuns note their affiliation early, sometimes alongside mention of the known natal family members.

Aside from the veneration that occurs in dedicated prayers, the legendary's only explicit appearance of Mary is her answer to the abbess Whitburgh's prayer in the form of two deer she sends to provide milk to the convent (fol. 67r). But MS 2604 opens with the *vitae* of two male saints whose mothers played an important role in socializing Mary into maternity, affirming childbed as a social space and childraising as a social exercise. As if to confirm the legendary's interest in Marian familial values, the *vita* of John the Baptist includes the story of his parents' infertility; the *vita* of John the Evangelist begins with a genealogy.[19] Given the generic conventions of the saint's birth narrative, to begin with John the Baptist is effectively to begin with Mary. The male saints' *vitae* incorporate holy versions of maternity through reference to their mothers.

Mary's first friend: Elizabeth

Cambridge 2604 opens with the annunciation to Elizabeth of John the Baptist, brought by the same angel who came to Mary.[20] Soon the news reaches her cousin:

> our blessyd lady that had than conceyued our lorde Ihesu Criste, hering say that hir cosyn Elizabeth was conceyued with childe, glad

and ioyfull she was that the reproue of the lawe was take from hir, cam ouer the hilles to hir and visited hir and, whan they mette to gedris, eche of hem gret other. And yit blessid Iohn, feling by the Holy Gost in his modir wombe that his lorde was come to him, for ioy he daunced and, as he myght, he gret him also.[21]

The Visitation, and this greeting scene in particular, was a wildly popular subject for devotional texts and visual art: two cousins, age gap notwithstanding, visibly pregnant with the holiest and second-holiest men ever to be born. Erler argues that English interest in the event began with the Feast of the Visitation in 1389 and continued for about sixty years; she has catalogued many of the places East Anglian women might see the Visitation depicted, including manuscript illuminations and church windows.[22] Elizabeth was considered a model for the infertile. Her touching Mary in greeting—in visual art, her hand variously caresses Mary's shoulder, abdomen, or breast—offers proof of their connection through genealogy and pregnancy. Elizabeth and Mary become spectacle because of whom they bear. Meg Twycross points out that the fetal John's being filled with Holy Spirit is what prompts Elizabeth's blessing of Mary: 'The children ... ventriloquise through their mothers'.[23] In visual art, the women's abdomens are often highlighted.

Yet what unfolds after the initial greeting in MS 2604 is less a meditation on the children than a focus on matrescence, a necessarily social process:

> This blessid virgyn, our lady Seynt Mary, bode stille with hir cosyn Elizabeth thre monthis aftir that she come and was to hir as a seruaunt. And whan the childe was borne, þat is the foure and twenty day of Iune, she was the first that sett honed vpon that childe and so was his godmodir and kept the childe in maner of a norse til the modir was vp.[24]

Mary's hands are the first to touch John, and she 'kept the childe in maner of a norse til the modir was vp'. This description is provocatively unclear, both 'norse' and 'vp': How long, and to what degree, was baby John 'kept' by Mary before Elizabeth took over? The author of MS 2604, leaving things vague, skips quickly ahead to John's adolescence, when he 'toke his leve of his modir' and escaped to the desert: what is important, now that Elizabeth has achieved matrescence and Mary has 'kept' the infant, is John's separation and independence from his mother. Other texts stretch or condense this moment. In the *Golden Legend*, Jacobus de Voragine pauses significantly at this point to highlight the parallels between John and Jesus. In the N-Town *Visit to Elizabeth* play, Mary tells Elizabeth that her three-month stay is 'yow to comforte and se' and to help take care of the baby.[25] Mirk's *Festial* explains that in doing so, she 'was mydwyff to Elizabeth, and toke Ion from þe erþe. And soo scho lernd all þat hur nedyd, forto come aȝeyne þe tyme þat hur sonne schuld be borne of hur'.[26] Mary, then, learned birthing techniques from Elizabeth, presumably so well that in many versions of the Nativity she was able to deliver her own child all alone.

Nicholas Love sets up the scene more suggestively. Before the birth, he describes Mary and Elizabeth, their children still in utero, sharing a bed: 'A lord god what house was þat, what Chaumbur & what bedde in þe whech duelleden to gedire & resteden so worþi Moderes with so noble sones, þat is to sey Marie & Elizabeth, Jesus & Jon'.[27] The husbands dwell nearby. When the infant John is born, Mary treats him as her own:

> Forþermore when þe tyme of Elizabeth was come she was liȝtnet & bare hir child, þe which in token of his grete holynes, oure lady first lift vp fro þe gronde, & after bisily diȝt & treted as it longet to him. And þe child as vndurstondyng what she was, sette hees eyene saddely vpon hire, & when she wolde take him to his modere *he turned his hed & his face to hire, als hauyng in hir al only his liking*, & she gladly pleide with him, & louely clipped & kissed him. And here mowe we se þe grete worþines of þis child, for þere was neuer none oþer before þat had so worþi a berere.[28]

John the Baptist prefers Mary to his own mother. The women's profuse sharing of the pre-partum experience here results in a blurring of maternal boundaries. Erler has shown how culturally important 'home visits' to elders were in late-medieval English culture for educating and socializing young women. Mary's offer to stay with Elizabeth results in a change in her status: she transforms from young girl to maternal authority, superior to Elizabeth, as a result of John's birth. Love credits the infant John for his discernment, but this is also the first occasion of Mary's maternal encroachment. The margins of maternal territories are always fluid. Mothers routinely feed, doctor, transport, discipline, and show affection for each other's children, a nearly-invisible nuance of parenting-based friendship that is often lost in popular portrayals of maternity but not, intriguingly, in these devotional narratives of Mary caring for Elizabeth's infant.[29] It is in this depiction of Mary doing motherwork for Elizabeth that we see her maternity being practiced, not merely embodied.

That maternal encroachment is hinted again in the second *vita* in MS 2604, that of John the Evangelist, which briefly features his mother, Mary Salome. Mary Salome is one of Anne's other daughters, often conflated in medieval understanding (despite careful distinction by clerical writers) with the Salome who doubted Mary's virginity at the Nativity. In MS 2604, she appears quite early in the text and is credited with John's clean living; he is 'vertuosly norysshed with his holy modir, Marie Salome, in childhode right clenly from al maner of vice'. The text does not mention the Crucifixion, where Christ famously presented his mother to John as her son in John 19:26–27. Rather, in what may be a claim of maternal territory, Mary Salome appears when her son John is to be imprisoned:

> I rede also that whan Mary Salome herde þat hir son Iohn was in prison and shulde be boyled in brennyng oyle, she went thedir ther he was for to speyke with him, *as tendernes axith of a modir to the childe*. And whan she come, he was outlawed. And than she went home ayen and passid deuoutly to God, whose holy body was beryed in a derk caue many yere vnto the tyme that Seynt Iames, hir son, was shewed by reuelacion where she laye. And he than translatid hir vnto the cite of Verulane in Campanye with moche reuerens and worship, where she dothe right gret miracles vnto this day.[30]

Mary Salome's act 'as tenderness axith of a modir to the childe' also establishes her maternal identity and territory. Showing up at jail is what mothers do. Readers of MS 2604 would certainly know the popular depiction of Mary Salome as someone who was also present and crucial at the Crucifixion, even as her own son was given by Christ to another woman.

By opening with texts that allow meditation on matrescence, MS 2604 speaks to interests that are gendered feminine even in its *vitae* of male saints. The texts are keenly Marian, as they focus precisely on the two women who were central to Mary's maternal social network. In doing so, the legendary cleverly alludes to Mary herself while also acknowledging the way that maternal labor is necessarily distributed beyond the natal family to figures who act as mother proxies—a useful concept for a convent's legendary to celebrate. This works well alongside the manuscript's emphasis on family relationships and genealogy in the narrative links between *vitae*. Still, according to several medieval sources, Mary will be alone during her own birthing experience. Erler has called attention to Love's emphasis on 'ordinary female conversation' at the Visitation.[31] In my reading, this normative affection only highlights that Elizabeth will not be similarly present for Mary. Mary is locked out of the 'conversation and good words' that Erler attributes to home visits for the remainder of her own pregnancy and parturition. This is partly because of her class: when Love tells us she lacks a servant to carry water, we should realize that she has no other women around. Mary does not have maternal peers present at her delivery. It is the Holy Spirit, not a birth assistant or relative, who teaches her to breastfeed, doubtless a knowledgeable source but hardly as warm and familiar as a chat with a cousin or girlfriend. We learn how that breastfeeding went from Bernard of Clairvaux, rather than from birth companions. Mary's solitary birth might be considered miraculous not only because it was painless but because no one was there to witness or share the experience. Salome eventually fills this role.

More troubling, given the historical discomfort with teenaged girls' bodies in public spaces, is that clerical writers admired Mary because she did not demand what was widely acknowledged as developmentally and situationally appropriate. Her age is very much a factor. Salome's verification of Mary's virginity is also a verification of her youth. *How can a virgin give birth* slides quickly into *how can this excellent mother be such a young girl?* Like the virgin martyrs, Mary's virginity is both tied inextricably to her youth and an identity that persists beyond it. Mary's solitude in childbed in *N-Town* and other late-medieval texts means that she does not take up a lot of space or human resources. She is tacitly praised for shrinking her body—a body that bears Christ!—to fit into a stable, for not requiring what readers felt was necessary for a healthy and manageable birth experience.

Salome

We see an alternate view in a small fourteenth-century alabaster relief that may have been part of an altarpiece in the Holy Trinity Church at Long Melford, a wool town in East Anglia. (See Plate 3.) It was found under the chancel floor during the eighteenth century, presumably hidden during the Reformation. Traces of vermillion and gold suggest the sculpture's former flamboyance; the bovine faces peeking out from under the bedskirts hint at its humor.[32] It is in many ways a conventional depiction of the Adoration of the Magi. Richard Marks describes this category of sculpture, known as 'Our Lady of Gesyn': the postnatal Mary reclining, Christ propped up on her thighs, often in the presence of visiting Magi or barn animals.[33] Here the Christ child appears to stand in a postpartum Mary's lap, stirring his new playthings in a proffered gold goblet. The nearest visitor warily tips his own crown at this infant king.

Everyone in the foreground, including Mary, gazes at the Christ child. But standing behind the furniture on which Mary reclines, her right hand arranging or fluffing a makeshift pillow, is a woman likely meant to be the doubting Salome. Mary's halo blocks Salome's line of sight so that she is unable to see the Christ child: she can only be looking at Mary. Salome's presence offers a counter-narrative within the scene. She is there not to nurse or worship the child, but to take care of his mother.

Her attention is, perhaps, a penance. Salome features in the *Protevangelium*, the *N-Town Nativity* play, Lydgate's *Life of Our Lady*, and other Nativity narratives not as a midwife or friend, but as a vocal doubter of Mary's bodily purity: she insists on verifying it with her own hand, in an impromptu cervical inspection that ignores Mary's bodily autonomy and results in Salome's hand shriveling, burning, or turning to clay.[34] She offers an anguished prayer of remorse. In language echoing Mary's act at Elizabeth's childbed, an angel instructs her to 'Put your hand to the infant, and carry it, and you will have safety and joy'. Salome obeys and leaves the cave cured. In Lydgate's *Life of Our Lady*, Salome goes dramatically public with her testimony, describing the miracle and affirming the virgin birth in the street to whoever will listen.

Gertrud Schiller notes that the doubting Salome was conflated with the 'believing midwife' and with Mary Salome, daughter of

Saint Anne and mother of John the Evangelist.[35] This conflation effectively establishes her as a companion to Mary throughout their adulthoods. According to Nicolas Love, it is also Mary Salome's son who is the groom at the wedding at Cana, although the text in MS 2604 disputes this.[36] Her son John is instructed to adopt Mary as his mother at the Crucifixion. In mystery plays, it is Mary Salome who shows up after the Crucifixion to get the word out about what's happened. In the *N-Town Play* 'Announcement to the Marys', the three Marys (Jacobi or Cleophas, Salome, and Magdalen) appear together as witnesses to the resurrection who share the news with the disciples. Mary Salome introduces herself as Christ's aunt, prepared to dress his wounds:

> To myghtfful God, omnypotent,
> I bere a boyst of oynement.
> I wold han softyd his sore dent,
> His sydys al abowte. (55–8)

Careful to explain her relation to Christ ('His modyr and I, systerys we be./Annys dowterys we be all thre—/Jhesu, we be thin awntys', 26–8), Mary Salome's description of her ointment suggests she acts as proxy for *Mary medica*: an othermother, reciprocating Mary's care for her son John. Mary Salome appears in a similar guise in the *Digby* 'Mary Magdalen' play, in which she suggests sharing news of the resurrection with Mary (1105–05), and in the *Townley* 'Resurrection' play, in which she calls Christ 'oure freynde' (398). Her roles in these post-Crucifixion scenes reframe the relationship: she has transformed from the doubter who invasively examines Mary's cervix to a full convert to Christianity within minutes of its origins. This gesture of solidarity contrasts with Salome's skeptical, uninvited touching of Mary and her punishment on contact in the period after Christ's birth.

With this in mind as we consider the Holy Trinity bas relief, it's clearer why Mary is, for Salome, the center. It will be Mary's voice that asks Jesus to replenish the wine supply at her son's wedding. It is Mary who is asked to step in for Mary Salome herself as Christ takes his last breaths. It is Mary's experience that will concern Mary Salome after the Resurrection. Salome's presence in this bas relief at Holy Trinity suggests that a church whose windows and brasses reinforce it as the very seat of the privileged, multigenerational elite is also interested in seeing Mary with a lifelong friend.[37] This permits a version of Mary and of maternity that is not rooted in the isolation of untouchable privilege but in the vulnerability of connection. Gail Gibson has explained how devoted Holy Trinity's congregants were to Anne and to family generally.[38] This is a community that believes even figures like Christ, like Mary, *need* a network of extended family.

The sculpture highlights, too, that birth is a social event, not only a medical or religious one. Scientific and documentary evidence of birth girdles indicates that they were lent out as circulating materials within social networks, and that their use, like that of other birth aids, would have required the help of other persons.[39] Only Mary experienced birth alone, and the presence of Salome in this image and in the medieval imagination suggests that medieval devotees wanted her to regain some of birth's social experience.[40] Birth requires dependence on other people: it is certainly possible to give birth alone, but most of us don't, and we often remember the social interactions, be they positive or negative, as much as the physical ones. Birth is a ritual at least as much as a physical process, and the performance of birth, like that of maternity, is socialized into us quite early.

Sue Niebrzydowski has suggested that the midwives' appearance at the Nativity in the N-Town and Chester plays 'brings Mary's experience closer to that of the women in the audience, and underlines the unique purity of the Mother of God'.[41] That certainly seems to be the goal in the Holy Trinity sculpture and other images that include Salome or other Marian birth supporters. However humanizing the midwives' presence might be, Mary's experience of birth is completely distinct from that of mortal birth mothers. In *Life of Our Lady* it's her engorged breasts, as much as the baby, that underscore the miracle of her virginity; her breast milk comes in immediately rather than a few days after the birth. *Life of Our Lady* also specifies that Mary can walk to the door immediately after giving birth. Depending on the source, she is understood to undergo a totally pain-free birth or to delay the pain by thirty-three years. In short, Mary is truly untouched by what was supposed to be the great bodily sacrifice of carrying and delivering the infant Christ. There is no reason, then, to associate the mothering (or 'motherwork') she might do with her own physiology. And if

Mary's mothering has little to do with her biological experience of birth, we need not expect other persons performing mothering work to have experienced their child's birth themselves. This division of biology from maternal status and work means that, for example, aunts can perform motherwork; fathers can perform motherwork; friends can perform motherwork; and in these legendaries, virgin martyrs can perform motherwork. This sharing of maternal duties is exemplified by Mary Salome, who introduces herself as an aunt and potential nurse of Christ shortly after her own adult child has been offered as proxy son to the Virgin Mary.

The depiction of Mary Salome as Mary's maternal peer upholds the Long Melford women's status quo of social networks and, potentially, power dynamics, tangled up in Mary's lifelong social and heart companion. The further development of the Holy Kindred—that is, Mary's relatives, including Mary Salome—in liturgical images and in the Digby, Towneley, and N-Town plays, gives Mary a whole extended family, complete with multiple maternal peers. We can see them in lay-sponsored screens at the Lady Chapel altar at St Helen's, Ranworth, Norfolk.[42] (See Plate 4.)

The figures are Mary Salome on the left, the Virgin Mary, and Mary Cleophas, next to Margaret of Antioch, patron saint of childbirth. In similar postures and sizes, with varying numbers of children, the women appear as equals. We can assume that Mary's sisters, unlike Mary, did experience pain in childbirth and the perceived shame of losing virginity, but even in their spiritual inequity they are presented as social and parenting peers.

Eamon Duffy first connected these images to the Bokenham list of patrons, calling them 'icons of the divine blessing on the earthiness of womanly things, of marriage and childbearing, of fruitfulness and heaven's blessing on woman's labour'.[43] Duffy's interpretation likely derives from the consensus that these images were viewed as part of a mother's churching ceremony, a ritual marking the return to public life after childbirth. The rood screens offer another means through which women could develop and demonstrate their devotional literacies.[44] Duffy's essentialist reading assumes that biological birth is required for mothering work, an implication that the images themselves discourage.[45] The mothers are, significantly, not only posed with their infants but are also gathered in each other's company and, nearby, the company of other saints. Parishioners approaching the screens would find them at eye-level, higher and larger than the screens of Christ's disciples a few steps away and equal in size to the adults at the John the Baptist chapel left of the chancel.[46] A devotee would not go to the Lady Chapel and be able to ignore all but one figure very easily; she would have to consider that they function as a group. At the Lady Chapel, that function is motherwork, for each other and to some degree for the viewer.

In acknowledging the maternity of the screens, then, we must include the connections and social support required for raising those children. The women are not only relatives of Christ or daughters of Anne but sisters, and carers for each other's children rather than only their own. The screens' placement is an homage not only to maternity but to sorority and camaraderie. Mary Cleophas, in particular, could not easily balance four children and their toys and emblems around her lap without help. The composition is framed, and her several children contained, not only by the boundary of the portrait but by the figures of the Virgin on the left and Margaret of Antioch on the right. Helpfully lacking the distraction of her own offspring, Margaret cuts her eyes at Mary Cleophas' children, her elongated cross positioned to corral them if necessary. The formality and stillness of the portraits should not belie what even first-time mothers would have learned deeply even by the time of their churching: that the infants control far more of that composition than their disproportionate size might visually suggest, that the presence of those sisters in the other panels keep the whole from entropy.

The children are not simply props to help identify the mothers. Like Christ nursing in Mary's arms, these boys also have spiritual destinies, and the mothers are shown growing them into their adult roles. The children of Mary of Cleophus play with a toy windmill and bubbles that humanize them beyond stereotype. Others also have identifying emblems. These are children who become recognizable adults: we know what the result of the mothering will be. Mary is surrounded by other maternal exemplars and encouragers: she is set among peers rather than acolytes, her daily tasks essentially the same as theirs. Motherhood is something regular people do, with recognizable tools and strategies.

The women are all sisters, related to each other through Anne; the children are all cousins of each other. We are looking at not a group of isolated mothers but a family gathering. This *family* of female saints and their children assemble to welcome and support other women into family-making.

Mary Salome's role as a post-Crucifixion witness means her presence alongside other Marys in the Ranforth screen is also a reminder of the Crucifixion and of Mary's sorrow, especially since we see foreshadowing in the children's trinkets of their destinies. Richard Marks explains that the simplest rood screen images depicted Mary and John at the foot of the rood beam.[47] Though serving a slightly different liturgical function, the Ranworth screens' grouping these other mothers and their infants as if in the Crucifixion moment centers the maternal peers of Mary alongside grief even as they celebrate social support. Duffy notes that other Lady Chapel screens usually depicted virgin martyrs.[48] The Ranworth ones highlight not martyrdom, but its maternal effects. The team of maternal peers and intercessors are valued not only for their support of Mary but because their experiences as mothers of martyrs are analogous to hers.[49]

Clearly East Anglian churchgoers wanted to restore social support to Mary's early mothering, as they depict her in the company of other women with children or infants. To express the need for companionship in birth and parenting experiences may seem to state the obvious after our own years of pandemic isolation. But it is a need missed by the clerics who composed so much Marian literature, and misrepresented by images of Marian maternity as a solitary role or achievement. Here we can distinguish a more palpable tension between the clerical party line on an isolated Mary and penitents' desire for her experience to mirror theirs—even affluent penitents who benefited from a status quo that protected property and bloodlines. The visual emphasis on Mary's need for friends humanizes her; it also humanizes the patrons who sponsored art so reflective of maternal experience. The screens here and, similarly, at Houghton St Giles near Walsingham acknowledge that successful birth and mothering require the help of a social network, and further, that the religious fabric of disciples and saints requires the work of mothers.

Holy Trinity and Arundel 327

Many of the texts in Arundel 327 were commissioned by women who attended Holy Trinity Church in Long Melford, the site of the sculpture of Salome at the Adoration of the Magi. Much of the fabric and the monuments of that church seem designed to confirm the local elite as locus of power: brasses of donors underfoot, clerestory windows with identifiable patrons overhead, Lydgatean verses inscribed on the wall. The Long Melford women's social and political networks have often been remarked by scholars of Arundel 327.[50] Some of their names still appear in stained glass and brasses in the church. In 1445, Bokenham began composing individual *vitae* about teenagers for these women, many of childbearing age. Most of them were already in the thick of mid-to-late childraising. Isabel Bourchier had borne a son in her first marriage at age fourteen; at age thirty-six and still mothering small children, she talked to Bokenham about Mary Magdalene at a party. Elizabeth Howard de Vere was thirty-five, also with small children; at age forty, Katherine Clopton Denston had a ten-year-old daughter. Another patron, Katherine Howard, was Elizabeth's mother. Agatha Flegge's daughter Joan was about to get married. These women and their patron saints were each other's maternal peers; engaging a local friar to write their favorite *vitae* was simply another step in deepening their own social ties.[51] Alexandra Verini points out that Bokenham's vita of Katherine is dedicated to two women, 'suggesti[ng] ... female friendship'.[52] Importantly, many of them also had cousins, sisters, and other relatives in convents.[53] Their enthusiasm for women's social bonds extends to their parish church's depiction of Mary.

Osbern Bokenham was a traveler, making multiple trips to Italy and at least one pilgrimage to Santiago de Compostela. In his prologue to Margaret's *vita*, Bokenham notes that Montefiascone, where Margaret's body rests, serves the Catalan Tribian wine rather than the Portuguese dessert wine Muscatel, which was popular in England while the Hundred Years' War hindered lighter French imports. He promises to divulge the story of Margaret's translation that is known there: 'who me not leue/Lete hym go thedyr & he shal it preue', he blusters.[54] He casually mentions having been in Venice when he benefitted from an item that had touched

Margaret's foot relic. Later, when summarizing Isabel Bourchier's family tree, Bokenham mentions her grandmother is from Spain and asks to delay writing the Magdalen *vita* that Bourchier has requested until he has finished his own pilgrimage to Compostela during jubilee year: despite his modesty tropes elsewhere, he claims as much right as she to piety and devotion in her ancestral home.

The compilation of his *vitae* in Arundel 327, however, is rootbound in tight constraints of place, the patrons of its contents mostly attending the same wool church in Long Melford, its beneficiary a nearby convent. The churchgoers at Holy Trinity didn't need another poet. They already had Lydgate down the road at Bury St Edmonds, composing poems to fill their books. Walsingham was a few hours' ride north; Mary was the patron saint of Clare Priory, Bokenham's home. The shrine at Holy Trinity's Lady Chapel would soon be larger than many whole churches in the area. From the mid-fifteenth century, as Bokenham was composing the Abbotsford legendary and Arundel 327 was read by a nearby convent, the Lady Chapel was soaked in Marian imagery, particularly the imagery of Marian maternal peers and 'friends'. A copy of Lydgate's 'Quis dabit' would be painted on the wall, the cognizance of loss spelled into churchgoers' Marian devotion.[55] The texts of Arundel 327, composed in the 1440s, anticipate this and the other Marian plays and images that revise the portrayal of Mary to include social context. A stained-glass window in Holy Trinity explicitly depicts female friendship, although it dates from much later in the fifteenth century, after Clopham's investments expanded and embellished the church's interior.[56]

To pause for a moment at Holy Trinity in 1447, with Thomas Burgh's compilation of Bokenham's *vitae* in Arundel 327, is to absorb the interest in Marian maternal peers and motherwork that was accumulating in churches and performances across East Anglia. The legendary's presentation of virgin martyrs as exemplars of friends help explain Margaret's presence in the Ranworth panels: maternal peers could cross the line between the quick and the dead.[57] While Bokenham's saints do not engage in 'home visits' to elder family members or friends, they do establish mentoring relationships: Katherine with the Queen, Margaret with her stepmother, Christine with her companions.[58] We can discern a flash of *imitatio Mariae* in their social connections that flesh out the relational aspect of maternity. This is sometimes camouflaged, since so many virgin martyrs are willing to eschew their natal family ties (and destabilize government authority) to protect their virginity. For Bokenham's patrons, the opposite is true, especially for those able to produce heirs. The support provided by maternal peers make such family-building fearsome in pro-Ricardian East Anglia: what might women sacrifice for their family members to accrue power? To them, a socially isolated Mary would look too politically vulnerable, a vulnerability only partly patched by the genealogies that appear in some of her narratives.

The collection is conscious of the importance of birth and its stabilizing social connections, for political alliances on the eve of the Wars of the Roses. Whom could one trust? How to make decisions about one's family in isolation? The period held various plausible definitions of 'family', as it did for 'friends'. Devotional texts often portrayed domesticity or family dynamics that were not necessarily rooted in actual practices of sending infants to wetnurses and children to court or the monastery, rather than sitting in a mother's lap to learn literacy, as Marian images depicted. But pious reading was otherwise useful. As Anne Dutton has noted, women in precarious political moments benefit from others' perception of their piety.[59] Equally pragmatically, devotional literacy was important to a group of women of childbearing age because the maternal mortality rate was so high. Maternity was not only a matter of life and death, but heaven and hell. Theological questions became much less abstract if one's neighbor, sister, or mother died in childbed.

Bokenham's *vita* of St Anne in Arundel 327 advises his readers to go read Lydgate's *Life of Our Lady*: 'But whoso wyl knowen, as I do gesse,/In Englysshe here laudes, lat hem looke/Of owre Ladyes Lyf Jhon Lytgates booke' (605–7). Mary may be excluded from Arundel 327 simply because Lydgate has already handled her, and Bokenham knows his readers' literary networks as well as the social one. We know that the household that owned Harley MS 4012, a text inscribed by Anne Wingfield and containing several short devotional texts including lives of Katherine, Margaret, and Anne, did in fact have a separate copy of Lydgate's *Life of Our Lady*.[60] At least two of Bokenham's patrons, Elizabeth de Vere and Isabell Bourchier, likely also owned a copy.[61] Bokenham's advice to go and read is not exclusive to those seeking more information about Mary: he also suggests in the same collection that readers go and read Capgrave to get Katherine's theological arguments, or the Gospels to learn more about the Magdalen, or Hippocrates about dysentery (in his *vita* of Lucy). He uses this technique frequently to make clear what material is outside his program, and Mary is viewed as slightly outside the scope, or at least the pages, of these legendaries. Even as he incites his own readers to consult multiple books, none of his saints read at all.[62] They are all brought to Christianity and to wisdom through socialization: a nurse, parents, the example of other saints.

Still, the social aspect of Marian maternity hovers over the devotional reading of Holy Trinity churchgoers. Among the network of other manuscripts with links to Bokenham's patrons, Suffolk, or Lydgate, we see further confirmation of birth as a social event.[63] Cambridge, Trinity College MS O.5.3 is a lectionary that contains several native saints (John of Beverley, Etheldreda, the translation of St Thomas, Kenelm, Oswald, Edith, and Wenefred) along with a selection of Marian texts (fol.157r ff); it includes Mary's visit to Elizabeth and an early focus on genealogy (158v). London, British Library, Yates Thompson MS 47, depicts the birth scene of Fremund with multiple visitors, male and female (fol. 61v). In the British Library Harley MS 2278 copy of the same poem, Edmund's birth is depicted with four midwives or birthing assistants, with gilted vessels and instruments (13v).[64] Gibson warns us not to read too much into such depictions: the 'woman's space of the birthing room enclosed women's bodies, women's discourse, and women's cultural performance but also existed, first and foremost, to produce the male children that were the essential links in the chain of male order and control'.[65] Yet the depiction of Mary as someone both as and with a maternal peer suggests pregnancy as a collective experience that passes the Bechdel test. Mary appears in Advocates Library Abbotsford MS, Bokenham's translation and expansion of the *Legenda Aurea*, which includes the Assumption, the Purification, and the Nativity along with documented theological explanations about why Mary had to be purified or why Christ was circumcised.[66] Abbotsford borrows Bernard's interpretation of Mary getting Elizabeth's annunciation as a means to 'encrees of hir ioye', partly because a miracle of infertility is matched by the miracle of a virgin birth. The text also explains how Mary's pregnancy erased 'the curs of al women'.[67]

The convent

No one who has written about Bokenham has ignored the social and political networks of his readers and patrons, a crucial piece of the context needed to understand the collection. He actively encourages readers' interest in his chatty, name-dropping introductions and epilogues. But we have Arundel 327 because Thomas Burgh was creating a compilation for a convent on behalf of his sister. In fact, if we accept Bokenham's account, it's Burgh who first requested he write the life of Margaret, patron saint of safe childbirth, the text that ultimately provoked the attentions of all the other patrons.[68] It is unclear whether Burgh's sister was still living at the time of his compilation of the manuscript; it is possible that, given Burgh's previous request for a life of Margaret and his subsequent request for prayers for her, she died in childbirth. No one talks about this unnamed sister of Thomas Burgh, but her part in the conception of Arundel 327 calls further attention to its emphasis on family relationships.[69]

While we know intimate details of Bokenham's patrons' social status and book ownership and even reproductive desires, we know little of Burgh's sister: only the saints in the legendary meant for a convent with which she may or may not have been affiliated outside her brother's dedication. Of the scholarly attention given to the legendary, the only mentions of the conventual audience have been with the purpose of identifying the convent.[70] A.I. Doyle has suggested that the nuns in question were the Franciscans of Aldgate and Denny, situated just northeast of Cambridge at a convent Margery Kempe visited in chapter 84 of her *Boke*.[71] I submit that another possibility is the Augustinian convent of Campsey Ash, also in Suffolk, a high-status convent that owned other vernacular legendaries and for whom the Virgin Mary was patron. My interest in what might have appealed to the conventual audience of Arundel 327 in addition to the readership of the original individual lives is an attempt to make sense of the manuscript that is extant rather than to speculate on booklets we no longer have. For example, the prefaces and names that are missing from the Abbotsford manuscript are left within the *vitae* of Arundel 327. These offered important intelligence to the convent: a list of locals demonstrably willing to sponsor pious activity was perhaps as useful to the nuns as a freshly translated legendary. The manuscript's marginal annotations identifying female patrons seems to confirm this value.

The *vitae* avoid of-the-moment cultural references apart from revealing personal details of patrons' lives. As Simon Horobin and Karen Winstead have each noted, the Abbotsford lives strip away even these details.[72] Writing in the 1440s, Bokenham assumed his *vitae* would be shared with other family members and future generations; they needed to be universally appealing. He was concerned with his patrons' and his religious house's legacies. He knew books had lasting influence, given the East Anglian regard of books as devotional objects and his own status as a frequent beneficiary of estate distribution. Bokenham was essentially writing textual heirlooms, a conservative endeavor, while Burgh was doing something relatively innovative by creating a women's legendary. What did Bokenham consider timeless? We find this in all the contemporary touches Arundel 327 lacks. There is no articulated threat of Lollardy or potential text-based heresy. There's no mysticism here, nor even private, internal voices: all of the saints' divine messages are witnessed by others, sometimes with accompanying miracles. Accordingly, Bokenham trims out doctrine from Margaret's interrogation of demons and Katherine's theological arguments. He leaves out the postmortem miracles from this collection that, as Horobin has shown, are in the Abbotsford. He makes only a vague gesture toward contemporary events in his references to 'witches', which itself suggests how well-read Bokenham must have been: it was only in the 1430s that witchcraft practices began to be codified in clerical texts; the most well known, *Hammer of Witches*, wouldn't appear until over twenty years after his death.[73] Rather than clever allusions to current events, Bokenham develops a focus on saints as family members and on the servants and witnesses that surround them to form community. This is true of the prologues and epilogues as well as the main content of the saints' lives. Even Thomas Burgh refers to himself as Bokenham's 'son'.

Burgh saw the focus on these social networks and attempts to build community as transcending convent walls. Both the conventual family and multi-layered social networks, not to mention the saints themselves, would be important to reading nuns. In a place where a book would be collectively owned, the intergenerational appeal of Bokenham's *vitae* would be desirable. Erler has argued that 'family connections were important in the movement of women's books' and observes that for enclosed women

> Acquisition of the book is itself meritorious, a preliminary to virtuous reading, and that preparatory act will radiate its benefits backward in time to the abbess' parents and forward to future members of her house. Book purchase is placed in a context doubly familial: both the abbess' natal family and her religious one are invoked in a way which makes it impossible to view reading as individual work.[74]

This must have been especially true for Burgh's sister, whose brother had the book copied for his sisters in religion, thus blurring some of the boundaries of enclosed life. Coming as they did from aristocratic or noble families, the nuns would be accustomed to thinking of themselves in terms of family connections. Many were still teenagers, much like the saints in the manuscript, their natal family relationships still an important means of social and emotional security despite their enclosure. Collective reading was one step toward the social cohesion that depended on intergenerational alliances, a gentle socialization into conventual identity that functions similarly to the matrescence we have already seen in Marian narrative.[75]

The legendary

Fittingly, almost as explicitly as Cambridge 2604, Arundel 327 defines its subjects in terms of family relationships.[76] Parents of the saints are often introduced before the saint herself, and grandparents and siblings make appearances as well. In Bokenham's virgin martyr legends, the virgins generally regard Christ as 'father' rather than the 'lover' he is in other versions of the lives. Those who do regard Christ as a replacement for pagan suitors (such as Faith, Dorothy, and Katherine) call him 'spouse'—a slightly more erotically neutral term—rather than 'lover'.[77] Family relationships, positive or negative, are central to many of the *vitae*, and readers are invited to see the saints as family members first and saints second.[78] The variety and flexibility of the natal family relationships represented here emphasize the saint's position as a family member, broadly defined, while maintaining that the metaphorical family of Christ supersedes biological ties. Once the saints are established as natal family members, they begin the transition to the metaphorical—and, in the context of the legendary, superior—family of Christ. While this pattern holds throughout the collection, I want to consider Margaret and Anne together, as they are first in the legendary, the pages decorated more sumptuously and copied by different scribes than the rest of the manuscript. Both Margaret and Anne were particularly cherished in East Anglia, and their roles as patron saints of safe childbirth confirm the collection's interest in maternity. Margaret and Anne's *vitae* establish the themes of filial roles and community that ground the whole collection in the atmosphere already established at Long Melford and attend to birth, infertility, motherhood, and parentage.

Margaret

Margaret appears in multiple texts and liturgical settings throughout late-medieval East Anglia; she is precious not only for her maternity but also her role as shepherd in an economy rooted in wool. Accordingly, Burgh opens the legendary with Margaret's birth to happy pagan parents and a public celebration in her honor. Margaret's father's enthusiasm over her birth does not develop into unconditional love for her. Here as elsewhere in the legendary, pagan familial love is misplaced and weak compared with the ties of Christianity. By the time Margaret's mother dies—and here, unusually, Margaret's mother does survive her birth—Margaret is more loyal to the nurse who taught her Christianity than to her father, who disowns her upon learning of her conversion. Margaret thus begins the second stage of her *vita* with no biological family ties: she is loyal only to her nurse and her belief in God. She has abandoned the natal definition of 'family' for a metaphorical Christian one.

Olibrius' first question of Margaret concerns her bloodline rather than her beliefs. Her attempt to evade the question by claiming Christianity results only in his repeating it ('"I aske of what kynrede thou art", quod he', 516). In clarifying Margaret's response, Olibrius refers to his own ancestry, noting that Christ is he 'whom that my fadrys crucyfye' (521). They agree that his ancestors crucified Christ. The reader familiar with Marian miracle stories might recall that Jews, not pagans or demons, were accused of killing Jesus, so this interpretation of Olibrius's faulty genealogy becomes something of an inside antisemitic joke. Margaret further condemns him for 'Sathanas werkys euere doost …/Thy fadyr' (627–8). Olibrius' ideological opposition to Margaret is confirmed by his genetic history: possibly Jewish and son of Satan, he cannot overcome his bad breeding.

Similarly, in Margaret's prison cell, her demon visitor refers to the dragon as his 'brothyr' and mentions his 'ospryng'. Margaret condemns him to go 'hom to thy kyn' as punishment. Neither Olibrius nor the demon has the option of choosing another definition of family: their evil is fixed and hereditary. In contrast, Margaret's own natal birth to pagan parents is portrayed as an inconvenience that can be overcome. The *vita* thus lays the framework for the message that builds throughout the legendary, to culminate in Elizabeth of Hungary's rejection of her own children in favor of Christian servitude: a Christian can and should [be willing to] abandon and replace her worldly biological family with Christ and fellow Christians. Margaret makes her choice explicit just before the appearance of the dragon in her cell, when she prays to see her enemy:

> Behold me, lord, thou art iuge.
> Doughtyr of my fader, and he hath me
> For the forsakyn, and so hym haue y.
> *Hens aftyr wil thou my fadyr be!* (673–6, emphasis mine)

In other versions of the *vita*, this prayer simply marks the move from Margaret's public encounter with Olibrius to that with the dragon in her cell, but in Arundel 327, it indicates her official shift from earthly family to heavenly one: not only has she rejected her biological father, but she declares that God will replace him. As a result of this prayer, she becomes the daughter of God. The curtailing of her interrogation of the demon highlights this change in emphasis.

The *vita* also highlights the importance of discerning good counsel, a requirement for building a strong support network for Margaret's metaphorical matrescence. At one point Margaret tells Olibrius she rejects his advice ('how lytyl that I sette by/Alle thy profyrs … For from the weys of trewthe neuere wyl y'). Margaret continually receives unsolicited bad advice from onlookers and from Olibrius himself, who urges her to 'lyst what I seye' (555). Previously she had asked God to send her an angel to advise her how to answer him. She demonstrates that, despite her youth, she is able to build a community of chosen family as she moves toward her martyrdom, knowing not to accept faulty counsel or the wrong peers.

Anne

Gibson has described the East Anglian cult of Anne as 'an undisguised celebration of family ties and the relationships of human kinship'. Noting that Holy Trinity had a St Anne altar, she argues that the veneration of Anne showed a belief in the family as venue of holiness and that Anne's portrayal as wealthy permitted a 'sanctity envisioned as a busy, pious, and comfortable life'.[79] Similarly, Carole Hill argues that the Marian cult at Walsingham should not be seen as distinct from the regional cult of Anne.[80] More specifically, Bokenham's *vita* of Anne is not only about choosing family but grounding a marriage or family unit in the faith community, an interpretation that would be especially appealing to a convent. It establishes that maternal peers can be retroactive, intergenerational, and beyond the grave, class, or a marriage. Bokenham's stated purpose in writing Anne's story was to request a son for his patron, Katherine Denston, who already had a daughter named Anne. The tale's focus on a would-be father's emotional response to social isolation offers a gentle reframing of infertility and the possibility of male maternity. In addition, her parents are commended for raising her properly. Arundel 327 handles parents who honor God quite differently from martyrs' pagan parents, whose daughters turn out holy in spite of rather than thanks to them. Bokenham's prologue invokes Mary, 'perles prencesse, of uirginyte/Synguler gemme' (1481–82) and 'of synners souereyn medeycyne' (1506) for help in telling her mother's story better, a prayer pointing out that Anne breastfed Mary for three years.

The inclusion of Anne in Bokenham's legendary to the near-exclusion of Mary is further testimony to the emphasis on family ties: Anne is important *because* she is biologically related to other holy people. But this is clumsily affirmed. In the opening of her *vita*, Bokenham praises Anne as 'commendyde' (1509) for a family tree that actually traces her husband Joachim's ancestors. The genealogy of Mary is absent from the Gospels but is, as Jacobus argues, the only possible venue through which Christ's lineage could be traced to David.[81] Jacobus lists Anne's other relatives, such as her sister Hismeria, Elizabeth's mother, and the grandchildren depicted on the Ranworth screens. Mirk includes multiple Annes in his 'genealogy', specifying which bore Christ's mother. Like Jacobus, Mirk only briefly mentions Anne's multiple husbands and daughters rather than offering any explanatory narrative. In his *vita* of Anne, Bokenham provides a genealogy of Mary that runs in both chronological directions, from David to the Holy Kinship of Anne's descendants. Most jarringly, Anne's father, unnamed in *Legenda Aurea*, is here 'Ysachar' (1514) or Isachar (1622), the same name as the high priest Isakar (1679) who casts Joachim from the temple, an eerie echo that is not in the other sources. The assignment of Anne to the tribe of Levi and the genealogical opening suggests this overlap in nomenclature is intentional, with Anne's father the priest who ostracizes Joachim, but it seems unnecessarily hurtful: Katherine Denston's own father died in 1446, and she never got the son she wanted. Why highlight a father who rejects his daughter's offering because of infertility? Perhaps it was meant to contrast with Joachim's own sensitivity and generosity.

Bokenham had several choices of how to tell the story of Anne's life. There are widely varying versions in the *Legenda Aurea*, in Mirk's *Festial*, in the stanzaic *Life of St Anne* taken from the Gospel of Pseudo-Matthew, even in Lydgate's invocation to her, though his attention to Anne and Joachim in *Life of Our Lady* was minimal.[82] The central conflict of Anne's *vita* is in how she and Joachim handle their twenty-year infertility. Most of the other fifteenth-century versions include substantial description of Mary's childhood and sometimes Christ's. Bokenham's innovation is in shaping the narrative to give as much attention to Anne's emotional state as to Joachim's. He edits the narrative to focus on their feelings about loneliness and isolation rather than the infertility itself. He mentions Mary only minimally. A few years later, the authors of the versions in Harley MS 4012, Chetham MS 8009, and *N-Town* would omit or condense Anne's experience while retaining or amplifying Joachim's.[83]

In all of the versions, Joachim bears more of the sudden public shame of decades-long infertility than does Anne. He fears additional rejection from his neighbors so much that he self-imposes exile from his wife. In Mirk, when a priest rejects his offering because he has no children, 'he went hom wepyng'. Jacobus also has him shamed in the temple 'among men who begot sons'.[84] The *N-Town Mary Play* slightly alters this dynamic by removing the element of surprise: Joachim knows before going to temple that he will be judged. Anne blames herself for Joachim's prophetic anticipation of the priest's scorn: 'Youre swemful wurdys make terys trekyl down be my face./Iwys, swete husbond, *the fawte is in me*'.[85] But Anne's claim of responsibility is absent from Bokenham. Joachim's distress is not at the years-long infertility itself, but in the denial of temple community, the exile from peers with children. Abashed, he goes to stay with his herdsmen for several months, seeking a new community among them as refuge from those who would shame him for infertility. He trains his energies on the sheep that he raises for charity, leaving Anne to mourn without news from him for five months.

In his absence, Anne receives an annunciation about 'how þe fruht of þi body in reuerence/& honour schal be & in mennys mende/Thorgh alle kynreddes to þe werdys ende' (1788–90). Shaken, Anne retreats to her bed in prayer for twenty-four hours. When she chastises her maid, 'which awt, me thynkyth, my confort han be' (1808) for not helping her, the maid insults her: 'Thow god thy wombe with barynesse/Hath shet, & thyn husbonde takyn a-way/Wenyst þu these myscheus I myht redresse?/Nay, nay!' (1813–16). The maid's retort is a subtle reminder that Anne lacks access to the Christian patrons of fertility who appear in Arundel 327 and *could* help her, such as Mary Magdalen, Margaret, Agnes, or, ironically, herself. She must seek comfort from an angel or her maid instead. As the Ranforth screens' grouping of Mary with her sisters and the virgin martyr Margaret suggests, maternal peers need not be social or even mortal peers. Anne's maid, falling short of the task of supporter, may be an unsympathetic companion, but Anne's complaint implies that proximity matters more than status when constructing a social network.

There is no such confrontation with a servant in Mirk or Jacobus, nor does it appear in later narratives that describe Anne's conception. Bokenham's choice to include this incident from Pseudo-Matthew raises the issue of inadequate maternal peers. If we continue reading in *Legenda Aurea* or the life of Anne that appears in Minnesota MS Z822 N81, we learn that the temple assigns the newly wed Mary a set of virgin helpers who turn out to be similarly poor substitutes for maternal peers.[86] Doing textile-based handwork with Mary, the virgins grow jealous of her skill and criticize her.[87] When Joseph learns Mary is pregnant, he blames the virgins for giving another man access to Mary. They defend her, but it is clear that the demands of Mary's situation are more than they can manage. This failure, coupled with Anne's humiliation by her maid, suggests there are limits to who can participate as maternal peers. I suggest those limits are rooted in age rather than class: given their own patterns of household employment, East Anglian readers would have expected the household servant, like Mary's virgin companions, to be a teenaged girl. Anne's maid speaks without the measure of compassion or experience we might expect from a longtime member of the household.

In contrast, gender is not a determining factor in who can be a worthy maternal peer to Anne, or more broadly, who can act maternal. Joachim's behavior speaks to bell hooks' pragmatic proposal that 'the word paternal should share the same meaning' as maternal.[88] He takes on emotional labor usually coded as maternal. It is Joachim, not Anne, who is publicly shamed for not having a child. In fact, his exile equates masculinity with parenthood. He explains his sadness to the angel in terms of virility. If his wife doesn't bear 'fruht', he's not a man, an unexpectedly vulnerable disclosure: 'I wante þe argumentes of a man; & whan men be reknyd I am lefth behynde' (1833–34). He expresses despair at the resulting social isolation. The couple have been infertile for twenty years; only when Joachim is denied fellowship by Isakar is he utterly distraught. Joachim exacerbates this exclusion by isolating from his wife. His decision to continue working with his sheep for charity suggests his exile has prompted him to put wider community needs over his personal ones. This signals that he is ready for parenthood, and they are both rewarded with a child. Perhaps ironically, Mary's miraculous conception in Joachim's physical absence restores his masculinity, the status that allows him social and spiritual connection.

By the time the couple are reunited, we have seen both Joachim and Anne engaging and commiserating with angels, herdsmen, and a handmaid, creating or attempting spontaneous pockets of brief community among unexpected peers until they are again home together in full temple fellowship. This anticipates the many virgin martyr narratives to come in Arundel 327 that will make a feature of saints creating spontaneous communities from witnesses and new converts. The text implies that even a companionate marriage is not enough on its own; the couple must also meet the approval of their temple community. This ensures Mary is born into a healthy social network, fully integrated into the life of her house of faith. Along with the social costs of infertility, the *vita* highlights the portability of maternal emotional labor. It also spotlights a father's active involvement in building a family and raising a child, opening with Joachim's painful isolation and closing as he waits with Anne for little Mary to mount the temple steps.

Mary's only appearance in the *vita* is as their independent three-year-old daughter. Seemingly unfamiliar with toddlers, Bokenham marvels that the tiny Mary climbs the temple stairs without looking at her parents. Both *Legenda Aurea* and the stanzaic *Life* clarify that this behavior is remarkable because the child, only recently weaned, ascends the staircase to be raised at the temple. Bokenham's omission of this explanation and of the popular elision of Anne's *vita* into Mary's childhood allows the child's agency to parallel that of the virgin martyrs in the rest of the legendary: she moves independently of her parents, seeking a new family in the community that supports her new religious goals.

Chosen family

In keeping with a maternal theme, Bokenham sometimes restores the mothers who are dead or absent in other versions, sometimes with a flash of humor. Christine's mother is dead in most versions of her *vita*, but in Arundel 327 she exclaims, 'thynk, dowghtir, þat I/Ten monethis þe bare in my body,/And wyth grete peyn into þis world þe brought'. Christine eventually answers, 'go hens, & labour nomore,/Clepe me not doughter' (2414–16; 2435–6). Otherwise, the text snaps quickly into a traditional virgin martyr dynamic, with a natal family that is not only insufficient but actively bad. The first half of Christine's vita features one-on-one conflict with her father Urban, who accuses her of witchcraft, an accusation that persists through her encounters with Zyon and Julian, particularly when snakes cling to her breasts. Christine, for her part, accuses each of them of being Satan's son. Christine's *imitatio Mariae* is not immediately obvious, although she does live in a high, gloomy tower in the company of twelve other virgins, much like Mary in Pseudo-Matthew's depiction of her early marriage. But then both Christ and God call her 'daughter': Christine slips out of her natal family and into a spiritual one. While torturing her, Julian orders Christine's breasts cut off. Milk flows out instead of blood, 'in tokyn of clennes of uirginite' (3017). A voice from heaven invites her, 'my doughtir dere', to ascend. Julian carries on the torment, demanding her tongue be cut out. In a perversion of Mary's projectile lactation on Bernard of Clairvaux, Christine spits a piece of her own tongue at Julian so that he is blinded. He is not only rejected but condemned to see partially and wrongly.

Other *vitae* in Arundel 327 offer examples of Christian 'family' acting as substitutes for biological ones. In the story of Faith, a young man named Caprasius is inspired by Faith's torment to follow her example. Faith and Caprasius are joined by two brothers, and the four of them act as a family unit, encouraging one another in converting others and driving the tyrant Dacien mad. Lucy, who maintains a healthy relationship with her biological mother, is also described as the 'sister' to Agatha, at whose grave she prays. Thus even the saints who do not explicitly claim Christ as father or spouse benefit from the metaphorical family formed by those who identify as Christian. In a departure from what is typical in virgin martyrs' lives, Bokenham's saints' biological families do not *have* to conflict with the spiritual one. In the vitae of Ursula, Cecilia, Lucy, and Elizabeth of Hungary, and to a lesser extent those of Mary Magdalene, Dorothy, and Agnes, the saints' families contribute to their success as holy women rather than acting as barriers. Elizabeth of Hungary lives out her role as daughter, wife, and mother in a supportive domestic environment before abandoning those roles for her metaphorical family. In each case, the saint benefits from familial support, but ultimately achieves true holiness by shedding her natal family identity in favor of identity with Christ. These are subtler, gentler versions of Mary's post-Crucifixion turn from Judaism to Christianity.

Such an emphasis on *chosen* family shifts slightly from the 'family ties' Gibson identified as an important theme in the legendary, particularly if we consider how maternal peers function in narratives of Marian maternity. The matrescence that Mary undergoes under the tutelage of Elizabeth allows Mary and, by extension, the saints to benefit from the often-invisible motherwork completed by others to help train them. Conventual readers of Arundel 327 would certainly be familiar with the maternal labor of socializing young novitiates into sisterhood. And Bokenham's first patrons were surrounded by visual evidence of the importance not only of maternity but of the sharing of motherwork. Burgh's compilation of Bokenham's texts avoids insisting on the compulsory rejection of one's natal family, but maintains that childraising and community-building happen via the collective labor of chosen family.

Pain

I want to close by briefly attending to pain as an element that links the concerns of Chapter 4 to the discussion in Chapter 3. Sara Ahmed describes pain as necessarily a social experience: we want it witnessed; we want to divulge it to others. It is even, she suggests via Sartre, what 'attaches this body to the world of other bodies, an attachment that is contingent on elements that are absent in the lived experience of pain'.[89] Pain not only becomes a binding element in human relationships but actively *requires* those other bodies in order to be fully experienced. By this metric, Mary could have an isolated Nativity in part because she had no pain to share. Her connections with Elizabeth and Salome give her a means to experience pain-based attachment. Mary is witness to the pain of Elizabeth's birth and to the pain in Salome's hand. In turn, the attendance of her sisters at her 'second birth', the Crucifixion, allows their witnessing of her pain.

If the pain of childbirth is a metaphor of choice in Douce 114, the sharing of that pain experience may be a useful way to think about the social emphases in Cambridge MS 2604 and Arundel 327. What is shared by readers of Bokenham's narratives is not only a connection to him or to their church's social and political circles, but the pain of childbirth, the pain of infertility, the potential pain of transfer from natal to sororal family and identity, shared and witnessed by others. Every acknowledgment of birth is also an acknowledgment of a pain that binds them socially and, perhaps, spiritually to one another. Mary's pain, as *dolorosa*, was certainly understood to be deeper, more unknowable. But Bokenham's frequent acknowledgments of his own bodily aches and pains, his aging, and even his preoccupations with Margaret's foot show he, too, is thinking of the consequences of life in a body and recognizing the value of sharing them. The *vitae* themselves focus on the pain of the suffering female body. These are the stories of young women who, like Mary and like the mystics of Douce 114, also suffered publicly witnessed bodily pain to advance readers' devotions or piety.

Notes

1 This poem also appears in Lambeth Palace Library MS. 853, c. 1430 and in Trinity College, Cambridge, R.3, 19. Printed in *Codex Ashmole 61: A Compilation of Popular Middle English Verse*, ed. George Shuffelton (Kalamazoo, MI,: Medieval Institute Publications, 2008).
2 Riddy argues that the fictional construct makes sense only if it's impossible for a daughter to learn simply by observation and example, which suggests a physical separation of mothers and daughters. Riddy and others have made clear that the medieval household did not equal the family as we now understand it; there was not a middle English term for 'family' to indicate an affective group as we now use it. Yet the poem's frequent addresses to a 'dere doughter' suggests an idealized filial relationship that accords with such a concept. See Felicity Riddy, 'Mother knows best: Reading social change in a courtesy text', *Speculum* 71.1 (1996), 66–86.
3 On this point, see the review of the field in Johnson, 'Divisions'.
4 We still see the effects of these concerns in architecture, landscape design, and urban planning, as most public spaces discourage the presence of teenagers. These attempts (and sometimes policies) disproportionately affect adolescent girls. The problem has been addressed directly by Rebecca Rubin and Angelica Åkerman at White Arkiteter in Stockholm and by Susannah Walker and Imogen Clark through their charity Make Space for Girls (makespaceforgirls.co.uk). See also Patty Eubanks Owens, 'No teens allowed: The exclusion of adolescents from public spaces', *Landscape Journal* 21.1 (2002),

156–63; and Sara Brunelle et al., 'Teens in public spaces and natural landscapes: Issues of access and design', *Handbook of Adolescent Development Research and its Impact on Global Policy*, ed. Jennifer E. Lansford and Prerna Banati (Oxford: Oxford University Press, 2018), 361–79.
5 Erler, 'Home visits'.
6 Dana Raphael provides an accessible definition in 'Matrescence, becoming a mother, a 'new/old' rite de passage', in *Being Female: Reproduction, Power, and Change*, ed. Dana Raphael (Berlin: De Gruyter, 1975), 65–71.
7 Catherine Sanok, *Her Life Historical: Exemplarity and Females Saints' Lives in Late Medieval England* (Philadelphia: University of Pennsylvania Press, 2007).
8 Sheingorn traces medieval approaches to Christ's genealogy from patrilineage in the eleventh century to the fifteenth-century development of the Holy Kinship, which centers Anne's extended family and support network, to the sixteenth-century focus on the Holy Family, which shifts to the idealization of the nuclear family in its centering of Joseph. See Sheingorn, 'Appropriating the Holy Kinship: Gender and family history', in Ashley and Sheingorn, *Interpreting Cultural Symbols*, 169–98.
9 Erler's *magnum opus* on the circumstances of women's reading and the movement of their books offers meticulous analysis of the connections among them. See Erler, *Women, Reading, and Piety in Late Medieval England* (Cambridge: Cambridge University Press, 2002).
10 See A.S.G. Edwards, 'Fifteenth-century English collections of female saints' lives', *The Yearbook of English Studies* 33 (2003), 131–41.
11 See Takševa.
12 Jessaca B. Leinaweaver, 'Practice Mothers', *Signs* 38 (2012), 405–30, especially at 424–5.
13 See Patricia Hill Collins, 'The meaning of motherhood in Black culture and Black mother-daughter relationships', *Double Stitch: Black Women Write About Mothers and Daughters*, ed. Patricia Bell-Scott. (New York: Harper Perennial, 1993), 42–60; and Stanlie M. James, 'Mothering: A possible Black feminist link to social transformation', *Theorizing Black Feminism: The Visionary Pragmatism of Black women*, ed. Stanlie James and A.P. Busia (New York: Routledge, 1999), 44–54.
14 Collins, 'Meaning', 45.
15 Knott, 'Theorizing'. See Sarah Blaffer Hrdy, *Mothers and Others: The Evolutionary Origins of Mutual Understanding* (Cambridge, MA: Harvard University Press, 2009).

16 For an edition, see *'Lyves and dethes' for Medieval English Nuns: An Edition of the Saints' Lives in CUL, MS Additional 2604*, ed. Veronica O'Mara and Virginia Blanton, MWTC (Brepols, forthcoming).
17 Veronica O'Mara and Virginia Blanton, 'Cambridge University Library, Additional MS 2604: repackaging female saints' lives for the fifteenth-century English nun', *The Journal of the Early Book Society for the Study of Manuscripts and Printing History* 13 (2010), 237–47, at 242, 245n. 5. On Denny, see note 71 below.
18 Fifteen of the nineteen female saints' *vitae* do so. This emphasis on family history is typical of the *vitae* of preconquest English saints, of course, but it is also a feature of the universal saints included in 2604.
19 This was possibly the same convent that received Burgh's legendary of Bokenham's saints; see note 71. Bookending the female saints with male saints calls attention to the gender of the women's legendary within.
20 Fol. 1r. 'his modir was warnyd for to bringe forth a chyld in hir olde age of the same aungell that our lady was gret with'. The author adds this detail, which is not in the *Golden Legend*. Transcriptions from this manuscript are my own, but Mara and Blanton's edition should appear in print shortly before this volume; I refer readers to their edition if it is available.
21 Fols 2v–3r.
22 Erler, 'Home visits'.
23 Meg Twycross, 'Kissing cousins: The four daughters of God and the Visitation in the N. Town *Mary play*', *Medieval English Theatre* 18 (1996), 99–141, at 103.
24 Fols 2v–3r.
25 *The N-Town Plays*, ed. Douglas Sugano (Kalamazoo, MI: Medieval Institute Publications, 2007), play 13, line 74.
26 *Mirk's Festial*, EETS. Vol. 96, 107.
27 Love, *Mirror*, 33.
28 *Ibid.*, emphasis mine.
29 Lucy Allen-Goss suggested to me that these passages' possible hints of cross-feeding may also have theological implications. Private communication.
30 Fol. 13v.
31 Erler, 'Home visits', 268.
32 Cows often show up in depictions of the Magi, as do patrons in the form of female figures.
33 Marks observes that about twenty of those surviving are alabaster and in parish churches; they seem to have been exported to north Germany and Poland, as well. See Marks, *Image and Devotion*, 143–7.

34 The *Protevangelium* provides the bones of the Salome narrative: she first appears when the midwife emerges from the Nativity cave to exclaim the miracle of a virgin birth. Salome declares that 'unless I thrust in my finger, and search the parts, I will not believe that a virgin has brought forth'. See Lily Vuong, *The Protevangelium of James* (Eugene, OR: Cascade Books, 2019), 99–100. Late medieval versions of this scene vary: in *N-Town*, her hand withers and turns to clay; in Lydgate's *Life of Our Lady* it dries up; in both she is told to touch the hem of the baby's garment. In the Chester play, her hand is rendered useless even before she begins the cervical test.
35 Gertrud Schiller, *Iconography of Christian Art*. Vol. 1, trans. Janet Seligman (Greenwich, CT: New York Graphic Society, 1971), 64.
36 Love, *Mirror*, 79.
37 The Coptic tradition, too, imagines Mary and Salome with an enduring friendship. See the Introduction to Wendy Belcher, *The Life and Struggles of Our Mother Walatta Petros: A Seventeenth-century African Biography of an Ethiopian Woman* (Princeton: Princeton University Press, 2015).
38 Gibson, 'Saint Anne'.
39 Sarah Fiddyment et al. 'Girding the loins? Direct evidence of the use of a medieval English parchment birthing girdle from biomolecular analysis', *Royal Society Open Science* 8.3 (2021), 202055.
40 Alaya Swann discusses the training and roles of midwives but does not dwell on the social aspect of their presence at births in '"By express experiment": the doubting midwife Salome in late medieval England', *Bulletin of the History of Medicine* 89.1 (2015), 1–24.
41 Sue Niebrzydowski, *Bonoure and Buxum: A Study of Wives in Late Medieval English Literature* (Oxford: Peter Lang, 2006), 159.
42 A similar set of screens is set up left of the rood screen at Houghton St Giles, the last stop for pilgrims en route to the shrine at Walsingham: Mary's aunt Emeria with, possibly, Servatius; Mary Salome with James and John; Mary and Christ; Mary Cleophas with Joseph, Jude, James, and Simon; Elizabeth with John the Baptist; and Anne teaching Mary to read. In such a small church, the images of intergenerational maternal peers with their children are even more dominant.
43 Eamon Duffy, 'Holy maydens, holy wyfes', *Studies in Church History* 27 (1990), 175–96.
44 See Virginia Blanton, *Signs of Devotion: The Cult of St Athelthryth in Medieval England, 695–1615* (Philadelphia: Pennsylvania State University Press, 2007), 263ff, for further discussion of the layers and depths to East Anglian parishioners' engagement with rood

screens. On the form, see Lucy Wrapson, 'East Anglian medieval church screens: A brief guide to their physical history', *Bulletin of the Hamilton Kerr Institute* 4 (2013), 33–47.

45 Conversely, Theresa Coletti sees this image as acknowledging the dangerous power of female sexuality and genetic ties, with Margaret a virginal balance to the fleshly mothers in 'Genealogy'. See also Blanton, *Signs of Devotion*, 285–6.

46 Richard Marks notes that 'All this emphasizes the nave and its fittings and furnishings predominantly as *lay space*', in 'Framing the Rood in Medieval England and Wales', *The Art and Science of the Church Screen in Medieval Europe: Making, Meaning, Preserving*, ed. Spike Bucklow, Richard Marks, and Lucy Wrapson (Woodbridge: Boydell & Brewer, 2017), 7–29, at 28.

47 In Richard Marks, 'Framing', at 13.

48 Duffy, *Stripping*, 171. Duffy specifies that several of the saints whose *vitae* appear in Arundel 327 are depicted on such screens.

49 In other visual depictions, the sisters are grouped together with Anne, known for her infertility and multiple marriages and widowhoods—another gesture toward maternal sorrow.

50 Sanok argues that Bokenham is creating a fictional textual and political community, seeing gender as the women's primary common bond. See *Her Life Historical*, 51–82.

51 Kim M. Phillips notes that Isabel Bourchier's aunt had similarly commissioned Lydgate to write a life of Margaret for her in 1429 or 1430 in 'Desiring virgins: Maidens, martyrs and femininity in late medieval England', *Youth in the Middle Ages*, ed. P.J.P. Goldberg and Felicity Riddy (Woodbridge: York Medieval Press, 2004), 45–59.

52 Alexandra Cassatt Verini, 'Reading between the lines: Female friendship in Osbern Bokenham's *Life* of St Katherine of Alexandria, *Magistra* 17.2 (2011), 53–70, at 59.

53 See A. I. Doyle, 'Books connected with the Vere family and Barking Abbey', *Transactions of the Essex Archaeological Society*, n.s., 25 (1958), 222–43, at 234ff, and Erler, *Women, Reading, and Piety*. Along similar lines, Virginia Bainbridge has done important work on the multigenerational social and political networks of families connected to Syon Abbey, e.g. 'Nuns on the run, or the "sturdy and wilful dames" of Syon Abbey and their disobedience to the Tudor state ca. 1530–1600', forthcoming in *Medieval and Renaissance Studies*. See also Marilyn Oliva, *The Convent and the Community in Late Medieval England: Female Monasteries in the Diocese of Norwich, 1350 to 1540* (Oxford: Boydell Press, 1998).

54 *Legendys*, 111–12.

55 See Matthew Evan Davis, 'Lydgate at Long Melford: Reassessing the *Testament* and "Quis dabit meo capiti fontem lacrimarum" in their local context', *The Journal of Medieval Religious Cultures* 43.1 (2017), 77–114.
56 Verini, 'Reading', 70.
57 I have discussed this point more fully in 'Saintly protection: The postmortem "mothers" of medieval hagiography', *Missing, Presumed Dead: The Absent Mother in the Cultural Imagination*, ed. Berit Åstrom (London: Palgrave Macmillan, 2017), 45–58.
58 See Osbern Bokenham, *Legendys of Hooly Wummen*, ed. Mary Serjeantson, EETS o.s. 206 (London, 1938), 188–90, 11, 61.
59 Anne M. Dutton, 'Piety, politics and person: MS Harley 4012 and Anne Harling', *Prestige, Authority and Power in Late Medieval Manuscripts and Texts*, ed. Felicity Riddy (Woodbridge: Boydell & Brewer, 2000), 133–46, at 140.
60 See Edwards, 'Fifteenth', 138. Erler has sorted out many more such connections in *Women, Reading, and Piety*.
61 Oxford, Bodleian Library MS Ashmole 39 has Bourchier's name inscribed; Edwards has argued for London, British Library MS Harley 3862 having been in the de Vere family in 'Transmission and audience', 166. See also Simon Horobin, 'Politics, patronage, and piety in the work of Osbern Bokenham', *Speculum* 82.4 (2007), 932–49, at 944.
62 This lack is made more obvious compared with Abbotsford. Karen Winstead argues that Bokenham had a change of education and perspective from Arundel to Abbotsford; see her 'Osbern Bokenham's "englische boke": re-forming holy women', *Form and reform: Reading across the fifteenth century*, ed. Shannon Gayk and Kathleen Tonry (Columbus: Ohio State University Press, 2011), 67–87.
63 Horobin lists several such books in his identification and discussion of Abbotsford, 'A manuscript found in the library of Abbotsford House and the lost legendary of Osbern Bokenham', *English Manuscript Studies 1100–1700* 14 (2008), 130–64, at 153.
64 Edwards and Scott believe the same scribe produced several Lydgate manuscripts at Bury St Edmunds. Yates Thompson MS 47 is the 'twin' of the Arundel Castle manuscript.
65 Gail McMurray Gibson, 'Scene and obscene: Seeing and performing late medieval childbirth', *Journal of Medieval and Early Modern Studies* 29.1 (1999), 7–24, at 11.
66 As Horobin has noted, the Abbotsford manuscript is missing the Arundel 327 lives of Anne, Katherine, Cecilia, and Elizabeth of Hungary. That absence is not necessarily significant; except for

Anne's, these saints' feast days appear later in the liturgical year than is covered by the Abbotsford. A quire is missing from the portion of the manuscript that would contain Anne's *vita* at July 26. See Horobin, 'Manuscript', 140, with relevant patrons listed at 149; see also his Introduction to Osbern Bokenham, *Lives of Saints*, EETS o.s. 356 (Oxford: Oxford University Press, 2020). Horobin argues persuasively for Cecily of York as the possible owner of Abbotsford, which may be the *Legenda Aurea* bequeathed to her granddaughter in her will, 150–1. Cecily was also a reader of Hilton and Love, per Riddy. Meale notes that British Library, Royal MS 19 A xix has Richard's seal in it but was likely meant for Cecily. Part of Horobin's argument for Abbotsford being Cecily's is that Bokenham's known audience was women.

67 Bokenham, *Lives*, 396, 394.
68 For Margaret's importance to convents, see Jenny Bledsoe, 'The cult of St Margaret of Antioch at Tarrant Crawford: The saint's didactic body and its resonance for religious women', *Journal of Medieval Religious Cultures* 39 (2013), 173–206.
69 Carol Meale speculates that this sister could have been a nun but does not offer evidence for the claim in '"alle the bokes that I haue of latyn, englisch, and frensch": laywomen and their books in late medieval England', *Women and Literature in Britain 1150–1500*, ed. Carol Meale (Cambridge: Cambridge University Press, 1993), 128–58, at 138.
70 On conventual reading generally, see Mary Erler, 'Private reading in the fifteenth- and sixteenth-century English nunnery', *The Culture of Medieval English Monasticism*, ed. James Clark (Woodbridge: Boydell, 2007), 134–46.
71 Doyle, 'Books', 236 n8.
72 See Horobin, 'Politics', and Winstead, 'Osbern'.
73 Sanok hypothesizes that the references to witchcraft in Margaret's *vita* allude to Margaret Jourdemain, the Witch of Eye, *Her Life Historical*, 68.
74 Erler, *Women, Reading, and Piety*, 25, 27.
75 See Warren, *Spiritual Economies: Female Monasticism in Later Medieval England* (Philadelphia: University of Pennsylvania Press, 2001).
76 This also seems to be true of the Abbotsford manuscript; see Horobin on Aubrey, who also appears in Cambridge 2604.
77 The only exception is Agnes, who continues to call Christ her lover and who describes him in erotic terms ('of þis louer my chaumbyr arayid is … and takyn of his mouth many a kys haue I,/swettyre þan

eythir milk or hony,/and fulle oftyn in armys he halsyd hath me', 4169–74).

78 Carroll Hilles connects the emphasis on genealogy and fertility in the lives to Bokenham's support for the Yorkist cause in 'Gender and politics in Osbern Bokenham's legendary', *New Medieval Literatures* 4 (2001), 189–212. Warren contends that Bokenham asserts masculine authority by subordinating his subjects to male relatives and by specific mention of his patrons' male relatives in *Spiritual Economies*. Neither Hilles nor Warren discusses the potential importance of family roles to the legendary's conventual audience.

79 Gibson, 'Saint Anne', at 100, 101.

80 Carole Hill, 'St Anne and her Walsingham daughter', *Walsingham in Literature and Culture from the Middle Ages to Modernity*, ed. Dominic James and Gary Waller (New York: Routledge, 2010), 99–111. Hill describes several examples of Anne's iconography in the region's small churches.

81 *The Golden Legend: Readings on the Saints*, ed. and trans. William Granger Ryan (Princeton: Princeton University Press, 2012), 535ff.

82 Minneapolis, University of Minnesota MS Z822 N81 contains an early fifteenth-century life of Anne based on the Latin apocryphal gospel of pseudo-Matthew, a version of the Protevangelium; it begins just after a selection from the *Northern Homily Cycle*. Here Joachim weeps when the priest refuses his offering (95), and Anne confronts her maid, as in Bokenham; much of the text is devoted to Christ's childhood. For an edition, see *Middle English Stanzaic Versions of the Life of Saint Anne*, ed. R.E. Parker, EETS o.s. 174 (London: Oxford University Press, 1928). For a description see J. Lawrence Mitchell, 'A "Northern Homilies Cycle" manuscript: Minnesota MS Z822 N81', *Scriptorium* 35.2 (1981), 321–30. On medieval manuscripts of the Gospel of Pseudo-Matthew, see Rita Beyers, 'The transmission of Marian apocrypha in the Latin Middle Ages', *Apocrypha* 23 (2012), 117–40. On this text's depiction of Christ's childhood, see Mary Dzon, 'Wanton boys in Middle English texts and the Christ Child in Minneapolis, University of Minnesota, MS Z822 N81', in *Medieval Life Cycles: Continuities and Change*, ed. Karen Smyth and Isabelle Cochelin (Turnhout: Brepols, 2013), 81–145.

83 Cambridge, Trinity College MS 601 contains the same version of Anne that appears in Chetham MS 8009 in the second half of the fifteenth century. It does not discuss Anne's reaction to infertility or her husband's absence at all, only Joachim's experience; the narrative then slides organically into the early biography of Mary. At the end of the fifteenth century, Harley 4012 contains the same succinct version

as Bodley 10234, Robert Reynys' commonplace book. Its genealogy focuses earlier and more closely on Anne's later husbands that produced Mary's relatives, as well as other relatives such as Anne's sister Ismeria. Here the angel goes to Joachim before Anne and makes a very brief annunciation to her, attending more extensively to Mary's childhood and youth. Trinity MS 601 and Bodley MS 10234 are edited in EETS 174.

84 Ryan, *Golden Legend*, 537.
85 *N-Town*, play 8, lines 66–7.
86 In the stanzaic life based on Pseudo-Matthew, the number is five; see *Middle English Stanzaic*, 16, line 590. Jacobus mentions seven virgins sent with Mary for this purpose but gives no details.
87 *Middle English Stanzaic*, 16–17.
88 bell hooks, *Feminist Theory from Margin to Center* (Boston: South End Press, 1984), 139.
89 Sara Ahmed, *Cultural Politics of Emotion*, 28–9.

Part III

The author: Chaucer as matricentric poet

This section turns to a single author, Chaucer, to consider how the late-fifteenth-century manuscript distribution of his Marian poems returns to the themes in Part I of the importance of space(s), the powers of speech and movement, and the expansions of our definitions of devotional literacies and Marian performance. The inclusion of Chaucer in collections that also include Lydgate's *Life of Our Lady*, such as Chetham 6709 and Harley 2382, suggests that readers and patrons considered Marian motherhood a literary theme. These texts, produced for women and often featuring women as speakers, re-present the longstanding Marian narratives that were largely created by and for men. Their inclusion in women's new books is curious, particularly because revised versions of Mary were appearing in newly composed poems and plays. As we've seen, fifteenth-century texts hint at a vernacular Marian maternity that pushes against a patriarchal rendering: the complexities constructed and performed by Margery Kempe, by the mystics in Douce 114, by saintly exemplars, and by the Marys and Annes who appeared onstage and in poetry illuminate how restrictive Chaucer's models are.

That Marian miracle stories and lyrics usually feature men as protagonists seems to support the common assumption that confessors or the Church pushed Marian devotion on women. In contrast, the Second Nun and the Prioress re-calibrate Marian devotion as something women do. In more typical Marian narratives, these nuns might be portrayed as temptations to monks or as competitors with Mary herself for attention. Here, as narrators, they center and normalize more conservative Marian versions of maternity, insisting on conformity that upholds the status quo. Chaucer borrows and highlights various aspects of that maternity: the persuasive virgin-mother in the *Second Nun's Tale*; the nurturing savior in the *Prioress's Tale*; the mediatrix of advocacy and intercession in the *ABC*. Pervading each are the Marian connections to literacy, intellect, and speech that Laura Saetveit Miles, Carolyn Collette, and Georgiana Donavin have written about. These three texts cover the spectrum of the Marian trinity of maiden, mother, and mistress that William Quinn notices in Chaucer's *ABC*.[1] Women reading them in mariales and household books—books Blurton and Johnson call 'devotional anthologies'—did so with the contexts of other Marian poems and practices rather than as two of many *Canterbury Tales*.[2] Centering both Mary and maternity in our own readings gives us a better sense of how they might have revised or internalized the Marian maternities they found there. Chaucer's texts have room for nuanced, vernacular interpretations of maternity and maternal practice but restrict his maternal protagonists to a clerical Marian model. In the *Prioress's Tale*, this adds to maternal loss; in the *Second Nun's Tale*, it affirms saintly power.

Notes

1 Notably, these manuscripts do not include the *Clerk's Tale*. For a nearly comprehensive list of Griselda's similarities to Mary, see Francis Lee Utley, 'Five genres in the "Clerk's Tale"', *Chaucer Review* 6.3 (1972), 198–228. That the *Clerk's Tale* was not included with other Marian texts in the fifteenth century suggests Chaucer's near-contemporaries did not find those similarities compelling.
2 Heather Blurton and Hannah Johnson, *The Critics and the Prioress: Antisemitism, Criticism, and Chaucer's* Prioress's Tale (Ann Arbor: University of Michigan Press, 2017), 134.

5

A Mary for every mother: mothers as agents of orthodoxy

Thomas of Cantimpré shares an anecdote about Thomas of Becket crouching in the cathedral choir: Becket is poised in sewing posture but mystified by how to mend the haircloth undergarments that are too tattered to stay in place.[1] To his great relief, Mary suddenly appears, consoles him, and stitches up the garments. They sit together as she makes quick work of the mending. 'The repair was instant and invisible', the text assures us.[2] This would make a delicious, faintly ridiculous scene in a *Tale*. That Chaucer resisted telling it may be evidence that he or his readers took Thomas and Mary too seriously to be amused. Because of frequent artistic depictions of her sewing skill, be the tool a mending needle, knitting needles, embroidery frame, or a loom, we don't question that Mary would rescue an archbishop from his incompetence at garment repair.

Becket's predicament underscores the gendering of male and female literacies. Becket, anxious about his undergarments, is 'ignorant and unskilled at this work'.[3] Literacy can be measured by any number of ways, including the artisanal form of knotting thread into fabric. When handwork is the standard, clerical definitions of literacy and power are, briefly, useless: even the Archbishop of Canterbury becomes illiterate, immobile, and ineffective. Importantly, Mary was closely affiliated with both handwork and textual literacy. Laura Saetveit Miles discusses the visual and theological replacement of Mary's sewing with a book.[4] Kathryn Rudy describes the routine use of books of hours as storage for stitched-in pilgrimage badges, a practice suggesting that sewing and literacy were of a piece.[5] Scholars of the early modern such as Bianca Calabresi and Wendy Wall have begun to tease out the interplay among women's textual and textile-based literacies.[6]

It is perhaps telling that Mary does *not* teach Becket how to sew, retaining that expertise and authority for herself and thereby leaving him dependent on her. While the anecdote may mean to show the demarcation between male and female realms, a late fifteenth-century reader might reach quite different conclusions about Mary declining to act as patient teacher. Her handwork was historically a marker of humility, a visual echo of her status as handmaiden. But Mary invokes an autonomy that allows her, like Margery Kempe, to sit in the choir and perform an action solidly gendered female. Rudy has described sewing as a physical means of asserting autonomy by enlarging, improving, or changing function in an object.[7] Further, the kind of leisure sewing that most literate women were doing in late-medieval England required extra space and resources. It was not merely functional but pleasurable. It was also becoming a site at which literacy education was transferred from mother to daughter: investing such a skill into the child asserted the mother's authority through education, changed the child by improving her function.

I begin this chapter about Chaucer with this anecdote because centering maternity rather than gender in Becket's encounter with Mary acknowledges the devotional literacies available to late fifteenth-century mothers. Asserting maternal authority included choosing which or whose Marian model to follow. Both Chaucer's *ABC* and the *Prioress's Tale*, in their way, recognize the kinds of choices mothers made about educating children. As we'll see, one opens myriad possibilities of Marian maternity, while the other closes them down. The visual appearance of the ABC allows a flexibility in the uses of Chaucer's text, and by extension in its depiction of Mary. Its form encourages an organic overlap of maternal practice with an ideal of Marian motherhood—teaching a child—and yet it may be, to judge from the more rigid model of Marian maternity we see in the *Tales*, a tease.

To pray or knot: stitching feminine authority into *An ABC*

By the late fifteenth century, when books of hours had long become commonplace among the literate, mothers could internalize some autonomy through their use of Marian texts in the realm of children's education. They could not easily decline to teach their own children about Mary, but there was room for discernment about content and methods. Heather Blurton and Hannah Johnson have argued persuasively that Chaucer was a Marian poet.[8] The *Prioress's Tale*'s manuscript overlap with Deguileville's Marian poetry and other texts with maternal themes further suggests a matricentric interpretation by fifteenth-century readers. British Library, Harley MS 2251 contains the *Prioress's Tale*, Chaucer's translation of Deguileville's *Prière*, and other Marian texts such as Lydgate's 'A Praise of St. Anne', 'Lamentacioun of our Lady Maria', and 'Child Jesus to Mary, the Rose'. Cambridge University Library Kk.1.3 includes a fragment of *The Prioress's Prologue* and *Tale* and Lydgate's *Life of Our Lady*. Harley MS 2382 includes several Marian texts with Lydgate's *Testament*, such as the *Prioress's Tale*, *Second Nun's Tale*, and Lydgate's *Life of Our Lady*. Whether these associations are simply Marian or specifically maternal is unclear, although the presence in some manuscripts of St Margaret, a saint often affiliated with safe childbirth, may be telling: Manchester, Chetham MS 6709 includes Lydgate's *Life of Our Lady*, the Life of St. Margaret, the *Second Nun's Tale*, and the *Prioress's Tale*; and New Haven, Yale University, Beinecke Library, Takamiya Deposit 24 appends Lydgate's life of St Margaret to the *Canterbury Tales*. Finally, copies of Deguileville's text being bound with Chaucer's *ABC* does not necessarily indicate a maternal interest, but does suggest readers were accustomed to thinking of their work in tandem. Glasgow, Hunter MS 239 contains Deguileville's *Pèlerinage de l'âme* with Chaucer's *ABC*.[9] Oxford Bodleian MS Laud Misc. 740 has English translations of *Le Pèlerinage de la vie humaine*, with Chaucer's *ABC* within the text.

With its abecedarian form and Marian content, *An ABC* already contains subtexts of Marian- and feminine-coded literacies.[10] Here I consider it as a vehicle of 'nonreading', as Leah Price has put it, or at least a different kind of reading.[11] Its position in fifteenth-century household books such as Harley MS 2251 suggests that *An ABC* could weave together a multitasking mother's desire for personal devotions with a template for teaching a child's letters, either written or stitched, and for composing one's own Marian narrative with needle and thread. It invites us to consider the forms of the maternal (as opposed to liturgical) day, of constative or performative literacies, and of domestic handwork.

The manuscripts of Chaucer's *ABC* thus provide a Marian space to consider connections among women's piety, the instruction of children, literacy, and handwork. This reading responds in part to Heather Blatt's challenge:

> [S]pace remains in which to push consideration of [devotional] reading further by examining the specific reading processes through which writers urged readers to make meaning of their works and, in the process, shed light on the role made for readers in late-medieval vernacular culture. ... Focusing on reading through the practice of participation helps illuminate the variety of processes that supported apprehension, as participation itself requires making readers work.[12]

Other scholars have written about readers as participants in the *ABC* specifically through prayer. William Quinn has argued that recitation as prayer gives the words new power for each reader; merely reading or hearing the text is too passive to engage with the text as it's meant to be used.[13] Quinn and Georgiana Donavin have each discussed the poem's formulaic similarity to prayer beads and their meditative, repetitive, circular patterns.[14] Such a form must have seemed natural to an abecedary: children routinely made the sign of the cross before reciting the alphabet and said 'Amen' afterward, as if in prayer.[15] To say one's letters was already to communicate with the divine.

As Quinn has argued, we should not necessarily consider the *ABC* juvenile or for children; it is performative, an adult prayer. But neither should we ignore its didactic acrostic form. I suggest we take its appearance in late fifteenth-century manuscripts at face value while acknowledging its possibilities and resonances. Donavin has noted that the capital letters stand out from the text. I submit that these letters served as patterns for both writing and stitching. The household books that contain the poem could thus teach how to pray but also how to write and stitch, and potentially, how to compose. The practice of stitching the letters, like saying the rosary, requires repetitive and meditative bodily action.[16] To return to a term I used in Chapter 1, whether the *ABC* is a prayer, a pedagogical tool, or a stitching pattern, it marks the occasion of a literacy event. Its potential to take any one of these forms imbues the text with devotional and literary flexibility and alters the social position of its reader.

Lucy M. Allen-Goss's meticulous analysis of Philomela's weaving demonstrates Chaucer's awareness of the mechanics, materials, and subtexts of textile work.[17] Chaucer keeps the textile arts visible.[18] He notices stockings, wimples, tapestries, weaving, and the stories they all tell; he sincerely admires the Wyf of Bath's talent. He frequently describes embroidered details on household fabrics and clothing, such as that worn by the Miller's Alison and the Squire. Needlepoint is everywhere, with its dueling connotations of sex work, as E. Jane Burns and Allen-Goss have noted, and its liturgical settings such as in stoles, altarclothes, and copes that Rozsika Parker has described.[19] Chaucer knew the political, economical, and narrative power of embroidery: His contemporary, embroiderer Thomas Carleton, was armorer to Edward III. Carleton owned a legendary that he may have used for embroidery patterns. By the end of his life, Carleton was an alderman and member of Parliament.[20]

The assumption that *ABC* was juvenile or for juveniles leaves out that mothers might be using the poem as they cared for children or practiced their devotions. The frequent visual and textual assertions that Mary and Anne were each constant and conscious teachers of their children added spiritual resonance to cherished norms that presumed maternal teaching of reading, devotions, and handwork.[21] Abecedaries were frequently used as a teaching tool, as psalters and books of hours had been in the recent past.[22] In England stitching was learned at about the same time as writing, rather than in earlier stages of reading literacy.[23] Chaucer was writing at least a full century before documentation of English alphabet samplers, but the temporal distance between late fifteenth-century household books and such samplers is much smaller.[24] Late fifteenth-century readers clearly felt the *ABC* needed to look as though it could serve the function of an embroidery pattern. This was a small conceptual step; books were already constructed and mended with needle and thread. Illuminators and embroiderers were often aligned and sometimes the same person, often using the same patterns, such as woodcuts, as Kate Heard has shown.[25] Jourdain notes that two thirteenth-century French embroiderers, 'Dame Margot and Dame Aalès … were both illuminators'.[26] The raw materials for embroidering cost roughly the same as those for practicing writing.[27]

Even before alphabet samplers became a common means of displaying one's needle-literacy prowess, textiles played a role in children's literacy. For appropriate childraising, the *Trotula* advises that 'there should be different kinds of pictures, *cloths of diverse colors*, and pearls placed in front of the child, and one should use nursery songs and simple words'.[28] Danièle Alexandre-Bidon notes that young children were given cloth squares with embroidered letters on them that were tossed up in a random heap.[29] They were meant to piece the squares together in order, like a puzzle, and could use the borders around the edges to help them before they recognized the letters. There were multiple routes to letter-level literacy, as Donavin has shown, not only various types of formal schooling, but also material means such as primers, prayer books, and embroidered squares.

Our grasp of the *ABC*'s use depends partly on how we interpret the presence of its offset or larger inset letters. I agree with George Pace that Chaucer's expectation of room for large initials in manuscripts is itself significant, although for a different reason.[30] The Lombardic capitals used in so many of the books containing the *ABC* were typically used in liturgical texts and decoration. In practice, having all these Lombardic letters set out in a few pages would make an efficient stitching pattern for someone working out their devotions on fabric. Donavin, discussing the appearances of the letters in various manuscripts, has argued that they are meant to teach Marian truths to new English speakers.[31] They could also teach the shaping to multiple users of the texts. What makes this liturgical script especially relevant to the *ABC* is that Mary herself is subject not only of Chaucer's poem but as subject of a large body of liturgical textiles such as copes and orphreys, especially those made to honor the Assumption and Coronation, as Rozsika Parker has shown. (See Plates 5 and 6.)

Saetveit Miles tells us that the iconography of Mary doing textile work was replaced by her reading by the twelfth century.[32] This is about when the English embroidery *opus anglicanum*, produced mostly by men, began developing as an industry. As the popularity of *opus anglicanum* waned in the late fourteenth century, images of Mary doing handwork resumed. This may indicate broadening of definitions of her literacy and, more subtly, a move of perceptions of embroidery from trade spaces to domestic ones and from men to women. Mary's handwork could be replaced by a book in icons and illuminations, but the shapes of the Lombardic letters remained part of ecclesiastical vestments and other devotional texts, a visual parallel with the Mary invoked in the *ABC*. Those same letters offer the chance for readers to narrate such stories.

Abecedaries were meant to teach children or the illiterate.[33] The sophistication of Chaucer's *ABC* lays subtle emphasis on Mary's literacy, itself an assertion of spiritual power, but it also suggests the potential resourcefulness of his readers. Claire Waters has shown that merely speaking Mary's name makes medievals 'lettered'; seeing or being seen by her image could change one's perspective or whole identity.[34] The additional results from engaging with Chaucer's Marian *ABC* by speaking the prayer, absorbing its narrative, teaching one's child, or practicing forming the letters—or revising the narrative—make this a text that richly repaid repeated uses.

The reader of the *ABC* can teach not only prayer or Marian devotion, but also the tools to create new prayers or narrative in text or textile. This use does not contradict Quinn's reminder that Chaucer's poem is a prayer: writing or knotting the *ABC* could easily serve as prayerful act. Modern theories of language and literacy can help us here. Borrowing terms from Austin's speech act theory, Karen Coats explains that the

> view of language as presented in [modern children's] alphabet books is changing from a traditional, linear, epistemological, masculine model, in which language is a way of knowing an existing reality, to a more performative, ontological, integrated model, in which language is recognized as a vehicle for actively constructing that reality.[35]

The shaping of 'Mary' into an alphabet suggests that just as every letter can signify an aspect of Mary, so can she be contained by twenty-three descriptors, as though the abecedary poem is exhaustive and static. Scholarship that sees the *ABC* as a text to be simply read or memorized depends on this constative view of the alphabet and this poem. But the form suggests the letters are there to be imitated—even, as Quinn has pointed out, prayed. If a reader can master *forming* those letters, she acquires power to create new Marian narratives with quill or needle. The performative autonomy permitted by these letters allows embroidery to become literary, narrative, and devotional practice.[36]

The poem's form allows that multiple Marian abecedaries—multiple Marys—are possible, in letters evoking the liturgical authority stitched by nuns. Through performative literacy, its readers can construct and perform the Marian maternity of their choosing. It is a shock, then, to turn to the Marian *Canterbury Tales* that were circulating simultaneously and see through the same matricentric lens that Chaucer's nuns discourage such an open view of Mary, shrinking her, in the *Prioress's Tale*, to the radical smallness of anti-semitism. The expansiveness granted by the 'auctoritee' to construct or revive Marian narratives here limits maternal authority.

The maternal authority of the clergeon's mother

The *Prioress's Tale* continues Chaucer's expectation of a reader's direct engagement with a Marian narrative, offering a version of Marian maternity that hews much closer to the clerical model than to the vernacular ones we have seen in previous chapters. Specifically, the clergeon's mother relies on and adopts antisemitism as a way to define her own Christian, bodily maternity. In doing so, she helps reinforce a system that privileges Christian identity and institutions even as it devalues her own maternal practice. For all its hawking of Mary as mother and the clergeon's mother's imitation of her, then, the *Prioress's Tale* is an anti-maternal text. It erases mothers of other faiths as well as denying the clergeon's mother full realization of her maternity. A value system in which Mary is so superior a substitute for the boy's mother that he is better off dead is one that does not trust a mother to raise her child without the input of institutions or power structures. The *Tale*'s portrayal of maternity as strictly Marian minimizes real maternal practice: it erases both the mothers who are not Marian and those who are. A matricentric reading exposes the *Tale* as more rather than less antisemitic, but it allows us to see how its bigotry and misogyny—specifically, anti-maternity—work in tandem. Constructing a Marian motherhood that depended in part on antisemitism was a project that began with Maximus of Constantinople, was refined by scholastics such as Aquinas, and continued through the fifteenth century, when the *Prioress's Tale* circulated in manuscript with Marian devotional texts.

The *Tale* is set up so the clergeon's mother is obliged to perform Marian maternity correctly, which here involves upholding institutional power structures. In other words, her mothering as depicted in the *Tale* is in service to something other than childrearing as its end. We do not meet her until her child is already harmed and missing, and she leaves before he speaks again: we never see her direct interactions with him, so all we know is by inference. Her maternal practice is largely invisible. We see some of the results, such as their urban residency, his school enrollment, and his Marian devotion, but not the particulars of maternal sacrifice, nourishment, or affection. Our best clue to the mother's circumstances is her demonstration of affective piety through *imitatio Mariae*, which requires time, access to a confessor, and likely her own literacy. That piety is also what gives her access to Marian maternity. Before examining that, I want to note the narrative choices Chaucer makes that minimize maternal values from the beginning.

Maternal and filial erasures

To center maternity is not only to consider the *Prioress's Tale* through the depiction of the clergeon's mother, but to notice the erasures of other mothers and of maternal concerns. Marian maternity is not available or desirable to everyone. As Patricia Hill Collins has pointed out, 'Motherhood occurs in specific historical situations framed by interlocking structures of race, class, and gender … For women of color, the subjective experience of mothering/motherhood is inextricably linked to the sociocultural concern of racial ethnic communities—one does not exist without the other.'[37] Similarly, the Jewish mothers in Chaucer's analogues do not have the same kind of access to the Marian model of maternity and the accompanying power of the church and law enforcement. That exclusion is made starker in the *Tale*, where the implied social isolation of the clergeon's mother contributes to the invisibility of Jewish mothers. Although she lives nearby, sends her child to school via the Jewish street, and is able to converse with Jewish people in a common language,[38] the mother does not seem to have personal connections in the neighborhood. So we meet no Jewish mothers. Despite the hyperbole in many Christian texts, Christian and Jewish mothers interacted regularly in daily continental life. Elisheva Baumgarten describes the practice of Jewish households hiring Christian wetnurses and even interfaith cross-feeding of infants in France and Germany.[39] Warnings to Christian men against sleeping with Jewish women or pledging sworn brotherhood to Jewish men suggests such mixed-faith activities were in practice.[40] As Baumgarten puts it, 'medieval Jews and Christians shared the same world'.[41] In declining to portray that reality, Chaucer preserves the illusion that only Mary or a Marian imitator can be maternal.

The *Tale*'s privileging of Marian maternity over maternal practice continues by not taking children seriously. The Prioress describes Christian children mostly as small bodies to fill a singing school ('Children an heep … to syngen and to rede/As smale children doon in hire childhede', 497–501). They may be preverbal venues for God's praise ('on the brest soukynge/Somtyme shewen they thyn heriynge', 458–9) or barely literate ones ('O grete God, that parfournest thy laude/By mouth of innocentz, lo, heere thy myght!', 607–8). Except for the brief, boasting exchange between the two schoolchildren that sets up the tale's premise, the Prioress does not depict Christian children beyond stereotype. She does not describe Jewish children at all, although they are surely living in the neighborhood that opens the *Tale*. Neither does her concern extend, later in the poem, to the orphaned children of the Jews killed en masse or to the children of any faith who must witness the victims' bodies tortured and hanged. Children are only a means to pathos, there to be trained or converted. This dismissal of them as individuals also erases the work done in raising them. We see a similar dismissal of mothers in the frequent allusions to the Holy Innocents in the *Prologue* and throughout the *Tale*. These are often considered evidence of the Prioress's adoration of children, but the story of the innocents was as much about mothers' protections and sorrows as children's vulnerability.[42] Invoking them only to highlight the purity of children discounts the labor and grief of those who mothered them.

Besides his explicit focus on Mary, Chaucer's main revision to the blood libel tale is to relocate it to 'Asye', a change that establishes a starker dynamic between 'Cristene folk' and 'Jewes' than is warranted and speaks little to maternal concerns. While

A Mary for every mother 197

Chaucer himself had traveled to religiously diverse regions and cities and likely interacted directly with Jews and Muslims, he knew many of his English Christian readers had not.[43] It is fair to suppose that he purposely left the setting of the *Prioress's Tale* as a flexible 'Asye', one that as easily indicated a real Asian city as a Semitic neighborhood within a European one.[44] That is not to say that his setting is amply described or wholly accurate. His 'greet cite' where 'Amonges Cristene folk' live 'a Jewerye' (488–9) leaves out Muslims altogether. We are told at the *Tale*'s beginning that the ghetto is 'Sustened by a lord of that contree' (490). The murder of a child, even one from outside the neighborhood, and the subsequent brutal punishment of so many of its inhabitants suggest he is not much of a sustainer. He neither protects the Jews under his care nor the child walking through the neighborhood, failing to sustain a community that values the safety of children. Chaucer describes both the Jewish residents' neighbors and the crowd who later appear as witnesses as 'cristene folk' (489, 614). We aren't told how to interpret this monolith, which omits many mothers other than the clergeon's, as well as other stakeholders. Where are the fellow song-school parents or teachers who might be concerned about a missing classmate in the school's neighborhood? Where are the Jewish mothers who would be distraught about a child's murder near their homes? Where, for that matter, are their children? Sheila Delany suggests that this Jewish street is a voluntarily mono-religious neighborhood built around a synagogue or similar.[45] There should, then, likely be a synagogue school nearby: is the safety of those children not an issue? In ignoring these questions, the *Tale* ignores other, non-Marian forms of maternal practice and exaggerates the clergeon's mother's isolation.

Assessing maternity: how Marian is she?

The artificially homogenous neighborhood provides more contrast to the clergeon's mother, who arrives there alone 'with moodres pitee in hir brest enclosed'. Her appearance midway through the *Tale* raises the question of whether she is a worthy maternal predecessor to Mary. Chaucer has assigned what maternity appears in the *Tale* to Mary instead: of the twenty uses of the term 'mooder', 'moodre', or 'mater', eighteen refer to Mary rather than the clergeon's mother.[46] The child victim of violence in the *Tale* does not call out for his mama in his hour of death or even acknowledge her. Mostly, she is a mystery until she begins her search for the child, a public debut that offers her multiple moral dilemmas amidst her grief. Faced with her child's disappearance, the mother has a narrow path of acceptable response: she must navigate not only filial loss but also public perception of her mothering and her faith.

She opts to perform Marian maternity: 'evere on Cristes mooder meeke and kynde/She cride' (597–8). The *Tale* has openly promoted Mary's motherhood from the beginning, from the *Prologue* to the clergeon's song. To emulate Marian motherhood within such a text is to submit to assessment and comparison. The maternal behaviors that are most accessible and assessable are her search and grieving. The *Tale*'s plot thus relies partly on its readers' familiarity with Mary's maternal mourning, a common subject for devotional meditation.[47] As we saw in Chapter 2, maternity and its attendant grief are at the heart of how and why Mary became an unlikely avatar for antisemitism. Late-medieval Christians believed her grief manifested in copious tears and delayed labor pains at the Crucifixion. Marian maternity is public: it does not allow maternity for its own sake, but for the edification and consumption of others. Mourning, especially, considers audience. Mary herself seems aware that her maternity is sometimes means to a penitent's end; in one poem Bernard of Clairvaux asks her for yet more details of Crucifixion events, and Mary snaps, 'Bernard, allas,/what woltou more aske me?'[48] The crack in her composure exposes irritation at her grief as product to be consumed.

Chaucer's fleshing out of the mother's behaviors in the *Prioress's Tale* departs from other versions of this blood libel narrative to suggest a particular interest in Marian maternity. The analogue in the Vernon manuscript (c. 1400) known as 'The Child Slain by Jews', set in Paris, includes the same antisemitism and violence we see in the *Tale* but does not implicate the mother and her maternity in a supporting role as Chaucer does.[49] In this analogue, when the child is killed, his corpse begins singing immediately, independent of his mother's actions. It is his singing voice rather than a gentle

A Mary for every mother

nudge from Christ that attracts his mother to the site. Neither her tears nor her engagement with Christ and Mary is required. Her Marian devotion, if it exists, is irrelevant. Rather, she is fluent and proactive in bureaucracy and law enforcement: she goes directly to the mayor and bailiffs to demand justice. Once she has identified the child and recruited the mayor to the cause, she disappears without swoon or further comment. There's no promise that Mary will adopt, no affiliation with a cathedral school, no maternal instruction in Marian adoration.

In the *Tale*, grief is raw material to be shaped and processed into devotion, certainly, but it also becomes a test of maternal competence. Mary's miracle will not complete without the mother's correct intervention. If the clergeon's mother channels her grief properly, she can act as accomplice to and representative of Mary to find peace for her son. But she must know to go to the Jewish neighborhood; she must audibly weep there in the vicinity of her child's body, as her tears will prompt his song, allowing his body to be found and his story to be told.

Marian tears and conflicting messages

The clergeon's mother is lucky to arrive at the right combination of location and action, given the range of messages to grieving mothers in Christian devotional texts. Whether a mother was entitled to grieve for her own child depended on the source. The *Lamentatio St. Bernardi de Compassione Mariae* was an imagined dialogue between Mary and Bernard of Clairvaux that circulated widely among Latinate Christian readers in both sermon and verse form. In the dialogue's poetic form, Christ advises pious mothers observing his death that their own children need their tears more than he does: 'Wepit not for me,/But wepiþ for ȝow & youre childer eke'.[50] But in a later 'Lament of Mary', Mary advises other mothers that they are not sufficiently reverent of Christ if they're crying over their own sons: 'make ye no mone for your chyld', she scoffs, portraying mothers' grief for their sons as a zero-sum game set against the requisite sorrow over the Crucifixion.[51] As we've seen, Marian lament (*planctus Mariae*) considered Christ's death and Mary's sorrow beyond what mortal Christian women might understand or imitate, although they were expected to try through affective meditation. Sarah McNamer notes that 'compassion as scripted in and through Middle English meditations on the Passion is largely a function of gender performance: to perform compassion is to feel like a woman'.[52] More specifically, in the *Tale*, it is to feel like a mother. Maternal tears were a moving target of regulation in Jewish grieving contexts, as well. Baumgarten observes that medieval Jewish sources recommended against mourning 'excessively', which suggests that Jewish mothers, too, were grieving more than their theologians were comfortable with.[53] The *Tale* does allow the mother to grieve briefly for her son, but she must also effectively turn him over to Mary and her superior maternity. The *imitatio Mariae* she is permitted is limited to the brief period during which she searches for him, processes the news of his death, and assigns blame for his loss.

The clearer message was that Mary and her imitators be antisemitic. The deployment of antisemitism in the *Tale*, as in multiple late-medieval depictions of Mary at the Crucifixion, affirms the mother's orthodoxy and defines her maternity: like Mary, the clergeon's mother claims Christian identity by turning sharply and vocally against Judaism at her child's death. The *Lamentatio St. Bernardi* reveals a sense of the antisemitic baggage packed into Marian devotional texts. In it, Mary describes her experience of the Crucifixion. Her suffering is directly linked to Christ's: seeing each other's pain increases their suffering in a cycle of accretion that is meant to implicate and ultimately redeem the penitent reader. In the Middle English verse adaptation of the *Lamentatio* text, Mary consistently frames this suffering as a result of Jewish actions rather than those of the Roman soldiers named in the Gospels: 'þe Jewis dide him gret wow'; 'þe Jewis led me him fro'; Þe Jewis harm had neuere non ende'; 'Þus þe Jewis sterne & stoute,/Mi sone þei held in hard bonde'; 'þe Jewis tuggid him al aboute'. When Mary wishes herself dead, Jewish participants witness her grief—'Þe Jewis sawe me þan sori'—but they are unmoved, coldly telling her to leave.[54] The habit of blaming Jews for the Crucifixion emerges here as a complex, illogical shorthand seemingly internalized by clerical writers and continually reiterated in Marian texts.

A Mary for every mother 201

Mothers seeking answers: the policing of maternity and the erasure of real mothers

Our first meeting with the clergeon's mother follows her sleepless night waiting for her child 'with face pale of drede and bisy thought'. Within the tale's allotment for her *imitatio Mariae*, that maternal concern helps define her as doctrinally correct: affective piety required Christians to train to feel empathy for Mary's distress at the Crucifixion. Since part of the Church's argument against Jews was that they lacked this compassion, such feeling was thought to affirm Christian identity. The clergeon's mother, 'moodres pitee in hir brest enclosed', 'goth, as she were half out of hir mynde' to demonstrate Christian maternal affection (593–4). Complicating this antisemitic trope are the similarly affectionate dynamics in Marian miracle stories that feature Jewish mothers who, against Christian stereotype, desperately seek their missing children. Rather than consider such behaviors natural maternal practice, the texts interpret these mothers' maternal instincts and affection as clues that reveal them as natural Christians, confirmed by their quick conversions to Christianity.[55] Chaucer did have relatively familiar maternal models in the form of the English blood libel tales about William of Norwich and Hugh of Lincoln. Thomas of Monmouth speculated that the mother of the twelve-year-old William of Norwich (d. 1144) sought him like Mary looked for Christ at temple. In Matthew Paris's *vita* of Hugh of Lincoln (d. 1255), the child's mother begins her own frantic multi-day search and 'by her cries and lamentations excited the grief and compassion of all the citizens who had flocked together to that place', her pathos contagious.[56] Such public worry and, sometimes, grieving would seem to put all these mothers in the same category.

Notably, however, the clergeon's mother is the only one of these who calls on Mary for help, a decision that also appears to prompt her entry into the Jewish neighborhood:

And evere on Cristes mooder meeke and kynde
She cride, and ate laste thus she wroghte:
Among the cursed Jues she hym soghte. (597–9)

Her Marian invocation seems intended to validate her accusation. A predisposition against Jews in blood libel tales was potentially histrionic, a narrative risk, especially as employed by women. Karma Lochrie argues that such bigotry was understood to be gendered: 'Considering the generic association of miracles of the Virgin with female readers, antisemitism, too, could well have been associated with female readership and devotional habits, if not with femininity itself.'[57] Thomas of Monmouth depicts William's mother as a gullible madwoman, 'screaming and crying' in the streets that the Jews have murdered her son; she convicts without evidence, 'with a woman's readiness of belief' that turns out to be accurate. The vita's language carefully distinguishes between 'woman' and 'mother': 'sometimes she behaved *like a mother* moved by all a mother's love, sometimes she bore *herself like a woman* with all a woman's passionate rashness'.[58] 'Mother' here is a trustworthy, recognizable category, as opposed to the unpredictable 'woman'. Upon finding her child's body, she rouses other Christians, who 'all cried out with one voice that all the Jews ought to be destroyed'.[59] Hugh of Lincoln's mother similarly believes the Jews are responsible for her son's death, and her 'cries and lamentations' constitute a public disturbance and potentially a political problem.[60] As we saw in Chapter 2, Katherine Goodland has discussed the concern that grieving mothers might disrupt the status quo.[61] While the mothers' targeting of Jews in these texts likely seemed a safe gamble to their writers, the scenes' wild energies edge close to those of riots. The search that Chaucer's *Tale* describes is similar to those of William's and Hugh's mothers, except that the clergeon's mother, although she is 'half out of hir mynde', does not act before consulting Mary. She, too, assigns Jews responsibility for her son's safety even before confirming his death, but Mary's proximity suggests that she is justified and, perhaps, mimetic. The danger of an irrational woman acting on impulse and riling fellow Christians into chaos eases. In the ethos of the genre, her doctrinally correct actions put the veneer of Marian maternity on misogyny and on antisemitism.

When the clergeon's mother asks her Jewish neighbors directly about her son, she is, briefly, Mary interrogating those who late-medieval Christians wrongly believed crucified her son. Their answers are noncommittal ('They seyde "nay"'). Her intuition triumphs over what appears to be a lie. She does this investigative work alone rather than raising the hue and cry or otherwise inflaming a crowd: that is, she does not disrupt the system that is already in place. That discernment and decorum is rewarded with a nudge from Christ, a hint of not only how but where to be:

> ... but Jhesu of his grace
> Yaf in hir thought inwith a litel space
> *That in that place* after hir sone she *cryde*,
> Where he was casten in a pit bisyde. (603–6, emphasis mine)

This means the clergeon's mother benefits from two miracles. Christ has noticed her doctrinally correct behaviors so far, showing maternal concern and maintaining decorum and the status quo as she asks passersby about her child's whereabouts. He thus guides her into the vicinity of her child's burial pit. Her tears there are Marian enough to complete Mary's miracle: her weeping provokes the child's Marian hymn in answer ('He Alma redemptoris gan to synge/So loude that al the place gan to rynge' 612–13). This sets the discovery and relocation of his body, and perceived justice, in motion. Mary's grain trick essentially requires that the boy's body be found by Christians: his song about her maternity must be heard and recognized. The child's impetus to sing is irrelevant until his mother cries nearby. Suddenly his song, as we might say now, goes viral.

> The Cristene folk that thurgh the street wente
> In coomen for to wonder upon this thing,
> And hastily they for the provost sente. (614–16)

Chaucer's description of the gathering crowd as only 'Cristene folk' suggests that there are no Jews or Muslims curious about why someone is singing a Christian song at top volume from the latrine. Neither is there specific mention of children or mothers in this crowd. These 'Cristene folk' share a confessional solidarity rather than a maternal one. They are drawn by the song that is prompted by her Marian tears. The clergeon's mother weeping in this space offers the pathos that might be expected from any recently bereaved parent, but her position, staged near his singing body, also makes a claim to Christian identity, signaling her affective devotion.

Tears as institutional power

Aside from their late-medieval Christian status as a spiritual gift, tears can also be a way for women with access to institutional, patriarchal power to invoke that power. This option is not available to the Jewish mothers in Marian miracle stories or blood libel tales. Chaucer's editing of the clergeon's mother to be more deferential to the church and more in alignment with law enforcement than her predecessors in the analogues gives her tears consequential power against the Jews wedged 'amonges Cristene folk' (489). Once she 'cride', the Jews are othered, even 'cursed'; when she 'cryde' again near her son's burial pit, his song draws the crowd who calls the magistrate. In the moment that she allows her tears to prompt official action, she exploits the vulnerable situation of the ghetto to align with power amid her own vulnerable grief. In Chaucer's story, a Jewish person really has committed the crime, which is what makes the story so dangerous: it elevates the Christian mother's tears to definitive judgment. Here, too, she briefly emulates Mary, who as Queen of Heaven routinely gets to be redeemer or persuader.

The mother's tears are answered with a Marian miracle that not only proves her orthodoxy and her son's innocence but also rains down more violence on the ghetto. The centering of antisemitism is 'correct' for her emulation of Mary, but it further endangers the Jewish population. As Mikki Kendall has shown in *Hood Feminism*, safe neighborhoods are a women's issue and especially a mothers' issue.[62] By inviting the police, who the magistrate's song makes clear are anti-Jewish, to do more surveillance and scrutiny, the 'Cristene folk' and the mother make the Jewish quarter significantly less safe for its inhabitants.

In addition, the mother's imitation and invocation of Mary bring the antisemitic subtexts of the late-medieval Crucifixion narrative to this Jewish space in Chaucer's 'Asye'. Her re-enactment of the Crucifixion composition, nudged into place by Christ himself (603–5) is legible as such to other characters. The magistrate's first act is not to assess the crime scene but to praise Christ and Mary, as if he is in church. Despite the Islamicate location, everyone with power in the *Tale* appears Christian: church and state authorities conflate against the Jewish population. As if to justify this dynamic, Chaucer has the *Tale*'s Jews acting more criminally than in the analogues or miracle tales, even as he bounces between singular and plural pronouns (565–73). They are prompted to action by Satan rather than their own discernment. They throw the child's body in a latrine rather than bury him. They show no remorse. There is certainly no mass conversion that might smooth them into

Christian conformity. The magistrate's arrival puts the seal of official law enforcement on the collective Christian action against the Jewish population, and he quickly self-identifies as part of their faith community, too. His arrest of the Jews is directly connected to his praise of Mary:

> He cam anon withouten tariyng,
> And *herieth Crist that is of hevene kyng*,
> *And eek his mooder*, honour of mankynde,
> And after that the Jewes leet he bynde. (617–20)

Whether he is actually Christian or not, he expresses solidarity with the crowd; 'heriyng' is the same verb used for the monks' praise of Mary at the end of the *Tale* and for the children's at the beginning.[63] The scene bears, briefly, cacophony: the mother is, presumably, still weeping; the magistrate is praising Christ and Mary; the child is singing so loudly the whole neighborhood rings. The Jewish street within an Islamicate city or neighborhood temporarily *sounds* Christian. We are still in a Semitic space, but it is clear that the justice system will take a Christian perspective. By the time the child's body rests on the bier in a predominantly Christian space, the magistrate's imposed punishment on the Jews will be brutal and final. There is no trial; he will operate on instinct. In the end, neither the abbot nor the monks of his convent will protest the violence: the Church approves.[64]

Marian mourning as maternal validation— and as antisemitic

Blurton and Johnson allude briefly to maternal grief in their discussion of the typology of the martyred child in the *Prioress's Tale* to the crucified Christ: 'boy singers, through their close association with mother figures, emphasize the maternal pain of loss that is such a prominent feature of biblical accounts of Christ's death'.[65] The 'maternal pain' mentioned here is explored most thoroughly in the tradition of *planctus Mariae* that Chaucer knew from reading and translating Guillaume de Deguileville and that his fifteenth-century readers would recognize from Hoccleve's and, later, Lydgate's translations.[66] Chaucer was a careful reader of Deguileville, a

Cistercian; Cistercian writers saw Mary's perfection as both singular and inimitable model of maternity. Chaucer's familiarity with the *planctus Mariae* emerges in the *ABC*:

> Ladi, *thi sorwe kan I not portreye*
> *Under the cros*, ne his greevous penaunce;
> But for youre bothes peynes I yow preye. (81–3, my emphases)

The image of a grieving Mary 'under the cros' and the co-suffering of mother and son are not present in Deguileville's version, whose L stanza praises only Mary's 'sweetness' ('douceur'). Helen Phillips has noted that Chaucer lingers more than does Deguileville on the Crucifixion, death, and womb, adding a 'clear echo of Stabat Mater to stanza L'.[67] The addition is less an echo than a shout. Chaucer's shift from 'sweet' to 'sorrowful' inserts the violence of the Crucifixion and Mary's *compassio* between stanzas that focus on Mary's purity and healing powers.[68] His linking of the 'greevous penaunce' and 'youre bothes peynes' of the Crucifixion to 'oure alder foo' makes Satan the cause of Mary's maternal pain at the Cross. This is a conscious choice. While Deguileville's L stanza avoids reference to the Crucifixion or to Jews' alleged role in it, his original *Lament*—the one Chaucer read—carefully preserves antisemitic tropes. As Mariamne Krummel has pointed out, Hoccleve also omits this antisemitism from his *Complaint,* so it does not necessarily have to be a component of Mary's sorrow.[69] Chaucer's leaving antisemitism out of his own L stanza only to make Mary an integral part of a blood libel tale that evokes *planctus Mariae* shifts attention from Mary's sorrow to a misplaced vengeance. In his corpus, a weeping Mary can exist without a Jewish-instigated murder, but not the reverse. Adding Mary to the blood libel tale weaponizes her maternity as incompatible with and antithetical to Jewishness.

The conversion of Mary's womb

When the 'cristene people' proceed with the clergeon's body to the abbey, 'His mooder swownynge by his beere lay' (625). That swoon at her child's bier is the mother's last appearance in the *Tale* before the abbot and monks take his body for burial. The figure of a mother openly grieving is absent from the funerals in the analogues.

The mother's swoon is Chaucer's innovation, a gesture that identifies her loss and her maternity as Marian. It also silently affirms her antisemitic stance. Chaucer positions the swooning woman at the altar, presumably in front of a screen attached to a Great Rood or templon beam,[70] with her child's corpse still eerily singing his postmortem hymn to Mary. It is a multisensory display for the convent and for readers.[71] Those familiar with late-medieval Christian depictions of the Crucifixion would recognize the typology: they knew that liturgical art made this moment a watershed for Marian maternity and a scapegoating for the Romans of the Jews. It particularly recalled Jewish disbelief in Mary's physical maternity.

As we saw in Chapter 2, for Christian theologians Mary's womb was not only the site of Christ's gestation but where her grief at the Crucifixion manifested as debilitating physical pain.[72] They argued that Mary had felt no discomfort in delivering Christ: her labor pains were realized later, under the Cross. Mary's Crucifixion swoon appears visually in *lo spasimo* paintings, poetically in the *planctus Mariae* genre, and doctrinally in sermons and devotional texts, as we have seen. When the clergeon's 'mooder swownynge by his beere lay' (625), she is not only expressing overwhelming grief but also promoting the claim that Mary, through her maternal grief, *had* felt the physical pain of birthing the church at Christ's death, affirming the womb as an important component of Marian maternity. The theology of *Maria compatiens* was developed fully in the Eastern church long before affective piety took hold in Western Christian practice.[73]

The seventh-century Old Georgian *Life of the Virgin*, composed in or near Constantinople by Maximus the Confessor, imagines the scene:

> she had no consolation, but as in an eternal night, she was surrounded by sadness and grief ... She stretched forth her hands, beat her breast, and groaned from the depths of her heart, and she endured her torments and drenched the earth with her tears. ... as her birthing was beyond nature, so also her sorrow ... she who suffered alone knows, and she alone completely understands the Lord who was born from her.[74]

Mary's Crucifixion swoon, linked to her anatomical womb, to her compassion at the Cross, and indirectly to her antipathy toward

Jews, is thus a concept first developed in 'Asye'.[75] Alleged Jewish skepticism of Christ's physical birth meant that Mary's birthing pains suffered at the Cross were not only confirmation of her biological and genealogical connection to Christ, but also a refutation of Judaism. The biological motherhood, seemingly free of human paternity, that is replicated in the *Prioress's Tale* and reiterated in the widowed mother's swoon at the child's bier, then, maintains a subtext of antisemitic feeling: only those whose hearts host Satan's 'waspes nest' could doubt the power of Marian bodily maternity, and by extension, doubt the pathos of maternal love.[76]

Punishing maternity

With law enforcement already activated, the mother's recreation of Mary's swoon with its accompanying messages aligns her with Mary's antisemitism and perpetuates falsehoods about and violence toward Jews. In case the point is too subtle, Chaucer cuts briefly away from the dulcet tones of the child's funeral Mass to a stanza describing the magistrate's brutal torture, dismemberment, and hanging of any Jews with knowledge of the child's death.

> This provost dooth thise Jewes for to sterve
> *That of this mordre wiste*,
> Yvele shal have that yvele wol deserve. (629–31, emphasis mine)

Who could claim ignorance of the mother's inquiries, the child singing, the unavailability of the latrine, the crowd of strangers passing through, the arrival of law enforcement? Such collective punishment of a whole community means even those who might have offered support or been concerned about child safety are killed. This shifts attention to Jewish mothers. The killing of Jews to avenge the Christian child's death ensures the suffering of more children and reduces the chances that a multifaith childraising community, such as what Baumgarten has shown was historically plausible, can be built or repaired.[77] The moment also sends a message to Jewish readers of the *Tale* that individual Christians will opt to align with the power of institutions rather than affirm Jewish humanity.

The expectation that one understands the system and that those carrying weapons share one's values is, like Marian motherhood itself, of limited accessibility. In the *Tale*, the mother's deference to this justice system—presented here as closely attuned to the Church—confirms her as suitably Christian. Yet despite this, and despite her close adherence to Marian behaviors, the responsibility for her son's body is left to the abbot and convent. This marks a departure from post-Crucifixion events. Some sources depict Mary arguing with disciples over possession of Christ's body; in others her friends and sisters go to prepare Christ's body for burial and discover it's missing. The clergeon's mother has no allies or argument over her child's body; she simply swoons and slips out of the narrative when the abbot and convent take over. That she has proven her ability to imitate Mary only to lose the ability to bury her own child reveals a gap between the alliance with or deference to power that Marian motherhood expects and the benefits Christian mothers actually get from such conformity.

The frequent allusions to the Slaughter of the Innocents in the *Prologue* and mention of Rachel in the *Tale*'s line 627 connote Jewish maternal loss and power. In Jeremiah 31.15, Rachel weeps for the Jewish children enslaved by the Assyrians. Christian scripture appropriates that image in Matthew 2.18 to suggest that Rachel wept similarly over the Jewish infants killed by Herod's decree. Reading typologically, Christian theology argued that the Gospel text promises restoration through the church itself, an explanation that fits neatly with the end of the *Tale*, which has the Christian convent organizing the child's transfer from his birth mother to Mary. Like Rachel whose tears would be answered by the Christian church, the clergeon's mother would in time understand the promise and meaning of her maternal sacrifice.

However, an eleventh-century midrash of the Jeremiah passage allows us to interpret line 627 quite differently. In Eikhah Rabbah, petihta 24, Rabbi Shlomo Itzhaki's exposition situates Rachel as a successful intercessor with God where Abraham, Issac, Jacob, and Moses failed.[78] This Rachel seeks compassion rather than justice. Describing her own past generosity of heart, she broadens her maternal love to include all Jewish children, not only her biological ones. God promises to restore Israel thanks to her intervention. As Caitlin Hamilton explains, 'What Rachel has in common with her "children" ... is not only genetics but a common relationship with God. ... In claiming this relationship before the throne of God with a demonstration of her love, Rachel shows herself to be a true mother to the whole people of Israel.'[79] If the clergeon's mother were truly a 'newe Rachel', she could intercede with the divine on behalf of her son by showing a similar generosity of heart, seeking compassion rather than revenge, rejecting the narrow biological definition of motherhood, and extending her maternal love to other children, including Jewish children. Yet instead of engaging in this way, she disappears from the text. She does not take on the additional task of intercession even to ask Mary to restore her child's life. Reading matricentrically here exposes her maternal limits.

How maternal is she? Sharing the mother(ing) load

Particularly for mothers who are not part of the dominant culture, maternal goals are often in conflict with the goals of patriarchal motherhood; they, too, are culturally specific. Ruddick states that 'Preserving the lives of children is the central constitutive, invariant aim of maternal practice.'[80] She defines such protection as 'to keep safe whatever is vulnerable and valuable in a child'.[81] This preservation or survival can often be assumed for white children but not for the children of those Collins calls 'racial ethnic' mothers. Secondary to this requirement of 'preservative love' are nurturing and training: these fall under the 'motherwork' category of maternal practice.[82] Collins notes that the goals of 'racial ethnic' mothers often differ from those of white mothers: she lists them as the physical survival of both children and of individuals and communities; reproductive justice; participating in motherwork for other children in the community ('othermothering', as opposed to being a 'bloodmother'); keeping one's children in one's own household; and controlling the education of one's children, including teaching them to resist and survive a racist culture.[83]

Applying these goals to the mothering depicted in the *Prioress's Tale* suggests the mother's attempt at Marian maternity achieves, at best, a mixed bag. She is able to keep her child and to choose his education, a task that for medieval Christian and Jewish families was the father's responsibility. We know that 'On Cristes mooder set was his entente' thanks to her teaching:

Thus hath this wydwe hir litel sone ytaught
Oure blisful Lady, Cristes mooder deere,
To worshipe ay, and he forgat it naught. (509–11)

That is, he's thinking about Mary rather than about his own mother or even his own safety. We 'meet' the mother first through this teaching of Marian reverence. It is thanks to his natal mother that he sings about Mary throughout the Jewish neighborhood, being sure to 'worshipe ay' even beyond the Ave Maria she herself taught him. That teaching seems to have come at the expense of the child's discretion and care for his own life. In sending her son to a Christian school through a neighborhood in which she has not built alliances, the clergeon's mother opts to focus on 'nurturance', a privileged ideal that takes for granted the child's survival, over 'preservation'.[84] She appears not to realize her child's vulnerability as a Christian, although we can infer it from the eagerness of the constable to avenge the child's death and the full attention of the bishop and convent. That naïveté is rooted in and reflected by the sparseness of her social network, a weakness that leaves her vulnerable to what we've seen: the responsibility of caring for the boy's body transfers away from the mother to the abbot and the convent, and ultimately to Mary.

Othermothering and maternal transfer

Mary's bodily expressions of tears and uterine pain rely on an essentialist physical definition of maternal grief, and by extension motherhood generally. There are obvious problems with this even besides its grounding in antisemitism: limiting maternity by genetics or by gender reduces the number of people equipped and recognized to meet maternal goals such as preservative love. bell hooks points out that

> As long as women or society as a whole see the mother/child relationship as unique and special because the female carries the child in her body and gives birth, or makes this biological experience synonymous with women having a closer, more significant bond to children than the male parent, responsibility for childcare and childrearing will continue to be primarily women's work.[85]

Matricentric theory resists essentialist language for motherhood: to consider the maternal is to examine all the work of mothering, not merely biological labor. As we saw in Chapter 4, the relational dynamics of mothering can be shared by multiple bodies, not only the 'bloodmother', as Collins calls the birth parent, but anyone in the community who participates in the work of raising a child ('othermother'). This practice is named variously; hooks uses the term 'childrearer' for anyone in the community doing parenting work.[86] Such labor looked different for medieval communities than it does for our own, but the dynamics are still familiar to us. As discussed in Chapter 4, Riddy has shown how household employers may have done the finishing work of parenting, and Erler suggests that older relatives may have taught crucial lessons to younger women.[87] In the *Prioress's Tale*, Mary can offer the boy protection and receive his love; the teacher can train him; the monks can attend his body; even his older classmate can instruct him to master and amplify the Marian devotion that his natal mother first introduced. Maternal care is not restricted to one person. Had his mother attempted the kind of interfaith friendship that Catholic texts warned against, Jewish mothers around the neighborhood might have kept a protective eye out too. To suggest all this care falls only to the natal mother is to reduce the full labor of childraising to the clerical imaginations that invented Marian motherhood.

As we've already seen, the solidarity of Christian othermothering requires the erasure of Jewish mothering. When Mary rejects her Jewish faith, she does not reject her Jewish sister Mary Salome, who has also converted at the Crucifixion. Mary Salome, whose son Christ offers to Mary as his proxy at the Cross, speaks up in Marian tones in the N-Town *Announcement to the Marys* play to criticize the Jews after the Crucifixion.

> Cryst — that Jewys dede sle,
> Oure Lord, that naylyd was on the rode
> And betyn out was his bodyes blode —
> He is aresyn, though they ben wode!
> A, Lorde, yitt wele thu be! (89–94)[88]

Such displays of shared motherhood reinforce Mary's maternal values, including her counterintuitive antisemitism, even when she is absent. The benefits of maternal peering appear to outweigh their religious devotion. There are similar erasures and preservations in an analogue of the *Tale* that appears in the *South English Legendary*.[89] A Jewish mother keeps her community ('that folk') close when she discovers her child sitting with a protective Mary in his father's hot oven. Aghast, the mother converts with her son and Jewish peers ('manie othere ... godemen bicome', 239–40) out of gratitude to Mary. She abandons her faith—and her husband, whom 'that folk' execute on the spot. The solidarity of the crowd softens her isolation in widowhood and conversion: 'manie othere' of 'that folk' are now new Christians with her. Conversion looks easy. But it also erases Jewish motherhood completely: she and her othermothers are now Christian. If Marian maternity cannot take Jewish motherhood or devotion seriously, it is effectively anti-maternal.

Compared with these examples, the clergeon's mother acts in relative isolation. She suffers a paucity of shared childrearing or 'motherwork'. In contrast to the mothers in the analogues, she searches for her child alone. The only community invested in this child apart from the mother is one rooted in institutions such as the church and law enforcement, not relatives or friends whom she can rely on as individuals. (Conversely, William of Norwich has an aunt and a father who play important roles in finding justice for him.) By this metric, the mother's community has failed her. hooks argues for society's 'need for collective parenting', particularly the informal, multigenerational networks that develop organically among family members and neighbors.[90] Such a system is crucial for single parents like the clergeon's mother, but her network is institutionally based: first Mary, then the legal system, and finally the Church step in when she cannot provide all the protection her child needs. Her maternal peers are noticeably absent; the action takes place in public settings such as the church, school, or in the street rather than in the private homes that sometimes appear in the analogues. Without a backup network of caregivers or support, the mother is at the mercy of the church; she is unlikely to challenge God, as did Rachel, or Christ as Mary herself does. The echoing of her values in the actions of other characters rings more of power than of collective care. No one guides the mother in what to do; her correct Marian behaviors result in changes to her son's status, but no one offers her comfort at the bier or brings her sustenance.

Those figures we might generously call 'othermothers'—the teacher, the older student—are nowhere to be seen.

In other words, the clergeon's mother has no friends. Into this breach steps Mary. The peering seems plausible; the mother has prepared her child to trust Mary as maternal figure. But it is unclear how Mary's maternity will extend to caring for the clergeon. If we accept that Mary shares in the motherwork for this child—and his testimony suggests that we should, as responsibility for him passes from his mother to Mary at his bier—we might also ask what kind of othermother she will be. We know from other miracle tales that Mary is capable of rescuing her devotees from condemnation to hell, curing their terminal illnesses, and healing from fatal accidents. She has not done these things here.

The placing of the grain to allow postmortem praises of herself but not to save or restore the child's life would not meet the basic maternal requirement of 'preservation'. Neither does the singing of a Marian hymn or the martyring of the child alter the Jewish neighborhood: more suffering ensues; the streets do not become safer for Christian or Jewish children; the 'justice' system remains the same; and interfaith relations worsen. To return to Collins' list of goals for maternity, Mary falls far short. Still, the tale ends with the promise of Mary's adoption of the boy:

> My litel child, now wol I fecche thee,
> Whan that the greyn is fro thy tonge ytake.
> Be nat agast; I wol thee nat forsake. (667–9)

An important goal of the *Tale* is the transfer of maternity from the clergeon's mother to Mary. There is no such promise in the analogues. The natal mother is left to mourn privately, having been excised from the scene as her child explains his relationship to the Virgin. Whether the mother's performance was close enough to Marian maternity that the transition was seamless is unclear. Compared with the mothers in the analogues, she is more devoted to Mary, less likely to cause a public disturbance, less socially connected, and more aligned with powerful institutions such as the police and the Church. She also follows a remarkably Marian pattern in her expression of grief. For this careful performance, her son will consider Mary his mother, and the convent will bury his body.

Chaucer's narrative innovations of introducing Mary and 'Asye' into old blood libel stories didn't change much. The Jews are still mortally punished; the child is still dead; the mother is still bereaved—although Mary has chipped away at her maternal status. What's left is antisemitism and anti-maternity. Reading matricentrically tells us that in the midst of horrific grief, a self-monitoring mother will sacrifice her neighbors' humanity and her own maternal practice to maintain her alignment with institutions of power, which will dismiss her despite her loyalty and conformity. Regardless of the ethos that the diversity of a 'greet citee' should teach, that mother will still unite with institutions of power against minorities if doing so seems even vaguely personally beneficial. These messages are not news, exactly, but paying attention only to the Prioress and not to the only other individual woman in the *Tale* can obscure them. Blurton and Johnson have warned of the critical tendency to suggest that 'it is the silly and unserious Prioress, rather than her theology or religious tradition, who is behind the dangerous concoction of emotion and antisemitism visible in her tale'.[91] As we saw in Chapter 2 and confirm here, the long revisionist history of Mary's role at the Cross makes clear that antisemitism was deliberately woven into the image of her as a grieving mother.

Obviously, the clergeon's mother is not the only one cheated by her maternal *imitatio Mariae*. Her choices in the moment of her son's death to highlight the Jewish connection to her son's death, to defer to authorities she surely knows will disproportionately punish Jewish bodies, to keep silence as those bodies are tormented, and to yield custody of her child to a powerful institution are not all predictable by the Marian model. But they help lead, over many centuries, to the reinforcements of institutional power and to deaths of more sons of mothers who do not conform as easily to institutional preferences. That is, her grief-fueled performance of Marian maternity only begets more grief.

Thinking of these Chaucerian mothers as agents of orthodoxy—whether 'mother' means the clergeon's mother, other mothers in the *Tales*, or the mother who might be reading the *ABC*—it becomes clear that their task of choosing or providing education for their children includes discernment about which Marian narrative to follow. Had the clergeon's mother access to the community-building Mary we saw in Chapters 3 and 4, she surely would have organized her young child's school experience differently. She has no margin for error in the delicate balance of familiarity with and implementation or imitation of Mary's maternal practices. Perhaps in part because she lacks the stitching authority to compose a more flexible imitable Mary or the broader perspective that maternal peers could share, she chooses a literal *imitatio Mariae* over potential preservation of her own child's life.

Notes

1 'die quadam solus in capite chori foris ecclesiam quasi reparaturus femoralia residebat', in *Materials for the History of Thomas Becket, Archbishop of Canterbury*, ed. James Craigie Robertson, Rolls Series 67. Vol. 2 (London: Longman, 1876), 292–5, at 293.
2 In the *Legenda Aurea*, the miracle is told differently: Becket has left his unmended undergarment under his bed, and the Virgin repairs it as a surprise; there, she leverages the repair to urge mercy for one of her devotees, in *Golden Legend*, 61.
3 'operis ergo hujus ignarus et expers', Robertson, 293.
4 Saetveit Miles focuses on depictions of the Annunciation but speaks more broadly about the implications for women's literacies in *Virgin Mary's Book*.
5 Kathryn Rudy, 'Sewing the body of Christ: Eucharist wafer souvenirs stitched into fifteenth-century manuscripts, primarily in the Netherlands', *Journal of Historians of Netherlandish Art* 8.1 (2016), 10.5092/jhna.2016.8.1.1.
6 See especially Bianca Calabresi, 'You sow, ile read: letter and literacies in early modern samplers', in *Reading Women: Literacy, Authorship, and Culture in the Atlantic World*, ed. Heidi Hackel and Catherine Kelly (Philadelphia: University of Pennsylvania Press, 2009) 79–104; and Wendy Wall, 'Literacies: Handwriting and handiwork', in *Recipes for Thought: Knowledge and Taste in the Early Modern Kitchen* (Philadelphia: University of Pennsylvania Press, 2016), 112–66.
7 Kathryn Rudy, 'Sewing as authority in the Middle Ages', *Zeitschrift für Medien-und Kulturforschung* 6.1 (2015), 117–31.
8 Blurton and Johnson, *Critics*.
9 Here and elsewhere I default to scholarly tradition, referring to Chaucer's translation of Deguileville's *Prière* as the *ABC* to avoid confusion, although I generally find arguments against that title persuasive.

10 On Mary's literacy, see especially Saetveit Miles and Donavin.
11 Leah Price, *How To Do Things with Books* (Princeton, NJ: Princeton University Press, 2012).
12 Heather Blatt, *Participatory Reading in Late-medieval England* (Manchester: Manchester University Press, 2018).
13 See William Quinn, 'Chaucer's problematic prière: *An ABC* as artifact and critical issue', *Studies in the Age of Chaucer* 23 (2001), 109–41, at 115.
14 See Quinn, 'Problematic'. Georgiana Donavin discusses the relationship between the rosary and Marian devotion in 'Alphabets and rosary beads in Chaucer's *An ABC*', *Medieval Rhetoric*, ed. Scott Troyan (New York: Routledge, 2004), 25–40.
15 Orme, *Medieval Children*, 237–72. See also Kathryn Rudy, 'An illustrated mid-fifteenth-century primer for a Flemish girl: British Library, Harley MS 3828', *Journal of the Warburg and Courtauld Institutes* 69 (2006), 51–94, at 60.
16 See Winston-Allen, *Stories of the Rose*, and Pamela H. Smith, *The Body of the Artisan: Art and Experience in the Scientific Revolution* (Chicago: University of Chicago Press, 2004).
17 Lucy M. Allen-Goss, *Female Desire in Chaucer's* Legend of Good Women *and Middle English Romance* (Cambridge: D.S. Brewer, 2020), 54–9.
18 See Laura Fulkerson Hodges, *Chaucer and Clothing: Clerical and Academic Costume in the General Prologue to the Canterbury Tales* (Cambridge: D.S. Brewer, 2005).
19 E. Jane Burns, *Sea of Silk: A Textile Geography of Women's Work in Medieval French Literature* (Philadelphia: University of Pennsylvania Press, 2009), and Rozsika Parker, *The Subversive Stitch: Embroidery and the Making of the Feminine* (London: Women's Press, 1984).
20 Hannes Kleineke, 'Carleton's book: William FitzStephen's "Description of London" in a late fourteenth-century common-place book', *Historical Research* 74.183 (2001), 117–26, at 124.
21 For Anne as Mary's teacher, see Pamela Sheingorn, '"The wise mother": The image of St. Anne teaching the Virgin Mary', in *Gendering the Master Narrative: Women and Power in the Middle Ages*, ed. Mary Erler and Maryanne Kowaleski (Ithaca, NY: Cornell University Press, 2003), 105–34; for Mary's literacy see Saetveit Miles, *Virgin Mary's Book*. On the expectation that mothers teach literacy, see Michael Clanchy, 'Did mothers teach their children to read?' in *Motherhood, Religion, and Society in Medieval Europe, 400–1400*, ed. Lesley Smith and Conrad Leyser (New York: Routledge, 2011), 129–53; Mary McDevitt, 'Mary, motherhood, and teaching in the

Book to a Mother and Chaucer's *ABC'*, *Marian Studies* 53 (2002), 23–42; and Donavin, *Scribit Mater*.
22 Rudy, 'Illustrated', 66.
23 Calabresi, 'You sow', 94.
24 Margaret Jourdain dates an English sampler reference as early as 1502, citing a payment for 'an elne of lynnyn cloth for a sampler for the Quene' from the Privy Purse account books, in *The History of English Secular Embroidery* (New York: Dutton and Company, 1912), at 177–8, n. 3. But according to Susan Frye, the earliest confirmed mention of an embroidered spot sampler occurs in a 1545 will, when the sampler's owner passes it on to another woman. This is also the OED's first recorded use of the word 'sampler', although it must have been in use for generations before. A few years earlier, in 1530, the first English stitch pattern book was published in Antwerp. See Susan Frye, *Pens and Needles: Women's Textualities in Early Modern England* (Philadelphia: University of Pennsylvania Press, 2013), 123, 128. Women were likely sharing or bequeathing their samplers informally long before legitimizing such gifts in legal documents.
25 See Kate Heard, *English Medieval Embroidery: Opus Anglicanum*, ed. Clare Browne, Glyn Davies, and M. A. Michael (New Haven: Yale University Press, 2016) 86 n. 40. See also Michael A. Michael in the same volume.
26 Jourdain, *History*, 6. See also Lanto Synge, *Art of Embroidery, History of Style and Technique* (Woodbridge: Antique Collector's Club, 2001), 2.
27 Figured by two ells linen cloth and one ounce silk thread against twenty-five sheets paper and ink. Gregory Clark, 'Lifestyles of the rich and famous: Living costs of the rich versus the poor in England, 1209–1869', in *Towards a Global History of Prices and Wages*, 2004. www.iisg.nl/hpw/papers/clark.pdf.
28 *Trotula*, 83, emphasis mine.
29 Danièle Alexandre-Bidon, 'La lettre volée: apprendre à lire à l'enfant au Moyen Âge', *Annales Économies, Sociétiés Civilisations* 44.4 (1989), 953–92, at 982.
30 George Pace, 'The adorned initials of Chaucer's A B C', *Manuscripta* 23 (1979), 88–98.
31 Donavin, *Scribit Mater*, 174.
32 Saetveit Miles, 'Origins', 633, 638.
33 B.L. Wolpe, 'Florilegium alphabeticum: Alphabets in medieval manuscripts', in *Calligraphy and Palaeography*, ed. A.S. Osley (London: Faber, 1965), 69–74.

34 Claire M. Waters, 'Maria mirabilis: Beholding Mary in the miracles', *Journal of Religious History* 44.4 (2020), 407–21.
35 Karen Coats, 'P is for patriarchy: Re-imaging the alphabet', *Children's Literature Association Quarterly* 25.2 (2000), 88–97, at 88. Rudy uses Austin's theory to consider sewing a means of establishing authority in 'Sewing as authority'.
36 To be clear, Chaucer often acknowledged the subversive ways embroidery and mother-daughter activities could tell women's stories, as in the *Knight's Tale*, *Troilus*, and *Legend of good women*. Similarly, Parker argues for feminist interpretations of liturgical textiles, completed by nuns and often featuring Mary or Margaret of Antioch. See her chapter 2 in *Subversive*. Jeffrey Hamburger's work on *nonnenarbeiten* points in similar directions.
37 Collins, 'Shifting the Center', 45, 47.
38 See lines 600–3. All citations of the *Canterbury Tales* are taken from *The Riverside Chaucer*, ed. Larry D. Benson, 3rd edn. (Boston: Houghton Mifflin, 1987).
39 Elisheva Baumgarten, *Mothers and Children: Jewish Family Life in Medieval Europe* (Princeton: Princeton University Press, 2004), especially chapter 4 and at 120 and 144, in which Baumgarten describes interfaith mothers discussing childcare.
40 Court decisions including the former appear in S. W. Baron, *A Social and Religious History of the Jews*, 18 vols. (New York: Columbia University Press, 1937), 2:53–4. As discussed in the Introduction, an Easter sermon warns of the latter in Ross, *Middle English Sermons*, 63–65.
41 Baumgarten, *Mothers*, 181.
42 Although Jewish and preverbal, the Innocents were considered the Christian church's first martyrs. The second-century Byzantine *Protevangelium* describes Elizabeth's command of a mountain to open to shelter the infant John. See Vuong, *Protevangelium*, 105. The Catholic Church estimated the number of victims as quite small, as low as six, while the Eastern and Coptic churches' estimates were as high as 144,000.
43 Sheila Delany describes Chaucer's travels to areas with Jewish and Muslim populations and the longtime Islamic presence in southern and central Europe that may have inspired his setting. See 'Chaucer's Prioress, the Jews and the Muslims', *Medieval Encounters* 5.2 (1999), 198–213, at 210.
44 It may even be one that holds true for someone like the Prioress, mixing her home-grown experiences and fetishes about the East to

apply to an imaginary space. Delany suggests that since the story is not, strictly speaking, possible in a real 'Asian' (or Islamic European) city, it must be that the Prioress or Chaucer is airlifting their own prejudices and stereotypes onto an imagined location. Emily Steiner points out we are 'asked to imagine' the setting as an English town in *Open Access Canterbury Tales*, https://opencanterburytales.dsl.lsu.edu/prt1/.

45 Delany, 'Chaucer's Prioress', 204.
46 Five of these are mentions of the *Alma redemptoris*, the clergeon's song honoring Mary as mother of the redeemer.
47 The *Maria dolorosa* as subject of affective piety in Christianity has been deeply studied; for a brief history, see Sandro Sticca, *The Planctus Mariae in the Dramatic Tradition of the Middle Ages*, trans. Joseph Berrigan (Athens, GA: University of Georgia Press, 1988); for its roots in the Greek tradition, see Stephen Shoemaker, 'Mary at the Cross, East and West: Maternal compassion and affective piety in the earliest "Life of the Virgin" and the High Middle Ages', *The Journal of Theological Studies* 62.2 (2011), 570–606.
48 From Richard Maidstone's translation in the Vernon manuscript. 'Lamentation of Mary to St Bernard' in G. Kribel, 'Studien zu Richard Rolle de Hampole II: *Lamentatio St. Bernardi de compassione Mariae*', *Englische Studien* 8 (1885), 85–114, at 108A, lines 593–4.
49 The text, from the Vernon manuscript, appears as 'Hou the Iewes in despit of Ure Lady threwe a child in a gonge', in Boyarin, *Miracles*, 60–3.
50 The poetic version quoted here is from Cambridge University Library, MS DD.I.1, fols 21r–29v: 'Lamentation of Mary to St Bernard', in Kribel, 'Studien', 88B, lines 77–8.
51 'The lament of Mary', in Shuffelton, *Codex Ashmole 61*, 274–7, at 275, line 11.
52 McNamer, *Affective Meditation*, 119.
53 Baumgarten, *Mothers and Children*, 165–7.
54 'Lamentation of Mary to St Bernard', in Kribel, 'Studien', 87B, 92B, 93B, 96B, 100B, lines 61, 187, 213, 273–4, 279, 389.
55 See the versions of 'The Jewish Boy' in the *South English Legendary* and in the Vernon manuscript, Boyarin, *Miracles*, 32–5 and 70–5.
56 *Matthew Paris's English History: From the Year 1235 to 1273*, ed. John Allen Giles, 3 vols. (London, 1852–54), 3: 139, especially *Of the Cruel Treatment of the Jews for Having Crucified a Boy*.
57 Lochrie, *Heterosyncracies* (Minneapolis, 2005), 66.
58 Emphasis mine. From Augustus Jessop and M. R. James, eds. *The Life and Miracles of St William of Norwich by Thomas of Monmouth*,

1896 (Cambridge: Cambridge University Press, 2011), 42. 'Hinc nimirum ceu mater materno pietatis tangebatur affectu; inde tanquam mulier muliebri ac temerario ferebatur ausu', qtd. in Diane Peters Auslander, 'Victims or Martyrs: Children, anti-Judaism, and the stress of change in medieval England', *Childhood in the Middle Ages and the Renaissance*, ed. Christoph Schwarze et al. (Berlin: De Gruyter, 2005), 105–34, at 112.

59 'omnes acclamabatur vocibus omnes radicitus debere destrui judeos', qtd. in Auslander, 'Victims', 118.
60 'orta est suspicio venemens inter Christianos, ipsum a Judaeis sublatum et interemptum', qtd. in Auslander, 'Victims', 113.
61 Goodland, '"Vs for to wepe"', 69–94.
62 Mikki Kendall, *Hood Feminism: Notes from the Women that a Movement Forgot* (New York: Viking, 2020), xiii, 20, 39.
63 Delany asserts that based on textual evidence the provost is 'imagined as also a Christian', 200 n. 5.
64 Kathy Lavezzo argues that both the neighborhood and church are mixed spaces in 'The minster and the Privy: Rereading the Prioress's Tale', *PMLA* 126.2 (2011), 363–82. While having the street open at both ends does mean it's never sealed off, an angry Christian mob would be, at best, unsettling to residents, particularly those with children.
65 Blurton and Johnson, *Critics*, 91.
66 Deguileville's portrayal of Mary's complaint appears in his *Lament of the Green Tree* in Book Four of *Le Pèlerinage de l'âme*; its English translation by Hoccleve, 'Complaint of the Virgin', is well known. Chaucer's *ABC* translates Deguileville's ABC from *Pilgrimage of Human Life*. Lydgate translated the 1355 recension of *Le pèlerinage de la vie humaine*, retaining Chaucer's translation of the Prière instead of composing his own.
67 Helen Phillips, 'Chaucer and DeGuileville: The "ABC" in context', *Medium Aevum* 62.1 (1993), 1–19, at 14.
68 Laila Z. Gross suggests this may be Chaucer's misreading of 'douceur' as 'douleur' in her notes in the *Riverside*, 1077 n. 81.
69 Krummel views Hoccleve's poem as a 'textual expression of kindness toward Jews', demonstrating that it is possible to read the same textual evidence but emerge with a different narrative. See Mariamne Krummel, 'Omissions of antisemitism: Thomas Hoccleve and the putative Jew', *Crafting Jewishness in Medieval England: Legally Absent, Virtually Present* (New York: Palgrave, 2011), 117–36, at 117.
70 Although a different architectural development, the Western rood screen was roughly visually equivalent to the templon beam or

iconostasis in Byzantine and Coptic churches. For a study of such screens especially in Byzantium, Jerusalem, and Egypt, see Sharon Gerstal, ed., *Thresholds of the Sacred: Architectural, Art Historical, Liturgical, and Theological Perspectives on Religious Screens, East and West* (Washington, DC: Dumbarton Oaks, 2006).

71 Philip Alexander notes that William of Norwich's crucifixion was depicted on a rood screen in Holy Trinity church, Loddon, Norfolk, further concentrating the blood libel focus. See Alexander, 'Madame Englentyne, Geoffrey Chaucer and the problem of medieval anti-semitism', *Bulletin of the John Rylands Library* 74.1 (1992), 109–20, at 119.

72 The full theology was first articulated in the West by the German Benedictine abbot Rupert (d. c. 1135): 'at this hour, she truly suffers the pains of childbirth. When [Jesus] was born, she did not suffer like other mothers: now, however, she suffers, she is tormented and full of sorrow, because her hour has come ... in the Passion of her only Son, the Blessed Virgin gave birth to the salvation of all mankind: in effect, she is the mother of all mankind', in *Commentaria in Evangelium Sandi Iohannis*, qtd. in Neff, 'Pain of *compassio*', 256. By the twelfth century, Christian belief that Mary accepted the role of universal mother at the Cross was commonplace.

73 Mary's puerperal swoon developed partly from the Byzantine idea of *compassio*, that Mary felt Christ's Crucifixion pains in her own body, which appears as early as the seventh-century Maximus the Confessor in Constantinople. See also Rubin, *Mother*, 243–55. The swoon incorporates the idea promoted by fourth-century bishop Ambrose of Milan that Mary became universal mother by birthing the Christian church at the Crucifixion. Neff notices the swoon first in the Byzantine Theodore Psalter, in the *Arrest of Christ, Virgin Supported by John*, London, British Library, Add. MS 19352, fol. 45v, dated 1066; it is a Greek manuscript originating in Constantinople, digitized and viewable at www.bl.uk/manuscripts/Viewer.aspx?ref=add_ms_19352_f045v. The swoon image appears in Byzantine and Western manuscripts, paintings, and sculpture through the fifteenth century, most famously in Rogier van der Weyden's *Descent from the Cross*.

74 Maximus the Confessor, *The Life of the Virgin*, trans. and ed. Stephen Shoemaker (New Haven: Yale, 2012), 107, 111.

75 Maximus assigns responsibility for the violence to Jews, but confusingly also frequently mentions Roman soldiers at the scene (104–5, 108–9).

76 See the discussion of Jewish doubt in Mary's bodily maternity in Chapter 2. In Ogier's meditation, Mary's body displays her grief: she

'lay prostrate', could 'scarcely hold herself up', 'stood as though dead', and was 'racked by many sobs'. She folds accusations against Jews into her vocal mourning: 'O wicked Jews! O wretched Jews, do not spare me! Since you crucify my only child, crucify the mother, or kill me with some other kind of cruel death, so long as I might die together with my son'. In Bestul, *Texts*, 173, 181.

77 See note 39 above.
78 Rabbi Shlomo Itzhaki, known as Rashi of Troyes, was born in Troyes in 1041; a translation of his exposition on Yirmiyahu 31.14 appears at www.jtsa.edu/torah/between-rachel-and-jeremiah/. A fuller discussion of this midrash is in Caitlin Hamilton's unpublished Ph.D thesis, *Jewish Suffering in Medieval Christian Drama* (Virginia: University of Virginia, 2017), 57–61. Hamilton notes Christians' 'live interest in Jewish exegesis in the twelfth century'.
79 Hamilton, *Jewish*, 59.
80 Ruddick, *Maternal*, 19.
81 *Ibid.*, 80.
82 'Motherwork' is the term Collins uses; from a labor-studies perspective, Evelyn Nakano Glenn calls it 'reproductive labor'.
83 Collins, 'Shifting', 49–50 and 55–6.
84 Collins describes 'nurturance' as a 'white' ideal; I broaden its application here to acknowledge the *Tale*'s different framework with an eye toward the mother's alignment with institutions of power.
85 bell hooks, *Feminist Theory*, 137.
86 *Ibid.*, 140–2.
87 See Felicity Riddy, 'Mother knows best', and Erler, 'Home visits'.
88 *N-Town*, 294, lines 89–94.
89 In Boyarin, *Miracles*, 32–5.
90 hooks, 'Feminist theory', 146.
91 Blurton and Johnson, *Critics*, 108.

6

A Marian, maternal Cecilia*

By the end of the fifteenth century, the consensus within Marian devotional literature was that Mary had sex appeal. The idea was not new. Theologically, the need for Mary to be beautiful had been recognized much earlier. If Mary was perfect, then her body must also be perfect, both in its virginity and the secular perfection of physical beauty. These attributes were portrayed as mutually supportive: Mary must be sexually desirable, else her virginity wasn't worth much; Mary's perpetual virginity meant she *could* be desirable without being tainted by that description. While her virginity was not official doctrine until much later, her desirability had long been codified.[1] In 1302, the 'Unam sanctam' of Boniface VIII had officially identified the bride portrayed in Canticles 6:8 as the church, represented in many popular texts by Mary. In effect, this papal linking allowed for Mary's role as a performer and subject of erotic poetry. Popular lyrics and narratives depicted Mary's rapport with Christ as if straight out of Canticles rather than the Crucifixion or Nativity.

Like her other qualities, Mary's beauty was impossible for normal women to replicate: as one writer put it, 'Mary had swylk natural fayrnes that I hope never woman in this lyfe had swylk fayrnes'.[2] Poems such as the Vernon manuscript's 'Salutation to Mary' build erotic steam by offering a part-by-part physical description in the style of portraiture.[3] Some lyrics deal with the tension of a sexy Mary through playfulness, as in the chansons d'aventure that place Mary in the role of a sought-after lady in a love quest, with the joke that she turns out to be the most-sought Lady of all. Several texts acknowledge or play up the dynamic by portraying Mary as a potential rival of wives or as a fantasy for men.[4] In an early miracle story, Mary temporarily shape-shifts to pass as a sinner's wife, stepping in as spouse as easily as she replaced the clergeon's mother in the *Prioress's Tale*.[5] In a later poem known as 'The Jealous Wife', the titular character, who is pregnant, kills her children and herself out of jealous rage over her husband's mysterious outings.[6] He has merely been at church praying to Mary. Such drama resulted from years' worth of accumulated evidence of Mary's desirability.

Importantly, her beauty persists despite childbearing. The *N-Town* midwives are shocked that a postpartum Mary hasn't been ravaged by childbirth. Her breasts and body nourish universally, forever, but are never aged, dysfunctional, or unattractive. Mary's power as Queen of Heaven depends at least partly on that persistent beauty. Frequently, Christ addresses her like a lover, a dynamic also common to mystical and hagiographical texts. Mary's beauty thus comes to play a role in her position as mother. The depiction of Mary as desirable, pushed to its logical boundaries, slides Christ into the role of sexual partner and blurs the lines between maternity and erotic play. That interchangeability of roles emerges in devotional texts. A lyric in Douce MS 322 has Mary declare, 'Quia amore langueo' (I languish for love) and ends with the line 'Take me for thy wyfe and lerne to synge' (95). Her desire is simply for people to pray, but the erotic element is unmistakable. By the third quarter of the fifteenth century, the version of this poem in Douce MS 78 has replaced 'wyfe' with 'modure'.[7] Even some of the Nativity poems adopt this tone:

> As sche hym held in hyr lape,
> *He toke hyr lovely by the pape,*
> *And therof swetly he toke a nappe,*
> And sok hys fyll of the lycowr.
> To hys modyr gen he seye,
> 'For this mylke me must deye;
> It ys my kynd therwith to playe,
> My swet modyr, *paramowr*'. (7–14, my emphases)[8]

The function of Mary's maternal breast mingles with the language of lovers. Similarly, Lydgate's *Life of Our Lady* describes nourishing milk shared from 'small pappes' that also suggest Mary's sexual desirability. Both poems, then, eroticize Mary's maternal breasts.[9] In the same vein, images in which Mary reminds Christ of her influential status by baring her breasts at him take on a sexualized tone.[10] The maternal cannot be separated from her sex appeal, even as that appeal is often tangled with her virginity.

Mary's post-Assumption relationship to Christ was thus understood as spousal as well as parental, a significant expansion of her maternal role. This is a different kind of motherly influence than at the wedding at Cana, for example, where Mary simply instructs the servants what to do and tells a dismissive Christ to produce more wine.[11] The heavenly phase of Mary's maternity is distinguished by her power as an intercessor whose appeal to Christ is at least partly due to her physical perfection. Mary *mediatrix* is never far from descriptions of the Queen of Heaven, although many texts elide the role of persuasion in Mary's power to help. Several of the *ora pro nobis* poems acknowledge the relational expectations of the 'blessid quene of heven' (6) as 'spowsesse of Crist, oure savyowre' (14).[12] Mirk's Assumption sermon, among many that play up bridal imagery, includes a poem that depicts Christ calling to Mary as 'my swete ... my flour' while also referring to her womb as 'my boure'.[13] Each penitent's appeal to Mary *mediatrix* had built into it at least a vague knowledge that the mother of Christ was also his bride, roles that coalesced in her power to help.

A Marian Cecilia: Harley 2382 and Chetham 6709

A material clue that Chaucer's Cecilia could be understood as participant in a similar kind of sexually flexible Marian maternity is the pair of late fifteenth-century devotional manuscripts that each contain Chaucer's version of her *vita*, the *Second Nun's Tale*. These are London, British Library Harley MS 2382 and Manchester, Chetham's Library MS 6709.[14] Both these manuscripts include the Marian *Prologue to the Second Nun's Tale* and the Prioress's *Prologue* and *Tale*, and both open with Lydgate's *Life of Our Lady*, the long biographical poem that glosses over Mary's maternal role during Christ's life in favor of a focus on her humility and virginity before his birth. Chetham 6709 opens with a cluster of Marian texts: Lydgate's *Life of Our Lady*, the *Second Nun's Tale*, the *Prioress's Tale*, and Lydgate's life of St Margaret, suggesting that not only Marian devotion but Marian maternity is an important theme.[15] Harley 2382 also contains Lydgate's 'Assumption of Our Lady', which picks up Mary's biography where *Life of Our Lady* leaves off, including her experience of the Crucifixion and her welcome as Queen of Heaven.

Why was the *Second Nun's Tale* bound among so many Marian texts? Its inclusion makes sense if Cecilia is considered a type for Mary. Certainly, Mary's presence in the *Prologue* invites direct and specific connections to Cecilia's behavior in the *Tale*.[16] The narrator even implies that the two are easily confused in lines 27–30, when she has to specify to whom each line is addressed: '*Thou* with thy gerland wroght [made] with rose and lilie—/*Thee* meene I, mayde and martyr, Seint Cecilie' (27–8, emphasis mine). One imagines the Second Nun pausing and casting her gaze heavenward as she then launches into the invocacio ad Mariam: 'And *thow that flour of virgines* art alle,/Of whom that Bernard list so wel to write (29–30). The narrator does not explain why she must take pains to articulate who is who, but the manuscripts' other Marian texts remind us that Mary's purpose as Queen of Heaven is to persuade. As we'll see, that is also Cecilia's primary task. The *Prologue* plays to the multiple familial facets of Mary's role as mediatrix early ('Thow Mayde and Mooder, doghter of thy Sone', 36) and calls on her directly for intercession ('O thou, that art so fair and ful of grace,/Be myn advocat in that heighe place', 67–8). The Virgin Mary's presence in the *Prologue* as wife, authoritative reader, and persuasive mother prompts us to ask how Cecilia's wifely role, authoritative preaching, and maternal behaviors fill the Marian void in the *Tale* itself. When we see Cecilia take on similar tasks, such as persuading her husband and his brother to convert, Mary's expanded brand of motherhood appears replicable. That Cecilia's *vita* is included in these manuscripts with Chaucer's explicitly Marian *Prologue* and with Lydgatean poems that emphasize Mary's strong influence on her son suggests we view Cecilia, too, through a maternal lens and consider how her status as a wife with persuasive skills justifies her *vita*'s presence in the manuscripts.

The Marian roles of wife and spiritual 'mother' that Cecilia embodies are not mutually exclusive. Rather, Cecilia's actions as a wife help broaden the definition of Marian maternity for a reading audience already familiar with the concept of Marian intercession. Rooted in her perceived sexual power, Cecilia's spousal persuasion recalls Mary's unfailing influence over the heavenly Christ more than child-nurturing and -raising. Like Mary on the throne, Cecilia uses her position as wife, especially through persuasion, to get what she wants.

The *vita*'s highlighting of Cecilia's speech allows readers a glimpse at Marian persuasion in action. Chaucer's splicing together of Dominican and Franciscan source texts in the *Second Nun's Tale* gives us Cecilia's authoritative voice in what first seem like two very different registers: as a sweetly persuasive wife to Valerian, and as a fierce, insulting preacher in her confrontation with Almachius.[17] Cecilia's social and rhetorical roles appear to shift dramatically from wife to widowed martyr. Her combative speech with Almachius attracts disproportionate attention from scholars, as does her preaching. Modern readers have been eager to describe Cecilia's speech as subversive despite its conformity to similar speeches in other virgin martyrs' *passiones*.[18] But the less-sexy truth is that Cecilia is a rule-follower, not -breaker: in Chaucer's hybrid translation of her *vita*, her consistent falling into line is highly rewarded. To grasp this, we can consider the biases of the *Tale*'s fifteenth-century audience, who would have read Cecilia's speeches along the short spectrum of orthodoxy and would have absorbed her preaching along with her private speaking by shoehorning both into the speech categories available to pious women. Her *vita* shows readers of Harley 2382 and Chetham 6709 how ordinary mothers and wives short of Mary's queenly status could use rhetoric effectively. Given that the post-assumption Christ and Mary behave like spouses, Mary's spousal maternity as demonstrated by Cecilia becomes a model for marriages as well as for parenting.

A Benedictine Cecilia

I have written elsewhere of the logic of reading this text as a hagiographical narrative modified to suit an audience with Benedictine, or at least pastoral, sympathies.[19] This is relevant for the Harley and Chetham manuscripts, which contain so many Marian texts by the Benedictine monk Lydgate.[20] The Second Nun, like the Prioress, is usually identified as Benedictine, as was the monastery that

Mary Giffin once posited was the original beneficiary of Chaucer's translation.[21] Giffin's suggestion that this tale was composed as a gift to the Benedictines at Norwich Cathedral Priory in honor of their former monk, Cardinal Adam Easton,[22] is plausible enough that it is often cited without question or comment.[23] Reading the *Tale* from the perspective of a Benedictine audience offers a way to understand Cecilia's speaking and persuasive behaviors and, by extension, how her *passio* is wholly congruent with the later Marian manuscripts where we find it. If Giffin is right, then the *Prologue* reminds Chaucer's later readers to interpret Cecilia as the Norwich Benedictines and users of their library would have, with an awareness of what their own books said and assumed about wives, women saints, and preachers. Those readers would have been thinking in pastoral as well as Marian terms. By those standards, the conventionality of Cecilia's first speech as a married woman helps us see that it, like her dialogue with Almachius, attempts to demonstrate women's potential agency within orthodoxy, and wives' and mothers' Marian agency within the family.

Both in the references to reading and in its form as a vernacular sermon, the *Prologue* makes clear that Mary's and Cecilia's authority to speak is rooted in Benedictine reading, an echo of Margery Kempe's training in Dominican reading. While elsewhere the Virgin Mary is occasionally shown preaching, she is more often depicted in visual art and popular perception as a reader, an association underscored by the recommendation in line 35 that readers who want to follow up 'may … reden in hir storie'.[24] A glance at the Benedictine Rule offers an explanation for the extensive sermon on idleness in the opening stanzas of the *Prologue*. Section 48 of the Rule explains that

> Idleness is the enemy of the soul. Therefore, the brothers should be occupied at set times in manual labor, and again at other set times in divine reading. … One or two senior monks [during Lent] should be assigned to go around the monastery during the hours the brothers are free for reading and see to it that there is no slothful brother who spends his time in idleness or gossip and neglects his reading; such a one is not only harmful to himself but also a distraction to others … If [on Sundays] somebody is so careless or lazy that he is unwilling or unable to meditate or read, let him be given some work to do so he will not be idle.[25]

Contrary to what some readers have inferred from the *Tale*'s references to Cecilia as a 'busy bee' who avoids idleness by converting others, this passage suggests that the opposites of idleness are manual labor and reading. In Lydgate's *Life of Our Lady*, the text that opens both Chetham 6709 and Harley 2382, 'to pray and *to rede*' is how Mary spends her time. The invocation to the Virgin Mary in the *Prologue* thus subtly underscores the need for careful reading and affirms the Benedictine theological understanding that is central to the *Tale*. As we see in the *Prologue*'s opening lines, idleness was regularly gendered female. For example, in New York, Morgan Library MS M.772, a copy of Deguileville's *Pilgrimage of Human Life*, idleness is personified as a lazy, impious, fashion-obsessed woman.[26] Reading, then, offers a way to rise above negative stereotypes of femininity by emulating Mary—a clever lesson for a book such as Chetham 6709 or Harley 2382 to suggest. The Second Nun describes book-based translation as her own shield against idleness. And the *Tale* itself reiterates literacy as an antidote to idleness: Urban converts Valerian from a book; Valerian cites from a book. Cecilia herself is not overtly literate but is clearly learned. Mary's spiritual authority, gained partly through reading, is a role Cecilia tries on as proselytizer and preacher. This may explain why the Chaucerian narrator has to clarify in line 28 that the speech against idleness invokes Cecilia, not Mary.

The *Prologue*'s criticism of idle speech and Cecilia's purposeful (rather than idle) speeches in the *Tale* make clear that this is a narrative interested in the outcomes of orthodox (rather than gossipy) women's speech that is obedient to confessional demands and geared toward proselytical productivity. Spoken by a Benedictine nun, the *Prologue* reminds us that our reading of the married Cecilia's words should be with an eye toward clerical expectations of wifely behaviors: amidst the many texts criticizing women's illicit speech, this tale explores what will happen if a woman's speech is *always* orthodox.[27] Specifically, the descriptions of women's speech and marital conversation in confessional manuals and hagiographical texts would prompt a pastoral reader's interpretation of the married virgin martyr Cecilia to consider first her speech as a wife, and only later as a preacher. By the standards of those genres, she is highly successful, achieving all her goals. When we do not read like Benedictines, we are less likely to notice the means of persuasion

Cecilia uses on her wedding night to convince her husband Valerian to remain chaste and ultimately convert to Christianity—a move that also makes him her spiritual son.[28] This address is her first, after a prayer, and is the linchpin of the whole narrative:

> O sweete and wel biloved spouse deere,
> Ther is a conseil, and ye wolde it heere
> Which that right fain I wolde unto yow seye,
> So that ye swere ye shul it nat biwreye. (144–7)[29]

With this bedroom speech and the ones that follow, Cecilia demonstrates what a good and orthodox wife she is and intends to remain. In a pastoral reading of the *Tale*, it is Cecilia's persuasion of Valerian on their wedding night that drives all the action that follows, from Valerian's agreement to keep the marriage chaste to Cecilia's own trial, when the widowed Cecilia abandons wifely persuasion in favor of a more conventional-hagiographical combative interaction with Almachius—that is, when she moves from acting like a good wife to acting like a good preacher. Even as she demonstrates her persuasive skills as a wife, Cecilia is also training Valerian in how to speak as a proselytizing Christian: she is, like a good Marian mother, *teaching* him. He respects her enough to trust her judgment. Cecilia herself becomes a public figure—that is, a speaker in the public sphere—only after her role and speech are legitimized by men. She thus reinforces wives' submissive roles as outlined by confessional manuals and other pastoral texts.

Speaking as a wife

Importantly, Cecilia's initial address to Valerian is spoken as his legal wife. That first line, 'O sweete and wel beloved spouse deere', suggests she is not interested in changing the status of their new relationship. Cecilia's identity as a Chaucerian wife has long been discussed; Donald Howard famously proposed that hers is the ideal Chaucerian marriage in part because it is chaste and ends in martyrdom, but he does not mention Cecilia's persuasive skills and glosses over her navigation of the late-medieval Christian role of wife.[30] Among saints, Cecilia's marital status is noteworthy because the *vitae* of female saints more often featured unmarried virgin martyrs.[31] Frequent admiring references to Cecilia in the biographies of would-be chaste women such as the married Margery Kempe and Marie d'Oignies make clear that female readers of her *vita* saw her primarily as a wife whose orthodoxy justified their citing her example.[32] Cecilia is mentioned more often as a model for wives than for unmarried virgins: it is her conduct within marriage that makes her admirable, as she manages to conform to parameters for wifely behavior without violating those of sanctity. Intriguingly, Cecilia does not acknowledge Mary as a model in the *Tale*. Mary's position either as the bride in Canticles or as wife to Joseph was not as popular as might be expected, although Bernard of Clairvaux and Jean Gerson, respectively, had tried to drum up interest in their sermons. Far more popular in pious art and narrative was Mary's role as Queen of Heaven, a position that, as we've seen, requires Mary's physical appeal. The incestuous dynamic that seeps into so many end-of-century Marian texts, including Chetham 6709 and Harley 2382, points to sexual desirability as a key element of the maternal authority that is available to Mary.

Cecilia's sex appeal is likewise crucial to her success, although the *Second Nun's Tale*, unlike typical virgin martyrs' narratives, does not dwell on her beauty. It focuses instead on her marital status, which seems, in hindsight, inevitable: the text opens with her desire to remain chaste, not to remain unmarried; her first words are a prayer uttered at her wedding; and as she speaks directly to Valerian for the first time, she instantly assumes a wifely persona. (Cecilia begins their conversation not with Christianity but with a tantalizing 'conseil' that carries the implication of sexuality: an 'angel', suspected by Valerian to be 'another man' in line 167, protects her. She knows what is on Valerian's mind on this wedding night.) In addition, Cecilia does not abandon the domestic setting of their first conversation until line 379, more than halfway through the tale. For the majority of the narrative, she remains in the nuptial bedroom, reminding us that however universal her faith and authority may be, her body is ensconced in domestic space for the duration of her marriage.

For pastoral readers, the validity of that marriage depends on her abilities to convert Valerian. According to Raymond of Peñafort, author of a thirteenth-century penitential manual and a *Summa de Matrimonio*, Christians were not held to a marriage contract with nonbelievers unless the latter converted: '[If] a believer contracts marriage with an unbeliever ... there is no marriage. However, a believer can contract an engagement with an unbeliever with the condition that the unbeliever be converted to the faith.'[33] It is not physical consummation of the marriage that matters to Raymond, who argues that a chaste marriage is consummated with holiness.[34] Rather, in a neat twist, the legality of Cecilia's marriage depends on Valerian's conversion, and as we will see, the strength and orthodoxy of her persuasive words depend on her being and staying married. Much hinges on Valerian's response to Cecilia: If he ignores or disbelieves her claims, the marriage can be invalidated; if he consequently attempts rape, her chastity will be threatened, and the angel will physically attack him. The integrity of Cecilia's legal and spiritual status, then, as well as Valerian's physical safety, all depend on Cecilia's powers of persuasion in this first speech and within this domestic space. The speech marks her acceptance of her role as Valerian's spouse and acknowledges that his validation of her words is crucial to his own conversion and, ultimately, her sanctity.

Further, the non-Chaucerian manuscript evidence points to the importance of this textual passage: nearly every version of Cecilia's life, with the exception only of a very few liturgical texts, includes the opening speech in its entirety, while the preaching and combative speech later in the text is more often minimized or omitted.[35] Sherry Reames has argued that such editing was with an eye toward providing good models of appropriate speech for laypersons, thus representing attempts to de-emphasize or even ignore Cecilia's confrontation with Almachius.[36] However, Cecilia's behavior in that exchange is consistent with that of other virgin martyrs in late-medieval hagiography. It is because pastoral readers privileged and endorsed Cecilia's nuptial persuasion, and not because her confrontation with Almachius is considered out of line, that the later speech is often omitted. Further, for readers of the Harley and Chetham manuscripts, the first conversation with Valerian offers a glimpse of the kind of rhetorical persuasion Mary must have employed with Christ in Heaven, which only rarely appears in the Marian corpus.[37] This is the case even when the importance of her influence is acknowledged, as in an appeal for Mary's protection that appears in Harley MS 2382 beginning: 'Bysek thi sone, hevene king' (43).[38]

Christ has promised always to honor Mary's intercessory requests, but those seeking an accessible model of Marian spousal maternity have few concrete examples of how she achieves persuasive success. Cecilia, as Marian type, offers this one.

Wifely persuasion and confessional manuals

It is, then, the nuptial speech to Valerian rather than that to Almachius to which we should be paying attention. In that address, Cecilia is a near-perfect example of the clerical ideal of wifely persuasion that appears in confessional manuals. Sharon Farmer first described this ideal in 1986, and Mary Carruthers has discussed it more recently in her work on the rhetoric of 'sweetness'.[39] Cecilia becomes 'sweeter' as a speaker, wife, and saint if we examine her opening speech through the lens of confessional manuals that often called attention to the danger of women's speech, but also to its power to encourage positive change in a man's behavior. She could potentially function not only as a model of how preachers and confessors were advising laywomen to influence their husbands morally but also as a model for how mothers could influence (on behalf of) their adult children. As David Herlily has argued, late-medieval mothers tended to be significantly closer in age to their children than were fathers; their roles in familial mediation relied on their status as wives as well as their rhetorical skills.[40]

The genre of confessional manuals had developed from the Fourth Lateran Council's requirement of yearly individual confession beginning in 1215.[41] These provided detailed analyses of types of sins and sinners and trained confessors on how to hear, understand, and handle each type.[42] Confessional manuals and other preaching manuals are certainly a relevant genre for Chaucer: his *Parson's Tale* has sources in Raymond of Peñaforte's *Summa penitentia* and Guillaume Peyraut's *Summa*. Cecilia herself does a fair amount of preaching, so pastoral readers might be remiss *not* to consider how preaching manuals might assess her behavior.[43] Chaucer could assume his first readers would be familiar enough with those arguments to note when the wives in his *Tales* strayed from or adhered to their precepts, especially about communication with their husbands.

While later readers of the Chetham and Harley manuscripts may not have had direct access to confessional manuals, they were certainly familiar with the church's hyper-attention to the speech of mothers and wives. Whether or not we accept Giffin's theory that Chaucer's translation was intended to honor an English priest in Rome (where Cecilia was considered a model of how women should treat their husbands), the *Second Nun's Tale*'s potential appeal becomes clearer when we accept Farmer's nudge to consider proscriptive descriptions of wifely behavior in confessional manuals such as the one by Thomas of Chobham, an English subdean of Salisbury cathedral, that now survives in over 160 manuscripts.[44] Chobham's *Summa* assigns the responsibility for a man's sins to his wife and argues that women's seductive powers of persuasion can be positively exploited for spiritual edification:

> In imposing penance, it should always be enjoined upon women to be *preachers* to their husbands, because no priest is able to soften the heart of a man the way his wife can. For this reason, the sin of a man is often imputed to his wife if, through her negligence, he is not corrected. Even in the bedroom, in the midst of their embraces, a wife should speak alluringly to her husband, and if he is hard and unmerciful, and an oppressor of the poor, she should invite him to be merciful; if he is a plunderer, she should denounce plundering; if he is avaricious, she should arouse generosity in him ... Therefore, this ought to be the first and foremost concern of the priest, that he instruct the wife in this way.[45]

Chobham's term 'preachers' ('predicatrices') suggests that he would consider Cecilia a 'preacher' from the very beginning of the *Tale*; the distinction between her private and public speeches is thus only a function of social context. Chobham's attitude toward wives' responsibility and ability to modify their husbands' behaviors appears in several clerical texts to which Chaucer, Easton, and the Norwich Benedictines would have had ready access. Chobham's contemporary Robert of Courson similarly expects a wife to exert influence 'emoliendo cor viri sui' ('by softening [her husband's] heart') and, if he is still 'impoenitens et incorrigible' ('unrepentant and incorrigible'), to refuse to accept financial support from him— though he clarifies 'sed numquam thori' (that she should 'never [refuse to share] his bed').[46] In both cases cited here, the wives exercise persuasive power in the bedroom, with its access to private speech and potential for sexual activity. Courson's stipulation that the wife continue to share her husband's bed acknowledges the implication of sexual bargaining with its insistence that the persuasion must occur verbally, not physically.[47]

Given Cecilia's status later in the poem as preacher, it makes sense that during the brief nuptial moment to which we are privy she adheres to the description of wifely behavior found in preachers' manuals. Cecilia's first words to Valerian convince him 1) not to consummate the marriage, 2) to convert to Christianity, and 3) to risk his life by seeking out an outlaw (here, a pope) to confirm her claims. Thanks largely to Cecilia's quick mastery of wifely rhetoric—she has, after all, only been a wife for a few hours—Valerian shows himself pliable to all her directions, confirming monastic assessments of wives' persuasive potential. Chaucer's portraying Cecilia as such a smooth talker required delicate dancing along the cultural party line on women's speech, which was legally and religiously suspect. As Sandy Bardsley has explained, 'wives were encouraged to speak gently, privately, and on appropriate topics, [but] speech outside these very circumscribed bounds was open to suspicion'.[48] This may be why so few Marian texts give specific examples of Mary's intercession: no one else would have her broad range of authority to speak. Bardsley's work has shown that women's public speech was highly regulated: women could be prosecuted for being 'scolds', for disturbing the status quo, and for slander; their public words could interfere with their husbands' social and spiritual standing.[49] Pastors' books contained plenty of examples of women's 'bad' speech, as well: Edwin Craun cites an anecdote from *Handlyng Sinne* that renders a mother's curse on her child literal and an exemplum of a man who pushes his talkative wife overboard.[50] Craun observes that pastoral tracts advise habitual silence to combat 'sins of the tongue', noting that the Benedictine Rule of silence was an attempt at 'breaking the tongue's habit of sinning'.[51] Too much talking was associated with lechery; idle speech risked attribution to minstrels; and Christians' words were expected to be salvific.[52]

Within that context, wives had a pastoral dispensation to speak at home, and their words are ascribed weight precisely because of their fleshly status.[53] Claire Waters clarifies that women's speech is 'suspect ... not ... because of its unimportance but because of its perceived power'.[54] Persuasion as a technique had feminine and sexual overtones. Chobham attributes wives a special power of speech in persuasion because he views women largely as sexual rather than intellectual beings.[55] Farmer notes that monastics considered 'speech as a sensuous and physical phenomenon, and they therefore associated speech with the physical realm and with women ... in part because they associated both women and oral persuasion with seduction and magic'.[56] The power and potential danger of wives' speech was perceived as merely a less-potent form of witchcraft.[57] These assumptions imbue significant authority to Cecilia's private speech to Valerian on their wedding night. Waters observes that 'beauty, intimacy and rhetoric' were considered particularly useful for persuasion—and of course, Cecilia achieves her first persuasive victory as Valerian's wife in their nuptial bedroom.[58]

Cecilia as sweetly persuasive wife

Chaucer's translation frames the wedding-night conversation with some sensitivity to its provocative implications. As Joseph Grossi and Lynn Staley have noted in other contexts,[59] he reworks its uses of terms such as 'secret' and 'hidden', removing the *Golden Legend*'s description of Cecilia's faith as 'nutrita absconditum' from lines 122–3 and from the bedroom itself ('cubiculi secreta silencia').[60] Absent these terms, Chaucer must locate the couple not merely in their chamber but 'to bedde ... as ofte is the manere' (141–2), and specify that Cecilia speak 'pryvely' (143) to her husband in that bed (promising intriguingly to reveal a 'conseil'). In this seemingly redundant phrasing, the 'intimacy' Waters mentions as useful to persuasion is clarified as close proximity, with implied sexual tension—but it is not hidden ('secreta'). This seems appropriate, since others are privy to Cecilia's faith as well as her bedroom: apart from the tale's readers, both Urban (by his inference) and Tiburce (by his presence) will have access to what transpires there. Given this dynamic, Cecilia's powerful bedroom talk always has potential to be public: while she may appear conventional, she will not be an ordinary wife, even as she borrows the persuasive speech of one. Throughout the scene, Chaucer's language reflects Cecilia's double role as Valerian's wife and pastor. For example, her greeting him as 'wel biloved' (144) rather than 'amantissime' does not just shift agency from him to herself: the 'biloved' she bestows can be interpreted as spousal or pastoral, even maternal. Yet while Chaucer's translation subtly reminds readers that Cecilia's speech serves multiple functions, the success of this scene depends on her taking on the guise of a wife and on Valerian's belief that she fully inhabits that role. She becomes a model of persuasion not by transcending her spousal role as a purely sexual being but by exploiting it in this conversation with her husband.

Mary Carruthers lists the specific Latin terms for 'sweetness' that appear in theological discussions of wives' potential influence on their husbands, chiefly, *suavitas*, meaning sweetness, pleasantness, agreeableness, and *persuadeo*, meaning to persuade. As Carruthers points out, 'persuadeo' or 'persuade' therefore means literally to sweeten, or as we still say in English, sweet talk.[61] This term comes to have a morally ambivalent sense for clerical writers, for it is most often women who employ sweetness to cajole their husbands; even seduction can be described as 'sweet'.[62] (We might note that the related 'suave' now has the connotation of slickness in English.) For medieval thinkers, eloquence or beauty can be suspect, for it distracts from the main message: Thomas Aquinas argued that while women's physical form and beauty do provoke lust, 'the *sweetness* of her voice and the pleasure of her words do so still more'.[63] For all these reasons monks were suspicious of women's speech, but as Farmer points out, persuasion was also (perhaps grudgingly) acknowledged as useful for both preachers and monks to influence others' behavior: men of God needed therefore to employ the rhetorical tools of a wife. Clerical writers' approval of wives' persuasive methods (particularly Thomas of Chobham's equating them with preachers) explains why Cecilia's ability to convert influential men with 'sweet persuasion' could be instructive. And as we've already seen, Deguileville describes Mary's 'douceur' or sweetness in his L stanza.

The opening line of Cecilia's first speech to Valerian, 'O sweete and wel biloved spouse deere' (144) is the only time Cecilia herself uses the word 'sweet'. In this scene, Cecilia is clearly employing sweet talk but cleverly attributing 'sweetness' to Valerian (who is, after all, learning on his wedding night that his wife wants to remain a virgin). I have yet to find 'sweetness' or its various Latin forms in any version of the *vita* referring to Cecilia herself; Cecilia is stunningly persuasive but is never called such directly in the *Tale* or in either of Chaucer's sources for the *vita*. Perhaps Chaucer's sources purposefully distanced Cecilia and her rhetoric from the concept of sweetness as persuasive technique because it might be perceived as overly slick or as undermining the seriousness of her message. However, it is more likely that Cecilia's persuasive talent is self-evident and need not be explicitly mentioned: we are seeing sweetness in action. When terms for sweetness do appear in the tale, they refer to her reputation ('soote savour' in the *Prologue*, 91); Valerian (144, as shown above); or the scent of the Marian lilies and roses that Cecilia's guardian angel gives them ('soote savour' or 'sweete smell', 229, 247, 251). Assuming Chaucer's sources were aware of the nuanced connotations of sweetness, we can read these other uses of the term as pointing to the effects of Cecilia's influence: the flowers symbolize her own purity and upcoming martyrdom, and their sweet scent renders Tiburce more susceptible to conversion. Given the positive effects, we can read these references to sweetness as an authorial vote in favor of her methods. They also recall the Virgin's popular association with those flowers, reminders to readers of her presence throughout the tale.[64]

Cecilia's commitment to orthodoxy, revealed early by her desire for chastity, both affirms and justifies her sweetness. When Cecilia does as Thomas of Chobham suggests, addressing Valerian 'in the bedroom, in the midst of their embraces ... [speaking] alluringly to her husband', her first goal is to convince him to be celibate. Her skill in doing so is a testament to Cecilia's ultimate powers of persuasion as a wife: using her proximity and potential sexuality to convince Valerian to abstain from taking advantage of these temptations. As is typical of virgin martyrs, Cecilia's virginity has been her chief concern up to this point. Preserving it assures her sanctity. But she must lay her virginity on the line in order to demonstrate her power as a sweet-talker. Her first words to Valerian—on their marriage bed—concern her desire (coupled with a threat) that he leave her untouched:

O sweete and wel biloved spouse deere,
Ther is a conseil, and ye wolde it heere ...
I have an aungel which that loveth me,
That with greet love, wher so I wake or sleepe,

> Is redy ay my body for to kepe.
> And if that he may feelen, out of drede,
> That ye me touche, or love in vileynye,
> He right anon wol sle yow with the dede. (144–5, 152–7)⁶⁵

Here Cecilia prefaces what amounts to a death threat with words of tenderness. The sweet talk (and, importantly, her status as wife) takes immediate effect: Valerian swears not to betray Cecilia in lines 148–50, *before* she mentions the angel or his potential violence. We see Cecilia employing a wife's method of sweet persuasion—one that conforms with Thomas of Chobham's ideal—to achieve the promise of her virginity, and by extension her sanctity. Her success in this rhetorical gamble validates her as a wife (because she is so good at persuasion) and as a saint (because she keeps her virginity). Further, it will point the way to her success as a preacher later on, as Valerian will mimic and validate her words here as well as the message she wants preached.

Cecilia as Marian maternal spouse

Cecilia's warning to Valerian not to 'touche' her here reminds us of Pierre Payer's observation that 'touch' in the confessional manuals is usually treated as a feature of illicit sexual situations. Pastoral readers would be primed to associate this warning with confessional manuals' treatment of sin and inappropriate behavior, contrasting Cecilia's holiness with Valerian's still-pagan status, a prompting that handily sets up Valerian's conversion and the couple's consequent teamwork as further evidence for clerical promotion of wifely persuasion. But readers of the Marian Chetham and Harley manuscripts would recognize this as the moment that Cecilia becomes Valerian's spiritual mother: this speech has set him in en route to becoming her 'fruit', as Urban will affirm, or her spiritual offspring. Touching her would not only mar Cecilia's chastity but would sully her role as the maternal spouse, modeled on Mary.

After their initial bedroom conversation, in which Cecilia achieves Valerian's chastity and conversion, Cecilia and Valerian develop an unusual level of trust and encouragement. The focus of the tale moves quickly from Cecilia's virginity to the way she carries out her persuasive role as wife. In fact, most of the narrative is missing the usual male/female faceoff of the virgin martyr genre. This is at least partially because Valerian—and nearly every other man in the story—acquiesces completely to Cecilia; except for a brief expression of doubt about the specifics of her guardian angel, Valerian follows all of her instructions without question. Cecilia convinces almost every man she encounters to convert, and they basically do so simply because she asks them to. Mary's model allows us to interpret Cecilia's authoritative rapport with various men as maternal rather than (merely) confrontational. Their susceptibility to feminine persuasion reveals a male aural vulnerability to women's words that is only implicit in the confessional manuals' emphasis on wifely persuasion. The clerical assumption that a wife can compel a husband's ears to hear her requires his willingness to be manipulated. It is only Cecilia's orthodoxy—and Valerian's adoption of it—that keeps him from looking foolish and weak.

By comparison, the spousal sweet talk between Mary and Christ that we see elsewhere in the late fifteenth-century Marian manuscripts is much more straightforward and transactional. In Harley MS 2382, Lydgate's 'Assumption' appears just before the *Testament* that contains the *Second Nun's Prologue*, as if to set the stage for spousal maternity. The poem establishes Christ and Mary's mutual desire to be together, with dialogue much closer to a nuptial tone than we see between Cecilia and Valerian:

> Sone thu art hider y-come
> *with* thyn angelis from a-bone.
> do þou now what thi wille ys;
> me hath longed to the, y-wys.
>
> Then Iesus to Marie sede,
> Moder, *with* ioye y woll the lede.
> of all wy*m*men the worth best,
> in heuene blisse that shal lest. (385–92)[66]

The exchange is one of affection and reunion. No trust need be earned, no conversion attained; the conversation doesn't have to achieve anything. The language quickly shifts into establishing Mary as partner with Christ in Heaven, naming their roles:

> ther *y am kyng; thu shalt be quene*;
> in grete ioye thu shall bene. (393–4)

Finally, Christ promises to do Mary's will concerning any intercession she might make for sinners:

> ... moder, for the loue of the,
> I woll of hym haue mercy.
> ... thogh a man had fully wroght
> all the synne that he had thought,
> and he on his laste day
> in none other wise may,
> yf he wepe and telle to the,
> in what synne that he be,
> full well y shall his bone here,
> for thi loue, my moder dere.[67] (432–3; 435–42)

Mary's persuasive power derives not from rhetoric but from her mere proximity to Christ, the 'kyng' to her 'quene'. Her success at intercession can be assumed from the outcomes of multiple miracle tales that omit heavenly cajoling or banter, but here Christ spells out the promise that his love for Mary, his 'quene' and 'lemman', will result in mercy every time, however undeserving the penitent. Christ's filial affection works as shorthand here: Mary will always get a yes, however undeserving the sinner. In other contexts, her occasional breast-flashing at Christ draws on the conflation of these joint maternal and spousal powers. In an anecdote that teases a namesake connection to Cecilia's Pope Urban, Mary casually explains to Bridget of Sweden how she influenced Pope Urban VI to settle in Rome: she led him 'as a mother leads her child whither she will, by showing him her breasts'.[68] A veteran of spousal maternity, Mary's confidence with Urban skips verbal rhetoric in favor of the visual. She needn't threaten overtly: her son(s) need only be reminded that her body establishes her status and influence.

Maternal persuasion

Cecilia does not appear to possess spectacular beauty or magnetic charm; the initial sweet talk with which she indulges Valerian carries her through the rest of the tale. It may be, like Mary as Queen of Heaven, that mere proximity does the trick. Cecilia's only secret, in personal persuasion as well as preaching, is in the detailed explanation she offers of what to do or what to believe: her (orthodox) knowledge gives her authority to be didactic—like a mother. Valerian and Tiburce are infantilized, asking basic questions that allow Cecilia to train them up right. She nurtures them as babies in faith before they leave the bedroom to go public. When she tells Valerian how to get baptized by Pope Urban, she explains exactly what to do and say: 'Sey hem right thus, as that I shal yow telle./ Telle hem that I, cecile, yow to hem sente' (175–6).[69] The message is clear: her connections are what matter, not his. Valerian does not even pause to ask questions about his newly-espoused doctrine before going to be baptized.

Likewise, it is only *after* declaring his belief in Christianity that Tiburce learns the implications of his decision or even major Christian doctrines. In their domestic setting, Cecilia preaches to Tiburce about subjects he should have known before converting, introducing some of Christianity's most basic mysteries. His questions express astonishment at the possibility of death (318: 'Algate ybrend in this world shul we be!') and confusion about the trinity (334–6: 'Ne seydestow right now in this manere,/Ther nys but o god, lord in soothfastnesse?/And now of thre how maystow bere witnesse?'). Such basic questions reveal that he was not fully aware of conversion's meaning. He was too swept up in her sweet talk, too easily persuaded to something he doesn't understand—and this despite the fact that he should be less susceptible to her words, since she is not his wife. It is Tiburce whose questions make explicit the risks he and Valerian are taking on. Given the perceived dangers of women's speech, he is lucky that Cecilia's is beyond reproach.

Importantly, Cecilia's words are not only believed by Valerian, but also confirmed by Urban. He acknowledges her success as a sweet-talker by expressing praise

> For thilke spouse that she took but now,
> Ful lik a fiers leoun, she sendeth here
> As meke as evere was any lamb. (197–9)

Readers have not seen evidence of Valerian's fierceness, but apparently what has rendered him as 'meek as a lamb' is Cecilia's speech: after all, at this point in the narrative, she hasn't actually done anything but talk. However, a few lines earlier, Urban has given thanks in prayer for 'The fruit of thilke seed of chastitee/That thow hast sowe in Cecile' (193–4). The 'fruit' here is, apparently,

Valerian himself: an interesting, if jarring, analog to the fruit of the chastity sown in the Virgin Mary that was Jesus. Urban's lack of clarity about whether it is Cecilia's chastity or her speech that produces the 'fruit' of Valerian underscores a sticking point for medieval theologians. The same clerical and biblical sources that affirm that women should try to convert their husbands tend to privilege holy deeds and behavior, such as chastity or altruism, over speech.[70] Outside the bedroom context, moral probity mattered as much as sweet talk; men like Urban and the pastoral readers of this *Tale* had to demonstrate virtue as well as rhetorical skill to be persuasive. And certainly the orthodoxy of Cecilia's speech, supported by the virtue of her behavior, matters: speaking God's rhetoric gets women permission and justification to speak publicly, even if they, like the Second Nun who is telling this story, are not wives or mothers.[71] To hear Urban tell it here, Cecilia has converted Valerian through both her chastity and her speech—a quiet reminder of theologians' belief that Christ got his humanity from Mary, and the implication that in Urban's mind Cecilia functions more like a mother than a wife. Urban confirms Cecilia's maternity. He is not privy to her pillow talk as we are: we know that she is able to preserve her virginity *because* of that pretty speech she gave Valerian, a speech whose effectiveness is dependent at least in part on her role as his wife. Further, Valerian himself values her rhetorical moves enough to imitate them when trying to convert his brother:

> I have an aungel which that loveth me,
> That with greet love, wher so I wake or sleepe,
> Is redy ay my body for to kepe ...
> And if that ye in clene love me gye,
> He wol yow love as me, for youre cleneness,
> And shewen yow his joye and his brightnesse. (Cecilia, 152–4; 159–61)

> Valerian seyde, 'Two corones han we,
> Snow white and rose reed, that shynen cleere,
> Whiche that thyne eyen han no myght to se;
> And as thou smellest hem thurgh my preyere,
> So shaltow seen hem, leeve brother deere,
> If it so be thou wolt, withouten slouthe,
> Bileve aright, and knowen verray trouthe'. (Valerian, 253–9)

Valerian's copying the structure of Cecilia's speech—making sure even to address Tiburce as 'leve brother deere', not too far from 'wel biloved spouse deere'—suggests he sees power in the rhetoric of her sweet talk and is willing to replicate it to produce more spiritual offspring. He has learned tools of persuasion as well as chastity from Cecilia's rendering his 'fiers leoun' into a 'meke lamb'. Significantly, despite his relative ignorance and lack of Christian experience, Valerian's imitation sweet talk works: Tiburce converts, and while it is Cecilia who then explains Christian doctrine to him, it is the rhetoric of her initial appeal to Valerian that engages Tiburce. In this text, then, sweet talk is not just for wives, but a useful all-purpose method of persuasion and spiritual reproduction. Cecilia's rhetoric is fruitful.

That Chaucer gives so much attention to Cecilia's eloquence— even switching to a source that cuts major events in the narrative to give proportionally more space to her words—suggests that he, like Thomas of Chobham, believes in the power of sweet talk and sees her preaching to and persuasion of Valerian of a piece with her vocal interactions with Almachius. Moreover, Cecilia's persistent chastity confirms that her sweet talk is not tainted by the dangerous temptation of female sexuality. Unlike the virgin martyrs who achieve mass conversions mostly by public performance (by undergoing bodily pain and enacting miracles), Cecilia persuades people one conversation at a time, as perhaps individual readers could, via promises, rewards and sometimes threats. As Mary Erler has explained, these small-scale conversions mean 'preaching and its desired outcome, conversion of heart, could now be reconceived— as conversation, a mode by definition private and personal'.[72] This text, then, validates Thomas's approval of the rhetoric of sweetness: Cecilia achieves and maintains authority throughout the tale largely as a function of having first persuaded her husband to accept her point of view.

Ironically, the success of Cecilia's methods requires her adherence to proscribed wifely behavior, and it is here that her status departs markedly from Mary's as Queen of Heaven. Cecilia's speech must first be validated by a pope and imitated by a husband before her message enters the public sphere, mediated through the preaching and ultimate martyrdom of her husband and brother-in-law. This suggests that her words cannot stand apart from male sanctioning: their effectiveness depends on her working within the gendered hierarchy that the confessional manuals reinforce. As a wife, Cecilia is not quite a threat to the status quo, as Winstead has suggested.[73] She consistently demonstrates that she respects male authority: in submitting to her father's arrangement of the marriage to Valerian, in making her husband's conversion central to the first episode in her own *vita*, in staying home while Tiburce and Valerian legitimate her words with their brief public ministry, and in waiting for the legal and economic status of widowhood before confronting Almachius and ultimately donating her legally-inherited house to the church.[74] Her acting like a submissive wife allows her to be taken seriously by the men she encounters.

This is most obvious in Cecilia's attention to Valerian's conversion. Her persuasive speech allows him to take center stage, preaching her message, ultimately to be martyred, in her own *vita*. In effecting Valerian's conversion, Cecilia fulfills the expectations of confessional manuals that see Christian wives as not only capable of persuasion but responsible for their husbands' souls.[75] Murray's work on confessional manuals has shown that women's agency is consistently compromised as ancillary to men's spiritual status.[76] Payer agrees, describing the confessional manuals as 'radically androcentric', noting that with few exceptions, the manuals are not addressed to women, nor do they offer much discussion of women's spiritual states.[77] Cecilia's job as wife, according to the manuals, is to ensure her husband behaves like a Christian, not to focus on her own spiritual development. She demonstrates her understanding and acceptance of doctrine by keeping Valerian in line: to 'submit' by temporarily biding her time as he takes the spotlight is to act in her own self-interest.

In other words, Cecilia earns her freedom to speak publicly— like a traditional virgin martyr or preacher—by first acting like a good wife and mother. She chooses to focus on Valerian's spiritual state, first as a convert (or spiritual 'child') and then as a preacher and martyr, rather than her own status as a potential saint and public speaker. Because of this adherence to form, Valerian and Tiburce are fully convinced by her speech, so much so that they proclaim her message publicly, anticipating and promoting her ideas so she can't later be confused with a gossip, scold, or rabble-rouser.[78]

The result is that Cecilia's preferences take center stage in the narrative even as she steps briefly out of the limelight. Cecilia easily avoids the 'idle speech' the Prologue warns about: she speaks with reason and orthodoxy, privately, and maintains her domestic identity until Valerian and Tiburce, as men preaching her message in the public arena, make her words more palatable.

Misreading Almachius, misreading the house

Until this point, Cecilia's success has largely been confirmed by men's responses to and assessments of her. Once she has proven herself as a wife, Urban has affirmed her orthodoxy, and Valerian and Tiburce have validated her speech, she is able to confront Almachius without attention to (Christian) male judgment. In this hagiographical public setting, his paganism matters more than his gender, just as her position as preacher, honed throughout the narrative, outweighs hers. The authority that Cecilia has built with her orthodox persuasion and proselytizing, mostly by proxy, can now be cashed in: because her speech and behavior are unquestionably orthodox, her manner of speaking to Almachius and his opinions of her are irrelevant. Cecilia's insults, defiance, and jeers are not surprising in the virgin martyr genre; Lydgate's Margaret of Antioch, included in Chetham MS 6709, employs similar language. Cecilia may call Almachius ugly names, but because she is and has consistently been speaking doctrine, she is no less or more a preacher than she was back in the bedroom with Valerian, any more than Mary's status changes when she angrily confronts antagonists in miracle tales. Cecilia's rhetorical techniques are no longer those of a wife, in part because persuasion or conversion of Almachius is not her goal: getting doctrinal truths uttered in public is, and she has already achieved that by persuading her husband to say them.

Part of what marks Almachius as pagan, and thus for readers wrongheaded in his reaction to Cecilia, is his misreading of her role in this scene and in previous events of the narrative. He assumes that removing Cecilia's voice from the public sphere will end her influence. Almachius condemns Cecilia to be boiled in a bathtub 'in hire hous' (514), where he also orders the executioner to behead her (523–34). Yet the importance and complexity of

Cecilia's voice are only underscored by her forced return 'home til her hous' (514) for her martyrdom, rather than the confinement in a government prison or execution at a public site that is more typical for virgin martyrs. In the context of this tale, Almachius does not realize the power of a Christian wife's words, of what she can achieve at home—in short, that a wife can be a preacher. As we have seen, until her confrontation with Almachius, most of Cecilia's speech has been uttered in domestic spaces, either her own or the convert Maxime's (368–90). That she preaches in her own home for three days before dying (537–9) makes explicit the connection between her roles as wife and as preacher. Almachius's misreading of what a wife can do ultimately allows the circumstances for the famous donation of Cecilia's house to the early Christian church, a contribution that for medieval readers derives directly from her role as a recent wife, now a widow and head of household.

The house reiterates readers' perceptions of Cecilia as maternal and offers a concrete example of domestic space made eternally significant. A line in the *Prologue* addressed to Mary, 'Withinne the cloistre blisful of thy sydis' (43), reminds readers of the metonymy of Mary's body, that through the incarnational trick of *ecclesia*, her womb becomes the church. The *Tale* offers an inversion of this: Cecilia's *house* is the productive womb, and the tale can be read as her maternal conversion and sanctifying of that house, which begins through her wifely persuasion. This transformation is first suggested by Cecilia's internal experiences of her own wedding ceremony and of the domestic space of her nuptial bedroom. After the undeniably Marian prologue, the *Tale* opens with Cecilia in pregnant solitude, as if awaiting an Annunciation. She even sings a prayer to parallel the Magnificat, asking to keep her body inviolate, perhaps as a reflection of Mary's pristine womb. But we are not then privy to an angel's announcement, even as Cecilia seems expectant: the very next scene, in answer to her prayer and fasting, has her inside the house, en route to her husband's bed. The 'birth' turns out to be baby Christian Valerian, conceived in a bedroom that is definitely not inviolate. Thus begins the conversion of the house to a holy space, and of Cecilia from wifely to maternal.

Within the tale, this space defines Cecilia. Valerian quotes to Tiburce a sermon from the famously bookish Ambrose, who says of Cecilia via the *Golden Legend*, 'The world *and eek hire chambre* gan she weyve' (276).[79] The delicate phrasing emphasizes the symbolic importance her bridal chamber will take on. Roughly half of the tale's action takes place in this house, much of it in this bedroom; in fact, domestic events get twice as many lines as those devoted to the confrontation between Cecilia and Almachius. But the house Cecilia gives away at the end is not the same one Valerian enters upon their marriage: once it has produced converts, its function and ownership change. Raymond of Penyafort felt that chaste marriage produces the 'fruit' of converts; Urban declares that the fruit of chastity that God 'hast sowe' in Cecilia is Valerian. When Valerian returns from seeing the Pope, Cecilia is hosting an angel in their nuptial bedroom, waiting with Marian rose-and-lily crowns. By the end, Cecilia has 'birthed' two Christians in that bedroom, who go out into the world to produce more 'fruit'. Later, in her martyrdom, her blood functions like Mary's breastmilk, pouring out grace to bless the house.

Displacing this spiritual fruitfulness to the house effectively outsources or externalizes Cecilia's spiritual reproduction. The text does not explain how the house became hers through marriage or widowhood. As late as line 219, their room is 'his' (Valerian's) chamber. Cecilia arguably makes it hers by inhabitation, remaining in the bedroom while sending Valerian off to meet Urban, hosting the angel there, staying in while Tiburce and Valerian go out to preach, and returning home for her own martyrdom to sanctify it with her blood before giving it to the church to produce more 'fruit'. The longer she stays in the house, the more prolific it becomes. The confrontation with Almachius becomes irrelevant: what matters is that the 'children' and the house get converted or sanctified to be more fruitful. (If the tale offers a parallel to the incarnation, it is this.) The house acting as her womb becomes an *ecclesia* that confirms Cecilia as Marian.

The suggestion that wives' orthodox submission leads to autonomy becomes heavy-handed by the end of the tale, when the very site at which a noblewoman has employed wifely persuasion becomes a holy place of worship. The types of sermons that Cecilia preached in her nuptial bedroom and from her bloody bathtub are presumably given now by men, as 'Men doon to Crist and to his seint servyse' (553). The *vita* thus allows us to track Cecilia's words from her domestic space to the public arena, showing that her speech and message are transferable, as worthy to be stated by men as by a young wife. She may appear to be a deviant speaker if we focus only on her public voice late in the tale or on Almachius's response to her, but in her deference to Christian male authority throughout the text and willingness to allow Valerian and Tiburce to 'go first' and speak her words for her, she upholds and reinforces the gendered expectations of the confessional manuals—and ultimately regains the central focus of the tale, along with her own sanctity.

Chaucer's choice of Cecilia as subject provides confirmation of the feminine behavior depicted in pastoral texts and offers a model for those thinking in terms of how to speak persuasively. There is much in this text to appeal to a pastoral readership: a good wife, whose piety is such that the Pope knows her personally, uses her persuasiveness to achieve her husband's conversion, which leads indirectly to her own validation. Chaucer, his target readers, and the Second Nun herself—who is, after all, also telling a story publicly, to be assessed by a man, and protected by the orthodoxy of her narrative—would recognize the registers of Cecilia's voices as congruent with their values.

Cecilia acts as spiritual mother to her husband, to his brother, and eventually to a range of people in her midst. To be sure, it is a Benedictine version of Marian motherhood. As we've seen, *imitatio Mariae* is often literal. Not here. Cecilia does not weep, lactate, or otherwise leak from her body. This is a sanitized, glorified, bodily-fluid-free form of motherhood, motherhood the way monks might envision it.[80] The 'children' are metaphorical: Cecilia does not have to touch, feed, or raise her converted offspring. It is maternity streamlined and simple, with only spiritual rewards. It is also, perhaps, as close as orthodox devotional literature gets to a Marian maternity that does not require a cisgendered woman's body.[81] For readers of the Chetham and Harley manuscripts, Cecilia offers a glimpse of what Marian maternity looks like apart from biological reproduction: she is a virgin who produces converts as her children, who survives attempted assassination, who performs postpartum miracles, and whose marriage presents a reinterpretation of marital and maternal roles.

A Marian, maternal Cecilia 251

Notes

* Portions of this chapter first appeared in Mary Beth Long, '"O sweete and wel biloved spouse deere": A pastoral reading of Cecilia's postnuptial persuasion in The Second Nun's Tale', *Studies in the Age of Chaucer* 39 (2017), 159–90.
1. Early Protestant reformers felt Marian sexualization had gone too far. Gary Waller discusses their responses to vulvic imagery, Marian breasts, and virginity, including Luther's lascivious mockery of Walsingham, in *The Virgin Mary in Late Medieval and Early Modern English Literature and Popular Culture* (Cambridge: Cambridge University Press, 2011), especially chapters one and four.
2. In the late fifteenth-century London, British Library MS Additional 37049, fol. 21; Boyarin, *Miracles*, 105–9.
3. Oxford, Bodleian MS Eng. poet. A.I, fols 121v–122v. Edited in *Minor Poems of the Vernon MS*, 121–31.
4. For Mary's sexuality in the *N-Town Plays*, see Solberg, *Virgin Whore*.
5. Ironically, it is the wife, not the husband, who is the Marian devotee. The anecdote appears in the *South English Legendary*.
6. Oxford, Bodleian MS Ashmole 61, fols 62r–65v. Edited in Shuffelton, *Codex Ashmole 61*, 170ff.
7. The poem, c. 1400, appears on fols 8v-9v in Douce 322; in Douce 78 it is on fol. 1v; the earlier version appears as Saupe, poem 79. Woolf comments that 'the language of love-longing is not fitting to a loving mother', *English Religious*, 302. Saupe argues that, as in *Pearl*, marriage should be considered here a metaphor for spiritual devotion.
8. 'Modyr, whyt os lyly flowr', in Oxford, Bodleian MS 29734 (Eng. Poet e.1), fol. 34; Saupe, poem 26.
9. This reading departs from scholarly convention. See e.g. Miles, who argues for a non-sexual interpretation of Mary's breast in the late medieval period in *A Complex Delight*, 33–53.
10. Williams Boyarin documents examples in fols 19r and 21r of London, British Library MS Additional 37049: 'Oure Blyssed Lady schewed unto hir son hyr breste and hir pappes, praying hym for thoes that he sowked to do mercy with the wretche', *Miracles*, 113. See also Salvador Ryan, 'The persuasive power of a mother's breast: The most desperate act of the Virgin Mary's advocacy', *Studia Hibernica* 32 (2002/2003), 59–74.
11. See Love's description of this event: 'she was þere in her sister house homely as in hir owne house, ordeynyng, & ministryng as maistrese þerof' and 'told priuely hir sone þerof for help & remedy', ultimately telling the servants 'þat þei shold do what þat he bad hem do'. Love

notes that Christ's first response, 'What is þat to me & to þe woman?' seems 'a harde & a buystes answere *as to his modere*'. Love, *Mirror*, 78–80, emphasis mine.

12 These lines are from Saupe, poem 56.
13 *Mirk's* Festial. Vol. 2, 202. In Saupe, poem 49, the line is amended to 'myn owne boure'.
14 Only two of the 55 extant manuscripts containing the *Second Nun's Tale* are not in collections of the *Canterbury Tales*. As Blurton and Johnson have noted, the *Tales* are buried within Lydgate's *Testament* in Harley 2382, which has been fully digitized by the British Library.
15 6709 is also known as Chetham's MS Mun. A. 4. 104. There are several echoes among the texts. Lydgate's *Life of Our Lady*, Margaret, and the two Chaucerian pieces are in rhyme royale. Lydgate highlights Margaret's humility and physical beauty; the prayer at the end of the *vita* emphasizes the health and comfort of the laboring mother rather than promising a lack of deformity for babies.
16 Samantha Katz Seal sees Mary's presence instead as a conceptive partner with the Second Nun as narrator in *Father Chaucer: Generating Authority in the Canterbury Tales* (Oxford: Oxford University Press, 2019), 101–5.
17 Chaucer's version of Cecilia's *vita* derives from two mendicant sources, the Dominican *Golden Legend* and a Franciscan breviary. See Sherry Reames, 'A recent discovery concerning the sources of Chaucer's "Second Nun's Tale"', *Modern Philology* 87.4 (1990), 337–61, and 'The Second Nun's Prologue and Tale', in *Sources and Analogues of the Canterbury Tales*. Vol. 1, ed. Robert M. Correale and Mary Hamel (Cambridge: D.S. Brewer, 2002), 491–527. Reames argues that Chaucer's manipulation of his sources highlights Cecilia's speech in 'The Office for Saint Cecilia', in *The Liturgy of the Medieval Church*, ed. Thomas J. Heffernan and E. Ann Matter (Kalamazoo, MI: Western Michigan Press, 2001), 219–42. Here and henceforth, like every other modern scholar of this tale, I am indebted to Reames' groundbreaking archival work.
18 Winstead, for example, includes Cecilia in a group of virgin martyrs she calls 'shrewish', and describes her 'aggressiveness' in *Virgin Martyrs*, 64, 83. Carolyn Collette calls her 'defiant' but contextualizes her claim that 'the central action of the tale revolves around Cecile's public confrontation with Almachius' with reference to the Virgin Mary's presence and influence in the *Tale* in *Performing Polity: Women and Agency in the Anglo-French Tradition, 1385–1620* (Turnhout: Brepols, 2006), 97.
19 See Mary Beth Long, '"O sweete and wel biloved spouse deere": A pastoral reading of Cecilia's post-nuptial persuasion in *The Second Nun's*

Tale', *Studies in the Age of Chaucer* 39 (2017), 159–90. Nancy Bradley Warren has done important archival work on Chaucer's texts in other religious houses, tracing Syon and Amesbury nuns' use of Chaucer for political and rhetorical purposes in 'Chaucer, the Chaucer tradition, and female monastic readers', *Chaucer Studies* 51.1 (2016), 88–106. For Chaucer's connections to theology and the church, see *Chaucer and Religion*, ed. Helen Phillips (Woodbridge: D.S. Brewer, 2010).

20 For Lydgate's female patrons and readership, see Julia Boffey, 'Lydgate's lyrics and women readers', *Women, the Book, and the Worldly*. Vol. 2, ed. Lesley Smith and Jane Taylor (Cambridge: D.S. Brewer, 1995), 139–49.

21 The Prioress has traditionally been affiliated with the St Leonard's Benedictine convent. On nuns' literary culture, see Erler, *Women, reading, and piety* on networks of women's reading materials passed across enclosure and generational lines slightly later than the period considered here, and *Nuns' Literacies in Medieval Europe: The Hull Dialogue* and *The Kansas City Dialogue*, ed. Virginia Blanton, Veronica O'Mara, and Patricia Stoop (Turnhout: Brepols, 2013, 2015).

22 The exact nature of Easton's role as cardinal and as inspiration for Chaucer's Cecilia has been debated. See Margaret Harvey, *The English in Rome 1362–1420: Portrait of an Expatriate Community* (Cambridge: Cambridge University Press, 1999), 206. Easton seemed interested in the subject of women's speech and authority; he wrote an Office for St Cecilia and was charged with determining the orthodoxy of Bridget of Sweden. See James Hogg, 'Adam Easton's Defensorium Sanctae Birgittae', *The Medieval Mystical Tradition: England, Ireland, and Wales*, ed. Marion Glasscoe (Cambridge: D.S. Brewer, 1999), 213–40.

23 See Mary Giffin, 'Hir hous the Chirche of Seinte Cecilie highte', *Studies on Chaucer and His Audience* (Québec: Les Editions L'Éclair, 1956), 29–48.

24 For Mary as a reader, see Donavin and Saetveit Miles.

25 The first set of ellipses replaces a list of all the specific hours monks are free to read. It is somewhat unclear whether the injunctions to read apply exclusively to Lent and Sundays or to ordinary hours as well. Translation from Bruce L. Venarde, ed. and trans., *The Rule of Saint Benedict* (Cambridge, MA: Dumbarton Oaks Medieval Library, 2011), 161, 163.

26 The digitized image can be viewed at www.themorgan.org/collection/Illuminating-Fashion/3

27 On women's speech, see Sandy Bardsley, *Venomous Tongues: Speech and Gender in Late Medieval England* (Philadelphia: University of Pennsylvania Press, 2006), and Susan E. Phillips, *Transforming*

Talk: The Problem with Gossip in Late Medieval England (University Park: Penn State University Press, 2007). See also Edwin D. Craun, *Lies, Slander and Obscenity in Medieval English Literature: Pastoral Rhetoric and the Deviant Speaker* (Cambridge: Cambridge University Press, 1997).

28 In fact, in a slightly different context, Reames has argued that 'the persuasive gifts of Cecilia are ultimately irrelevant. God does not use persuasion'; 'Disappearance', 51.

29 This phrasing is consistent with that of Chaucer's sources, the *Golden Legend* and the Franciscan abridgement, i.e., 'O dulcissime atque amantissime iuvenis, est misterium quod tibi confitear si modo tu iuratus asseras tota te illud observantia custodire', in Reames, 'Second Nun's', 505; 'O sweetest and most loving young man, I have a secret to confess to you, on condition that you swear to keep this secret entirely to yourself', in Ryan, *Golden Legend*, 705–5; and from the abridgement, 'O dulcissime atque amantissime iuvenis, est secretum quod tibi confitear, si modo tu iuratus asseras tota te illud observantia custodire', in Reames, 'A recent discovery', 357.

30 Howard muses that Cecilia's marriage 'involves something more than the subjugation of the woman to the man's will. There is a kind of mutuality in their relationship, a lack of any noticeable element of "maistrye"'—though I suspect most modern readers would agree that Cecilia is very much in charge. See Donald Howard, 'The conclusion of the marriage group: Chaucer and the human condition', *Modern Philology* 57.4 (1960), 223–32, at 229. Reames reads the relationship as 'an alternative model of marriage' in 'Mary, sanctity and prayers to saints: Chaucer and late-medieval piety', in Phillips, *Chaucer and Religion*, 81–96, at 94.

31 See Marc Glasser, 'Marriage in medieval hagiography', *Studies in Medieval and Renaissance History*, n.s. 4 (1981), 3–34, and Dyan Elliott, *Spiritual Marriage: Sexual Abstinence in Medieval Wedlock* (Princeton: Princeton University Press, 1993); Donald Weinstein and Rudolph M. Bell, *Saints and Society: The Two Worlds of Western Christendom, 1000–1700* (Chicago: University of Chicago Press, 1982); *A Companion to Middle English Hagiography*, ed. Sarah Salih (Woodbridge: D.S. Brewer, 2006); and Jocelyn Wogan-Browne, *Saints' Lives and Women's Literary Culture c. 1150–1300: Virginity and its Authorizations* (Oxford: Oxford University Press, 2001).

32 See Sharon Farmer, 'Persuasive voices: Clerical images of medieval wives', *Speculum* 61.3 (1986), 517–43, at 536. Wives are not her only admirers; Sanok opens *Her Life Historical* with Cecilia as prime example of a saint whose imitable behaviors might vary depending on readers' historical and social contexts.

33 '[Si] fidelis contrahit cum infideli ... nullum est matrimonium. Sponsalia tamen potest fidelis cum infideli contrahere sub conditione ut infidelis convertatur ad fidem', from Raymond of Penyafort, *Summa de matrimonio*, ed. Xaverio Ochoa and Aloisio Díez, Universa Bibliotheca Iuris. Vol. 1, tomus C (Rome: Commentarium pro religiosis, 1978), 951. Trans. in Raymond of Penyafort, *Summa on Marriage*, trans. and ed. Pierre Payer (Toronto: Pontifical Institute of Mediaeval Studies, 2005), Title X, 'Dissimilar Religion', 51ff.

34 'Quod perfectum et consummatum dicitur coniugium sanctitate, etiam ante carnalem copulam', Raymond, *Summa* (ed. Ochoa and Díez), 923; 'a marriage is called completed or consummated through holiness, even before carnal copulation', Raymond, *Summa* (ed. Payer), 27.

35 Even in the liturgy, the wedding night dominates. Reames' work on late-medieval breviaries shows that what was most often heard at Matins as lessons from the saint's life was the nuptial scene: '[I]t is probably no accident that the breviaries with verbatim excerpts from the Cecilia legend tend to reproduce the same portions of the legend that were emphasized in the chants for her Office: the initial description of her piety, her hair shirt and fasts and fervent prayers before her wedding, *her wedding-night conversation with Valerian*, his baptism, and his return to find the angel made visible', in Reames, 'Office for St. Cecilia', 233–4, emphasis mine.

36 Reames, 'Office for St Cecilia', 239.

37 The miracles generally portray intercession only from the penitent's perspective; the lyrics give a sense of Christ and Mary's dynamic, but few examples of the intercessory conversations. One exception is Johannes Herolt's portrayal of the weighing of a sinner's deeds against his devotions; Christ says to Mary, 'It is impossible to deny you anything.' Love's *Mirror* ends before Mary's assumption; *N-Town* has a play devoted to it, but does not portray Mary's interactions with Christ.

38 From the poem 'Marie Moder, wel thee be', which appears on fol. 86v and as Saupe, poem 59.

39 In Farmer, 'Persuasive voices', and in Mary Carruthers, 'Sweetness', *Speculum* 81.4 (2006), 999–1013.

40 This dynamic required women to hold dual roles as wife and mother: Herlily also points out that widowed mothers who outlived their welcome were sometimes regarded as obstacles to children's financial and social success. See David Herlily, *Medieval Households* (Cambridge, MA: Harvard University Press, 1985), 120–5.

41 Raymond of Peñafort wrote his *summa* between 1220–45; Guillaume Peyraut wrote his *Summa de vitiis* in the 1230s; Thomas of Chobham

began *Summa cum miserationes* well before the Fourth Lateran Council, edited it just after the end of 1215, and completed and circulated it in 1216. Thomas Tentler counts one or two dozen *summa*, depending on the definition, from 1215 to 1520, in 'The summa for confessors as an instrument of social control' in *The Pursuit of Holiness in Late Medieval and Renaissance Religion*, ed. Charles Trinkaus and Heiko A. Oberman (Leiden: Brill, 1974), 103–26. Around 1303, Robert Mannyng of Brunne composed the first English version of the genre, *Handlyng synne*, a Middle English verse translation of *Manuel des peches*. See also F. Broomfield, ed., *Thomae de Chobham summa confessorum* (Louvain: Éditions Nauwelaerts, 1968), lxii.

42 In language echoing that of the *Prologue*, Phillips, *Transforming Talk* notes that confession works in line with, rather than in opposition to, penitential rules, 17, although it is 'continually besieged by idle talk, vulnerable to gossip at almost every stage of its process', 42.

43 While the Benedictines are not primarily known as preachers, there is evidence that they were preaching to the laity in late medieval England. See Siegfried Wenzel, *Monastic Preaching in the Age of Chaucer* (Kalamazoo, MI: Medieval Institute Publications, 1993), and Patrick Horner, 'Benedictines and preaching in fifteenth-century England: The evidence of two Bodleian Library manuscripts', *Revue Bénédictine* 99 (1989), 313–32. As Joan Greatrex notes, Adam Easton himself was so valued for his preaching that the prior recalled him to Norwich at least twice during his studies at Oxford for preaching duties, in 'Benedictine sermons: preparation and practice in the English monastic cathedral cloisters', in *Medieval monastic preaching*, ed. Carolyn Muessig (Leiden: Brill, 1998), 257–78, at 261.

44 According to Neil Ker, a fourteenth-century copy of Thomas's *Summa* (Cambridge University Library MS Ii. I. 22) was at the Priory of Holy Trinity in Norwich, so these Benedictine readers would have been familiar with its arguments as they read the life of Cecilia; one inventory of the Priory's books lists a *Summa Confessorum* along with a *legenda aurea*. See Neil Ker, 'Medieval manuscripts from Norwich Cathedral Priory', *Transactions of the Cambridge Bibliographical Society* 1.1 (1949), 1–28. See also Ker, *Medieval Libraries of Great Britain: A List of Surviving Books*, 2nd edn. (London: Royal Historical Society, 1964), 284–6 of which cover Norwich Cathedral library. Broomfield argues that English readers were Chobham's target audience.

45 Emphasis mine. 'Mulieribus tamen semper in penitentia iniungendum est quod sint *predicatrices* virorum suorum. Nullus enim sacerdos ita potest cor viri emollire sicut potest uxor. Unde peccatum viri sepe

A Marian, maternal Cecilia 257

mulieri imputatur si per eius negligentiam vir eius non emmendator. Debet enim in cubiculo et inter medios amplexus virum suum blande alloqui, et si durus est et immisericors et oppressor pauperum, debet eum invitare ad misericordiam; si raptor est, debet detestari rapinam; si avarus est, suscitet in eo largitatem ... Prima ergo sacerdotis et precipua providentia ista debet esse ut mulierem hoc modo instruat.' Thomas of Chobham, *Summa confessorum*, at 375. Trans. in Farmer, 'Persuasive voices', at 517.

46 Both Thomas of Chobham and Robert of Courson had been concerned with wives of men who committed usury, a major thirteenth-century theological issue. The full passage from Courson: 'Cum uxor feneratoris agit causam spoliaterum, vivat parce de iis quae ministrat ei vir suus de spoliis usurae, non quia ipse possit ei dare, cum non sint suae, sed quia ipsa advocatrix est spoliatorum pro melioranda corum causa, emoliendo cor viri sui, & inducendo virum suum ad faciendam condignam restitutionem sic ablatorum. Si autem invenerit cor viri sui impoenitens & incorrigible, & se nihil erga ipsum perficere posse pro facienda debita restitutione; tunc tenetur modis omnibus quaerere separationem mensae ejus & convivii; sed numquam thori, ut prius mendicet ab amicis vel aliis quo veseatur & vestiatur, quam hujusmodi tam morticino & quasi idolotito foedae usurae contra Deum pascatur', in 'Consilium Parisiensis, 1212', pt. 5, chap. X, *Sacrorum Conciliorum Nova et Amplissima Collectio*, ed. J.D. Mansi, 31 vols. (Florence, 1759–98), 22: 852.

47 In related discussions, Paul Strohm expresses skepticism about how much actual power this role granted queens in *Hochon's Arrow: The Social Imagination of Fourteenth-century Texts* (Princeton: Princeton University Press, 1992), 95–120. Collette emphasizes the power as well as the danger of Cecilia's private-to-public speech as sanctioned and authorized by Mary in *Performing Polity*, 79.

48 Bardsley, *Venomous Tongues*, 68.

49 Ibid., 6, 47, 48, 51.

50 Craun, *Lies*, 1, 51.

51 Ibid., 53. Gilchrist notes that silence was the default in the monastery in *Norwich Cathedral Close*, 13.

52 Ibid., 26–47, 172n.47, 173.

53 Bardsley discusses several examples of wives whose husbands should beware their wives' speech, including Eve, Noah's wife, and the Wife of Bath, in *Venomous Tongues*, 58–62.

54 Claire M. Waters, *Angels and Earthly Creatures: Preaching, Performance, and Gender in the Later Middle Ages* (Philadelphia: University of Pennsylvania, 2004), 97.

55 Among other things, he argues that women should be churched early so their husbands won't seek sex elsewhere, and allows the husband's sins and preferences to overshadow those of the wife's even in her confession and penitence. See Murray, 'Absent penitent', 23. In Murray's words: 'the very structure of confessors' manuals reinforced the notion of women as primarily, even exclusively, sexual. In the process, therefore, the salvation of women's souls was linked to their sexuality and to their sexuality alone', 'Gendered souls', 83.

56 Sharon Farmer, 'Softening the hearts of men: Women, embodiment, and persuasion in the thirteenth century', *Embodied Love: Sensuality and Relationship as Feminist Values*, ed. Paula Cooey et al. (San Francisco: Harper & Row, 1987), 115–34, at 116. Farmer continues, 'Christian theologians associated false rhetoric—that in which men and women were persuaded of something that was contrary to Christian doctrine—with magic or seduction, while they associated true rhetoric—that which persuaded men and women to believe and obey Christian doctrine—with divine inspiration or assistance', 117.

57 Jacqueline Murray provides Serlo's and Robert of Flamborough's citations of women's non-verbal influence over men through potions and other physical means in 'Absent penitent', 21.

58 Waters, *Angels*, 96.

59 See Joseph Grossi, 'The unhidden piety of Chaucer's "Seint Cecilie"', *Chaucer Review* 36.3 (2002), 298–309, at 300, and Lynn Staley, 'Chaucer and the postures of sanctity', in David Aers and Staley, *The Powers of the Holy: Religion, Politics, and Gender in Late Medieval English Culture* (University Park: Penn State University Press, 1996), 179–259, at 206.

60 Reames, 'Second Nun's', *Sources and Analogues*, 505.

61 Carruthers, 'Sweetness', 1008.

62 *Ibid.*, 1003.

63 Waters, *Angels*, 100, emphasis mine.

64 See Rubin, *Mother of God*, 310–11.

65 Again, from the *Golden Legend*: 'O dulcissime atque amantissime juvenis, est misterium quod tibi confitear si modo tu juratus asseras tota te illud observancia custodire ... Angelum Dei habeo amatorem, qui nimio zelo custodit corpus meum. Hic si vel leviter senserit quod tu me polluto amore contingas, statim feriet te, et amittes florem tue gratissime juventutis', in Reames, 'The Second Nun's Prologue and Tale', *Sources and Analogues*, 505; 'O sweetest and most loving young man, I have a secret to confess to you, on condition that you swear to keep this secret entirely to yourself ... I have a lover, an angel of God, who watches over my body with exceeding zeal. If my angel senses that you are touching me with lust in your heart, he will strike

you and you will lose the flower of your gracious youth', in Ryan, *Golden Legend*, 704–5.
66 Fols 80v–81r. Printed in *King Horn, Floriz and Blauncheflur, The Assumption of Our Lady*, ed. J.R. Lumby, EETS o.s. 14 (1886, 1901), 125.
67 Fol. 81v. In another version of the poem (British Library, Addit. MS. 10036, fol. 62r), Christ's welcome to Mary is even more suggestive:

> He dide his mod*er* ful moche ri3t,
> As a sone au3t his moder to done,
> He callid þe aungeles eue*r*ychone,
> And alle þe mayne þat was i*n* heuene,
> And seide to hem with mury steuene:
> '*Commeþ with me to my lemman!*'
> Sche is my moder; hure sone I am (414–20, emphasis mine).

68 Johannes Jørgensen, *Saint Bridget of Sweden*, trans. Ingeborg Lund. Vol. 2 (London, Longmans, Green, 1954), 221–2. 'Sicut mater ducit filium suum ad locum, ubi sibi placet, dum ostendit sibi ubera sua ...' chapter 138 of *Revelaciones* IV, ed. Hans Aili (Uppsala: Almqvist & Wiksell), 387.
69 In the *Northern Homily Cycle* version of the *vita*, Cecilia explicitly requires Valerian to go to Urban for confession before he can be baptized: 'And tell him all thi life till end,/No so that he may thi mis amend' (109–10). In Bertha Ellen Lovewell, *The Life of St Cecilia: From MS Ashmole 43 and MS Cotton Tiberius E. VIII*, Yale Studies in English 3 (Boston: Lamson, 1898), 93.
70 Farmer synthesizes the arguments of Augustine and the author of 1 Peter in 'Persuasive voices', 528, 532, 540.
71 For a fuller discussion of women's 'good' speech, see Bardsley, *Venomous Tongues*. See also Craun, *Lies*, 97ff.
72 Erler, 'Home visits', 260.
73 See her chapter 'Unruly virgins and the Laity', in *Virgin Martyrs*, 64–111.
74 Here, Cecilia uses her secular, economic power as a widow for spiritual benefit. Having had her speech authorized by Valerian and Tiburce, she is only now legally authorized to donate her property to the church. See Michael Sheehan, 'The influence of canon law on the property rights of married women in England', *Medieval Studies* 25 (1963), 109–24. Sanok reads this as confirmation of Cecilia's authority as preacher: 'When Cecilia turns her house into a church, it gives her a forum for the pastoral work reserved in late medieval England to male clerics. She now "preaches" to those she had once "fostered" ... the Second Nun refuses to circumscribe Cecilia's authority', *Her Life Historical*, 169.

75 Christine de Pisan also advocated that women should take some responsibility for their husbands' spiritual well-being in her 1405 *Livres de trois virtues*.
76 Murray, 'Absent penitent', 20–4. For example, consensual adultery is a violation of another man's bed, with penance ascertained according to the status of the woman whom a man has violated, rather than a sin equally committed by men and women.
77 Payer, *Sex and the New*, 8, 9 n. 15.
78 See Phillips, *Transforming talk*, and Bardsley, *Venomous Tongues*.
79 'Ipsum mundum est cum thalamis execrata'. The text is from Ambrose's preface to the Cecilia mass; see Millett Henshaw, 'The preface of St. Ambrose and Chaucer's *Second Nun's Tale*', *Modern Philology* 26.1 (1928), 15–16.
80 Similarly, there are no literal or physically messy 'mothers' in Lydgate's *vita* of Margaret, in which the pearls in her name's etymology may stanch bleeding; no pain in childbirth, but lots of spiritual 'fruit' in the form of conversions.
81 I hope to be proven wrong on this point; there is significant work still to be done on Marian maternity and hagiography.

Conclusion: 'Show yourself a mother'

'Losing a child is very, very difficult. You feel the pain in your womb, just like the day when you made that child.' Allison Jean, mother of Botham Jean[1]

'When everything happened I told everyone I hurt in my womb. I still hurt there.' Nelba Márquez-Greene, mother of Ana Grace Greene[2]

'No tongue can speak, no mind will conceive, how much sorrow affected the holy womb of Mary.' Ogier of Locedio, *Meditacio de lamentacione beate virginis*[3]

Mary still embodies visceral maternal mourning, as is clear from the epigraphs above and from art such as Mark Doox's *Our Lady of Ferguson* and Jon Henry's photographic series *Stranger Fruit*.[4] In the United States, mothers of the victims of gun violence and police brutality, overwhelmingly women of color, have borne a disproportionate share of contemporary maternal grief. That imbalance points up the ironies and inconsistencies of turning a maternal lens on, for example, the *Prioress's Tale*, whose bereft mother is both victim and beneficiary of racial tensions. The modern mothers of color whose grieving wombs inflict pain are not eagerly defended or avenged by law enforcement as is the clergeon's mother. I have defined medieval Marian maternity in Chapter 5 as an extension of institutions such as the Church and law enforcement, weaponized against Jewish people. However, Mary was first a Jewish mother whose child became a political target. That truth of Marian maternity is refracted in many harrowing maternal experiences that are invisible in late-medieval depictions. If, through an absence or delay of birth pains, Mary was perhaps denied resilience, or as Monagle puts it the ability to 'make and remake' herself, then other modern mothers have disproportionately honed that skill. The systemic racism and policies that harm mothers and children of color, transgender children and mothers, and children and mothers in vulnerable geopolitical circumstances—namely by sharply narrowing the parameters of *who gets to be a mother*—are also part of the legacy of Marian motherhood and should be included as we consider more broadly what the Marian model of maternity can teach us.

While not a book that is overtly about race or racism, this study has examined Marian maternity through matricentric feminism, a theoretical lens shaped largely by the intellectual work of Black mothers. My aim has been to render its concepts of mothering—of maternal practice—more legible in these late-medieval texts. We should know where the culturally dominant standards for modern Western motherhood come from, and in what they're embedded. Mothering, as we've seen, is learned behavior; a full education includes recognizing the limitations and possibilities of its cultural codes. So, too, should we all be aware of the work and resources that go into raising children. As we are learning in the United States, the political urge toward forced birth works in tandem with the hiding of maternal labor. If birthing and maternity are no longer a choice, they should at least be visible.

Reading matricentrically, then, means noticing maternity where it doesn't announce itself. Among the 'mothers' discussed in this study, Cecilia, though she more obviously behaves as a wife, puts maternity in a public space, making it legible and visible. Margery claims more spiritual authority than she otherwise would because of her *imitatio Mariae*, which has her imagining herself as the church. While Marian maternity contracts acceptable maternal practice to narrow parameters, it expands maternal authority for those who can claim to embody it. The mystics in Douce 114 gain status in part because their community-building is rooted in bodily pain that looks like Mary's *compassio*. And sometimes that same *compassio*, practiced by Marian devotees, expands the possibilities for Mary herself: the reluctance of the *planctus Mariae* to affirm the collective experience of grieving mothers is answered, in a way, by the readers of legendaries and rood screens who insist on developing a stronger network of friends and family for the Virgin.

Given the Marian model's influence, how can we open it up to make it more inclusive of the maternity that many of us actually practice? To begin to answer that—and though the end of a book, this is only a beginning—I'd like to look briefly to one more medieval text. The *Alphabet of Tales* includes a miracle in which an abbess gets pregnant. Mary intervenes, giving the child to a hermit to raise. The abbess maintains her position without discovery, and the child is given to the church at age seven to become a bishop. The abbess's role as spiritual mother takes precedence over her biological connection to a child. The tale welcomes this maternal transfer as a means of social reproduction. Importantly, it respects the mother's preference not to raise the child, a departure from examples I've discussed that ignore the mother's volition: in Chapter 3, Catherine of Siena attempts to replace her young Dominican protégé's mother, and in Chapter 5, the child's body is deemed more useful to the Church than to his mother. Other Marian miracle tales routinely remove Jewish children from their natal families.

The church's history of such involuntary removals has caused much more pain than a brief essay can address. But the practice as described in the *Alphabet of Tales* miracle inadvertently acknowledges that biological or natal motherhood is not the only means through which a child *can* be mothered. It also suggests mothering, or not mothering, is a choice. These are cracks in the usual shape of 'Marian maternity' through other forms of maternity might be introduced. Nancy Bradley Warren discusses the ramifications of what she calls 'spiritual maternity' in a different context:

> When maternity is made spiritual, its female particularity is obliterated. Maternity is removed from the sphere of the carnal and the feminine, a move that enhances its value. Maternity is no longer solely the province of women; spiritual maternity—which is 'bettur þan' bearing Christ bodily—is not uniquely female work.[5]

Warren's comments regard the Church's attempts to replace physical maternity with its own practices, a re-codifying of reproduction and nurturing with institutional values. In her reading, to remove not only biological reproduction but gender from maternity is to devalue women, to make Mary, and thus women, fungible. If patriarchal definitions of motherhood are all we have, this is indeed the only reading available to us, and I argue for a very similar reading of the *Prioress's Tale* in Chapter 5.

But matricentric theory makes room for other, positive long-term effects that can come even from this effort by the medieval church. I have not always taken an optimistic view of the elements of Marian maternity that arise in this study's primary texts or get practiced by its subjects, largely because they sometimes seem harmful to the children or mothers affected and to those who do not or cannot practice them. But what if 'Marian maternity' can be isolated from not only Mary's body, but from all female bodies? Might maternity, as bell hooks once imagined, float free from the biological, separate from the baggage it was assigned by patriarchal motherhood and from its most harmful elements? Mary's imitators do not *have* to adopt the medieval Mary's antisemitism or the exploitation of the maternal body. They do not have to be gendered female: Mary's father Joachim committed to reinventing himself and strengthening his community in preparation to parent her. Even in its conception of spiritual maternity, the church relies on the concept of shared motherwork. As we've seen, thanks in large part to vernacular and lay revisions of Marian narrative, fifteenth-century devotional texts *did* carve out positive and replicable interpretations of Marian maternity among its representatives and proxies: they heal and nurture the sick, build friendships, share maternal labor, express vulnerability and emotional wholeness, act with authority, persuade others to do good. A caregiver or set of caregivers who can manage these tasks might be one every kid should have. These practices are recognizable in the visual art, the play performances, and the texts that lay devotional readers were commissioning, hearing, compiling, and sharing. Imagining a Marian maternity without its entanglement in patriarchal expectations of a cisgendered female body might get us closer to a parenting model worth building on.

Notes

1 Radio Caribbean International interview, *She Speaks*, February 12, 2019, eight months before the conviction of police officer Amber Guyger, who fatally shot Jean's son Botham as he ate ice cream in his own apartment in Dallas. Jean repeated the declaration shortly after Guyger's conviction: 'When you lose a child, you feel the labor pains in your womb again'.

2 Tweet, now deleted, from Márquez-Greene's Twitter account on December 11, 2020. Márquez-Greene's six-year-old daughter Ana Grace was fatally shot in her classroom at Sandy Hook Elementary School on December 14, 2012.
3 'Non lingua loqui, non mens cogitare valebit, quanto dolore afficebantur pia viscera Marie'. Attributed to Bernard of Clairvaux in Bestul, *Texts*, 176. Translation mine.
4 Both artists employ Marian imagery to depict maternal mourning of children lost to violence: https://markdoox.com/work#/our-lady-of-ferguson-missouri-and-all-killed-by-gun-violence; www.lensculture.com/articles/jon-henry-stranger-fruit
5 Here Warren is discussing *Book to a Mother* in *Spiritual Economies*, 89.

Bibliography

Manuscripts

Brussels

Bibliothèque Royale Albert I MS 7917
Bibliothèque Royale Albert I MS 8609–20

Cambridge

Cambridge University Library MS 2604
Cambridge University Library MS DD.I.1
Cambridge University Library MS Ii. I. 22
Cambridge University Library MS Ff. 5. 48
Corpus Christi College MS 218
Trinity College MS R.3
Trinity College MS 601

Liège

Bibliothèque du Grand Séminaire MS XV 6L21
Archives d'État de Liège Charte no. 4, Hôpital Tirebourse et St Christophe
Archives d'État de Liège Charte no. 7, Hôpital Tirebourse et St Christophe
Archives d'État de Liège Fonds Tirebourse et S Christophe April 24, 1307
Université de Liège MS 135
Université de Liège MS 260

London

British Library MS Harley 2253
British Library Royal MS B XXIII

British Library Addit. MS. 10036
British Library MS Additional 37049
British Library Additional MS 20059
British Library Royal 12 E 1
British Library MS Harley 3862
British Library MS Additional 37049
British Library Harley MS 2382
British Library Harley MS 4012
British Library Arundel MS 327
Lambeth Palace Library MS 853

Manchester

Chetham 6709/Chetham's MS Mun. A. 4. 104
Chetham MS 8009
Rylands Library 18932 (Latin 395)

New York

Morgan Library MS M.772

Oxford

Bodleian MS 240
Bodleian MS 10234
Bodleian MS 29734 (Eng. Poet e.1)
Bodleian MS Ashmole 61
Bodleian MS Douce 78
Bodleian MS Douce 114
Bodleian MS Douce 322
Bodleian MS Eng. poet. a. 1 (Vernon)
St. John's College MS 182

San Marino

Huntington Library MS 115

Stonyhurst

Stonyhurst College Blackburn MS 24

Primary sources

(Pseudo-)Albertus Magnus. *Sermones de tempore et de sanctis.* Cologne, 1475.
Angela da Foligno. *Il Libro della Beata Angela da Foligno.* Ed. Ludger Their and Abele Calufetti. Grottaferrata: Editiones Collegii S. Bonaventurae ad Claras Aquas, 1985.
Bokenham, Osbern. *Legendys of Hooly Wummen.* Ed. Mary Serjeantson. EETS o.s. 206. London, 1938.
———. *Lives of Saints.* Ed. Simon Horobin. EETS o.s. 356. Oxford: Oxford University Press, 2020.
Bridget of Sweden. *Revelaciones* IV. Ed. Hans Aili. Uppsala: Almqvist & Wiksell, 1992.
———. *The Liber Celestis of St Bridget of Sweden.* Ed. Roger Ellis. Vol. 1. EETS o.s. 291. Oxford: Oxford University Press, 1987.
———. *Saint Bridget of Sweden.* Ed. Johannes Jørgensen, trans. Ingeborg Lund. Vol. 2. London: Longmans, Green, 1954.
Cartulaire de Notre-Dame de Chartres. Ed. E. de Lepinois and Lucien Merlet. 3 vols. Chartres, 1865.
Catherine of Siena. *The Letters of Catherine of Siena.* Vol. 2. Ed. Suzanne Noffke. Tempe: Arizona Center for Medieval and Renaissance Studies, 2000.
Chaucer, Geoffrey. *The Riverside Chaucer.* Ed. Larry Benson. 3rd edn. Boston, 1987.
Codex Ashmole 61: A Compilation of Popular Middle English Verse. Ed. George Shuffelton. Kalamazoo, MI: Medieval Institute Publications, 2008.
A Critical Edition of and Commentary on MS Douce 114. Ed. Jennifer Brown. Turnhout: Brepols, 2003.
Dives and Pauper. Ed. Priscilla Heath Barnum. EETS o.s. 275. Oxford: Oxford University Press, 1975.
The Early English Carols. Ed. R.L. Greene. 2nd ed. Oxford: Clarendon Press, 1977.
The Exempla or Illustrative Stories from the Sermones Vulgares of Jacques de Vitry. Ed. Thomas Crane. London: Folklore Society, 1890.
The Golden Legend: Readings on the Saints. Ed. and trans. William Granger Ryan. Princeton: Princeton University Press, 2012.
Henry of Grosmont. *Le Livre de Seyntz Medicines/The Book of Holy Medicines.* Ed. Catherine Batt. Tempe, Arizona: ACMRS, 2014.
———. *Le Livre de seyntz Medicines: The Unpublished Devotional Treatise of Henry of Lancaster.* Ed. E.J. Arnould. Anglo-Norman Text Society. Vol. 2. Oxford: Basil Blackwell, 1940.
Hilton, Walter. *Walter Hilton's Latin Writings.* Ed. John P.H. Clark and Cheryl Taylor. 2 vols. Analecta Cartusiana 124. Salzburg: Institut für Anglistik und Amerikanistik, 1987.

Hoccleve, Thomas. *Hoccleve's Works: The Minor Poems*. Ed. F.J. Furnivall and I. Gollancz. EETS e. s. 61. London: Kegan Paul, Trench, and Trübner, 1892.
Isidore of Seville. *The Etymologies of Isidore of Seville*. Ed. and trans. Stephen A. Barney, W.J. Lewis, J.A. Beach, and Oliver Berghof. Cambridge: Cambridge University Press, 2006.
Jacobus de Voragine. *Materials for a Life of Jacopo da Varagine*. Ed. E.C. Richardson. New York: H.W. Wilson, 1935.
———. *Sermones aurei de Maria Virgine Dei Matre, omni doctrina & magnis Sacre Scripture Sensibus Referti*. Venice, 1590.
———. *Sermones quadragesimales*. Ed. Giovanni Paolo Maggioni. Edizione Nazionale dei Testi Mediolatini 13. Florence: Sismel, 2005.
Jacques de Vitry. 'Texts on hospitals: Translation of Jacques de Vitry's *Historia occidentalis* 29'. Ed. Jessalyn Bird. *Religion and Medicine in the Middle Ages*. Ed. Peter Biller and Joseph Ziegler. Woodbridge: York Medieval Press, 2001. 109–34.
Kempe, Margery. *The Book of Margery Kempe*. Ed. Lynn Staley. Kalamazoo, MI: Medieval Institute Publications, 1996.
King Horn, Floriz and Blauncheflur, The Assumption of Our Lady. Ed. J.R. Lumby. EETS o.s. 14. London: Kegan Paul, Trench, and Trübner. 1886, 1901.
The Lanterne of Liȝt. Ed. Lilian M. Swinburn. EETS o.s. 151. London: Kegan Paul, Trench, and Trübner, 1917.
The Life of St Cecilia: From MS Ashmole 43 and MS Cotton Tiberius E. VIII. Ed. Bertha Ellen Lovewell. Yale Studies in English 3. Boston: Lamson, 1898.
Love, Nicholas. *The Mirror of the Blessed Life of Jesus Christ*. Ed. Michael G. Sargent. Exeter: University of Exeter Press, 2004.
'Lyves and Dethes' for Medieval English Nuns: An Edition of the Saints' Lives in CUL, MS Additional 2604. Ed. Veronica O'Mara and Virginia Blanton. Turnhout: Brepols, forthcoming.
Materials for the History of Thomas Becket, Archbishop of Canterbury. Ed. James Craigie Robertson. Rolls Series 67. Vol. 2. London: Longman, 1876.
Maximus the Confessor. *The Life of the Virgin*. Ed. and trans. Stephen Shoemaker. New Haven: Yale, 2012.
Middle English Marian Lyrics. Ed. Karen Saupe. Kalamazoo, MI: Medieval Institute Publications, 1998.
Middle English Stanzaic Versions of the Life of Saint Anne. Ed. R.E. Parker. EETS o.s. 174. London: Oxford University Press, 1928.
The Minor Poems of the Vernon Manuscript. Ed. Carl Horstmann. EETS o.s. 98, 117. London: Kegan Paul, Trench, Trübner & Co., 1892.
Miracles of the Virgin. Ed. Adrienne Williams Boyarin. Peterborough, ON: Broadview Press, 2015.
Myrc (Mirk), John. *Instructions for Parish Priests*. Ed. Edward Peacock and F.J. Furnivall. EETS o.s. 31. London: Oxford University Press, 1868.

———. *John Mirk's Festial*. Ed. Susan Powell. 2 vols. Oxford: Oxford University Press, 2010, 2011.
The N-Town Plays. Ed. Douglas Sugano. Kalamazoo, MI: Medieval Institute Publications, 2007.
Paris, Matthew. *Matthew Paris's English History: From the Year 1235 to 1273*. Ed. John Allen Giles. Vol. 3. London: HG Bohn, 1852.
Patrologiae Cursus Completas. Series Latina. Ed. Jacques-Paul Migne. 217 vols. Paris, 1841–55.
Petrarch, Francis. *Letters of Old Age (Rerum Senilium Libri)* I-XVIII. Trans. by Aldo S. Bernardo, Saul Levin, and Reta A. Bernardo. Vol. 1. Baltimore and London: Johns Hopkins University Press, 1992.
'Prosalegenden: die Legenden des MS Douce 114'. Ed. Carl Horstmann. *Anglia* 8 (1885), 119–34.
The Protevangelium of James. Ed. Lily Vuong. Eugene, OR: Cascade Books, 2019.
Raymond of Capua. *The Life of St Catherine of Siena*. Trans. George Lamb. Charlotte, NC: Tan Books, 2009.
Religious Lyrics of the Fifteenth Century. Ed. Carleton Brown. Oxford: Clarendon Press, 1939.
Robert of Courson. *Sacrorum Conciliorum Nova et Amplissima Collectio*. Ed. J.D. Mansi. 31 vols. Florence, 1759–98.
The Rule of Saint Benedict. Ed. Bruce L. Venarde. Cambridge, MA: Dumbarton Oaks Medieval Library, 2011.
Stacions of the Cross. Ed. Frederick J. Furnivall. EETS 25. London: N. Trübner, 1867.
'Studien zu Richard Rolle de Hampole II: *Lamentatio St. Bernardi de compassione Mariae*'. Ed. G. Kribel. *Englische Studien* 8 (1885), 67–114.
Suger, Abbot. *Abbot Suger on the Abbey Church of St.-Denis and its Art Treasures*. Ed. and trans. E. Panofsky. 2nd edn. by G. Panofsky-Soergel. Princeton: Princeton University Press, 1979.
Suso, Henry. 'Orologium Sapientiae or The Seven Poyntes of Trewe Wisdom, Aus MS. Douce 113'. Ed. Carl Horstmann. *Anglia* 10 (1887), 323–89.
———. *Henry Suso: The Exemplar, with Two German Sermons*. Trans. and ed. Frank Tobin. New York: Paulist Press, 1989.
Thomas of Cantimpré and Jacques de Vitry. *Two Lives of Marie d'Oignies*. Ed. and trans. Margot King and Hugh Feiss. Toronto: Peregrina Press, 1987.
Thomas of Chobham. *Summa de arte praedicandi*. Ed. Franco Morenzoni. CCCM 82. Turnhout, 1988.
———. *Thomae de Chobham Summa Confessorum*. Ed. F. Broomfield. Louvain: Éditions Nauwelaerts, 1968.
Thomas of Monmouth. *The Life and Miracles of St William of Norwich by Thomas of Monmouth, 1896*. Ed. Augustus Jessop and M. R. James. Cambridge: Cambridge University Press, 2011.

The Trotula: An English Translation of the Medical Compendium of Women's Medicine. Ed. Monica Green. Philadelphia: University of Pennsylvania Press, 2002.
Two Wycliffite Texts. Ed. Anne Hudson. EETS o.s. 301. Oxford: Oxford University Press, 1993.

Secondary sources

Ahmed, Sara. *The Cultural Politics of Emotion*. Edinburgh: Edinburgh University Press, 2004.
Alexander, Philip. 'Madame Englentyne, Geoffrey Chaucer and the problem of medieval anti-semitism'. *Bulletin of the John Rylands Library* 74.1 (1992), 109–20.
Alexandre-Bidon, Danièle. 'La lettre volée: Apprendre à lire à l'enfant au Moyen Âge'. *Annales Économies, Sociétiés Civilisations* 44.4 (1989), 953–92.
Allen, Hope Emily. Notes. *The Book of Margery Kempe*. Ed. Sanford Brown Meech. EETS o.s. 212. London: Oxford University Press, 1940.
Allen-Goss, Lucy M. *Female Desire in Chaucer's* Legend of Good Women *and Middle English Romance*. Woodbridge: D.S. Brewer, 2020.
Andrews, David. 'A lost Essex hospital: the College of St Mark at Audley End'. *Essex Archaeology and History* 26 (1995), 276–7.
Appleford, Amy. *Learning to Die in London: 1380–1540*. Philadelphia: University of Pennsylvania Press, 2015.
―――― and Corinne Saunders. 'Reading women in the medieval information age: *The Life of Elizabeth of Spalbeek* and *The Book of Margery Kempe*'. *Studies in the Age of Chaucer* 42 (2020), 253–81.
Aston, Margaret. 'Gold and images'. *Faith and Fire: Popular and Unpopular Religion 1350–1600*. London: Hambledon Press, 1993, 219–29.
Auslander, Diane Peters. 'Victims or martyrs: Children, anti-Judaism, and the stress of change in medieval England'. *Childhood in the Middle Ages and the Renaissance*. Ed. Albrecht Classen. Berlin: De Gruyter, 2005, 105–34.
Ball, Philip. *Universe of Stone: Chartres Cathedral and the Triumph of the Medieval Mind*. London: The Bodley Head, 2008.
Bardsley, Sandy. *Venomous Tongues: Speech and Gender in Late Medieval England*. Philadelphia: University of Pennsylvania Press, 2006.
Baron, S.W. *A Social and Religious History of the Jews*. Vol. 2. New York: Columbia University Press, 1937.
Barton, David and Mary Hamilton. 'Literacy practices'. *Situated Literacies: Reading and Writing in Context*. Ed. by David Barton, Mary Hamilton, and Roz Ivanič. New York: Routledge, 2000, 7–14.
Baumgarten, Elisheva. *Mothers and Children: Jewish Family Life in Medieval Europe*. Princeton, 2004.

Belting, Hans. *Likeness and Presence: A History of the Image Before Art.* Trans. Edmund Jephcott. Chicago: University of Chicago Press, 1994.

Bestul, Thomas H. *Texts of the Passion: Latin Devotional Literature and Medieval Society.* Philadelphia: University of Pennsylvania Press, 1996.

Beyers, Rita. 'The transmission of Marian apocrypha in the Latin Middle Ages'. *Apocrypha* 23 (2012), 117–40.

Biddick, Kathleen. 'Genders, bodies, borders: Technologies of the visible'. *Speculum* 68.2 (1993), 389–418.

Bird, Jessalyn. 'Medicine for body and soul: Jacques de Vitry's sermons to hospitallers and their charges.' *Religion and Medicine in the Middle Ages.* Ed. Peter Biller and Joseph Ziegler. Woodbridge: York Medieval Press, 2001, 91–108.

Blanton, Virginia. *Signs of Devotion: The Cult of St Athelthryth in Medieval England, 695–1615.* Pennsylvania: Pennsylvania State University Press, 2007.

———, Veronica O'Mara, and Patricia Stoop, eds. *Nuns' Literacies in Medieval Europe: The Hull Dialogue* and *the Kansas City Dialogue.* Turnhout: Brepols, 2013, 2015.

Blatt, Heather. *Participatory Reading in Late-medieval England.* Manchester, UK: Manchester University Press, 2018.

Blurton, Heather and Hannah Johnson. *The Critics and the Prioress: Antisemitism, Criticism, and Chaucer's* Prioress's Tale. Ann Arbor: University of Michigan Press, 2017.

Boffey, Julia. 'Lydgate's Lyrics and Women Readers'. *Women, the Book, and the Worldly.* Ed. Lesley Smith and Jane Taylor. Vol. 2. Cambridge: D.S. Brewer, 1995, 139–49.

Boswell, John. *The Kindness of Strangers: The Abandonment of Children in Western Europe from Late Antiquity to the Renaissance.* New York: Pantheon, 1988.

Bradley, Ritamary. 'Backgrounds of the title *Speculum* in mediaeval literature'. *Speculum* 29.1 (1954), 100–15.

Brenner, Elma. 'The leprous body in twelfth- and thirteenth-century Rouen: Perceptions and responses', *The Ends of the Body: Identity and Community in Medieval Culture*, ed. Jill Ross and Suzanne Akbari. Toronto: University of Toronto Press, 2013.

Brown, Jennifer N. *Fruit of the Orchard: Reading Catherine of Siena in Late Medieval and Early Modern England.* Toronto: University of Toronto Press, 2019.

Brundage, James. *Law, Sex, and Christian Society in Medieval Europe.* Chicago: University of Chicago Press, 1987.

Brunelle, Sara, Mariana Brussoni, Susan Herrington, M. Kyle Matsuba, and Michael W. Pratt, 'Teens in public spaces and natural landscapes: Issues of access and design', *Handbook of Adolescent Development Research and its Impact on Global Policy*, ed. Jennifer E. Lansford and Prerna Banati. Oxford: Oxford University Press, 2018, 361–79.

Bryan, Jennifer. 'Hoccleve, the Virgin, and the politics of complaint'. *PMLA* 117.5 (2002), 1172–87.
Bynum, Caroline Walker. *Holy Feast and Holy Fast: The Religious Significance of Food to Holy Women*. Berkeley: University of California, 1988.
———. *Fragmentation and Redemption: Essays on Gender and the Human Body in Medieval Religion*. New York: Zone Books, 1991.
Cadden, Joan. *Meanings of Sex Difference in the Middle Ages*. Cambridge: Cambridge University Press, 1993.
Calabresi, Bianca. 'You sow, Ile read: Letter and literacies in early modern samplers'. *Reading Women: Literacy, Authorship, and Culture in the Atlantic World*. Ed. Heidi Hackel and Catherine Kelly. Philadelphia: University of Pennsylvania Press, 2009, 79–104.
Camille, Michael. *The Gothic Idol: Ideology and Image-making in Medieval Art*. Cambridge: Cambridge University Press, 1990.
Carruthers, Mary. *The Book of Memory*. Cambridge: Cambridge University Press, 2008
———. 'Sweetness'. *Speculum* 81.4 (2006), 999–1013.
Ciresi, Lisa Victoria. 'Maria Ecclesia: The Aachen Marienschrein as an alternate body for the Virgin Mary' in *Binding the Absent Body in Medieval and Modern Art*. Ed. Emily Kelley and Elizabeth Rivenbark. London: Routledge, 2017.
Clanchy, Michael. 'Did mothers teach their children to read?' in *Motherhood, Religion, and Society in Medieval Europe, 400–1400*. Ed. Lesley Smith and Conrad Leyser. New York: Routledge, 2011, 129–53.
Clark, Anne. 'Guardians of the sacred: The nuns of Soissons and the slipper of the Virgin Mary'. *Church History* 76.4 (2007), 724–49.
Coats, Karen. 'P is for patriarchy: Re-imaging the alphabet'. *Children's Literature Association Quarterly* 25.2 (2000), 88–97.
Cohen, Esther. *The Modulated Scream: Pain in Late Medieval Culture*. Chicago: University of Chicago Press, 2010.
———. 'The animated pain of the body'. *American Historical Review* 105.1 (2000), 36–68.
Cohen, Jeremy. *The Friars and the Jews: The Evolution of Medieval Anti-Judaism*. Ithaca, NY: Cornell University Press, 1982.
———. 'The Jews as the killers of Christ in the Latin tradition, from Augustine to the Friars'. *Traditio* 39 (1983), 1–27.
Coletti, Theresa. 'Social contexts of the East Anglian saint play: The Digby Mary Magdalene and the late medieval hospital?' *Medieval East Anglia*. Ed. Christopher Harper-Bill. Woodbridge, UK: Boydell Press, 2005, 287–301.
Collette, Carolyn. *Performing Polity: Women and Agency in the Anglo-French Tradition, 1385–1620*. Turnhout: Brepols, 2006.
Collins, Patricia Hill. 'The meaning of motherhood in Black culture and Black mother-daughter relationships'. *Double Stitch: Black Women*

Write about Mothers and Daughters. Ed. Patricia Bell-Scott. New York: Harper Perennial, 1993, 42–60.

———. 'Shifting the center: Race, class, and feminist theorizing about motherhood'. *Mothering: Ideology, Experience, and Agency*. Ed. Evelyn Nakano Glenn, Grace Chang, and Linda Rennie Forcey. New York: Routledge, 1994, 45–65.

Corboz, André. 'Le territoire comme palimpseste'. *Diogène* 121 (1983), 14–35.

Craun, Edwin D. *Lies, Slander and Obscenity in Medieval English Literature: Pastoral Rhetoric and the Deviant Speaker*. Cambridge: Cambridge University Press, 1997.

Davis, Adam J. 'Preaching in thirteenth-century hospitals'. *Journal of Medieval History* 36 (2010), 72–89.

Delany, Sheila. 'Chaucer's Prioress, the Jews and the Muslims'. *Medieval Encounters* 5.2 (1999), 198–213.

Depres, Denise. 'Cultic anti-Judaism and Chaucer's litel clergeon'. *Modern Philology* 91.4 (1994), 413–27.

Dewez, Léon and Albert van Iterson, 'La lactation de Saint Bernard: legende et iconographie'. *Citeaux in de Nederlanden* 7 (1956), 165–89.

Donavin, Georgiana. *Scribit Mater: Mary and the Language Arts in the Literature of Medieval England*. Washington, DC: Catholic University of America Press, 2012.

———. 'Alphabets and rosary beads in Chaucer's *An ABC*'. *Medieval Rhetoric*. Ed. Scott D. Troyan. Routledge: New York, 2004, 25–40.

Doyle, A.I. 'Books connected with the Vere family and Barking Abbey'. *Transactions of the Essex Archaeological Society*. n.s., 25 (1958), 222–43.

Duden, Barbara. *Disembodying Women: Perspectives on Pregnancy and the Unborn*. Cambridge, MA: Harvard University Press, 1993.

Duffy, Eamon. *The stripping of the Altars*. New Haven: Yale University Press, 1993.

———. 'Holy maydens, holy wyves: The cult of women saints in fifteenth- and sixteenth-century England'. *Studies in Church History* 27 (1990), 175–96.

Dutton, Anne M. 'Piety, politics and person: MS Harley 4012 and Anne Harling'. *Prestige, Authority and power in late medieval manuscripts and texts*. Ed. Felicity Riddy. Woodbridge: Boydell & Brewer, 2000, 133–46.

Dyas, Dee. *Pilgrimage in Medieval English Literature, 700–1500*. Cambridge: D.S. Brewer, 2001.

Edwards, A.S.G. 'Fifteenth-century English collections of female saints' lives'. *The Yearbook of English Studies* 33 (2003), 131–41.

———. 'The transmission and audience of Osbern Bokenham's *Legendys of Hooly Wummen*'. *Late-medieval Religious Texts and Their Transmission: Essays in Honour of A.I. Doyle*. Woodbridge: Boydell and Brewer, 1994, 157–67.

Ellington, Donna Spivey. *From Sacred Body to Angelic Soul: Understanding Mary in Late Medieval and Early Modern Europe*. Washington, DC: Catholic University of America Press, 2001.

Elliott, Dyan. *Spiritual Marriage: Sexual Abstinence in Medieval Wedlock*. Princeton: Princeton University Press, 1993.

Erler, Mary C. *Women, Reading, and Piety in Late Medieval England*. Cambridge: Cambridge University Press, 2002.

———. 'Private reading in the fifteenth- and sixteenth-century English nunnery'. *The Culture of Medieval English Monasticism*. Ed. James G. Clark. Woodbridge: Boydell, 2007, 134–46.

———. 'Widows in retirement: region, patronage, spirituality, reading at the Gaunts, Bristol'. *Religion & Literature* 37.2 (2005), 51–75.

———. 'Home visits: Mary, Elizabeth, Margery Kempe and the Feast of the Visitation', in *Medieval Domesticity: Home, Housing and Household in Medieval England*. Ed. Maryanne Kowaleski and P.J.P Goldberg. Cambridge: Cambridge University Press, 2008, 259–76.

Evans, Joan. *History of Jewellery 1100–1870*. London: Faber and Faber, 1953.

Farmer, Sharon. 'Low Country ascetics and Oriental luxury: Jacques de Vitry, Marie of Oignies, and the treasures of Oignies'. *History in the Comic Mode: Medieval Communities and the Matter of Person*. Ed. Rachel Fulton and Bruce W. Holsinger. New York: Columbia University Press, 2007, 205–22.

———. 'Persuasive voices: Clerical images of medieval wives'. *Speculum* 61.3 (1986), 517–43.

———. 'Softening the hearts of men: Women, embodiment, and persuasion in the thirteenth century'. *Embodied Love: Sensuality and Relationship as Feminist Values*. Ed. Paula Cooey, Sharon Farmer, and Mary Ellen Ross. San Francisco: Harper & Row, 1987, 115–34.

Fiddyment, Sarah, Natalie Goodison, Elma Brenner, Stefania Signorello, Kierri Price, and Matthew Collins. 'Girding the loins? Direct evidence of the use of a medieval English parchment birthing girdle from biomolecular analysis'. *Royal Society Open Science* 8.3 (2021), 202055.

Finucane, R.C. 'The use and abuse of medieval miracles'. *History* 60.198 (1975), 1–10.

Flood, Gavin. *The Ascetic Self: Subjectivity, Memory, and Tradition*. Cambridge: Cambridge University Press, 2004.

Franck, Karen A. and R. Bianca Lepori. *Architecture from the Inside Out*. 2nd ed. Chichester: Wiley-Academy Press, 2007.

French, Katherine. 'The material culture of childbirth in late medieval London and its suburbs'. *Journal of Women's History* 28.2 (2016), 126–48.

Frye, Susan. *Pens and Needles: Women's Textualities in Early Modern England*. Philadelphia: University of Pennsylvania Press, 2013.

Gelfand, Laura D. and Walter S. Gibson. 'The "Rolin Madonna" and the late-medieval devotional portrait'. *Simiolus: Netherlands Quarterly for the History of Art* 29.3/4 (2002), 119–38.

Gerstal, Sharon, ed. *Thresholds of the Sacred: Architectural, Art Historical, Liturgical, and Theological Perspectives on Religious Screens, East and West*. United Kingdom: Dumbarton Oaks, 2006.

Gibson, Gail McMurray. 'Scene and obscene: Seeing and performing late medieval childbirth'. *Journal of Medieval and Early Modern Studies* 29.1 (1999), 7–24.

———. 'Saint Anne and the religion of childbed: Some East Anglian texts and talismans', in *Interpreting Cultural Symbols: Saint Anne In Late Medieval Society*. Ed. Kathleen Ashley and Pamela Sheingorn. Athens: University of Georgia Press, 1990, 95–110.

Giffin, Mary. 'Hir hous the Chirche of Seinte Cecilie highte'. *Studies on Chaucer and his Audience*. Québec: Les Editions L'Éclair, 1956, 29–48.

Gilchrist, Roberta. *Norwich Cathedral Close: The Evolution of the English Cathedral Landscape*. Woodbridge: Boydell and Brewer, 2005.

Glasser, Marc. 'Marriage in medieval hagiography'. *Studies in Medieval and Renaissance History* n.s. 4 (1981), 3–34.

Glucklich, Ariel. *Sacred Pain: Hurting the Body for the Sake of the Soul*. New York: Oxford University Press, 2001.

Goldberg, Benjamin. *The Mirror and Man*. Charlottesville: University of Press of Virginia, 1985.

Goodland, Katharine. '"Veniance, Lord, apon thaym fall": Maternal mourning, divine justice, and tragedy in the Corpus Christi plays'. *Medieval & Renaissance Drama in England* 18 (2005), 166–92.

———. '"Vs for to wepe no man may lett": Accommodating female grief in the medieval English Lazarus plays'. *Early Theatre* 8.1 (2005), 69–94.

Goodman, A.E. *Margery Kempe and her World*. London: Routledge, 2002.

Graef, Hilda. *Mary: A History of Doctrine and Devotion*. Notre Dame, IN: Ave Maria Press, 2009.

Green, Monica. 'Documenting medieval women's medical practice'. *Practical Medicine from Salerno to the Black Death*. Ed. Luis García-Ballester, Roger French, Jon Arrizabalaga, and Andrew Cunningham. Cambridge: Cambridge University Press, 1994, 322–52.

———. 'Women's medical practice and health care in medieval Europe'. *Signs* 14.2 (1988–89), 434–73.

———. 'Gender, health, disease: Recent work on medieval women's medicine'. *Studies in Medieval and Renaissance History*. ser. 3, 5 (2005), 1–46.

Grossi, Joseph. 'The unhidden piety of Chaucer's "Seint Cecilie"'. *Chaucer Review* 36.3 (2002), 298–309.

Halberstam, Jack. *Female Masculinity*. Durham: Duke University Press, 1998.

Hamburger, Jeffrey F. 'The use of images in the pastoral care of nuns: The case of Heinrich Suso and the Dominicans'. *The Art Bulletin* 71.1 (1989), 20–46.

———. *Nuns as Artists: The Visual Culture of a Medieval Convent*. Berkeley: University of California Press, 1997.

———. *The Visual and the Visionary: Art and Female Spirituality in Late Medieval Germany*. New York: Zone Books, 1999.

Hamburgh, Harvey. 'The problem of *Lo Spasimo* of the Virgin in cinquecento paintings of the Descent from the Cross'. *The Sixteenth Century Journal* 12.4 (1981), 45–75.

Hamilton, Caitlin. *Jewish Suffering in Medieval Christian Drama*. Unpub. Ph.D thesis, University of Virginia, 2017.

Harding, Wendy. 'Medieval women's unwritten discourse on motherhood: A reading of two fifteenth-century texts'. *Women's Studies* 21 (1992), 197–209.

Harris-Stoertz, Fiona. 'Pregnancy and childbirth in twelfth- and thirteenth-century French and English law'. *Journal of the History of Sexuality* 21.2 (2012), 263–81.

Harvey, Margaret. *The English in Rome 1362–1420: Portrait of an Expatriate Community*. Cambridge: Cambridge University Press, 1999.

Heard, Kate. 'Ecclesiastical embroidery in England from 1350 to the Reformation'. *English Medieval Embroidery: Opus Anglicanum*. Ed. Michael A. Michael. New Haven: Yale University Press, 2016, 77–90.

Heath, Shirley Brice. 'What no bedtime story means'. *Language in Society* 11.1 (1982), 49–76.

Herlily, David. *Medieval Households*. Cambridge, MA: Harvard University Press, 1985.

Hill, Carole. 'St Anne and her Walsingham daughter'. *Walsingham in Literature and Culture from the Middle Ages to Modernity*. Ed. Dominic James and Gary Waller. New York: Routledge, 2010, 99–111.

Hilles, Carroll. 'Gender and politics in Osbern Bokenham's legendary'. *New Medieval Literatures* 4 (2001), 189–212.

Hilmo, Maidie. *Medieval Images, Icons, and Illustrated English Literary Texts from the Ruthwell Cross to the Ellesmere Chaucer*. New York: Routledge, 2004.

Hodges, Laura Fulkerson. *Chaucer and Clothing: Clerical and Academic Costume in the General Prologue to the Canterbury Tales*. Cambridge: D.S. Brewer, 2005.

Hollywood, Amy. *The Soul as Virgin Wife: Mechthild of Magdeburg, Marguerite Porete, and Meister Eckhart*. Notre Dame: University of Notre Dame Press, 1995.

———. *Sensible Ecstasy: Mysticism, Sexual Difference, and the Demands of History*. Chicago: University of Chicago Press, 2001.

Holmes, Megan. 'Disrobing the Virgin: The Madonna Lactans in fifteenth-century Florentine art'. *Picturing Women in Renaissance and Baroque Italy*. Ed. S. Matthews Grieco and G. Johnson. Cambridge: Cambridge University Press, 1997, 167–95.

hooks, bell. *Feminist Theory from Margin to Center*. Boston: South End Press, 1984.

Horden, Peregrine. 'A non-natural environment: Medicine without doctors and the medieval European hospital'. *The Medieval Hospital and Medical Practice*. Ed. Barbara Bowers. Aldershot: Routledge, 2007, 133–45.

Horie, Ruth. *Perceptions of Ecclesia: Church and Soul in Medieval Dedication Sermons*. Turnhout: Brepols, 2006.

Horobin, Simon. 'Politics, patronage, and piety in the work of Osbern Bokenham'. *Speculum* 82.4 (2007), 932–49.

———. 'A manuscript found in the library of Abbotsford House and the lost legendary of Osbern Bokenham', *English Manuscript Studies 1100–1700* 14 (2008), 130–64.

Hostetler, Margaret, '"I wold thow wer closyd in an hows of ston": Reimagining religious enclosure in the Book of Margery Kempe', *Parergon* 20.2 (2003), 71–94.

Howes, Laura. 'Romancing the city: Margery Kempe in Rome', *Studies in Philology* 111.4 (2014), 680–90.

Hrdy, Sarah Blaffer. *Mothers and Others: The Evolutionary Origins of Mutual Understanding*. Cambridge, MA: Harvard University Press, 2009.

Izbicki, Thomas. 'The immaculate conception and ecclesiastical politics from the council of Basel to the Council of Trent: the Dominicans and their foes'. *Archiv für Reformationsgeschichte* 96 (2005), 145–70.

James, Stanlie. 'Mothering: A possible Black feminist link to social transformation'. *Theorizing Black Feminism: The Visionary Pragmatism of Black Women*. Ed. Stanlie James and A.P. Busia. New York: Routledge, 1999, 44–54.

Jamroziak, Emilia. *The Cistercian Order in Medieval Europe 1090–1500*. New York: Routledge, 2013.

Johnson, Rebecca Wynne. 'Divisions of labor: Gender, power, and later medieval childbirth, c. 1200–1500'. *History Compass* 14.9 (2016), 383–96.

Jones, Peter, and Lea Olsan. 'Performative rituals for conception and childbirth in England, 900–1500', *Bulletin of the History of Medicine* 89.3 (2015), 406–33.

Jourdain, Margaret. *The History of English Secular Embroidery*. New York, Dutton and Company, 1912.

Kalas, Laura. *Margery Kempe's Spiritual Medicine: Suffering, Transformation and the Life Course*. Woodbridge: Boydell and Brewer, 2020.

Keiser, George. 'The Middle English *Planctus Mariae* and the rhetoric of pathos'. *The Popular Literature of Medieval England*. Ed. Thomas J. Heffernan. Knoxville: University of Tennessee Press, 1985, 167–93.

Ker, Neil. 'Medieval manuscripts from Norwich Cathedral Priory'. *Transactions of the Cambridge Bibliographical Society* 1.1 (1949), 1–28.

———. *Medieval Libraries of Great Britain: A List of Surviving Books*. 2nd edn. London: Royal Historical Society, 1964, 284–6.

Knott, Sarah. *Mother Is a Verb: An Unconventional History*. New York: Sarah Crichton Books, 2019.

———. 'Theorizing and historicizing mothering's many labours'. *Past and Present* Supplement 15 (2020), 1–23.

Korpiola, Mia and Anu Lahtinen. 'Cultures of death and dying in medieval and early modern Europe: An introduction'. *Collegium: Studies across Disciplines in the Humanities and Social Sciences* 19 (2015), 1–31.

Krug, Rebecca. *Margery Kempe and the Lonely Reader*. Ithaca, NY: Cornell University Press, 2017.

Krummel, Mariamne. 'Omissions of antisemitism: Thomas Hoccleve and the putative Jew'. *Crafting Jewishness in Medieval England: Legally Absent, Virtually Present*. New York: Palgrave, 2011, 117–36.

Kurtz, Patricia Deery. 'Mary of Oignies, Christine the Marvelous and medieval heresy'. *Mystics Quarterly* 14 (1988), 186–96.

Lang, Richard. 'The dwelling door: Towards a phenomenology of transition'. *Dwelling, Place and Environment* Ed. D. Seamon and R. Mugerauer. Dordrecht: Martinus Nijhoff Publishers, 1985, 201–13.

Lauwers, Michel. '"Noli me tangere": Marie Madeleine, Marie d'Oignies et les pénitentes du XIIIe siècle'. *Mélanges de l'École Française de Rome: Moyen Age* 104 (1992), 209–68.

———. *La mémoire des ancêtres, le souci des morts: morts, rites et société au Moyen Age: Diocèse de Liège, XIe–XIIIe siècles*. Paris: Beauchesne, 1997. 410–13.

Lavezzo, Kathy. 'The minster and the privy: Rereading the *Prioress's Tale*'. *PMLA* 126.2 (2011), 363–82.

Leinaweaver, Jessaca B. 'Practice mothers'. *Signs* 38 (2012), 405–30.

Lidova, Maria. 'Empress, Virgin, Ecclesia: The icon of Santa Maria in Trastevere in the early Byzantine context'. *IKON* 9 (2016), 109–28.

Lloyd, Joan Barclay. 'The river of life in the medieval mosaics of S Maria Maggiore in Rome'. *Reading Texts and Images* Ed. Bernard Muir. Exeter: University of Exeter Press, 2002, 35–55.

Lochrie, Karma. *Margery Kempe and Translations of the Flesh*. Philadelphia: University of Pennsylvania Press, 1994.

Long, Mary Beth. '"O sweete and wel biloved spouse deere": A pastoral reading of Cecilia's post-nuptial persuasion in The Second Nun's Tale'. *Studies in the Age of Chaucer* 39 (2017), 159–90.

Majérus, Pascal. *Ces femmes qu'on dit béguines … Guide des béguinages de Belgique. Bibliographie et sources d'archives*, 2 vols. Bruxelles: Archives générales du Royaume, 1997.

Mâle, Emile. *The Gothic Image: Religious Art in France of the Thirteenth Century*. New York: Harper and Row, 1972.

Marks, Richard. *Image and Devotion in Late Medieval England*. Stroud: Sutton, 2004.

———. 'Framing the rood in medieval England and Wales'. *The Art and Science of the Church Screen in Medieval Europe: Making, Meaning,*

Preserving. Ed. Spike Bucklow, Richard Marks, and Lucy Wrapson. Woodbridge: Boydell & Brewer, 2017, 7–29.

McAvoy, Liz Herbert. *Authority and the Female Body in the Writings of Julian of Norwich and Margery Kempe*. Woodbridge: Boydell & Brewer, 2004.

———. 'Virgin, mother, whore: The sexual spirituality of Margery Kempe'. *Intersections of Sexuality and the Divine in Medieval Culture: The Word Made Flesh*. Ed. Susannah Chewning. Hampshire: Ashgate, 2005, 121–40.

———. *Medieval Anchoritisms: Gender, Space and the Solitary Life*. Woodbridge: D.S. Brewer, 2011.

McDevitt, Mary. 'Mary, motherhood, and teaching in the *Book to a Mother* and Chaucer's *ABC*'. *Marian Studies* 53 (2002), 23–42.

McDonnell, Ernest. *The Beguines and Beghards in Medieval Culture, with Special Emphasis on the Belgian Scene*. New York: Octagon Books, 1969.

McDowell, Linda. *Gender, Identity, and Place: Understanding Feminist Geographies*. Minneapolis: University of Minnesota Press, 1999.

McNamer, Sarah. *Affective Meditation and the Invention of Medieval Compassion*. Philadelphia: University of Pennsylvania Press, 2010.

Miles, Margaret R. *A Complex Delight: The Secularization of the Breast, 1350–1750*. Berkeley: University of California Press, 2008.

Monagle, Clare, *Scholastic Affect: Gender, Maternity and the History of Emotions*. Cambridge: Cambridge University Press, 2020.

Morse, Mary. 'Margery Kempe, Venice, and Marian iconology'. *Studia Mystica* 19 (1998), 56–67.

Müller, Wolfgang. *The Criminalization of Abortion in the West: Its Origins in Medieval Law*. Ithaca: Cornell University Press, 2012.

Murray, Jacqueline. 'Absent penitent: The cure of women's souls and confessors' manuals in thirteenth-century England'. *Women, the Book and the Godly*. Ed. Lesley Smith and Jane H.M. Taylor. Cambridge: D.S. Brewer, 1995, 13–25.

———. 'Gendered souls in sexed bodies: The male construction of female sexuality in some medieval confessors' manuals'. *Handling Sin: Confession in the Middle Ages*. Ed. Peter Biller and A. J. Minnis. York: York Medieval Press, 1998, 79–93.

Nakano Glenn, Evelyn. 'Social construction of mothering: An overview'. *Mothering: Ideology, Experience, and Agency*. Ed. Evelyn Nakano Glenn, Grace Chang, and Linda Renney Forcey. New York: Routledge, 1993, 1–32.

———. 'From servitude to service work: Historical continuities in the racial division of paid reproductive labor'. *Signs* 18.1 (1992), 1–43.

Neff, Amy. 'The pain of *compassio*: Mary's labor at the foot of the Cross'. *The Art Bulletin* 80.2 (1998), 254–73.

Newman, Barbara. 'What did it mean to say "I saw"? the clash between theory and practice in medieval visionary culture', *Speculum* 80 (2005), 1–43.

Niebrzydowski, Sue. *Bonoure and Buxum: A Study of Wives in Late Medieval English Literature*. Oxford: Peter Lang, 2006.
———. 'Marian literature'. *The History of British Women's Writing, 700–1500*. Ed. Liz Herbert McAvoy and Diane Watt. Basingstoke, 2012, 112–20.
Noreen, Kirstin. 'The icon of Santa Maria Maggiore, Rome: An image and its afterlife'. *Renaissance Studies* 19.5 (2005), 660–72.
O'Mara, Veronica and Virginia Blanton. 'Cambridge University Library, Additional MS 2604: Repackaging female saints' lives for the fifteenth-century English nun'. *The Journal of the Early Book Society for the Study of Manuscripts and Printing History* 13 (2010), 237–47.
O'Reilly, Andrea. *Matricentric Feminism: Theory, Activism, and Practice*. Toronto: Demeter Press, 2016.
Orme, Nicholas. *Medieval Children*. New Haven: Yale, 2001.
——— and Margaret Webster. *The English Hospital, 1070–1570*. New Haven: Yale, 1995.
Owens, Patty Eubanks. 'No teens allowed: The exclusion of adolescents from public spaces'. *Landscape Journal* 21.1 (2002), 156–63.
Owst, G. R. *Literature and the Pulpit in Medieval England*. 2nd ed. New York: Barnes and Noble, 1961.
Park, Katherine. *Secrets of Women: Gender, Generation, and the Origins of Human Dissection*. New York: Zone Books, 2006.
Parker, Kate. 'Lynn and the making of a mystic'. *A Companion to* The Book of Margery Kempe. Ed. John Arnold and Katherine Lewis. Cambridge: D.S. Brewer, 2004, 55–74.
Parker, Rozsika. *The Subversive Stitch: Embroidery and the Making of the Feminine*. London: Women's Press, 1984.
Partridge, Loren. 'Urbanism: Rotting cadeavors and the New Jerusalem'. *The Art of Renaissance Rome, 1400–1600*. New York: Harry N. Abrams, 1996, 19–40.
Pearsall, Derek. 'Hoccleve's *Regement of Princes*: The poetics of royal self-representation'. *Speculum* 69.2 (1994), 386–410.
Pevsner, Nikolaus. *Suffolk*. 2nd ed. Harmondsworth: Penguin, 1974.
Phillips, Helen. 'Chaucer and DeGuileville: The "ABC" in context'. *Medium Aevum* 62.1 (1993), 1–19.
———, ed. *Chaucer and Religion*. Woodbridge: D.S. Brewer, 2010.
Phillips, Kim M. 'Desiring virgins: Maidens, martyrs and femininity in late medieval England'. *Youth in the Middle Ages*. Ed. P.J.P. Goldberg and Felicity Riddy. Woodbridge: York Medieval Press, 2004, 45–59.
Phillips, Susan E. *Transforming Talk: The Problem with Gossip in Late Medieval England*. University Park: Penn State University Press, 2007.
Price, Leah. *How to Do Things with Books*. Princeton, NJ: Princeton University Press, 2012.
Quinn, William. 'Chaucer's problematic Prière: *An ABC* as Artifact and Critical Issue'. *Studies in the Age of Chaucer* 23 (2001), 109–41.
Raguin, Virginia Chieffo. 'Real and imaged bodies in architectural space: The setting for Margery Kempe's *Book*'. *Women's Space: Patronage, Place,*

and *Gender in the Medieval Church*. Ed. Virginia Chieffo Raguin and Sarah Stanbury. Albany, NY: SUNY Press, 2006, 105–40.

Raphael, Dana. 'Matrescence, becoming a mother, a "new/old" rite de passage'. *Being Female: Reproduction, Power, and Change*. Ed. Dana Raphael. Berlin: De Gruyter, 1975, 65–71.

Rawcliffe, Carole. 'Medicine for the soul: The medieval English hospital and the quest for spiritual health'. *Religion, Health and Suffering*. Ed. John R. Hinnels and Roy Porter. New York: Routledge, 1999, 316–38, at 323.

———. *Leprosy in Medieval England*. Woodbridge: Boydell & Brewer, 2006, 337–43.

Reames, Sherry. 'A recent discovery concerning the sources of Chaucer's "Second Nun's Tale"'. *Modern Philology* 87.4 (1990), 337–61.

———. 'The Second Nun's Prologue and Tale' *Sources and Analogues of the Canterbury Tales*. Vol. 1. Ed. Robert M. Correale and Mary Hamel. Cambridge: D.S. Brewer, 2002, 491–527.

———. 'The Office for Saint Cecilia'. *The Liturgy of the Medieval Church*. Ed. Thomas J. Heffernan and E. Ann Matter. Kalamazoo, MI: Western Michigan Press, 2001, 219–42.

———. 'Mary, sanctity and prayers to saints: Chaucer and late-medieval piety'. *Chaucer and Religion*. Ed. Helen Phillips. Woodbridge: D.S. Brewer, 2010, 81–96.

Rice, Nicole R. 'The feminine prehistory of the York Purification: St. Leonard's Hospital, civic drama, and women's devotion'. *Speculum* 94.3 (2019), 704–38.

Rich, Adrienne. *Of Woman Born: Motherhood as Experience and Institution*. Norton, 1976, 1995.

Riddy, Felicity. 'Mother knows best: Reading social change in a courtesy text'. *Speculum* 71.1 (1996), 66–86.

Ritchey, Sara. *Acts of Care: Recovering Women in Late Medieval Health*. Ithaca, NY: Cornell University Press, 2021.

Roffey, Simon. 'Medieval leper hospitals in England: Archaeological perspective'. *Medieval Archaeology* 56 (2012), 203–33.

Rose, Gillian. *Feminism and Geography: The Limits of Geographical Knowledge*. Minneapolis: University of Minnesota Press, 1993.

Rose, Jacqueline. *Mothers: An Essay on Love and Cruelty*. New York: Farrar, Straus and Giroux, 2018.

Rosenwein, Barbara. *Emotional Communities in the Early Middle Ages*. Ithaca: Cornell University Press, 2006.

Ross, Woodburn O., ed. *Middle English Sermons*. EETS o.s. 209. London: Oxford University Press, 1940.

Rowe, Nina. *The Jew, the Cathedral, and the Medieval City*. Cambridge: Cambridge University Press, 2014.

Rozenski, Steven, Jr., 'Henry Suso's *Horologium Sapientiae* in fifteenth-century France: Images of reading and writing in Brussels Royal Library MS IV 111'. *Word & Image* 26.4 (2010), 364–80.

Rubin, Miri. *Corpus Christi: The Eucharist in Late Medieval Culture.* Cambridge: Cambridge University Press, 1991.
———. *Mother of God: A History of the Virgin Mary.* New Haven: Yale, 2009.
———. '*Ecclesia* and *Synagoga*: The changing meanings of a powerful pairing'. *Conflict and Religious Conversation in Latin Christendom.* Ed. Ram Ben-Shalom and Israel Jacob Yuval. Turnhout: Brepols, 2014, 55–86.
Ruddick, Sara. *Maternal Thinking: Toward a Politics of Peace.* Boston: Beacon Press, 1989.
Rudolph, Conrad. *The 'Things of Greater Importance': Bernard of Clairvaux's Apologia and the Medieval Attitude Toward Art.* Philadelphia: University of Pennsylvania Press, 1990, 282–3.
Rudy, Kathryn. 'An illustrated mid-fifteenth-century primer for a Flemish Girl: British Library, Harley MS 3828', *Journal of the Warburg and Courtauld Institutes* 69 (2006), 51–94.
———. 'Sewing as authority in the Middle Ages'. *Zeitschrift für Medien- und Kulturforschung* 6.1 (2015), 117–31.
Ryan, Salvador. 'The persuasive power of a mother's breast: The most desperate act of the Virgin Mary's advocacy'. *Studia Hibernica* 32 (2002/2003), 59–74.
Saetveit Miles, Laura. 'Origins and development of the Virgin Mary's book at the Annunciation'. *Speculum* 89.3 (2014), 632–69.
———. *The Virgin Mary's Book at the Annunciation.* Woodbridge: Boydell & Brewer, 2020.
Salih, Sarah. *Versions of Virginity in Late Medieval England.* Woodbridge: Boydell & Brewer, 2001.
———. *A Companion to Middle English Hagiography.* Woodbridge: D.S. Brewer, 2006.
———. 'At home; Out of the house'. *The Cambridge Companion to Medieval Women's Writing.* Ed. Carolyn Dinshaw and David Wallace. Cambridge: Cambridge University Press, 2006, 124–40.
Sanok, Catherine. *Her Life Historical: Exemplarity and Females Saints' Lives in Late Medieval England.* Philadelphia: University of Pennsylvania Press, 2007.
Scarry, Elaine. *The Body in Pain: The Making and Unmaking of the World.* Oxford: Oxford University Press, 1987.
Schiller, Gertrud. *Iconography of Christian Art.* 2 vols. Trans. Janet Seligman. Greenwich, CT: New York Graphic Society, 1971.
Schultze, Dick. 'Wisdom in the margins: Text and paratext in *The Seven Points of True Love and Everlasting Wisdom*'. *Études Anglaises* 66.3 (2013), 341–56.
Schwarz, Heinrich. 'The mirror of the artist and the mirror of the devout'. *Studies in the History of Art.* London: Phaidon, 1959, 90–105.
Seal, Samantha Katz. *Father Chaucer: Generating Authority in the Canterbury Tales.* Oxford: Oxford University Press, 2019.

Sheehan, Michael. 'The influence of canon law on the property rights of married women in England'. *Medieval Studies* 25 (1963), 109–24.
Sheingorn, Pamela. '"The wise mother": The image of St. Anne teaching the Virgin Mary'. *Gendering the Master Narrative: Women and Power in the Middle Ages*. Ed. M.C. Erler and M. Kowaleski. Ithaca, NY: Cornell University Press, 2003, 105–34.
Shoemaker, Stephen. 'Mary at the cross, east and west: Maternal compassion and affective piety in the earliest "Life of the Virgin" and the High Middle Ages'. *The Journal of Theological Studies* 62.2 (2011), 570–606.
Shoham-Steiner, Ephraim. 'The Virgin Mary, Miriam, and Jewish reactions to Marian devotion in the high Middle Ages'. *AJS Review* 37.1 (2013), 75–91.
Simons, Walter. 'Reading a saint's body: Rapture and bodily movement in the *vitae* of thirteenth-century béguines'. *Framing Medieval Bodies*. Ed. Sarah Kay and Miri Rubin. Manchester: Manchester University Press, 1994, 10–23.
———. *Cities of Ladies: Beguine Communities in the Medieval Low Countries, 1200–1565*. Philadelphia: University of Pennsylvania Press, 2001.
Simpson, James. *Reform and Cultural Revolution*. The Oxford English Literary History. Vol. 2. Oxford: Oxford University Press, 2002.
Smith, Pamela H. *The Body of the Artisan: Art and Experience in the Scientific Revolution*. Chicago: University of Chicago Press, 2004.
Solberg, Emma Maggie. *Virgin Whore*. Ithaca: Cornell University Press, 2018.
Sperling, Jutta. 'Squeezing, squirting, spilling milk: The lactation of Saint Bernard and the Flemish *Madonna Lactans* (ca. 1430–1530)'. *Renaissance Quarterly* 71.3 (2018), 868–918.
Spreadbury, Jo. 'The gender of the church: The female image of *Ecclesia* in the late Middle Ages'. *Gender and Christian Religion*. Ed. R.N. Swanson. Woodbridge: Boydell, 1998, 93–103.
Staley Johnson, Lynn. 'Chaucer's tale of the Second Nun and the strategies of dissent'. *Studies in Philology* 89.3 (1992), 314–33.
———. 'Chaucer and the Postures of Sanctity'. *The Powers of the Holy: Religion, Politics, and Gender in Late Medieval English Culture*. Ed. David Aers and Lynn Staley. University Park: Penn State University Press, 1996, 179–259.
Stargardt, Ute. 'The beguines of Belgium, the Dominican nuns of Germany, and Margery Kempe'. *The Popular Literature of Medieval England*. Ed. Thomas Heffernan. Knoxville: University of Tennessee Press, 1985, 277–313.
Sticca, Sandro. *The Planctus Mariae in the Dramatic Tradition of the Middle Ages*. Trans. Joseph Berrigan. Athens, GA: University of Georgia Press, 1988.
Stock, Brian. *The Implications of Literacy*. Princeton, NJ: Princeton University Press, 1983.

Strohm, Paul. *Hochon's Arrow: The Social Imagination of Fourteenth-century Texts*. Princeton: Princeton University Press, 1992.
Suydam, Mary. 'Beguine textuality: Sacred performances'. *Performance and Transformation: New Approaches to Late Medieval Spirituality*. Ed. Mary A. Suydam and Joanna E. Ziegler. New York: St. Martin's Press, 1999, 169–210.
Swann, Alaya. '"By Expresse Experiment": The doubting midwife Salome in late medieval England'. *Bulletin of the History of Medicine* 89.1 (2015), 1–24.
Synge, Lanto. *Art of Embroidery: History of Style and Technique*. Woodbridge: Antique Collector's Club, 2001.
Takševa, Tatjana. 'One is not born but rather becomes a mother: Claiming the maternal in women and gender studies'. *Journal of the Motherhood Initiative* 10.1–2 (2019), 27–44.
Tasioulas, J.A. 'The portrayal of Mary in the N-Town Plays'. *Medieval Women in Their Communities*. Ed. Diane Watt. Toronto: University of Toronto Press, 1997, 222–45.
Tryon, Ruth. 'Miracles of Our Lady in Middle English verse'. *PMLA* 38.2 (1923), 308–88.
Twycross, Meg. 'Kissing cousins: The four daughters of God and the Visitation in the N. Town Mary play'. *Medieval English Theatre* 18 (1996), 99–141.
Utley, Francis Lee. 'Five genres in the "Clerk's Tale"'. *Chaucer Review* 6.3 (1972), 198–228.
Vandeburie, Jan. '"Sancte fidei omnino deiciar"': Ugolino dei Conti di Segni's doubts and Jacques de Vitry's intervention'. *Studies in Church History* 52 (2016), 87–101.
Vander Veen, Brian C. 'The *vitae* of Bodleian Library MS Douce 114'. Unpub. Ph.D. thesis, University of Nottingham, 2007.
Varnam, Laura. 'The crucifix, the pietà, and the female mystic: Devotional objects and performative identity in *The Book of Margery Kempe*'. *The Journal of Medieval Religious Cultures* 41:2 (2015), 208–37.
———. 'The importance of St Margaret's Church in *The Book of Margery Kempe*: A sacred place and an exemplary parishioner'. *Nottingham Medieval Studies* 61 (2018), 197–243.
Vauchez, André. *La spiritualité du Moyen Âge occidental (VIIIe–XIIIe siècles)*. 2nd edn. Paris: Editions du Seuil, 1994.
Verini, Alexandra Cassatt. 'Reading between the lines: Female friendship in Osbern Bokenham's *Life* of St Katherine of Alexandria'. *Magistra* 17.2 (2011), 53–70.
Vines, Amy. 'Lullaby as lament: Learning to mourn in middle English nativity lyrics'. *Laments for the Lost: Medieval Mourning and Elegy*. Ed. Jane Tolmie and M. Jane Toswell. Turnhout: Brepols, 2010, 201–23.
Wall, Wendy. *Recipes for Thought: Knowledge and Taste in the Early Modern Kitchen*, Philadelphia: University of Pennsylvania Press, 2016.

Waller, Gary. *The Virgin Mary in Late Medieval and Early Modern English Literature and Popular Culture*. Cambridge: Cambridge University Press, 2011.

Ward, Jennifer C. 'Joan de Bohun, Countess of Hereford, Essex and Northampton, c. 1370–1419: Family, land and social networks'. *Essex Archaeology and History* 32 (2001), 146–53.

Warren, Nancy Bradley. *Spiritual Economies: Female Monasticism in Later Medieval England*. Philadelphia: University of Pennsylvania Press, 2001.

———. 'Chaucer, the Chaucer tradition, and female monastic readers'. *Chaucer Studies* 51.1 (2016), 88–106.

Waters, Claire M. *Angels and Earthly Creatures: Preaching, Performance, and Gender in the Later Middle Ages*. Philadelphia: University of Pennsylvania, 2004.

———. 'Maria Mirabilis: beholding Mary in the miracles'. *Journal of Religious History* 44.4 (2020), 407–21.

Watson, Nicholas. '"Et que est huius ydoli materia? Tuipse": Idols and images in Walter Hilton'. *Images, Idolatry, and Iconoclasm in Late Medieval England*. Ed. Jeremy Dimmick, James Simpson, and Nicolette Zeeman. Oxford: Oxford University Press, 2002, 95–111.

Watt, Diane. 'Mary the physician: Women, religion and medicine in the Middle Ages'. *Medicine, Religion and Gender in Medieval Culture*. Ed. Naoë Kukita Yoshikawa. Woodbridge: D.S. Brewer, 2015, 27–44.

Wechsler, Judith. 'A change in the iconography of the Song of Songs in 12th and 13th century Latin Bibles'. *Texts and Responses: Studies Presented to Nahum N. Glatzer*. Ed. Michael Fishbane and Paul Flohr. Leiden: Brill, 1975, 73–93.

Weinstein, Donald and Rudolph M. Bell. *Saints and Society: The Two Worlds of Western Christendom, 1000–1700*. Chicago: University of Chicago Press, 1982.

Weissman, Hope Phyllis. 'Margery Kempe in Jerusalem'. *Acts of Interpretation: The Text in its Contexts, 700–1600*. Ed. Mary Carruthers and Elizabeth Kirk. Norman, OK: Pilgrim Books, 1982, 201–17.

Wenzel, Siegfried. 'The Dominican presence in middle English literature'. *Christ among the Medieval Dominicans*. Ed. Kent Emery and Joseph Wawrykow. South Bend: University of Notre Dame Press, 1998, 315–31.

Williams, Tara. 'Manipulating Mary: Maternal, sexual, and textual authority in *The Book of Margery Kempe*'. *Modern Philology* 107.4 (2010), 528–55.

Wilson, Janet. 'Communities of dissent: The secular and ecclesiastical communities of Margery Kempe's *Book*'. *Medieval Women in Their Communities*. Ed. Diane Watt. Toronto: University of Toronto Press, 1997, 155–85.

Winstead, Karen. *Virgin Martyrs: Legends of Sainthood in Late Medieval England*. Ithaca: Cornell University Press, 1997.

———. 'Osbern Bokenham's "englische boke": Re-forming holy women'. *Form and Reform: Reading Across the Fifteenth Century*. Ed. Shannon

Gayk and Kathleen Tonry. Columbus: Ohio State University Press, 2011, 67–87.
Winston-Allen, Anne. *Stories of the Rose: The Making of the Rosary in the Middle Ages*. University Park: Pennsylvania State University Press, 1997.
Wogan-Browne, Jocelyn. *Saints' Lives and Women's Literary Culture c. 1150–1300: Virginity and its Authorizations*. Oxford: Oxford University Press, 2001.
Wolpe, B. L. '*Florilegium alphabeticum*: Alphabets in medieval manuscripts'. *Calligraphy and Palaeography*. Ed. A.S. Osley. London: Faber, 1965, 69–74.
Wood, Charles T. 'The doctors' dilemma: Sin, salvation, and the menstrual cycle in medieval thought'. *Speculum* 56.4 (1981), 710–27.
Woolf, Rosemary. *English Religious Lyric in the Middle Ages*. Oxford: Clarendon Press, 1968.
Yoshikawa, Naoë Kukita. 'Searching for the image of new Ecclesia: Margery Kempe's spiritual pilgrimage reconsidered'. *Medieval Perspectives* 11 (1996), 125–38.
———. *Margery Kempe's Meditations: The Context of Medieval Devotional Literatures, Liturgy and Iconography*. Cardiff: University of Wales Press, 2007.
———. 'Holy medicine and diseases of the soul: Henry of Lancaster and Le Livre de Seyntz Medicines'. *Medical History* 53 (2009), 397–414.
———. *Medicine, Religion and Gender in Medieval Culture*. Woodbridge: D.S. Brewer, 2015.
Young, Iris Marian. 'Pregnant embodiment: Subjectivity and alienation'. *On Female Body Experience: Throwing Like a Girl and Other Essays*. Oxford: Oxford University Press, 2005, 46–61.
Ziegler, Joanna. *Sculpture of Compassion: The Pietà and the Beguines in the Southern Low Countries, c.1300–c.1600*. Brussels: Institut Historique Belge de Rome, 1992.
Ziegler, Tiffany. *Medieval Healthcare and the Rise of Charitable Institutions*. New York: Palgrave, 2018.
Zimbalist, Barbara. *Translating Christ in the Middle Ages*. Notre Dame: University of Notre Dame Press, 2022.

Index

Anne, mother of Mary 55, 58, 145, 146, 152, 155, 156, 158, 159, 162, 167, 169–73, 177n.8, 179n.42, 180n.49, 181n.66, 183n.82, 183n.83, 191
antisemitism 1, 7, 8, 9n.2, 53n.87, 56, 68, 69–70, 72, 84, 93n.60, 168, 194–216, 222n.76, 264

Bernard of Clairvaux 2, 10n.7, 21, 22, 44n.23, 49n.61, 52n.84, 67, 68, 69, 153, 163, 174, 198, 199, 232
birth 1, 2, 3, 5, 8, 9n.3, 20, 28, 29, 31, 44n.23, 54n.100, 55, 56, 57, 58, 59–60, 63, 69, 70, 71, 72, 75–7, 78, 79, 80, 83, 86, 87, 89n.16, 94n.72, 104, 106, 115, 123, 124, 143–9, 151, 153, 154, 156, 157, 159, 162, 163, 164, 167, 175, 176, 207, 208, 248, 249, 262
Black, mothering while 94n.83, 148, 195, 204, 210, 261–2
blood 60, 62, 63, 124, 128, 249
blood libel 1, 70, 195, 196, 198, 201, 203, 204, 206, 213, 214, 215

Bokenham, Osbern 99, 146, 149, 157, 160–76
breastfeeding 3, 25, 44n.23, 60, 63–5, 66–8, 70, 74, 79, 91n.44, 102, 104, 118, 119, 148, 153, 156, 169, 174, 178n.29, 196, 225
Bridget of Sweden 13, 21, 25, 58, 88n.14, 94n.72, 114, 122, 125, 242

caregiving and healing 5, 25, 55, 77, 87n.3, 104, 105–7, 110, 111, 112, 113, 120, 122, 123, 125, 126, 127, 129, 131, 132, 148, 151, 154, 155, 156, 158–9, 174, 191, 211, 212, 213, 264
Catherine of Siena 8, 13, 25, 105, 109, 122–5, 129, 130, 132, 263
Cecilia 8–9, 61, 90n.28, 139n.87, 146, 174, 224–50, 262
Chaucer 7, 8, 47n.43, 185–6
  An ABC 8, 188–94, 206
  Prioress's Tale 8, 188–9, 194–216
  Second Nun's Tale 8–9, 189, 224–50

Index

child[ren] 1, 2, 3, 4, 5, 55, 56, 65, 74, 76, 80, 81, 82–3, 87, 87n.3, 104, 106, 144, 150–1, 152, 157–9, 160, 163, 168, 172, 188–9, 190, 193, 194, 196–9, 201, 203–9, 210, 211, 213–14, 215, 219n.42, 221n.64, 225, 234, 236, 246, 249, 250, 261–4
  Mary as 173
Christ 15, 16–17, 21, 23–7, 29–30, 56, 58–9, 61, 63–5, 83–4, 101, 122, 129, 130, 203, 225–6, 241–2
  as child 1, 3, 4, 23, 25, 29, 30, 31, 56, 57, 67, 73, 79–81, 83, 154, 156–8, 199
Christina *mirabilis* 8, 105, 109, 115–20, 123, 130, 132
church
  as institution 5, 9, 19, 28, 205, 209, 213, 214
  Gothic cathedrals 7, 23, 32–5, 36, 39
  liturgical space 7, 19, 23, 24, 27, 30, 33, 35, 36, 37, 38, 40, 157–9, 180n.46
  Mary as 7, 19, 23, 31, 32, 33, 34, 35, 36, 37, 53n.92, 58, 68, 224, 248
  Pentecost, 59, 68, 70, 109, 207
community 111, 112, 113, 115, 117, 118, 119, 120, 121, 122, 123, 126, 127, 132, 143, 145, 146, 148, 156, 157, 158–9, 164–5, 167, 172–3, 174–5, 209, 211, 212–13, 215, 262
compassio 101–2, 104, 113–14, 116, 120, 122, 126, 128, 132, 200, 201, 206, 207, 222n.73, 262
Crucifixion 3, 7, 28, 29, 40, 56–8, 60–2, 70–2, 75, 78–9, 87, 101, 102, 109, 111, 115, 152, 155, 159, 198, 200, 201, 202, 204, 206, 207, 209, 212, 215

death 73–5, 78–9, 198, 205, 206, 208, 211, 215, 243
devotional literacies 4, 5, 6, 8, 13, 15–41, 55, 60, 75, 116, 125, 126, 132, 144, 145, 157, 162, 165–6, 185, 187–9, 190, 192, 193, 195, 207, 228–9, 235

Ecclesia see Maria Ecclesia
Elizabeth, cousin of Mary 57, 73, 147, 149–53, 175
Elizabeth of Spalbeek 8, 105, 109, 110–13, 115, 116, 120, 123, 130, 132
Eucharist 1, 7, 9n.3, 36, 40, 56, 60, 61, 62, 63, 64, 65, 70, 72, 90n.37, 113, 124, 130–1

fathers 123, 157, 167, 168–9, 170, 173, 174, 210, 213, 234, 264
flesh 2, 58, 60, 62, 109, 111, 118, 121, 124, 131, 236

Gesine 28, 35, 38, 154

Hoccleve 72–3, 74, 76, 80, 205, 206

imitatio Mariae 4, 6, 7, 8, 13, 17–21, 23–4, 27, 29, 31–8, 65, 71, 72, 74, 83, 86, 131, 199, 204, 227, 228, 230, 249, 250, 262
  via tears 29, 30, 37, 40, 64, 70, 72, 79, 83–5, 87, 120, 121–2, 174, 194, 195, 198–204, 209, 211, 214, 215, 216, 231, 250, 262

incarnation 1, 19, 20, 22, 23–4, 34, 38, 58, 60, 61, 62, 65, 71, 72, 249
incorporation 22–3, 33, 38, 58–60, 63, 89n.16, 107
infertility 149, 150, 163, 169, 170–3
inhabitation 7, 22–4, 34, 35, 36, 38, 40, 56, 107, 232, 249

Jacobus de Voragine 21, 115, 151, 170, 171
Jacques de Vitry 77–8, 107–8, 113, 120–1, 122, 131–2, 136n.40
John the Evangelist 28, 29, 51n.73, 61, 71, 72, 85, 111, 147, 148, 149, 152, 155, 159

Kempe, Margery 6–7, 13, 15–87, 164, 185, 188, 229, 232, 262
  Book 105–6, 122, 125

law enforcement 78, 85, 195, 199, 203, 204–5, 208, 209, 211, 213, 214, 261
Long Melford, Holy Trinity Church 49n.59, 154, 157, 160–1
Lydgate 3, 144, 154, 157, 160, 161, 162, 163, 170, 185, 189, 205, 225, 226–7, 228, 230, 241, 247, 252n.15, 260n.80

Margaret of Antioch 57, 146, 157–8, 160, 161, 164–5, 167–9, 171, 180n.51, 189, 226, 247, 260n.80
Maria [Mater] dolorosa 29, 32, 70, 81, 83, 84, 101, 132, 146, 176, 198, 205, 206, 207, 211, 261
Maria Ecclesia 7, 19, 31–3, 34, 36, 37, 52n.84, 53n.87, 56, 58, 60–2, 68, 72, 89n.19, 248, 249
Maria lactans 7, 31, 60, 64, 67, 68
Maria mediatrix 225–6, 227–8, 231, 233–4, 241–2
Maria medica 8, 55, 56, 66, 99, 101, 104, 106, 109, 131, 155
Maria Regina see Queen of Heaven
Marian body 5, 56, 57, 58, 60, 69, 99, 211, 224, 225, 242, 248
  as beautiful 224–6, 230
  as healing agent 101–4, 110
  as parturient 2, 3, 61, 62, 65, 68, 69, 130, 156, 207
  as virginal 2, 3, 10n.7, 21, 153, 224, 226
Marian poetry 73–5, 78, 79, 80, 81, 82, 104, 188–94, 198, 199, 225, 241, 259n.67
Marie d'Oignies 8, 43n.14, 105, 106, 107, 108, 109, 113, 120–2, 123, 129, 130, 131–2, 232
marriage 30–1, 32, 121, 144, 157, 166, 231, 233–7
  persuasion within 61–2, 227–8, 243–4, 230–1, 233–4, 236–7, 238–40, 245, 247
  teaching within 227, 231, 243–4
Maria sponsa 225, 241–2
[Mary] Salome 147, 152, 153, 154–9, 160, 175, 179n.34, 179n.37, 212
maternal body 80, 105, 107, 108, 109, 110, 115, 116, 119, 122, 126, 131, 147, 194, 211, 224, 248, 250, 264
maternal grief 8, 21, 29, 73–5, 76–9, 80, 81, 82–6, 115, 143,

196, 198, 199, 200, 202, 203, 205, 207, 209, 211, 214, 215, 261–2
maternal labor 3, 5, 8, 9, 55, 83, 104, 106, 147, 157, 173, 175, 190, 210, 212
  shared with others 5, 8, 83, 99, 107, 110, 143, 147, 148, 151, 152, 153, 156, 157, 159, 175, 196, 210, 211, 212, 213–14, 262, 264
maternal peers 5, 8, 99, 110, 123, 143, 144, 145, 146, 147, 148, 149, 150–4, 156, 157, 158, 159, 160, 161, 163, 169, 171, 172, 173, 174–5, 209, 212, 213–14, 216, 262
maternal practice 4, 5, 6, 7, 8, 9, 13, 55, 64, 144–5, 149, 152, 188–9, 190, 191, 194, 195, 201, 210, 216, 262–3
maternal teaching 4, 143, 188, 189, 190, 191, 193, 199, 210, 215, 217n.21
matrescence 144, 145, 147, 149, 150, 151, 152, 159, 166, 168, 175, 177n.6, 262
mendicant culture 13, 15–20, 22–3, 24, 25, 26, 28, 29, 31, 38, 42n.10, 43n.14, 56, 58, 63, 68, 70, 116
miracle tales 1, 66, 102, 106, 109, 114, 194–216, 225, 242, 247, 263

Nativity 1, 25, 40, 58, 79, 151, 154, 156
nuns 5, 26, 58, 119, 120, 145–6, 148–9, 160–1, 164–5, 166, 175, 180n.53, 185, 194, 209, 230, 263

pain 1, 8, 55, 71, 72, 80, 86–7, 94n.72, 99, 101–4, 106–7, 109, 110, 111, 113, 114, 115, 116, 117, 118, 121, 122, 123, 124, 126, 132, 132n.1, 137n.44, 148, 149, 157, 175–6, 207–8, 211, 261–3
patriarchal motherhood 4, 5, 9, 185, 203, 210, 263, 264
Pietà 28, 29, 40, 58, 79, 101
pilgrimage 7, 13, 16–17, 19, 23, 26, 29, 30, 34–5, 40
pregnancy loss 74–8, 82, 83

Queen of Heaven 8, 23, 27, 30, 31, 32, 114, 204, 225, 226, 227, 232, 242, 245

relics 22, 28–9, 34, 35, 38, 68, 90n.45, 107–8, 132, 136n.38, 136n.40, 161

sleeplessness 121, 201
Suso, Henry 8, 20, 25, 27, 28, 45n.27, 57, 58, 62, 102, 104, 105, 109, 113, 126–8, 130
swoon 70–1, 72, 83, 102, 115, 132n.1, 206–8, 209, 222n.73

teenagers 143–5, 153, 160, 166, 172, 176, 176n.2, 176n.3, 176n.4

Visitation 57–8, 147, 150, 153
visual art 7, 13, 18–20, 23, 24, 26, 27, 28, 38, 58, 61, 72, 148, 150, 154, 157–9, 179n.42, 191, 207

EU authorised representative for GPSR:
Easy Access System Europe, Mustamäe tee 50,
10621 Tallinn, Estonia
gpsr.requests@easproject.com

www.ingramcontent.com/pod-product-compliance
Lightning Source LLC
Chambersburg PA
CBHW050925240426
43668CB00021B/2436